Interpretations of Native North American Life

Published in cooperation with The Society for Historical Archaeology

Florida A&M University, Tallahassee
Florida Atlantic University, Boca Raton
Florida Gulf Coast University, Ft. Myers
Florida International University, Miami
Florida State University, Tallahassee
University of Central Florida, Orlando
University of Florida, Gainesville
University of North Florida, Jacksonville
University of South Florida, Tampa
University of West Florida, Pensacola

Interpretations of
Native North American Life
Material Contributions to Ethnohistory

Edited by Michael S. Nassaney and Eric S. Johnson

University Press of Florida
Gainesville · Tallahassee · Tampa · Boca Raton
Pensacola · Orlando · Miami · Jacksonville · Ft. Myers

149246

05 04 03 02 01 00 6 5 4 3 2 1

LIBRARY OF CONGRESS CATALOGING-IN-PUBLICATION DATA
Interpretations of Native North American life: material contributions
to ethnohistory / edited by Michael S. Nassaney and Eric S. Johnson.
p. cm.
Includes bibliographical references and index.
ISBN 0-8130-1783-1 (cloth: alk. paper)
1. Indians of North America—Material culture. 2. Indians of North
America—Ethnic identity. 3. Indians of North America—Historiography. I. Nassaney, Michael S. II. Johnson, Eric S., 1956–.
E98.M34 I57 2000
305.897—dc21 99-056331

The University Press of Florida is the scholarly publishing agency for
the State University System of Florida, comprising Florida A&M
University, Florida Atlantic University, Florida Gulf Coast University,
Florida International University, Florida State University, University
of Central Florida, University of Florida, University of North Florida, University of South Florida, and University of West Florida.

University Press of Florida
15 Northwest 15th Street
Gainesville, FL 32611
http://www.upf.com

Contents

Tables

Figures

Foreword

Reflections on the Importance of Material Culture

Any analysis of material culture as a dimension of human society must start with a series of elemental assumptions that are as old as material culture itself. We hominids, along with our closest primate relatives, have a very long history of purposefully modifying material objects into useful artifacts. In this process of making things, two components are of importance: namely, our imaginative ability to visualize the transformation of a raw material into a new form, coupled with the mechanical means to achieve the desired transformation. In this sense the artifact is the product of an event or a series of events.

The stone-tool industry begun by our hominid ancestors at least two and one half million years ago shows some distinctive characteristics. In retrospect it may be ascertained that, unlike the tools manufactured by nonhominids, the stone tools produced by our ancestors indicate patterned behavior. That is, the mechanical process of manufacture is sequential, resulting in uniform types of tools. Once this routine process, however simple, is in place, we may observe tool-making traditions. That is, the innovations of one generation were systematically incorporated in the technological procedures of subsequent generations. This important distinction is the basis for technological and stylistic continuity, which today are basic elements in analyzing material culture.

We might ask why tradition developed at all? Leaving aside critical evolutionary elements such as the mechanical advantage of improving hand-eye coordination and the ability to invent and manipulate symbols in communication, tool traditions were undoubtedly motivated by improved function. Here we might reflect on Leslie White's premise that cultural complexity is ultimately linked to energy from the environment. Extracting energy is in turn dependent on the development of new energy sources and/or the improvement of the instrumental means of energy production—that is, more effective and efficient tools. Since our earliest hominid ancestors could not yet tap new energy resources, it was the manufacture of increasingly effective tools that conferred a distinct evolutionary advantage. This is still the case. Our species is forever linked to our ability to make and improve the *things* that stand between ourselves and extinction.

As our ancestors ultimately spread from Africa and began to meet the challenges posed by distant places and new environments, technology became not only increasingly complex but diversified as well. Regional and local traditions developed and added rich content to the nexus between artifacts and their makers. Beyond the blend of expedient form with function, artifacts themselves became symbols. Things came to communicate identity, beauty, power, grief, and practically any other conceivable expression of intellect or emotion. It is in this symbolic relationship between humans of particular cultures and their self-created material world that we find the means to gain insight into their minds and behavior. To paraphrase Lévi-Strauss, artifacts are not only useful, they are good to think with.

This volume on material culture in the historic past of Native North America edited by Michael Nassaney and Eric Johnson provides a broad spectrum of case studies that show how artifacts can provide a window into the structure of human society—why artifacts are good to think with. This is especially the case where our vision is necessarily diminished by the absence of modern informants. Here we enter the realm of the archaeologist. When it comes to the study of material culture, we must pay tribute to the archaeologist. Undoubtedly the study of artifacts in substance and in theory has reached its highest form not at the hand of the art historian nor the curator, the collector nor the preservationist, but of the archaeologist. It is the archaeologist who is dependent upon the thing, who contemplates absence as well as presence, the broken and the whole, the beautiful and the ugly, the discarded as well as the curated. It is the archaeologist who gives notice to the nuance of style, not for aesthetics alone but for hints of identity, invention, and diffusion. It is the archaeologist who longs for context and treasures it more than any value that uniqueness might bring.

Whereas the prehistorian has only the artifacts themselves to bear witness to behavior and value, the historical archaeologist often has access to contemporary written documents and oral tradition to help put the artifact into cultural context. The use of documents and oral testimony in the analysis of material things provides both theoretical and methodological advantages. Many of these are amply illustrated by the studies included in this volume. Unlike the prehistorian, who must depend solely on the analysis of the variability within and between collections in order to explicate cultural context, the historical archaeologist may formulate and test hypotheses by the use of two complementary yet contrasting data sets. One is drawn from the excavated artifacts and the other from written and oral sources.

Michael Nassaney, Eric Johnson, and the contributors to this book are to be congratulated on an interesting and useful volume. Collectively the following chapters provide an excellent addition to the literature on material culture and to the history and historic archaeology of Native North America.

Charles E. Cleland
East Lansing, Michigan

Preface

This volume brings together a variety of material-based approaches to the examination and interpretation of Native North American life in historical and anthropological perspective. The studies assembled here address three broad, interrelated themes: ethnogenesis or the creation, maintenance, and transformation of ethnic identity; change and continuity in daily life; and ritual, iconography, and ideology. The investigation of past Native American lifeways has traditionally been the domain of two distinct disciplines: anthropology and history. Practitioners working under the umbrella of historical archaeology, ethnohistory, and material culture studies are increasingly blurring older disciplinary boundaries. We see this trend as a positive outcome of interdisciplinary approaches to Native American studies as demonstrated in this volume.

The contributors to this collection represent diverse academic fields including archaeology, material culture studies, and art history, and they discuss case material drawn from throughout North America. The diversity and geographic breadth of their work reflect the development of interrelations among these fields, and the important contributions, both realized and potential, that research on the material world has to offer. We think that this work will appeal to ethnohistorians interested in exploring new sources of information as well as archaeologists with an interest in Native American history and culture.

The idea for this book emerged in 1995, when we began discussing a proposal for a symposium at the annual meeting of the American Society for Ethnohistory (ASE), hosted by Western Michigan University (WMU) in Kalamazoo. At the time, we envisioned a session focusing primarily on archaeology and other material culture studies, one that would add a new dimension to the meetings and attract many of our archaeological colleagues who do not routinely attend this conference. (This was the first ASE meeting for both of us.) The aim was to highlight how material objects could, indeed should, be routinely integrated into ethnohistoric studies of Native America. As both familiar and new scholars began responding to our call for papers, we were quickly impressed by the high quality of the submissions, their thematic and methodological breadth, the enthusiasm in the tone of the correspondence, and the level of interest. Our final program consisted of twenty-seven individual papers organized into four sessions and delivered over two full days. The meeting itself was an intense and exhilarating experience, as we (and several others) listened to all of the presentations, participated in many discussions and debates, and made and renewed acquaintances with colleagues from all over North America. Even before the last session ended, we had resolved to create an edited volume that captured the intellectual excitement of that memorable weekend in Kalamazoo. This book is that creation. We are pleased with the material outcome and hope that this volume stimulates further investigations on the common ground of archaeology, ethnography, and history.

In the process of preparing this volume, we have benefited from the assistance of several individuals and organizations. The program chair for the 1995 annual meeting of the American Society for Ethnohistory, Donald Fixico, helped to ensure that our outrageous proposal for such an enormous session was accepted and that the meeting sponsored by WMU ran smoothly. The many participants in the symposium, including presenters and audience, helped to create a stimulating environment for the presentations and discussions. While we regret that some presenters chose not to submit their papers for publication in this collection, a second volume would have been required if each one had been included. All of the chapters in this book are expanded versions of the 1995 ASE symposium papers with the exception of the contribution by Larissa Thomas, which was solicited later. We would like to commend the contributors to this volume for their efforts in preparing their manuscripts and responding to our editorial comments.

We thank Ronald Michael of the Society for Historical Archaeology for soliciting the book manuscript and William Turnbaugh for securing the four conscientious reviewers who provided useful commentary on an earlier draft. Meredith Morris-Babb and her able associates at the University Press of Florida facilitated the publication process. We also appreciate Charles Cleland's cheerful willingness to contribute the Foreword.

Finally, we acknowledge the institutional support provided by Western Michigan University during the preparation of this volume. The WMU Computing Center provided the personnel and material resources to assist in preparing several of the line drawings in this collection, including the frontispiece. Much of the final editing was facilitated by the release time Michael Nassaney was granted during his sabbatical leave in 1998–99, including the time spent as a research fellow at the John Nicholas Brown Center at Brown University.

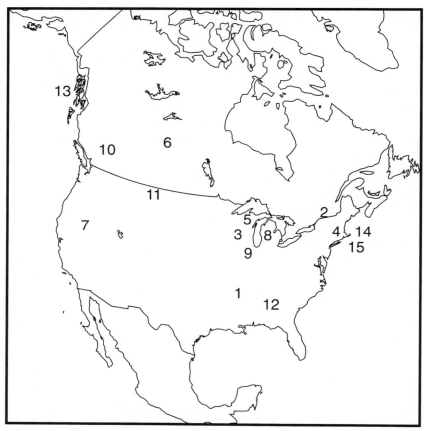

Map of Native North America showing the locations of study areas in this volume by chapter number

The Contributions of Material Objects to Ethnohistory in Native North America

Michael S. Nassaney and Eric S. Johnson

Moccasins and feathered headdresses were among the material symbols Native peoples used in the early 20th century to create public awareness of their ethnic survival and to counter the prevalent belief that Indians had vanished from New England and other parts of eastern North America. The beaded belts, plastic-tipped spears, and "Indian" tom-toms that were conspicuous commodities of the 1960s tourist trade in the White Mountains of New Hampshire and many other parts of the United States carried unambiguous messages about ethnicity, despite the labels identifying their Asian manufacture. These recent patterns of material posturing have deep roots in human history; artifacts define humanity and our social groups. In North America, elements of dress, weaponry, household technology, architecture, and other classes of artifacts have served to create, reproduce, and transform social identities of individuals, families, communities, and nations since the earliest arrivals to the continent. Given the pervasiveness and importance of tangible objects and the built environment in peoples' lives, students of Native culture and history can ill afford to ignore the potential of the material world as a source of information about the past.

Indeed, scholars in the humanities and social sciences have long recognized that historical and anthropological data can be drawn from a variety of different sources. To derive information on Native American life, researchers have relied upon a wide range of documents such as maps, photographs, letters, diaries, biographies, field notes, and other written accounts, as well as participant observation, personal interviews, oral tradition, narratives, folklore, myth, art, and artifacts (see, for example, Axtell 1997). Material objects from ethnographic and archaeological contexts are increasingly a focus of research, particularly among societies that until recently had not developed or adopted a written form of language (see Bradley 1987; Burnham 1992; Penney 1992; Rogers and Wilson 1993). In many cases, the analyses of ethnographic specimens and archaeological data provide important insights into the process of cultural change and continuity in the lives of indigenous peoples and are valuable supplements to written texts and oral accounts.

The purpose of this essay is to suggest that tangible objects can be analyzed in conjunction with other sources of historical data to expand our understanding of Native culture and history in various parts of North America from the pre-Columbian era into the contemporary world. Our approach grows out of the related fields of ethnohistory and historical archaeology and the agreement among practitioners in these fields that history and anthropology have much to say to each other (Krech 1991). Ethnohistory combines not only diverse sources but also diverse approaches: history, with its focus on particular events, and anthropology, with its emphasis on generalization. Archaeology, situated within anthropology and its concern for general patterns and processes, yet faced with data that are the products and precedents of particular behaviors, may be especially well suited to combine these approaches, as many of the authors in the volume demonstrate.

Given the limited number of written sources that may be available for a specific area or time period, historical anthropologists often need to move beyond disciplinary boundaries in an attempt to reconstruct a cultural context that affords a more nuanced understanding of human agency and historical development. For various reasons, the analysis of material objects in historical interpretation can lead to results that complement or contradict information derived from other data sets. Multiple sources can be used to describe and understand events, patterns, and processes more fully (Spores 1980:579). For example, material culture studies and archaeology can inform about geographic areas that lack documents, segments of society that were ignored in the written record, and aspects of life that went unrecorded. Of course, multiple lines of evidence may not lead to concordant interpretations. Contradictions among diverse data sets allow us to ask new questions, recognize ambiguities, test hypotheses, evaluate the reliability of assumptions, or contextualize documentary sources (Leone and Crosby 1987; Spores 1980).

It is the dynamic interplay that accompanies the process as well as the outcome of material analysis that contribute to the complexity and richness of this interpretive endeavor. In the remainder of this introduction we define the scope of our inquiry by discussing the significance of material culture and the spatial-temporal parameters of the case studies in this volume. We also discuss some of the ways in which archaeology and material culture studies can make a valuable contribution to Native history, and explore how the material record can be integrated with other sources of information. The works presented in this collection underscore the interplay among documentary, archaeological, ethnographic, and oral sources in ethnohistoric research. Comparing and integrating these sources is a research strategy that most practitioners of the interdisciplinary fields of ethnohistory and historical archaeology find extremely rewarding (see Andren 1998; Beaudry 1988; Bragdon 1996; Leone and Potter 1988:11–14; Rogers and Wilson 1993). And like any endeavor that is rewarding, it is also challenging.

A Material Culture Primer

Most of the contributions to this collection have as their points of departure the concrete, tangible expressions of Native American culture that were the deliberate products of Native American activities. Native peoples, like all human beings, made and used artifacts to meet their basic needs of food, shelter, and clothing, and as a means of participating in social, religious, and intellectual life. Thus, all aspects of society were created and reproduced at least partly through material objects. For the authors in this book, these objects are a rich source of information about the people who produced, used, viewed, and discarded them.

Over the past twenty-five years, archaeologists and other material culture specialists have revised their thinking about the significance and interpretive potential of the products of human labor and artistic expression (see DeCunzo and Herman 1996; Ferguson 1977; Glassie 1975; Hodder 1982; Kingery 1995; Martin and Garrison 1997; Prown 1988; Quimby 1978; Schlereth 1979, 1980; St. George 1988; Winner 1980; Wobst 1977). Binford (1962) was among the first practitioners to describe explicitly the multidimensionality of artifacts based on their technomic, sociotechnic, and ideotechnic functions. He saw technomic artifacts as those used to cope directly with the physical environment, whereas sociotechnic artifacts functioned in the social realm of culture. Binford classified artifacts that signify and symbolize the ideologies of society as ideotechnic. One could argue, however, that many artifacts embody each of these dimensions—the technological, social, and ideological—simultaneously. For example, the main function of a ceramic vessel may be to hold liquid, yet its context of use in a public ceremony and its distinctive decorative treatment also express social and ideological meanings to the object's users and viewers. Among many Native groups, "even the most utilitarian objects include an important artistic or decorated component, for which there is usually a particular spiritual association" (Tanner 1992:viii). It is this multivalency of material goods that makes them so potentially powerful as interpretive tools but at the same time challenges the analyst to decode them from an emic point of view.

Scholars are likely to disagree over the interpretation of material objects; they are, after all, material *symbols,* and the meanings of symbols are arbitrary by definition. Yet many of the authors in this volume would subscribe to the following tenets of material objects.

(1) Material culture is tangible. Unlike the values, ideas, attitudes, and assumptions of a society (which may be inferred from artifacts), objects of material culture have length, width, and mass. "Material culture is the object-based aspect of the study of culture" (Prown 1988:22).

(2) Material culture is often fragmentary and incomplete due to differential preservation caused by the processes that create the archaeological record (Schiffer 1976). Organic materials, in particular, are subject to decay and deterioration under deleterious conditions. Selective curation also affects the sample of ethnographic objects available for study.

(3) Material culture consists of both artifactual and documentary remains. While we usually equate artifacts with material culture, documents are also tangible and can be subjected to external analysis to determine, for example, their authenticity by examining the paper, ink, and writing implements used to produce them (Barber 1994:8). Moreover, the conceptualization of material culture as a "text" further blurs the distinction between artifacts and documents since each can be "read," albeit in different ways (Beaudry 1988; Hodder 1982; Patrick 1985).

(4) Material culture occurs in both systemic and archaeological contexts (Schiffer 1972). Here it is important to make the distinction between ethnographic and archaeological specimens. Whereas archaeological remains are typically recovered from contexts in which they were once abandoned, discarded, or lost, ethnographic objects are usually intentionally curated from systemic contexts. Thus, the history of an object is important because objects can be used for purposes other than those originally intended.

(5) Material culture has formal, spatial, and temporal dimensions (Spaulding 1960; Deetz 1977b:64). Fortunately for the material culture specialist, the form of an object of analysis varies across space and through time. The formal attributes (such as shape, raw material, color) of an object are temporally and spatially diagnostic, making it possible to identify, even at a glance, a ceramic vessel, for example, as an indigenous product of eastern Arkansas at the time of European contact.

(6) Material culture serves as a medium of communication that embodies meaning to its makers, users, and viewers (Wobst 1977). While objects convey meaning, they are multivocal and do not convey a single meaning, in part due to the social contexts of the observers, which may vary according to age, gender, status, and ethnicity (see, for example, Garman 1994).

(7) Finally, material culture is actively constituted and has recursive qualities. It is both a product and precedent of human action rather than a passive by-product of human behavior (Hodder 1982, 1986; Potter 1992; Shanks and Tilley 1987; Tilley 1984; Winner 1980; Wobst 1977).

Armed with these perspectives, material analysts find objects to be powerful interpretive tools to explore culture and history. The approaches that we advocate to the study of material culture are drawn from art history and archaeology, perhaps the two disciplines most relevant to the actual work of investigating the material conditions of human life (Prown 1988:23). Archaeologists are especially well suited to use material objects in the service of historical and cultural reconstruction because their main focus of interest is interpreting the formal, spatial, and temporal dimensions of the archaeological record—the combined detritus of humanity from time immemorial that covers all corners of the globe and beyond. In contrast, art historians often work with curated objects like baskets, clothing, and beadwork, which are commonly made of more perishable materials, though these distinctions are by no means hard and fast.

Although archaeologists typically unearth their data, once out of the ground such finds are available for a wider audience to ponder and reinterpret. Moreover, new archaeological records (artifacts and their spatial relations) await discovery. This is important because it means that archaeology offers a continually evolving database that can serve as a cross-check against insights gained through other approaches. Archaeologists are also trained to pay particular attention to provenience and association—in short, context—and to employ a comparative perspective in assessing the significance of their observations for historical and anthropological reconstruction. What they lack in the completeness of the record is offset by context. And lastly, archaeologists have access to the products of behavior over large spatial arenas and long segments of time (Wobst 1978), even though they cannot observe behavior directly. This perspective allows them to utilize the comparative approach to its fullest potential.

Whither Prehistory?

Archaeologists have spent considerable effort trying to determine the goals of their discipline. There has been serious debate over whether archaeology should be oriented toward creating a narrative of human history or deriving nomothetic laws of human behavior (Deetz 1977a, 1983; Flannery 1967; Preucel 1991; Taylor 1948; Trigger 1989). This has created a healthy tension in the field today between the discipline's generalizing and particularistic tendencies. Trigger (1980) was among the first to criticize the thrust of processual archaeology for its generalized treatment of Native American pasts. He rightfully argued that archaeology would remain irrelevant to indigenous peoples so long as practitioners used the archaeological record only as a laboratory to test models of human behavior. Such an approach lacked any appreciation of the historical developments that were unique to indigenous peoples. Trigger sounded a call for a reconsideration of the notion of historical process. This did not "entail simply the building of chronologies and the construction of typologies" that marked the earlier cultural-historical paradigm (Cobb and Nassaney 1995:216). Rather, it called for a renewed interest in the historical contexts in which groups reproduced their social relations through time and across space.

Native peoples were creating and reproducing their social identities through encounters with neighboring groups soon after they settled the continent and began to fill its niches more than ten thousand years ago (Nassaney and Sassaman 1995). The important point to be made is that the dynamics of Native societies changed more in degree than in kind and content after their contacts with Europeans and Africans (Wilson and Rogers 1993). Native peoples had histories long before European chroniclers were on hand to record their observations of Native life and the passage of events (cf. Rowlands 1989; Trigger 1980). Thus, we acknowledge the importance of historical documents for elucidating some aspects of Native pasts, and we recognize that fundamentally different methodologies can be applied to material remains when written documents are available. However, we do not find it useful to retain the concept of "prehistory" in our study of the events and activities that structured the lives of Native Americans prior to 1492 (see also Axtell 1989, 1997:18; Deagan 1988; Lightfoot 1995; Robinson 1994:88–89). By rejecting "prehistory," we adopt a perspective that challenges the artificial division between so-called "prehistoric" and historical archaeology (Rubertone 1996:81; see also Nassaney 1999).

Moreover, we realize that written documents as well as other potential sources of information (for example, paintings, photographs) must be subjected to critical source analysis to contextualize the work. To understand a document we have to understand its author, the milieu in which it was written, as well as the author's qualifications as an observer and his or her purpose for writing (Galloway 1993:81). Many researchers have underscored the potential problems associated with documents written by white, male Europeans who lived in stratified societies (Axtell 1997:14; Deetz 1977b). Unquestionably, Native societies were often significantly transformed through contact by the time Europeans began to record their observations (Dunnell 1991; Wolf 1982). This does not, however, render those observations useless. Although we must retain a healthy dose of skepticism regarding the ability of any and all documents to inform about Native culture prior to contact, we think that the historical record can be used cautiously to frame questions regarding the meaning of material goods. Indeed, the strengths of the approaches showcased in this volume lie in their unabashed efforts to draw exhaustively on a multitude of data sources to shed light on a particular ethnic identity (Part I), daily activity (Part II), or ritual practice (Part III). The result is an attempt to understand more clearly the forces that created and conditioned change and continuity in all aspects of Native American life.

The Rise of Interdisciplinary Studies

The vitality of ethnohistory and historical archaeology is testimony to the expanded interest in interdisciplinary studies in the postmodern world. One of the clearest indicators of this trend is the number of new journals devoted to exploring the interstices and common ground of traditional disciplines, and the fruitful results brought about by cross-fertilization. A good example is the *Journal of Material Culture,* which was launched in

1996 and claims to "fill the last serious gap in the structure of the social sciences." It was designed to cater to the increasing interest in material culture studies and the relationship between artifacts and social relations irrespective of time and space. The linkages between material, thought, and action are the focus of the studies assembled here, and each chapter is meant to illustrate the potential benefits of the interdisciplinary approaches that we are advocating. An exhaustive material history of the continent would require an encyclopedic treatment well beyond the scope of this endeavor. Instead, we have selected case studies that take as their starting point objects of material culture that can be juxtaposed with other source materials to elucidate change and continuity in the sociopolitical, cultural, and ritual lives of Native North Americans. These studies can be seen as examples of text-aided archaeology (for example, Little 1992) with the purpose of writing culture histories. Although other sources of information are available to document past lifeways (for example, written accounts, oral tradition), we think that material culture is essential because it is potentially more representative than documents and more enduring than oral accounts. Artifacts may be less constrained by some of the biases of written works because they are the direct products of Native hands and therefore originate within a Native worldview.

The Scope of This Book

Native Americans have always made and modified material objects; their earliest examples are more than ten thousand years old. Their material culture has been the subject of curiosity by early antiquarians and, later, of careful scrutiny by archaeologists and art historians. The contributors to this volume focus on analyses and interpretations of the objects that were produced over the past several hundred years. Artifacts from this recent period are often associated with written documents and oral accounts. At the same time, these artifacts also reflect to a significant degree the changes and continuities of Native Americans who came into contact with Europeans and Africans.

An early focus of ethnohistory as well as the study of Native Americans in historical archaeology was an examination of the process by which indigenous peoples became acculturated to European lifeways, often by examining changes in artifact assemblages (Brain 1979; G. Quimby 1966; Quimby and Spoehr 1951; Spicer 1961). Anthropologists often believed that the adoption of elements from Euroamerican culture marked a process by which Native cultures became transformed. Ultimately, a prolonged period of sustained acculturation would lead to assimilation, whereby Natives lost all vestiges of their original cultural identities and came to resemble the dominant society (Linton 1940). This problematic is now phrased in different terms since simple acculturation models have proven inadequate to explain the complexity of Native responses during the Contact period (see Bradley 1987; Branstner 1992; Brenner 1988; Burton 1976; Fitzhugh 1985; Rubertone 1989; Spicer 1971; Thomas 1979). For example, in their encounters with colonial powers, Native Americans often created new societies that were similar to, yet different from, their parent cultures (Merrell 1988:96; see also Hill 1996). This process of ethnogenesis—the creation and recreation of ethnic and tribal entities—poses significant challenges to anthropologists who attempt to identify pre-Contact archaeological complexes with historical peoples. The theme of ethnogenesis is taken up in Part I of this collection.

Ethnogenesis: The Creation, Maintenance, and Transformation of Ethnic Identity

Anthropologists have long recognized that archaeology is a unique technique for monitoring long-term history, particularly in areas that lack a continuous written record. Demographers (for example, Cook 1976; Dobyns 1983) were among the first to question the accuracy of written documents compiled after sustained contact with Europeans. Their suspicions are supported by the work of epidemiologists, who argue that European diseases were transmitted to non-European populations (often well in advance of direct European contact) with devastating impacts. Thus, the introduction of foreign diseases brought about one of the earliest disruptions in Native American societies (A. Crosby 1972; Dobyns 1983; Hill 1996:4; Ramenofsky 1987). These biological insults had expectable cultural and social ramifications. The immediate population decline that followed in the wake of numerous epidemics led to demographic upheaval and subsequent migrations as groups coalesced to form viable social and biological units. Population movements created a domino effect by the 17th and 18th centuries, as groups along the Atlantic seaboard retreated inland and encroached on the territories of their neighbors. The ethnic composition of many Native groups was in almost constant flux as adjustments were made to the biological and social impacts of Europeans. Groups moved, amalgamated, fragmented, disappeared, emerged, and persisted.

These demographic changes were accompanied by changes in social organization, ideology, and political structure. These disruptions were particularly common among the tribes of the Great Plains, where cultural changes give the impression of historical discontinuity (Albers 1996; Hickerson 1996). Historic tribes of the region exhibit an "intermingling of previously disparate cultural traits and complexes" that distinguish them from their pre-Contact ancestors (Hickerson 1996:71). Structural changes in Native societies of the lower Mississippi Valley had occurred by the end of the 17th century, although diseases may not have been directly responsible (Burnett and Murray 1991, cited in Hoffman 1993). The populous groups with hereditary chiefs that occupied the walled towns of Pacaha and Casqui, which the de Soto chroniclers observed in the 1540s, were reorganized beyond recognition by the time the French traveled downstream 130 years later (see Cande, chap. 1). Population decrease, migration, and amalgamation were constantly taking place on the borders of centralized political entities, leading to the creation and recreation of ethnic groups—a process anthropologists call ethnogenesis (see Sturtevant 1971). As a result of ethnogenesis, archaeologists have struggled to identify materials associated with the historic antecedents of a given people at the time of their earliest contact with Europeans. While the process of ethnogenesis was not confined to the post-Contact period (see Nassaney and Sassaman 1995), it apparently accelerated and intensified after 1492.

Archaeologists and historians are devising innovative ways to identify ethnogenesis and recognize ethnic identity using material objects and archaeological remains. For example, recent archaeological investigations in the lower Mississippi Valley coupled with Native migration accounts have convinced some archaeologists that the Quapaw were likely newcomers to the valley. Late Mississippi period and protohistoric sites in east-central Arkansas are now believed to be associated with the Tunica (Hoffman 1994; Jeter 1986, 1990). Jeffrey Brain (1988) and others have traced Tunica movements from central Arkansas in the mid-16th century to their current homeland in eastern Louisiana.

Similar forced migrations have been documented elsewhere in the midcontinent. For example, William Cremin (1995, 1996) has identified ceramics in his investigations of Berrien-phase (A.D. 1400–1600) sites in southwestern Michigan that resemble early historic Potawatomi materials at the mouth of Green Bay. These stylistic similarities, which suggest a cultural connection, are supported by documentary evidence that indicates that the Potawatomi were recent arrivals in northeast Wisconsin, probably a result of displacement caused by Iroquois incursions from the east. The changes wrought by population movements challenge ethno-historians to recognize ethnic identities in the absence of written documentation.

The displacement of Native peoples in the Eastern Woodlands during the 16th through 18th centuries had profound implications for ethnogenesis throughout much of North America. Thus, archaeological remains are not always easily linked to historic tribes who later came to reside in a region. The populous, hierarchical, palisaded towns of northeast Arkansas observed by de Soto are archaeologically conspicuous. We know them as the materials associated with the Nodena and Parkin phases. Researchers are comparing records from the de Soto *entrada* with Spanish finds from archaeological sites in the region to gain a better understanding of Native politics and social organization prior to and after Spanish contact (see contributors to Young and Hoffman [1993] among others). These data are crucial because the late Mississippi period and early historic inhabitants of northeast Arkansas left few descendants into the historic period. Archaeologists and historians have struggled to understand the processes responsible for such a significant settlement reorganization, if not wholesale abandonment, of the region by the time the French arrived in the 1670s.

Kathleen Cande (chap. 1) compares ritual activity and its material implications during the initial two centuries of culture contact to explain the relationship between the Mississippian peoples encountered by de Soto and the Quapaw that greeted the French in the late 17th century. She identifies a number of rituals such as gift giving, feasting, and the Sacred Pole that exhibit continuity from the Mississippian occupation of northeast Arkansas to the late 17th-century Quapaw. Her analysis also points to the complexities of interpreting the fragmentary documentary records and material remains that were collected with other research questions in mind. Until more problem-oriented archaeology is conducted in the region, it appears that the jury will still be out over whether the Quapaw are recent migrants into the region, or whether they represent survivors in an attenuated form of their more hierarchically organized ancestors of a century and a half earlier.

The potential contradictions between material and documentary evidence are highlighted in James Pendergast's contribution to this collection (chap. 2). He provides a thorough history of scholarly attempts to establish the ethnic identity of the people of Jacques Cartier's Stadacona and Hochelaga sites near present-day Montreal in the St. Lawrence River Valley. For various reasons, historians have been reluctant to incorporate archaeological findings in their assessments of the Native groups first encountered by the French in this region. Archaeologists also have sometimes prematurely judged an archaeological site to be a specific place mentioned in written documents. For example, the apparent misidentification of the Menard site in the lower Arkansas Valley as the Quapaw village of Osotouy (Ford 1961) led investigators to believe that the Quapaw were descended from local populations, a conclusion that has yet to be demonstrated. Despite these problems in identification both in the lower Arkansas and St. Lawrence river valleys, practitioners are ill advised to give up the direct historical approach, although it must be used with the utmost caution for the reasons alluded to above (see also Fenton 1957; Galloway 1992).

The formation of the Winnebago as an ethnic entity is another problem that has defied a simple explanation after nearly one hundred years of investigation in the upper Midwest. Neither archaeological nor documentary approaches to identifying Winnebago origins are by themselves satisfactory. John Staeck (chap. 3) uses material drawn from oral tradition to help reconcile differences in interpretation brought about by varying data sources. He suggests that archaeologists have been looking at the antecedents of the Winnebago all along, but were unable to make the connection because of facile expectations. If the Winnebago are seen as a post-Contact amalgamation of groups from the western Great Lakes, then their ancestors are probably represented by segments of the Oneota, Effigy Mound, and countless other contemporaneous archaeological complexes and cultural variants in the region.

As an outgrowth of his interests in political process, Eric Johnson (chap. 4) considers the ways in which material culture was implicated in the creation of political alliances and community identity in southern New England. He uses the discordance between ceramic styles and Native homelands to suggest the absence of permanent social boundaries and the relative instability of political alliance. After the Pequot War (1636–37), some Native communities were flooded with refugees even as increasing political tensions created unprecedented social boundaries between some groups. Under these conditions a distinctive ceramic style emerged. Johnson argues that the development of so-called Shantok-style pottery both reflected and sustained these new political realities among the Mohegans, who sought to distinguish themselves from their neighbors and promote internal solidarity.

Ethnic markers permeate the material world and are not confined to ceramics. Moreover, the relative permanence of artifacts makes them good candidates for spatial analysis. Even though artifacts are portable by definition, their location can still lead us to the person behind the artifact. Objects need not be abandoned, lost, or discarded to be of interest to the ethnohistorian, as museum anthropologists well know. Many Native products of clay, stone, wood, hide, and cloth that have either been passed down through the ages or reinvented in the 20th century provide insights into the ways in which objects express social relations, often through elaborate symbolic codes (for example, Burnham 1992; Penney 1992).

The tradition of Native ribbon work from the Great Lakes region has left physical remains that can be profitably subjected to material analysis. Susan Neill (chap. 5) uses ethnographic specimens collected in the 19th and 20th centuries to explore the role of cloth in the expression of cultural identities. Her comprehensive material-culture study led her to create a large database and annotated bibliography that enabled her to synthesize information from museum collections, photographs, secondary documents, and oral interviews. Her study shows that stylistic attributes of ribbon work reflect the cultural, economic, and political concerns of indigenous peoples over the past two centuries. The analysis has many parallels with the study of beadwork among Plains Indian groups in which various colors and configurations served to identify ethnic groups in the 19th century (Byers 1995; Logan and Schmittou 1995). Woodsplint baskets from colonial and historic New England as well as basketry from other regions of North America have also yielded similar insights (for example, McMullen 1995; McMullen and Handsman 1987; Turnbaugh and Turnbaugh 1986).

Change and Continuity in Daily Life

Native peoples and their distinctive identities persist into the 21st century, despite the challenges they have had to face over the past five hundred years. Perhaps the most devastating effect of European contact was the introduction of epidemic diseases, to which Native people had no natural immunities. European efforts at military, political, and cultural conquest were frequently met with more successful resistance. The material and documentary records of Native North America are replete with cases of resistance to cultural and political domination. These efforts are exemplified in the so-called "Indian Wars," which began as soon as Europeans came ashore and continue in parts of the Americas to this day. Native peoples had much to lose, and they often challenged the new systems of hegemony that their would-be conquerors sought to impose upon them through economic, political, military, and ideological means.

A major theme in ethnohistory and historical archaeology has been the consequences of interactions between Native Americans and Europeans, particularly in the realm of material exchange. Europeans often drew Native Americans into the world economic system and relations of dependency by offering them finished goods in exchange for valued raw materials such as fur, fish, wampum, and land (Wolf 1982). Simple models that argue for the technological superiority of European goods to account for their rapid adoption have been replaced in recent years with interpretations that emphasize the Native point of view. As might be expected, Native responses to exchange were quite variable and were likely negotiated repeatedly. George Hamell's (1983) study of the way in which trade goods such as beads, mirrors, and shiny metal objects fit into preconceived Native symbolic categories underscores the fact that trade goods had different meanings in various social contexts. These goods were not necessarily superior to Native counterparts and were often used in different ways than their producers had intended as they came to serve new functions only explicable from a Native perspective.

It is also well established that European goods often served as symbols of social prestige among individuals who could command access to such goods. Native peoples' responses to European commodities varied widely depending on the goods themselves, the traders, the status of Native clients, and a host of other factors (see, for example, Brenner 1988; Rubertone 1989). Peter Thomas (1979) was among the first ethnohistorians to discuss the complexity of the exchange relationship and noted that for Native peoples, objects served primarily as tangible representations of social alliances. This is not to say that European markets did not sometimes provide new economic opportunities that Native peoples exploited to transform their roles and responsibilities within a rapidly changing society (Nassaney 1989). If one constant has emerged from these studies it is that no single model can account for the motivations that initiated exchange and the conditions that made Native peoples receptive to the goods being offered (cf. Trubowitz 1995). It would be extremely informative to explore how exchange relations changed over time and varied within and between groups. Continuing analysis of the types and frequency of traded objects, as well as their contexts of use and deposition, will help to refine their meanings over time and space.

The study of exchange need not be confined to the realm of technology. While technological products were the dominant medium of exchange,

and one that is often preserved archaeologically, trading activities had implications for the social, political, and ideological spheres of Native life. Alice Kehoe (chap. 6) uses Native artifacts (ceramic pots and a stone knife blade) from a late 18th-century "pedlars' post" in Saskatchewan to identify Indian women residents of the post who were traders' wives. Limited documentary evidence is used to frame the possibility of this interpretation. This raises the interesting issue of the mechanisms involved in interactions on the frontier. Marriage, as a potentially long-term bond that serves to create formidable alliances across ethnic boundaries, is a practice whose material implications remain understudied and undertheorized to our knowledge (but see White 1999:128–37).

Technological products were frequently exchanged between Natives and newcomers throughout North America. Since technology is by definition a means of enhancing human labor to extract energy from the environment, it should come as no surprise that new technologies had far-reaching implications for subsistence practices. At the same time, anthropologists note that foodways are one of the most conservative aspects of culture. Thus, we should expect patterns of both change and continuity in the dietary choices and food-acquisition strategies that Natives practiced, particularly as European goods became increasingly available.

Brooke Arkush (chap. 7) presents a comparative study of the long-term use of animal traps in the Mono Lake Basin of east-central California. The archaeological remnants of features that have been in use over the past several hundred years have contributed important information to our understanding of cultural continuity and change among the Mono Basin Paiute. Arkush notes that even though various aspects of Paiute culture were dramatically altered through direct and indirect contact with Euroamericans, traps used to capture big game were in use (sometimes continuously) from the pre-Contact period (18th century) into the 20th century. Material evidence of these activities complements written accounts of material culture modification and retention among the Mono Basin Paiute.

Another well-known feature used by Native Americans is the storage or cache pit. Recent archaeological investigations conducted by Sean Dunham (chap. 8), at a mid-19th-century Native homestead in Newaygo County, Michigan, revealed several depressions that appear to represent the cache pits described in the local ethnohistoric literature. Dunham uses ethnographic, historic, ethnobotanical, and archaeological approaches to understand the function of these pits. These distinctive features were likely used well before Europeans settled in Michigan and may be useful markers to distinguish between contemporaneous Native and Euroamerican occupations in the 19th century.

Carol Mason and Margaret Holman (chap. 9) also raise the question of continuity in subsistence practices. Each author has previously studied the practice of maple sugaring in the Midwest and each has come to differing conclusions regarding its antiquity (Holman 1984; Mason 1985). Historic accounts document the sugar-making process in considerable detail, and illustrations survive from the early 18th century. Lafitau (cited in Holmes 1903:32–33) described the tapping of the trees, the collecting of the sap, the boiling of the water, and the shaping of the soft sugar into cakes. What is yet to be established is whether this craft was performed in "recent aboriginal times, if not in very ancient times," to use the words of W. H. Holmes (1903:31). Although the debate continues to simmer, Mason and Holman agree that material evidence is likely the only way that we can know for sure who invented maple sugaring.

A similar debate revolves around the origins of fish fertilizer in New England. Traditionally held to be a Native American practice taught to the settlers of Plimoth Plantation by their Patuxet ally Tisquantum (Squanto), it was recently suggested that the practice originated in Europe, where it was observed by Tisquantum, who introduced it to Massachusetts (Ceci 1975). More recently, ethnohistoric (Nanepashemet 1993) and archaeological studies (Mrozowski 1994) have offered compelling evidence that the technique was indeed of Native origin.

Archaeologists no longer assume that the presence of Europeans and the changes that they brought necessarily led to a complete transformation in Native lifeways. Late 19th-century ethnographers of the Canadian Plateau were concerned with recording what appeared to be "traditional" Native culture, while ignoring changes that came about in order to preserve and maintain ethnicity. Catherine Carlson (chap. 10) has recently begun to investigate the archaeology of a Salishan village adjacent to a trading post established by the Hudson's Bay Company in British Columbia. Her findings document a record of material culture that exhibits both change and continuity in the context of European expansion. She argues that traditional architectural features, storage facilities, portable technological objects, and faunal remains recovered from Native encampments near the fort were used to reproduce Native social identity in the face of early cultural interactions with the British and Eurocanadians. Comparisons of differing contact settings can help to identify broad-scale patterning in the changes associated with Native lifeways. For instance, how do the sequences of goods adopted by Native groups from their European trading partners vary among different groups? Which aspects of Native culture are most resistant or most susceptible to change and how does this vary from group to group? What are the material expressions of resistance, accommodation, continuity, and change, and again, how do these vary in different circumstances?

The still-life images of Natives left to us by Samuel de Champlain, Edward Curtis, Theodore De Bry, Joseph François Lafitau, John White, and others constitute important media that provide yet another avenue to the past. While many of these early travelers were not trained artists, their graphic renditions often corroborate other types of evidence. For example, Stephen Mrozowski (1994) has recently uncovered archaeological evidence of Native corn hills associated with a shelter at Sandy's Point in eastern Massachusetts that are remarkably similar to features shown in Champlain's engravings from the early 17th century. In the North American West, where the ethnographic present lasted well into the 19th century, Plains Indian groups created a rich tradition of pictographic drawings on buffalo hides (Lanford 1995). This was later replaced by an artform known as "ledger drawings," so called because many were made on paper from the bound ledgers that soldiers and traders used to inventory their goods (see Lovett and DeWitt 1998). These pictorial narratives often include scenes proclaiming a man's prowess in activities such as buffalo hunting, warrior exploits, and hand-to-hand combat. In nonliterate societies, such images could serve as mnemonic devices that would prompt the oral historian of a group in recounting the stories passed down from generation to generation by word of mouth. These Native forms of graphic art can be juxtaposed with the Euroamerican drawings and photographs that became popular in the 19th century.

Mark Parker Miller (chap. 11) uses pictographic self-portraits made by Mahtotohpa to evaluate the historical accuracy of some of George Catlin's paintings of the Mandan created in 1832. Catlin is one of the best known among numerous 19th-century professional artists who left us a legacy in oil, canvas, bronze, and printed images. These works of art are an interesting form of material culture even though many are the products of Euroamerican artisans using Western conventions to depict Native subjects (see Katakis 1998). Miller analyzes a few of Catlin's paintings in relation to archaeological data, scenes by other artists, and ethnographic specimens to evaluate the utility of the paintings for understanding the historical Mandan. His analysis shows that even though Catlin's paintings are rooted in Euroamerican traditions of representation, they nevertheless depict important details of Mandan material culture. In the end, the analyst is able to transcend Catlin and his culture and learn something about the Mandan themselves.

Ritual, Iconography, and Ideology

Ethnohistorians who seek to understand the meaning of ritual, iconography, and ideology are heavily dependent upon the clues that they can extract about symbolic systems from historical accounts (both oral and written), along with insights that living descendants may be able and willing to offer. For many archaeologists, ideology lies on the top rung of the ladder of inference (Hawkes 1954). Although American archaeology has a strong materialist grounding, numerous voices espouse the important role of belief in structuring the material world and, in turn, social relations (for example, Beaudry 1989; Conrad and Demarest 1984; C. Crosby 1988; Hall 1979; Leone 1984; Seeman 1995). Since ethnohistorians and historical archaeologists have access to the products of both historical and anthropological research, they are uniquely poised to study ritual through synthesizing the particulars of historical inquiry with the generalizing tendencies of the anthropological enterprise.

Unfortunately for the archaeologist, unambiguous evidence of ritual or ideological systems is seldom directly recoverable from the archaeological record. Yet despite the rarity of ritual artifacts in most archaeological contexts, significant quantities of objects with ideological messages have been recovered from Mississippi-period (ca. A.D. 900–1700) sites in the Southeast, particularly at the cult centers of Spiro in Oklahoma and Etowah in Georgia. Larissa Thomas (chap. 12) takes the opportunity to use female representations in Mississippian iconography to explore the role of women in ritual practice and belief immediately prior to and during the early Contact period. Her study focuses on a large sample of objects in stone, ceramic, copper, and shell, including figurines, smoking pipes, bottles, plates, gorgets, and cups from sites across the region. Ethnohistorical sources and the archaeological contexts of discovery provide a framework to interpret the objects' symbolic contents and social-ritual contexts of use. Thomas's analysis forces us to rethink the role of women in the ritual world of Native American chiefly societies and reconsider their importance in the social, political, and ideological realms of everyday life.

Another class of ritual objects that are found in hierarchical societies are the mortuary masks of the Northwest Coast. Barbara Brotherton (chap. 13) uses these ethnographic objects as primary documents from historical contexts that have limited reliable written records. As an art historian, Brotherton persuasively demonstrates how art can act as a mirror of social change and cultural continuity. Her focus is the mortuary art of the Tlingit shamans of southeast Alaska, which embodies information on the role of the traditional healer, changes in curing implements, and Tlingit views about health, medicine, and the spiritual world. She uses the rich body of ethnographic data collected by Boas and his students to support her claims about the meanings of what must be highly sensitive cultural objects. Paying close attention to stylistic conventions in this art form, Brotherton is able to identify individual carvers or schools of carvers who trained or worked together. This type of attribute analysis goes well beyond the comparatively crude stylistic analyses that archaeologists use to link artifact types with ethnic groups (cf. Johnson, chap. 4; Neill, chap. 5). Brotherton's approach may be worth emulating in the study of other highly plastic and visually expressive forms of material culture such as beadwork, decorated basketry, clothing, or ceramics. Another group of objects that may be particularly amenable to a similar type of analysis are the well-known human effigy head pots of southeast Missouri and northeast Arkansas. Specialized artisans may have produced these ceramic portraiture vessels, which are typically found in 14th to 16th century mortuary contexts, in the likeness of the newly deceased to commemorate their death. A careful analysis might reveal clusters of stylistic attributes that may be associated with individual artists or artistic traditions that have heretofore gone unrecognized.

A group's cosmology is often expressed in various aspects of the ritual treatment of the dead, which usually follows culturally specific prescriptions. For this reason, early archaeologists and museum collectors were attracted to mortuary sites where the placement, orientation, and accompaniments of the dead reflected ideas about the afterlife and other ideological dimensions. As the last two papers in this collection illustrate, mortuary ritual occurs in an ideologically charged environment. Native peoples commonly demarcate sacred areas for the burial of the dead, which are accorded ritual and sometimes supernatural significance. Moreover, cemeteries can be used to resolve social and ideological conflicts from which the living cannot easily escape.

Paul Robinson (chap. 14) discusses the rich historical record that describes the ancient, continuing, and complex Native use of Conanicut Island in the state of Rhode Island. The island first came to the attention of ethnohistorians through the work of William Simmons (1970), a well-known anthropologist, folklorist, and ethnographer of the Narragansetts.

In the 1960s, Simmons collected valuable information from a threatened burial ground called the West Ferry site. Subsequent work has redefined and extended the boundaries of the site (McBride 1989). It has become clear that the island was an important ritual location for millennia. However, secondary historical accounts deny the ritual importance of the burial ground, despite the claims made by the Narragansetts over their concern for past activities on the island. Two contradictory ideologies have emerged regarding the history and contemporary significance of Conanicut Island. Robinson suggests that the attitudes toward this place, and the role of archaeological materials in shaping those attitudes, is a function of social and political circumstances. With the 1990 passage of the Native American Graves Protection and Repatriation Act (NAGPRA), there appears to be a positive change of attitude among some local residents, who are beginning to express respect and concern for the graves of their Narragansett predecessors. One would like to think that the work of archaeologists and ethnohistorians was instrumental in bringing about this new sensitivity and will continue to promote respect and empathy between peoples who have held conflicting perspectives on the past.

The final paper in the collection by Michael Nassaney (chap. 15) also explores the mortuary ritual beliefs of the Narragansetts. Just as the Narragansetts were gaining federal recognition, the accidental discovery of a remarkably well preserved 17th-century cemetery less than three miles from Roger Williams's trading post in Rhode Island came to the attention of local archaeologists. Most investigators involved with the cemetery have welcomed a body of ethnographic information collected through the years, beginning in 1643 with Roger Williams's *A Key into the Language of America* (1936), arguably the first Native North American ethnography. The cemetery has spawned some debate over the reaction of Native Americans to the European presence, and the ways in which 17th-century mortuary ritual was implicated (Nassaney 1989; Robinson 1990; Robinson et al. 1985; Rubertone 1989). Nassaney's paper combines archaeology and oral history to make sense of two intrusive pits identified in the 1983 excavations and the postmortem interment of a soapstone smoking pipe.

The concordance of oral history and archaeological evidence points to increasing tensions between men and women as gender roles were being transformed in the process of European contact. As women and children gained access to tobacco for recreational use, men responded by revitalizing the tradition of carving stone pipes to restrict smoking behavior to ritual contexts. As a result, stone pipes came to reinforce notions of male identity. This cultural prescription was so rigidly adhered to that a stone pipe was returned to its rightful owner after death. Nassaney suggests that the lessons that emerged from conflicts between men and women as social roles became restructured during the turbulent 17th century were codified and passed on to subsequent generations through oral traditions. Such an interpretation would not have been possible had there not been multiple lines of evidence available to explore the meaning of ritual, ideology, and gender relations in the Contact period of southeastern New England.

Conclusion

The chapters in this volume are intended to showcase the vitality of material analysis in historical and anthropological studies today, particularly among scholars who work across disciplinary boundaries and derive their observations from various source materials. They also demonstrate that historical archaeologists are increasingly concerned with Native Americans, a trend that we predict will accelerate in the future (see Rubertone 1996). As the importance of material objects for contemporary Native groups has increased in the wake of recent legislation like NAGPRA, there is renewed interest in ways of extracting historical and cultural information from the tangible and the concrete. Archaeologists are not alone in this endeavor, but they can certainly lead the way. As experts in the analysis of the material world, archaeologists and their associates in art history and other related disciplines are well poised to unlock the hidden meanings that art, artifacts, and landscapes held to their makers, users, and viewers. Using a holistic and comparative methodology, they juxtapose objects, texts, oral accounts, and other source materials from the present and the past to explore structure, action, and outcome.

The case studies in this collection serve to complement and enhance our historical and cultural understandings of Native Americans. Indeed, change and continuity in their daily activities, social identities, and belief systems are encoded in the material symbols that they employed to create and recreate the cultural systems of everyday life. Needless to say, the process of cultural creation is not confined to Native Americans or to the past. Therefore, we maintain that the theoretical approaches and research methodologies highlighted in this volume have broader spatial and temporal applications and implications. For example, witness the importance of material symbols in contemporary Native displays of their identities in pow-wows and other public settings.

Moreover, the encounters that Native peoples experienced as a result of the creation of the modern world that was set in motion by the European Age of Discovery more than five centuries ago have parallels in Africa, Asia, and Australia. Societies with divergent values, viewpoints, and material assemblages have been repeatedly forced into contact with profound results (Wolf 1982). The formation of the Zulu state, the Irish potato famine, raiding for captives in West Africa, the Chinese opium wars, the emergence of Palmares in colonial Brazil, and the mass production and consumption of commodities in industrial settings are historical events of global significance that had their genesis in the creation of a world economic system and the subsequent clash of cultures (see Orser 1996; Paynter 2000a, 2000b; Wallerstein 1974; Wolf 1982). The conditions that gave rise to these developments and their consequences are ideally amenable to investigation through material objects as the flows of people, goods, and information were diverted in different directions and historically transformed by a host of new social, political, and economic processes. Importantly, the bearers and creators of culture accommodated themselves to these new demographic, social, and ideological conditions through artifacts and artificial spaces. By imposing meaning on their material lives, both the powerful and the disenfranchised attempted to rationalize a new world order. Fortunately for the material analyst, tangible traces of that physical world have often survived in the form of rusty nails, decorated potsherds, post-mold patterns, broken smoking pipes, and numerous other "small things forgotten" (Deetz 1977b). Such tangible evidence and its context form the interpretive springboards from which fuller historical and cultural understandings can be launched. Together with other sources of information about the human condition, material objects do indeed have much to contribute to the culture history of Native North America and any other place where people left traces of their activities, identities, and lives.

References Cited

Albers, Patricia C. 1996. Changing Patterns of Ethnicity in the Northeastern Plains, 1780–1870. In *History, Power, and Identity: Ethnogenesis in the Americas, 1492–1992,* ed. J. D. Hill, 90–118. University of Iowa Press, Iowa City.

Andren, Anders. 1998. *Between Artifacts and Texts: Historical Archaeology in Global Perspective.* Plenum Press, New York.

Axtell, James. 1989. *After Columbus.* Oxford University Press, New York.

———. 1997. The Ethnohistory of Native America. In *Rethinking American Indian History,* ed. D. L. Fixico, 11–27. University of New Mexico Press, Albuquerque.

Barber, Russell. 1994. Source Analysis. In *Doing Historical Archaeology,* by R. J. Barber, 8–16. Prentice Hall, Englewood Cliffs, N.J.

Beaudry, Mary C. 1989. The Lowell Boot Mills Complex and Its Housing: Material Expressions of Corporate Ideology. *Historical Archaeology* 23:18–32.

———, ed. 1988. *Documentary Archaeology in the New World.* Cambridge University Press, Cambridge.

Binford, Lewis. 1962. Archaeology as Anthropology. *American Antiquity* 28:217–25.

Bradley, James W. 1987. *Evolution of the Onondaga Iroquois: Accommodating Change, 1500–1655.* Syracuse University Press, Syracuse, N.Y.

Bragdon, Kathleen J. 1996. *Native People of Southern New England, 1500–1650.* University of Oklahoma Press, Norman.

Brain, Jeffrey P. 1979. *Tunica Treasure.* Papers of the Peabody Museum of Archaeology and Ethnology 71. Harvard University, Cambridge.

———. 1988. *Tunica Archaeology.* Papers of the Peabody Museum of Archaeology and Ethnology 78. Harvard University, Cambridge.

Branstner, Susan M. 1992. Tionontate Huron Occupation at the Marquette Mission. In *Calumet and Fleur-de-Lys: Archaeology of Indian and French Contact in the Midcontinent,* ed. J. A. Walthall and T. E. Emerson, 177–201. Smithsonian Institution Press, Washington, D.C.

Brenner, Elise. 1988. Sociopolitical Implications of Mortuary Ritual Remains in 17th Century Native Southern New England. In *The Recovery of Meaning: Historical Archaeology in the Eastern United States,* ed. M. P. Leone and P. B. Potter, Jr., 147–81. Smithsonian Institution Press, Washington, D.C.

Burnett, Barbara A., and Katherine A. Murray. 1991. Death, Drought and de Soto: The Bioarchaeology of Depopulation. Revised paper delivered at the 1989 "De Soto in Arkansas" symposium, Fayetteville.

Burnham, Dorothy K. 1992. *To Please the Caribou: Painted Caribou-Skin Coats Worn by the Naskapi, Montagnais, and Cree Hunters of the Quebec-Labrador Peninsula.* University of Washington Press, Seattle.

Burton, William John. 1976. Hellish Fiends and Brutish Men: Amerindian-Euroamerican Interaction in Southern New England, An Interdisciplinary Analysis, 1600–1750. Ph.D. diss., Kent State University, Kent, Ohio.

Byers, Stan. 1995. Arapaho Assimilation and Distinction. Paper presented in the symposium "Expressions of Ethnicity: Evolutionary and Historical Perspectives on Plains Indian Art," the Frank McClung Museum, University of Tennessee, Knoxville.

Ceci, Lynn. 1975. Fish Fertilizer: A Native North American Practice? *Science* 188:26–30.

Cobb, Charles R., and Michael S. Nassaney. 1995. Interaction and Integration in the Late Woodland Southeast. In *Native American Interactions: Multiscalar Analyses and Interpretations in the Eastern Woodlands,* ed. M. S. Nassaney and K. E. Sassaman, 205–26. University of Tennessee Press, Knoxville.

Conrad, Geoffrey W., and Arthur A. Demarest. 1984. *Religion and Empire*. Cambridge University Press, Cambridge.

Cook, Sherburne F. 1976. *The Indian Population of New England in the Seventeenth Century*. University of California, Publications in Anthropology vol. 12. University of California Press, Berkeley.

Cremin, William. 1995. Identifying the Potawatomi in Late Prehistory: The Contribution of Archaeology in Establishing the Ethnicity of the Berrien Phase People of Southwest Michigan. Paper presented at the annual meeting of the American Society for Ethnohistory, Kalamazoo, Mich.

———. 1996. The Berrien Phase of Southwest Michigan: Proto-Potawatomi? In *Investigating the Archaeological Record of the Great Lakes State*, ed. M. B. Holman, J. G. Brashler, and K. E. Parker, 383–413. New Issues Press, Western Michigan University, Kalamazoo.

Crosby, Alfred W. 1972. *The Columbian Exchange: Biological and Cultural Consequences of 1492*. Greenwood Publishing, Westport, Conn.

Crosby, Constance A. 1988. From Myth to History, or Why King Philip's Ghost Walks Abroad. In *The Recovery of Meaning: Historical Archaeology in the Eastern United States*, ed. M. P. Leone and P. B. Potter, Jr., 183–209. Smithsonian Institution Press, Washington, D.C.

Deagan, Kathleen. 1988. Neither History nor Prehistory: The Questions that Count in Historical Archaeology. *Historical Archaeology* 22(1):7–12.

DeCunzo, LuAnn, and Bernard L. Herman, eds. 1996. *Historical Archaeology and the Study of American Culture*. Henry Francis du Pont Winterthur Museum, Winterthur, Del.

Deetz, James F. 1977a. Historical Archaeology as the Science of Material Culture. In *Historical Archaeology and the Importance of Material Things*, ed. L. G. Ferguson, 9–12. Special Publication 2, Society for Historical Archaeology, Tucson, Ariz.

———. 1977b. *In Small Things Forgotten*. Anchor Books, Garden City, N.Y.

———. 1983. Scientific Humanism and Humanistic Science: A Plea for Paradigmatic Pluralism in Historical Archaeology. *Geoscience and Man* 23:27–34.

Dobyns, Henry F. 1983. *Their Number Become Thinned: Native Population Dynamics in Eastern North America*. University of Tennessee Press, Knoxville.

Dunnell, Robert. 1991. Methodological Impacts of Catastrophic Depopulation on American Archaeology and Ethnology. In *Columbian Consequences*, vol. 3, *The Spanish Borderlands in Pan-American Perspective*, ed. D. H. Thomas, 561–80. Smithsonian Institution Press, Washington, D.C.

Falk, Lisa, ed. 1991. *Historical Archaeology in Global Perspective*. Smithsonian Institution Press, Washington, D.C.

Fenton, William N. 1957. *American Indian and White Relations to 1830: Needs and Opportunities for Study*. University of North Carolina Press, Chapel Hill.

Ferguson, Leland, ed. 1977. *Historical Archaeology and the Importance of Material Things*. Special Publication 2, Society for Historical Archaeology, Tucson, Ariz.

Fitzhugh, William, ed. 1985. *Cultures in Contact: The Impact of European Contacts on Native American Cultural Institutions, A.D. 1000–1800.* Smithsonian Institution Press, Washington, D.C.

Flannery, Kent. 1967. Culture History vs. Culture Process: A Debate in American Archaeology. *Scientific American* 217:119–22.

Ford, James A. 1961. *Menard Site: The Quapaw Village of Osotouy on the Arkansas River.* Anthropological Papers of the American Museum of Natural History, vol. 49, part 2.

Galloway, Patricia. 1992. The Unexamined Habitus: Direct Historic Analogy and the Archaeology of the Text. In *Representations in Archaeology*, ed. J. Gardin and C. S. Peebles, 178–95. Indiana University Press, Bloomington.

———. 1993. Ethnohistory. In *The Development of Southeastern Archaeology*, ed. J. K. Johnson, 78–108. University of Alabama Press, Tuscaloosa.

Garman, James C. 1994. Viewing the Color Line through the Material Culture of Death. *Historical Archaeology* 28(3):74–93.

Glassie, Henry. 1975. *Folk Housing in Middle Virginia.* University of Tennessee Press, Knoxville.

Hamell, George R. 1983. Trading in Metaphors: The Magic of Beads. In *Proceedings of the 1982 Glass Trade Bead Conference*, ed. C. F. Hayes III, 5–28. Rochester Museum and Science Center, Research Records 16.

Hall, Robert L. 1979. In Search of the Ideology of the Adena-Hopewell Climax. In *Hopewell Archaeology: The Chillicothe Conference*, ed. D. S. Brose and N'omi Greber, 258–65. Kent State University Press, Kent, Ohio.

Hawkes, Christopher F. 1954. Archaeological Theory and Method: Some Suggestions from the Old World. *American Anthropologist* 56:155–68.

Hickerson, Nancy P. 1996. Ethnogenesis in the Southern Plains. In *History, Power, and Identity: Ethnogenesis in the Americas, 1492–1992*, ed. J. D. Hill, 70–89. University of Iowa Press, Iowa City.

Hill, Jonathan D. 1996. Introduction: Ethnogenesis in the Americas, 1492–1992. In *History, Power, and Identity: Ethnogenesis in the Americas, 1492–1992*, ed. J. D. Hill, 1–19. University of Iowa Press, Iowa City.

Hodder, Ian. 1982. *Symbols in Action.* Cambridge University Press, Cambridge.

———. 1986. *Reading the Past: Current Approaches to Interpretation in Archaeology.* Cambridge University Press, Cambridge.

Hoffman, Michael P. 1990. The Terminal Mississippian Period in the Arkansas River Valley and Quapaw Ethnogenesis. In *Towns and Temples along the Mississippi*, ed. D. H. Dye and C. A. Cox, 208–26. University of Alabama Press, Tuscaloosa.

———. 1993. The Depopulation and Abandonment of Northeastern Arkansas in the Protohistoric Period. In *Archaeology of Eastern North America: Papers in Honor of Stephen Williams*, ed. J. B. Stoltman, 261–75. Archaeological Report No. 25. Mississippi Department of Archives and History, Jackson.

———. 1994. Ethnic Identities and Cultural Change in the Protohistoric Period of Eastern Arkansas. In *Perspectives on the Southeast: Linguistics, Archaeology, and Ethnohistory,* ed. P. B. Kwachka, 61–70. Southern Anthropological Society Proceedings no. 27. University of Georgia Press, Athens.

Holman, Margaret. 1984. The Identification of Late Woodland Maple Sugaring Sites in the Upper Great Lakes. *Midcontinental Journal of Archaeology* 9(1):63–89.

Holmes, William Henry. 1903. Aboriginal Pottery in the Eastern United States. In *20th Annual Report of the Bureau of American Ethnology for the Years 1898–1899,* 1–201. Government Printing Office, Washington, D.C.

Jeter, Marvin D. 1986. Tunicans West of the Mississippi: A Summary of Early Historic and Archaeological Evidence. In *The Protohistoric Period in the Mid-South: 1500–1700,* ed. D. H. Dye and R. C. Brister, 38–63. Proceedings of the 1983 Mid-South Archaeological Conference. Mississippi Department of Archives and History, Archaeological Report 18, Jackson.

———. 1990. Summary, Conclusions, and Alternative Interpretations. In *Goldsmith Oliver 2 (3PU306): A Protohistoric Archeological Site Near Little Rock, Arkansas,* vols. I–III, ed. M. D. Jeter, K. H. Cande, and J. J. Mintz, 507–37. Arkansas Archeological Survey, Fayetteville.

Katakis, Michael, ed. 1998. *Excavating Voices: Listening to Photographs of Native Americans.* University of Pennsylvania Museum, Philadelphia.

Kingery, W. David, ed. 1995. *Learning from Things: Method and Theory of Material Culture Studies.* Smithsonian Institution Press, Washington, D.C.

Krech, Shepard, III. 1991. The State of Ethnohistory. *Annual Review of Anthropology* 20:345–75.

Lanford, Benson. 1995. Proto-Historic and Early Historic Plains Indian Hide Painting. Paper presented in the symposium "Expressions of Ethnicity: Evolutionary and Historical Perspectives on Plains Indian Art," the Frank McClung Museum, University of Tennessee, Knoxville.

Leone, Mark P. 1984. Interpreting Ideology in Historical Archaeology: The William Paca Garden in Annapolis, Maryland. In *Ideology, Power, and Prehistory,* ed. Daniel Miller and Christopher Tilley, 25–35. Cambridge University Press, Cambridge.

Leone, Mark P., and Constance Crosby. 1987. Epilogue: Middle Range Theory in Historical Archaeology. In *Consumer Choice in Historical Archaeology,* ed. S. M. Spencer-Wood, 397–410. Plenum Press, New York.

Leone, Mark P., and Parker B. Potter, Jr. 1988. Introduction: Issues in Historical Archaeology. In *The Recovery of Meaning: Historical Archaeology in the Eastern United States,* ed. M. P. Leone and P. B. Potter, Jr., 1–22. Smithsonian Institution Press, Washington, D.C.

Lightfoot, Kent G. 1995. Culture Contact Studies: Redefining the Relationship between Prehistoric and Historical Archaeology. *American Antiquity* 60:199–217.

Linton, Ralph. 1940. The Distinctive Aspects of Acculturation. In *Acculturation in Seven American Indian Tribes,* ed. Ralph Linton, 501–20. Appleton-Century, New York.

Little, Barbara J., ed. 1992. *Test-Aided Archaeology.* CRC Press, Boca Raton, Fla.

Logan, Michael H., and Douglas A. Schmittou. 1995. The Crow Problem: A Test of the Boyd and Richerson Hypothesis. Paper presented in the symposium "Expressions of Ethnicity: Evolutionary and Historical Perspectives on Plains Indian Art," the Frank McClung Museum, University of Tennessee, Knoxville.

Lovett, John R., Jr., and Donald L. DeWitt (compilers). 1998. *Guide to Native American Ledger Drawings and Pictographs in United States Museums, Libraries, and Archives.* Bibliographies and Indexes in American History, no. 39. Greenwood Press, Westport, Conn.

Martin, Ann Smart, and J. Ritchie Garrison, eds. 1997. *American Material Culture: The Shape of the Field.* Henry Francis du Pont Winterthur Museum, Winterthur, Del.

Mason, Carol. 1985. Prehistoric Maple Sugaring Sites? *Midcontinental Journal of Archaeology* 10(1):149–52.

McBride, Kevin. 1989. *Phase I and II Investigations, West Ferry Site, RI 84, Jamestown Elementary School.* Jamestown School Committee, Jamestown, R.I.

McMullen, Ann. 1995. Under the Bridge: Woodsplint Basketry and the Identification of Hidden Native Communities in Historic New England. Paper presented at the annual meeting of the American Society for Ethnohistory, Kalamazoo, Mich.

McMullen, Ann, and Russell G. Handsman, eds. 1987. *A Key into the Language of Woodsplint Baskets.* American Indian Archaeological Institute, Washington, Conn.

Merrell, James H. 1988. The Indians' New World: The Catawba Experience. In *Material Life in America, 1600–1860,* ed. R. B. St. George, 95–112. Northeastern University Press, Boston.

Mrozowski, Stephen A. 1994. The Discovery of a Native American Cornfield on Cape Cod. *Archaeology of Eastern North America* 22:47–62.

Nanepashemet. 1993. It Smells Fishy to Me: An Argument Supporting the Use of Fish Fertilizer by the Native People of Southern New England. In *Algonkians of New England: Past and Present,* ed. Peter Benes, 42–50. Dublin Seminar for New England Folklife Annual Proceedings 1991, Boston University Press, Boston.

Nassaney, Michael S. 1989. An Epistemological Enquiry into Some Archaeological and Historical Interpretations of 17th Century Native American–European Relations. In *Archaeological Approaches to Cultural Identity,* ed. S. J. Shennan, 76–93. Unwin Hyman, London.

———. 1999. The Historical Development of Late Woodland Societies. Paper presented at the annual meeting of the Society for American Archaeology, Chicago.

Nassaney, Michael S., and Kenneth E. Sassaman, eds. 1995. *Native American Interactions: Multiscalar Analyses and Interpretations in the Eastern Woodlands.* University of Tennessee Press, Knoxville.

Orser, Charles E., Jr. 1996. *A Historical Archaeology of the Modern World.* Plenum Press, New York.

Patrick, Linda. 1985. Is There an Archaeological Record? In *Advances in Archaeological Method and Theory,* vol. 8, ed. M. B. Schiffer, 27–62. Academic Press, New York.

Paynter, Robert. 2000a. Historical and Anthropological Archaeology: Forging Alliances. *Journal of Archaeological Research* 8(1):1–37.

———. 2000b. Historical Archaeology and the Post-Columbian World of North America. *Journal of Archaeological Research* (in press).

Penney, David W. 1992. *Art of the American Indian Frontier.* Detroit Institute of Arts and the University of Washington Press, Seattle.

Potter, Parker B., Jr. 1992. Critical Archaeology: In the Ground and on the Street. *Historical Archaeology* 26:117–29.

Preucel, Robert W., ed. 1991. *Processual and Postprocessual Archaeologies.* Center for Archaeological Investigations, Occasional Paper No. 10. Southern Illinois University, Carbondale.

Prown, Jules. 1988. Mind in Matter: An Introduction to Material Culture Theory and Method. In *Material Life in America, 1600–1860,* ed. R. B. St. George, 17–37. Northeastern University Press, Boston.

Quimby, George I. 1966. *Indian Culture and European Trade Goods: The Archaeology of the Historic Period in the Western Great Lakes Region.* University of Wisconsin Press, Madison.

Quimby, George I., and Alexander Spoehr. 1951. *Acculturation and Material Culture.* Fieldiana 36(6). Chicago Natural History Museum, Chicago.

Quimby, Ian M. G., ed. 1978. *Material Culture and the Study of American Life.* W. W. Norton, New York.

Ramenofsky, Ann. 1987. *Vectors of Death: The Archaeology of European Contact.* University of New Mexico Press, Albuquerque.

Robinson, Paul A. 1990. The Struggle Within: The Indian Debate in Seventeenth-Century Narragansett Country. Ph.D. diss., Department of Anthropology, State University of New York at Binghamton.

———. 1994. Archaeology, History, and Native Americans: Preserving the Richness of the Past. In *Cultural Resource Management: Archaeological Research, Preservation Planning, and Public Education in the Northeastern United States,* ed. J. E. Kerber, 87–95. Bergin and Garvey, Westport, Conn.

Robinson, Paul A., Marc A. Kelley, and Patricia E. Rubertone. 1985. Preliminary Biocultural Interpretations from a Seventeenth-Century Narragansett Indian Cemetery in Rhode Island. In *Cultures in Contact: The Impact of European Contacts on Native American Cultural Institutions, A.D. 1000–1800,* ed. W. Fitzhugh, 107–30. Smithsonian Institution Press, Washington, D.C.

Rogers, J. Daniel, and Samuel M. Wilson, eds. 1993. *Ethnohistory and Archaeology: Approaches to Postcontact Change in the Americas.* Plenum Press, New York.

Rowlands, Michael. 1989. The Archaeology of Colonialism and Constituting the African Peasantry. In *Domination and Resistance,* ed. Daniel Miller, Michael Rowlands, and Christopher Tilley, 261–83. Unwin Hyman, London.

Rubertone, Patricia. 1989. Archaeology, Colonialism and 17th-Century Native America: Towards an Alternative Interpretation. In *Conflict in the Archaeology of Living Traditions,* ed. Robert Layton, 32–45. Unwin Hyman, London.

———. 1996. Matters of Inclusion: Historical Archaeology and Native Americans. *World Archaeology Bulletin* 7:77–86.

St. George, Robert, ed. 1988. *Material Life in America, 1600–1860.* Northeastern University Press, Boston.

Schiffer, Michael B. 1972. Archaeological Context and Systemic Context. *American Antiquity* 37:372–75.

———. 1976. *Behavioral Archaeology.* Academic Press, New York.

Schlereth, Thomas J. 1979. Material Culture Studies in America: Notes Towards a Historical Perspective. *Material History Bulletin* 8:89–98.

———. 1980. *Artifacts and the American Past.* American Association for State and Local History, Nashville, Tenn.

Seeman, Mark F. 1995. When Words Are Not Enough: Hopewell Interregionalism and the Use of Material Symbols at the GE Mound. In *Native American Interactions: Multiscalar Analyses and Interpretations in the Eastern Woodlands,* ed. M. S. Nassaney and K. E. Sassaman, 122–43. University of Tennessee Press, Knoxville.

Shanks, Michael, and Christopher Tilley. 1987. *Social Theory and Archaeology.* University of New Mexico Press, Albuquerque.

Simmons, William S. 1970. *Cautantowwit's House: An Indian Burial Ground on the Island of Conanicut in Narragansett Bay.* Brown University Press, Providence, R.I.

Spaulding, Albert C. 1960. The Dimensions of Archaeology. In *Essays in the Science of Culture,* ed. G. E. Dole and R. L. Carneiro, 437–56. Thomas Y. Crowell, New York.

Spicer, Edward H. 1971. Persistent Cultural Systems: A Comparative Study of Identity Systems That Can Adapt to Contrasting Environments. *Science* 174(4011):795–800.

———, ed. 1961. *Perspectives in American Indian Culture Change.* University of Chicago Press, Chicago.

Spores, Ronald. 1980. New World Ethnohistory and Archaeology, 1970–1980. *Annual Review of Anthropology* 9:575–603.

Sturtevant, William. 1971. Creek into Seminole: North American Indians. In *Historical Perspective,* ed. Eleanor Leacock and Nancy Lurie, 92–128. Random House, New York.

Tanner, Adrian. 1992. Foreword. In *To Please the Caribou: Painted Caribou-Skin Coats Worn by the Naskapi, Montagnais, and Cree Hunters of the Quebec-Labrador Peninsula,* by Dorothy K. Burnham, vii–ix. University of Washington Press, Seattle.

Taylor, Walter W. 1948. *A Study of Archeology*. American Anthropological Association, Memoir 69. Menasha, Wisc.

Thomas, Peter A. 1979. In the Maelstrom of Change: The Indian Trade and Cultural Processes in the Middle Connecticut River Valley, 1635–1665. Ph.D. diss., Department of Anthropology, University of Massachusetts, Amherst.

Tilley, Christopher. 1984. Ideology and the Legitimation of Power in the Middle Neolithic of Southern Sweden. In *Ideology, Power, and Prehistory*, ed. Daniel Miller and Christopher Tilley, 111–46. Cambridge University Press, Cambridge.

Trigger, Bruce. 1980. Archaeology and the Image of the American Indian. *American Antiquity* 45:662–76.

———. 1989. *A History of Archaeological Thought*. Cambridge University Press, Cambridge.

Trubowitz, Neal. 1995. A General Research Model for Trade in the Columbian Exchange: An Archaeological and Ethnohistoric Perspective. Paper presented at the annual meeting of the American Society for Ethnohistory, Kalamazoo, Mich.

Turnbaugh, Sarah Peabody, and William A. Turnbaugh. 1986. *Indian Baskets*. Peabody Museum of Archaeology and Ethnology, Harvard University, and Schiffer Publishing Ltd., West Chester, Penn.

Wallerstein, Immanuel. 1974. *The Modern World-System*, vol. 1. Academic Press, New York.

White, Bruce M. 1999. The Woman Who Married a Beaver: Trade Patterns and Gender Roles in the Ojibwa Fur Trade. *Ethnohistory* 46(1):109–47.

Williams, Roger. [1643] 1936. *A Key into the Language of America*. 5th ed. The Rhode Island and Providence Plantations Tercentenary Commission, Providence.

Wilson, Samuel, and J. Daniel Rogers. 1993. Historical Dynamics in the Contact Era. In *Ethnohistory and Archaeology: Approaches to Postcontact Change in the Americas,* ed. J. D. Rogers and S. M. Wilson, 3–15. Plenum Press, New York.

Winner, Langdon. 1980. Do Artifacts Have Politics? *Daedalus* 109:121–36.

Wobst, H. Martin. 1977. Stylistic Behavior and Information Exchange. In *Papers for the Director: Research Essays in Honor of James B. Griffin,* ed. C. E. Cleland, 317–42. Anthropology Papers 61. Museum of Anthropology, University of Michigan, Ann Arbor.

———. 1978. The Archaeo-Ethnology of Hunter-Gatherers, or The Tyranny of the Ethnographic Record in Archaeology. *American Antiquity* 43:303–9.

Wolf, Eric. 1982. *Europe and the People without History*. University of California Press, Berkeley.

Young, Gloria A., and Michael P. Hoffman, eds. 1993. *The Expedition of Hernando de Soto West of the Mississippi, 1541–1543*. University of Arkansas Press, Fayetteville.

I

Ethnogenesis: The Creation,
Maintenance, and Transformation
of Ethnic Identity

I

Ritual and Material Culture as Keys to Cultural Continuity

Native American Interaction with Europeans
in Eastern Arkansas, 1541–1682

Kathleen H. Cande

Charles Hudson recently opined that "the sixteenth century is, for all practical purposes, simply missing from southern history" (1987:6). Yet the quincentennial of Columbus's "voyage of discovery" (1992) and the 45oth anniversary of the Hernando de Soto entrada to the southeastern United States (1989–1993) have reminded historians and anthropologists of the entailments brought about by the interactions between European explorers and Native Americans (Brain 1985; Hudson 1992; Thomas 1992; Wylie 1992). As Hudson pointed out, the sixteenth-century Southeast was not an empty stage or a "borderland" where rival colonial powers fought for supremacy. Rather, it was the home of highly developed chiefdoms, among the most centralized aboriginal societies in North America, which are of both historical and anthropological interest. The process of studying the events and activities of the 16th and 17th centuries, however, is complicated by the paucity of written records. Consequently, an interdisciplinary approach that draws together various sources of information—including archaeological evidence, linguistic survivals, oral traditions, and ethnographic analogy—is needed to interpret the social history of Native Americans during the early Contact period.

Although much attention has focused on the earliest interactions between European explorers and Native Americans in Arkansas during the 16th and 17th centuries, most emphasis has been placed on the actions and reactions of the Europeans (for example, Dickinson 1986; Dye and Brister 1986; Hudson 1985, 1993; Swanton 1939, 1952; Whayne 1995; Young and Hoffman 1993). This is particularly true of the written accounts of the explorations, since they were penned entirely by the travelers. Nonetheless, the documents contain valuable information about Native American material culture, social life, and cultural changes brought about by subsequent permanent European settlement in the region.

This chapter examines the interactions between Native Americans and Europeans in eastern Arkansas from the 1540s through 1682. It is intended as a summary of our understanding of the problem to date, and a prospectus for future research. Social conventions that the Indians used in dealing with Europeans can be inferred from the documentary record and compared with expectations derived from other data sources. The ways these conventions varied in accordance with the status and role of the Europeans and how they changed over time provide insights into the effects of European exploration and settlement on Native Americans in eastern Arkansas. By examining these interactions we may also ascertain the significance of Native American cultural influences in the development of European institutions in colonial America (Sabo 1993:193). The underlying goal is to understand the dynamism of ethnic groups (and the fluidity and instability of ethnicity) in the context of cultural interaction.

Of equal importance is the vexing question of the ethnic identities of the groups encountered in 1541 by de Soto in eastern Arkansas. Resolution of this issue may shed light on the ethnogenesis of the Quapaw, who appear at the dawn of history yet have no clear pre-Contact predecessors in the central Mississippi Valley. Thus, the origins of the Quapaw represent a missing link in the chain between the pre-Contact and early historic period in Arkansas. The Quapaw are identified as a historic Indian tribe that lived in eastern Arkansas during the late 17th century and into the early 19th century, when they were removed into eastern Oklahoma (Baird 1989). Their encounters with the French can be compared with Spanish accounts of interactions to assess their degree of similarity (equivalent instances of interaction). If it was the Quapaw who met de Soto and his men, how did their interactions in the 1540s compare with subsequent dealings with the French? Was Quapaw sociopolitical organization transformed over time, and if so, were these structural changes brought about by internal or external forces?

Like the long-standing efforts to define de Soto's route and interactions with Native Americans through the Southeast, the pursuit of the origins of the Quapaw has been inconclusive, prompting one researcher to call it the

"Quapaw paradox" (Hoffman 1986). This pursuit has its roots in the search for the site of Osotouy, the Quapaw village where La Salle's aide, Henri de Tonti, established the first European occupation on the Mississippi River in 1686 (Ford 1961; Phillips et al. 1951; Swanton 1939). An important source of information in this inquiry is archaeological evidence, especially in the culturally sensitive modes of decoration on ceramic vessels. One of the more durable forms of material culture, thousands of fragments of pots and many whole vessels have been found at pre-Contact archaeological sites in eastern Arkansas. Since the ceramic morphology and decoration were intertwined with the lives and beliefs of Native Americans, these artifacts are just as valuable as written documents in our attempt to reconstruct the past.

Exploring Quapaw Ethnogenesis

The Quapaw are members of the Dhegiha Siouan language group, which includes the Kansa, Omaha, Osage, and Ponca tribes. Quapaw oral tradition holds that once the Dhegiha Sioux all lived together in the Ohio River Valley. Later the five tribes moved westward with the Quapaw going "downstream" and settling at the confluence of the Arkansas and Mississippi rivers (fig. 1.1). The other tribes continued west to the eastern Plains. The tribal name may be derived from Ug'akhpa, meaning the "downstream people" (Nieberding 1976:1). By 1673, when Marquette and Jolliet traveled down the Mississippi River, they met Indians living in four villages near the mouth of the Arkansas River. Marquette called these Indians Akansea, the name given them by their Illinois neighbors to the north. They called themselves Ogaxpa, the "broken off" segment of the Siouans, and today are known as the Quapaw (Nieberding 1976:18).

Galloway (1994, 1995) and Hudson (1992) have convincingly reconstructed the evolution of Native American social organization during the protohistoric period for the Choctaw in Mississippi and the chiefdom of Coosa and others in northern Georgia, respectively. These examples provide two possible models of Quapaw social organization during the protohistoric period. Through a study of documentary and archaeological evidence, Hudson inferred that chiefdoms of differing levels of complexity existed in 16th-century northern Georgia. He also noted that chiefdoms were in various stages of ascendancy and decline. Fortification of towns implied that these chiefdoms were engaged in expansion of territories. Finally, alliances were often formed among polities for mutual benefit, as in 1560 when Coosa became allied with the Spanish (see also McKivergan 1995). Galloway demonstrated that the Choctaws were a multiethnic con-

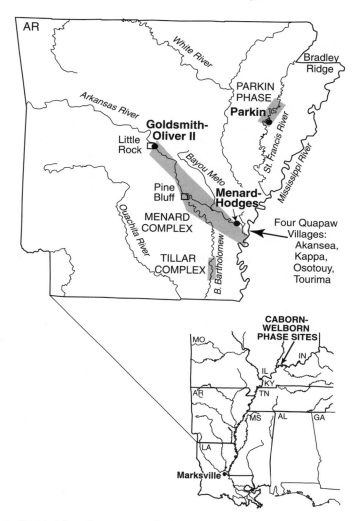

Fig. 1.1. General location map, including pre-Contact archaeological sites and phases discussed in the text

federacy with members from different failed or "devolved" Mississippian chiefdoms. She contends that there was a cyclical development between tribal and chiefly forms of social organization in the Southeast and that a new social form, confederations, emerged in protohistoric Mississippi. Epidemic diseases introduced by Europeans had disrupted the chiefdoms. Galloway argues that there is evidence of multiple locations of origin for constituent peoples, supported by variability in material culture consistent with amalgamation.

Using Friedman's (1975) model of "transformations," Galloway argues that some forms of tribal organization may have represented a developmental cycle on a continuum from segmentary tribes to simple chiefdoms, and finally to paramount chiefdoms. With each step toward greater complexity comes increased efficiency in agricultural production along with population concentration, soil exhaustion, and depletion of other essential natural resources. She contends that confederation was a viable response not only to collapsing chiefdoms but also to the effects of European contact. The option of confederation was flexible and could balance the centralizing and decentralizing tendencies of the various stresses on the populations. Forces that would work to destabilize the confederation might include conflict over overlapping hunting territories or an individual's ambition to build personal status. The Choctaw confederation in Mississippi shared the experiences of epidemic disease, a location that was home to none, a common language group (western Muskogean), and a suite of shared beliefs and traditions.

The two models suggested by Hudson and Galloway may be applicable to understanding historical development among Native American groups in eastern Arkansas; each author recognizes temporal instability and spatial variation. Other investigators have also noted fluctuations in southeastern political and social organization. For instance, Anderson (1995) concludes that "cycling"—the emergence, expansion, and fragmentation of late prehistoric chiefdoms—was common in the Savannah River basin (and elsewhere in the Southeast) in the period ca. A.D. 1000–1600. Nassaney (1992a, 1994) has made a similar argument to explain the spatial and temporal discontinuities in the social and political landscape of central Arkansas over the past two millennia. Furthermore, he suggests that fluctuations between egalitarian, kin-based societies and more centralized, ranked structures characterized much of the aboriginal Southeast. Historical documents related to Native encounters with the Spanish and French and archaeological data relevant to Quapaw ethnogenesis are summarized in this chapter in order to evaluate the applicability of these models.

The de Soto Entrada in Eastern Arkansas, 1541–1542

In recent years much research and debate among archaeologists and historians has focused on reconstructing the route of the de Soto entrada through Arkansas and tying it to 16th-century archaeological sites (Early 1993; Hudson 1993; P. Morse 1993; Schambach 1993). Sabo (1993) analyzed key passages in four European narratives that described turning points for the Spaniards, including the crossing of the Mississippi River and encounters at several Native American villages in eastern Arkansas. His study centered on the ways in which Native American perceptions and actions were reported by the Spanish chroniclers.

The Spanish members of the de Soto entrada were primarily motivated by the acquisition of wealth, and also the extension of Catholicism into the New World (Jones 1997). In short, they were concerned with appropriation on both the material and spiritual levels. They also desired to form alliances with the Indians that would be strategically and materially advantageous and were willing to resort to violence if necessary to achieve these ends. De Soto was carefully chosen to lead the expedition because he was "an entrepreneur with military experience" (P. Hoffman 1990:91).

The Indians approached encounters with the Spanish from a completely different perspective. They were concerned with forming alliances involving mutual reciprocity. They had no interest in acquiring property, but were preoccupied with group relationships determined by kinship ties and reciprocal obligations (see McKivergan 1995). They wanted to achieve prestige in their relationships by whatever means necessary.

A key point in Sabo's analysis of the de Soto accounts is that although the narratives identify paramount chiefdoms in eastern Arkansas, they do not provide firm evidence that the leaders acted as paramount chiefs. Instead, independent hereditary-lineage societies regulated by group competition are indicated. In contrast, when the de Soto entrada encountered Indian groups in southwest Arkansas, these clearly were paramount chiefdoms.

When the surviving members of the de Soto entrada departed La Florida (southeastern U.S.), the curtain fell on the Indians of eastern Arkansas. For more than 130 years there were no known contacts between them and Europeans, and their fate during this "protohistoric dark age" (ca. 1542–1673) is unknown. Did epidemic disease break out in the wake of the Spaniards? Did a killing drought ruin crops for a period of almost fifty years? Were massive groups of people moving across present-day Arkansas as a means of survival? What was the legacy of the first encounter with Europeans?

The French on the Mississippi River, 1673–1682

In May 1673, Father Jacques Marquette and Louis Jolliet traveled down the Mississippi River from Canada. Their task was to discover if the Mississippi met the sea and to spread the word of God. This voyage marked the end of the "protohistoric dark age," once again providing a glimpse of the Indians of Arkansas. Surviving records chronicling these events include letters written by Catholic missionary priests, often to superiors, reporting on their encounters with Native Americans. When Marquette, Jolliet, and their party reached the Quapaw village of Akansea, they were met by Quapaws holding a sacred pipe (fig. 1.1). They were warmly welcomed, and Father Marquette's speech about the "Holy Faith" was so well received that the Indians wanted to hear more. The Quapaws' actions suggest that they were eager both to open trade relations and to use Marquette and Jolliet as potential agents to gain access to supernatural powers (the force called Wahkonda) important in the Quapaws' day-to-day activities (Sabo 1991:108). The sacred pipe dance was convened for the French travelers, and the pipe was presented to them as a symbol of alliance.

René-Robert Cavelier, Sieur de La Salle, established a number of bases after being granted a trading concession along the Mississippi River in 1677. He descended the Mississippi, reaching its mouth on April 7, 1682. Before arriving at the Gulf, La Salle, his men, and their Illini Indian guides encountered the Quapaw at their village of Kappa on the west bank of the Mississippi above the mouth of the Arkansas River (fig. 1.1). La Salle presented a calumet to the Quapaws; six Quapaw chiefs returned with sacred pipes (Sabo 1991:109). The Quapaws gave the French food, constructed cabins for them, and honored them with a ceremony. The sacred pipe dance was described by Nicolas de La Salle as follows:

> In order to dance the calumet they all come into the place, especially the warriors, and the chiefs set poles all about, as for drying linen, and upon them they display what they intend to give. They brought two calumets adorned with plumage of all colors, and red stones full of tobacco. These were given to the chiefs, who were in the middle of the place. These chiefs and the warriors have gourds full of pebbles and two drums, which are earthen pots covered with dressed skin. The first began a song accompanied by the chime of their gourds. These having ended, others struck up the same thing; then those who have done brave deeds go to a post set in the midst of the place and smite it with their tomahawks. And, after relating their gallant achievements, they gave presents to M. de La Salle, for whom they made the festival. . . .
>
> Meanwhile, the chiefs are smoking the calumet and are having it carried to everyone in succession to smoke. M. de La Salle received fifty or sixty oxhides. The Frenchmen, with the exception of M. de

La Salle, also struck the post, relating their valorous deeds, and made gifts from that which M. de La Salle had given them for the purpose. (Anderson 1898:19–21)

La Salle ceremoniously claimed possession of the territory in the name of King Louis XIV. More feasting and gift giving took place. In the Quapaw village of Kappa, a large cross was erected on an apparently artificial earthen mound. A member of La Salle's group, Father Membre, communicated to the Quapaw using sign language about the Christian God and his saving powers. The Quapaw received this information with interest. La Salle and his group visited each of the four Quapaw villages near the mouth of the Arkansas River, where they were honored with more gift exchanges, feasts, and ceremonies. La Salle's group subsequently left the area, stopping again on the return visit. The Quapaw were impressed with the fact that La Salle had traveled a long distance through enemy territory without losing a man, proof to them of the protection of the Christian God. Father Membre noticed that in the interim, the cross erected by the French at Kappa had been surrounded by a circle of stakes.

The Quapaw wanted the priests to stay in their villages so that they could benefit from the spiritual power of the Christian God that was channeled through the priests. They saw the cross as the outward sign of their alliance with the French, as well as a symbol of the French God. The Quapaw had responded to each overture by the French with the expectation that a lasting alliance could be formed, but each time they were disappointed.

Other encounters between the French and Quapaw occurred in the late 1680s, and by participation in the Native American ceremonies, the Quapaw believed an alliance had been formed, with attendant rights and obligations. Performance of the Quapaw rituals served to bring order and predictability to otherwise unpredictable and uncontrollable events. Unfortunately, the French did not want to fulfill or did not understand the reciprocal obligations of the alliance perceived by the Quapaw and, into the 18th century, remained "inconsistent kin" (Sabo 1991:128).

Comparison of the Rituals of Encounter

Several similarities between Native American rituals of encounter observed by the Spanish in 1541 and those seen by the French in the late 1600s can be identified. Gift giving, competition for prestige, the symbolism of the circle, and a desire to receive power from the Christian God appear to have continuity from the mid-16th century into the late 17th century. Additionally, the Quapaws' sacred pipe and sacred pole ceremonies may have had antecedents in 16th-century northeast Arkansas. One of the de Soto accounts tells of a cross erected by the Spanish atop an earthen mound. The Indians believed that the power of the Christian God ended a drought, and they later placed a fence of cane stalks around it. This action may be similar to that of the Quapaw, when Father Membre, a member of La Salle's group, observed that a cross erected in the village of Kappa by the missionaries was later surrounded by "a circle of stakes" (Shea 1861:169).

Knight (1986:685) emphasizes that Mississippian societies of the eastern United States should be broadly defined as having a "prevalent variety of socio-religious organization crosscutting other cultural and ecological boundaries," recognizable by shared symbolic objects for ceremonial use and display. Religion and ritual may have effected a stabilizing and amalgamating influence on Native groups, and thus the rituals and religious symbols seen in common by the Spanish and French explorers can be argued to represent cultural continuity through the protohistoric period.

The rituals of encounter can also be examined for differences and contradictions that might indicate that different ethnic groups were involved between the mid-16th and late 17th centuries. The 16th-century towns of northeast Arkansas visited by de Soto are all described as being paramount chiefdoms in eastern Arkansas. A paramount chiefdom (as opposed to a simple chiefdom) is an organization of several polities, each with a leader or chief, who are subject to a single, paramount leader (Hudson 1988:600–601). A paramount chiefdom also implies a social hierarchy in which lineages are ranked. In contrast, the Quapaw were not a paramount chiefdom; they were a tribe. The Quapaw were not a hierarchically organized society; each clan had responsibilities reciprocated by other clans that fostered stability, and decision-making was a consensual activity (Sabo 1995:79).

The two organizational forms, clans and paramount chiefdoms, were the historically dominant types of social organization among Mississippian groups of the Southeast (Knight 1990:19). The hierarchically organized societies, however, were plagued with chronic political instability, and at times may have "regressed" to simpler forms of social organization to avoid submitting to "governance by a disconnected, despotic, and self-absorbed nobility" (Knight 1990:18).

Accounts of the de Soto entrada do not describe a formalized greeting ritual that resembles the sacred pipe or calumet ceremony. That is not to say that such a ritual, or one like it, did not exist. Brown (1989:315) has suggested that the playing of flutelike instruments may have served an analogous role among many Indian groups. The Spanish were greeted very ceremoniously in some instances. It is also possible that the 16th-century Indians took a more adversarial stance (at least initially) against the Spanish than did the Quapaw with the French. When de Soto's party landed on the Florida coast in 1539, it included 600 armored soldiers, 213 horses, and hundreds of pigs and mastiff dogs (P. Hoffman 1990:91). Three of the de Soto accounts describe Natives bearing shields made of cane with arrows at the ready during the Spaniards' crossing of the Mississippi River into Arkansas. In contrast, the French groups were vastly smaller, comprising a few soldiers and unarmed priests arriving by canoe. Some of the subtle differences and similarities in the ways in which these Indian groups greeted outsiders may not have been observed by the European chroniclers, or were observed but not recorded. The archaeological record is essential in providing material-cultural details that may shed light on some of the data gaps.

Archaeological Evidence

A number of scenarios, based in part on archaeological evidence, have been suggested as possible explanations of how the 16th-century Native American groups in eastern Arkansas may have been the antecedents of the Quapaw (see M. Hoffman 1990). Determining the origins of the Quapaw should lead to a clearer understanding of events affecting other Indian groups in eastern Arkansas at this time. Some archaeologists have recently realized that what had been identified as the "Quapaw phase" (that is, a group of pre-Contact cultural traits and objects found at a number of archaeological sites in eastern Arkansas and up the Arkansas River to Little Rock) has not been connected or reconciled with what is known of the ethnographic Quapaw tribe described by the various 17th-century French explorers. That is, an "ethnic Quapaw archeological assemblage has not yet been identified" (House 1991:21). The archaeological Quapaw phase has recently been renamed the Menard complex to avoid confusion (Hoffman 1995; House 1997:49; Jeter 1990a:95–96).

The first scenario is that Quapaws of the historic period were recent (17th century) arrivals in Arkansas from the Ohio Valley. They filled the vacuum created by the demise of the hierarchically organized 16th-century group(s), who disappeared due to disease epidemics, warfare, or migration. It is further suggested that the Quapaw adopted the ceramic forms and general lifestyle of the antecedent groups as well.

The first part of this scenario is consistent with Quapaw origin stories describing a recent separation from the related Dhegiha groups and then movement "downstream" (Henning 1993: 255). The second part of the proposition, however, is harder to envision. If the Quapaw took up the cultural traits of the preceding groups, they would have been extremely adaptable, a trait which M. Hoffman (1990) states the Quapaw possess. If the Quapaw lived in the Ohio Valley earlier, however, there should be an archaeological manifestation ancestral to them there.

M. Hoffman (1986, 1990) has observed that several pre-Contact Caborn–Welborn phase sites (ca. A.D. 1400–1600) in southwestern Indiana and north-central Kentucky (at the confluence of the Wabash and Ohio rivers) yielded ceramic vessels similar to those of the Menard complex (fig. 1.1). Occurrences (albeit rare) of typical Menard-complex ceramic types (for example, Barton Incised, Carson Red on Buff, Wallace Incised) have been noted in Caborn-Welborn site assemblages (Green and Munson 1978:302). Other artifacts characteristic of this phase include Nodena arrow points, small thumbnail or snubnose end scrapers, disk pipes (some made of catlinite), and European trade goods such as glass beads, brass tinkling cones, bracelets and kettle fragments, and Dutch and French gunflints (Green and Munson 1978:303, 307).

In an alternative scenario, Morse and Morse (1983:321) have suggested that the Quapaw picked up the shattered pieces of the 16th-century, Siouan-speaking Mississippian cultures and put them together in a way expressed by the documented interaction with the French. More recently the Morses (1990:208) propose that the population composing the four Quapaw villages on the Arkansas River observed by the French were people who migrated from Bradley Ridge in northeast Arkansas (fig. 1.1). They suggest that Bradley Ridge may have supported sixty acres of people in four stockaded towns by ca. 1625. This idea is called "shreds and patches" by M. Hoffman (1990:221), but most likely would have involved consolidation of allied groups that were not traditional enemies. To take this idea a step further, it is possible that a confederation, like that described in Mississippi by Galloway for the Choctaw, was created to weather cultural breakdown caused by unstable hierarchical social organization and by European encroachment.

In a study of pottery vessels from several Menard complex archaeological sites in the lower Arkansas River Valley, House (1991:20) concludes that the ceramic evidence indicates that the Menard complex does not represent a single short-lived occupation during the time of early French contact. Rather, it is a diverse archaeological assemblage spanning more than two hundred years (1991:20). He now believes that mortuary vessel assemblages from the Menard-Hodges site (type site for the Menard complex) locality are atypical of the Menard complex in general because they show definite northeast Arkansas influences (John H. House, personal communication, 1995).

The formation of a multiethnic confederation in protohistoric eastern Arkansas may have been the result of the natural cycle of chiefdom development and devolution and the upheavals caused by the introduction of epidemic disease during the mid-16th century. If the 17th-century Quapaw were an amalgamation of Mississippian peoples from northeast Arkansas and southeast Missouri, there should be indications of patterned diversity in material culture (including pottery) indicative of coalescence by constituent peoples (Galloway 1994:394). To date, ceramic assemblages studied show no such patterning.

Linguistic data, however, do not support the interpretation that the Quapaw are an amalgamation of a number of distinct groups (Rankin 1983). Further, the names of the 16th-century towns (appearing in the de Soto accounts) are not Siouan words, although this may be a factor of the ethnic identity of the Indian interpreters used by de Soto. M. Hoffman (1990:221) points out that the Quapaw oral tradition does not support amalgamation either.

A third scenario is that the Menard-complex archaeological phase actually represents not the Quapaw, but a completely different cultural group, the ancestors of the historic Tunicans. (The Tunicans were living near Marksville, Louisiana, when "discovered" in the early 19th century; see fig. 1.1.) This tribe is thought by some archaeologists to have lived in southeast Arkansas and northeastern Louisiana into the 16th century, and possibly several hundred years earlier. The Tunicans were displaced southward during the late 16th and early 17th centuries by the Quapaw, and left Arkansas between 1650 and the early 1700s (Jeter 1986:58). According to this model, the Indians living in eastern Arkansas in the 1500s were Tunicans. In cultural terms as well as ceramic styles, the Tunicans were part of the Mississippian tradition, with particular affinities with lower Mississippi Valley phases related to the historic Tunicans (Brain 1979:224).

If the Native American groups living in eastern Arkansas during the protohistoric period were Tunicans and not Quapaw, then cultural assemblages should reflect a long period of in situ development. Jeter (1986:52) has demonstrated that ceramics from the protohistoric Tillar complex in southeast Arkansas bear similarities to decorative modes on Tunican pottery from northern Louisiana dating to the same time frame. In fact, he concludes (1986:58) "'Tunicans'... were the principal occupants [of this area]... possibly for several hundred years before the De Soto entrada." He bases this conclusion on the widespread presence of regional variants of Mississippi Plain, Barton Incised, and Winterville Incised pottery (Jeter 1990b:534). He goes on to suggest, in a provocative "maximum Tunican scenario," that various Tunican groups may have "once occupied a truly huge area on both sides of the Mississippi River, northeastern Louisiana, and virtually all of eastern Arkansas, plus a western extension well up the Arkansas Valley" (Jeter 1990b:528).

As an alternative to these three scenarios, it can also be argued that the same ethnic group or groups were represented in both the 16th- and 17th-century European accounts. How could such cultural continuity or adaptability be explained? House (1991) has suggested that the Menard-complex peoples may have persisted relatively intact into the 17th century because of their more peripheral geographical location (above the confluence of the Arkansas, White, and Mississippi rivers) and lower population densities at the beginning of the 16th century. This is in stark contrast to other 16th-century floodplain societies living on major communication routes, who suffered rapid population decline in due to introduced diseases.

Friedman's (1975) model for the "devolution" or transformation of chiefdoms is one way in which to explain the proposition of continuity in eastern Arkansas Indian groups. His model holds that cyclical progression from tribe to chiefdom (in pre-state societies) and back to tribe is a function of population density, ecological constraints, and other factors that affect long-term development along this continuum. This cycling back and forth between greater and lesser social complexity is thought to be a natural developmental response heightened by the stresses caused by European exploration. Further integration on a larger scale into state-level societies (the most complex form of social organization) apparently never happened in the Southeast. The alternative was dissolution (Galloway 1994:395–96). The mass migrations of populations out of northeastern Arkansas at the end of the 16th century as well as disease epidemics may have forced the amalgamation of various Native American groups visited by de Soto into a confederation based upon common needs.

A paramount chiefdom can no longer function when most of its constituents—those who do the labor—are gone. Similarly, oral traditions, rituals, material culture traits, and even languages are lost with depopulation. Galloway (1994:397–98) posits that "chiefdoms would suffer more than segmentary tribes. Chiefdoms would lose their organization, and . . . this would mean their destruction . . . [while] segmentary tribes or the remnants of devolved chiefdoms would suffer far less, since they retained the web of tradition at a lower level of distributed expertise and since their dispersed settlement pattern and infrequent gatherings would not favor the spread of disease."

Currently there are no conclusive bioarchaeological data from northeast Arkansas to support the contention that the de Soto entrada spread epidemic disease, although depopulation did occur within some groups (Burnett and Murray 1993). This is not for lack of study but because of the incompleteness of the osteological sample (Murray 1989). There are, similarly, no documentary records of such outbreaks, although the epidemics would not have begun until after the Spanish had left the region, and there are no written records of events in eastern Arkansas during the protohistoric period between 1541 and 1673 (Dye 1986:xii; Jeter 1990b:537). However, in 1699 Father St. Cosme described the Quapaw as having suffered through a smallpox epidemic that killed many people (Kellogg 1917:359).

Recent study of skeletal remains representing fifty-eight individuals from two Parkin-phase archaeological sites (Big Eddy, Cummings) and three Menard-complex sites (Menard-Hodges, Greer, Kinkead-Mainard) revealed a pattern of high mortality as well as chronic malnutrition particularly among Menard-complex peoples. The Parkin-phase peoples were also experiencing stress, possibly caused by epidemic disease (evidence for tuberculosis and treponematosis has been found in the skeletal population). However, these results are equivocal since genetic affinity between northeast Arkansas Parkin-phase and Menard-complex peoples has not been established (through study of nonmetric cranial traits) and skeletal samples are not representative (Murray 1989:138–139, 1998:30–31). Another complicating factor is the lack of skeletal evidence for epidemic disease, since individuals who are infected often succumb rapidly with no impact to bone. Instead, a prolonged drought in eastern Arkansas between 1541 and 1577, along with an increase in interpersonal violence, are suggested as more likely agents of depopulation (Burnett and Murray 1993:235–236; Rose and Harmon 1999: 65–66; Stahle et al. 1985).

Additional, fine-grained analyses of ceramic assemblages from 16th-century Native American archaeological sites in eastern and central Arkansas believed to have been visited by the de Soto entrada may shed light on the issue of Quapaw ethnogenesis. Archaeologists have long studied ceramic vessels from the Mississippi Valley; as malleable items of material culture, their form, decoration, and method of construction transmit important information about the social identities of their makers. Ceramics may also express variations in activities and levels of complexity in social relations (House 1990:15). If ceramic styles transmit information about ethnicity and social boundaries, then greater stylistic homogeneity would be expected between regions in eastern Arkansas after European contact. As groups declined in number and moved from region to region and faced drought, soil exhaustion, and other upheavals, ethnic boundaries may have become less defined and more permeable (Nassaney 1992b:5).

A multi-year study of material-culture assemblages from Menard-complex sites in eastern Arkansas reveals considerable variation in mortuary ceramics, but an apparent distinctive localized tradition in utilitarian wares (House 1997). Observable temporal variation has allowed for the definition of two horizons within the Menard complex. The Poor horizon includes those sites dating to the 16th century, while 17th century sites are subsumed under the Douglas horizon. The later sites may represent "movement of Menard Complex peoples into nucleated villages on the south bank of the Arkansas River below Pine Bluff" (House 1997:93).

Since a true Quapaw archaeological assemblage has yet to be defined, this task should have priority. Jeter (1990b:537) suggests that this analysis be done using materials from the four Akansea-Quapaw settlements documented in historical records.

Conclusions

In this chapter I have attempted to gather and compare information on the encounters between Native Americans and Europeans in protohistoric eastern Arkansas, A.D. 1541–1682. The goal of this synthesis is to determine if there was stability in indigenous ethnic groups from the mid-16th through the late 17th centuries. There are parallels between the 16th-century groups' actions in greeting and alliance-formation rituals, and those of the late 17th-century Quapaw, but this alone is insufficient evidence to establish cultural continuity.

There is no hard evidence of devolved chiefdoms in northeastern Arkansas, although Morse and Morse (1990:208) estimate a population decline in Arkansas from almost 75,000 to 15,000 inhabitants during this period. As mentioned above, the residents of four villages on Bradley Ridge may have moved south to form the four villages of the Quapaw on

the Arkansas River. There is skeletal evidence that protohistoric populations in the Arkansas River Valley were malnourished and dying in their reproductive years, but this has been attributed to a major drought that occurred between 1531 and 1577 (Burnett and Murray 1993). There is, however, continuity in artifact styles, suggesting that mechanisms were developed to husband these important cultural traits.

Despite the ambiguity of the historic accounts and the archaeological data, there is a logical next step in the study of the role of ritual in cultural continuity. First, the fundamental structural differences between groups, what Rappaport (1971) calls "ultimate sacred principles," must be identified. Sabo has successfully done this in Arkansas for the Quapaw, a group organized according to complementary opposites, and the Caddo, a hierarchically structured group. Second, it must be determined if these same principles structured the archaeological record. Since the "Mississippianism" of late prehistoric societies carried with it a prevalent type of socioreligious organization crosscutting other cultural and economic boundaries, it follows that these principles structured the material world as well. An examination of settlement patterns (on both the inter- and intrasite levels) could shed light on the differences between hierarchically structured societies like the Caddo, Tunica, and Natchez, and nonhierarchically structured societies such as the Quapaw. Are the 16th-century archaeological sites in eastern Arkansas organized hierarchically? There is a recognized settlement hierarchy within and between sites, indicating that the groups occupying them were not Quapaw, but possibly a Dhegihan group that was hierarchically structured.

In addition to these tasks, several other avenues of research include genetic comparison between modern Quapaw with late pre-Contact human remains from Menard-complex archaeological sites. Cordage made of human hair from the Goldsmith-Oliver II site (ca. 1500–1700) could also be utilized (Cande 1992). The location and study of archaeological sites in eastern Arkansas, and particularly in the Arkansas River Valley, have been hampered by decades of agriculture (including land leveling) and channelization of the Arkansas River. Fluctuations in water levels over time have contributed to untold losses of archaeological data.

Precisely what changes occurred in eastern Arkansas during this early Contact period and their far-reaching effects may never be fully appreciated. It seems clear, however, that the role of ritual and material culture in the realm of the sacred and the profane may be the keys to understanding cultural continuity in the face of revolutionary change.

Acknowledgments

This research began as part of Dr. Elliott West's graduate history seminar at the University of Arkansas on "Native American–EuroAmerican Interactions in the Trans-Mississippi West." I thank him and my fellow graduate students for their constructive criticism. George Sabo III suggested this topic to me and provided many helpful comments and insights. Robert C. Mainfort, Jr., and Jamie C. Brandon read and commented on earlier versions of this chapter and tracked down elusive references. I am grateful for the use of Hester A. Davis's extensive library. Mary Lynn Kennedy cheerfully created the location map. This chapter would not have reached its final form without the support, editorial skills, and firm guidance of Michael Nassaney and Eric Johnson. I also appreciate the editorial suggestions of two anonymous reviewers; they have considerably strengthened the chapter.

References Cited

Anderson, D. G. 1995. *The Savannah River Chiefdoms: Political Change in the Late Prehistoric Southeast.* University of Alabama Press, Tuscaloosa.

Anderson, M. B. (translator). 1898. *Relation of the Discovery of the Mississippi River, written from the Narrative of Nicolas de la Salle, otherwise known as the Little M. de La Salle.* The Caxton Club, Chicago.

Baird, W. D. 1989. *The Quapaws.* Chelsea House, New York.

Brain, J. P. 1979. *Tunica Treasure.* Papers of the Peabody Museum of Archaeology and Ethnology 71. Harvard University, Cambridge.

———. 1985. Introduction: Update of De Soto Studies since the United States De Soto Expedition Commission Report. In *Final Report of the United States De Soto Expedition Commission,* ed. J. R. Swanton, xi–lxxii. Smithsonian Institution Press, Washington, D.C.

Brown, I. W. 1989. The Calumet Ceremony in the Southeast and Its Archaeological Manifestations. *American Antiquity* 54:311–31.

Burnett, B. A., and K. A. Murray. 1993. Death, Drought, and de Soto: The Bioarcheology of Depopulation. In *The Expedition of Hernando de Soto West of the Mississippi, 1541–1543,* ed. G. A. Young and M. P. Hoffman, 227–36. University of Arkansas Press, Fayetteville.

Cande, K. H. 1992. Cordage from the Goldsmith Oliver II Site, Arkansas: The Human Touch. Paper presented at the tenth annual conference on textiles, Colorado State University, Ft. Collins.

Dickinson, S. D. 1986. The River of Cayas: The Ouachita or the Arkansas River? *Arkansas Archeological Society Field Notes* 209:5–11.

Dye, D. H. 1986. Introduction. In *The Protohistoric Period in the Mid-South: 1500–1700,* ed. D. H. Dye and R. C. Brister, xi–xiv. Proceedings of the 1983

Mid-South Archaeological Conference. Mississippi Department of Archives and History, Archaeological Report 18, Jackson.

Dye, D. H., and R. C. Brister, eds. 1986. *The Protohistoric Period in the Mid-South: 1500–1700.* Proceedings of the 1983 Mid-South Archaeological Conference. Mississippi Department of Archives and History, Archaeological Report 18, Jackson.

Early, A. M. 1993. Finding the Middle Passage: The Spanish Journey from the Swamplands to Caddo County. In *The Expedition of Hernando de Soto West of the Mississippi, 1541–1543,* ed. G. A. Young and M. P. Hoffman, 68–77. University of Arkansas Press, Fayetteville.

Ford, J. A. 1961. *The Menard Site: The Quapaw Village of Osotouy on the Arkansas River.* Anthropological Papers of the American Museum of Natural History, vol. 48, pt. 2. New York.

Friedman, Jonathan. 1975. Tribes, States, and Transformations. In *Marxist Analyses and Social Anthropology,* ed. Maurice Bloch, 161–202. John Wiley and Sons, New York.

Galloway, Patricia. 1994. Confederacy as a Solution to Chiefdom Dissolution: Historical Evidence in the Choctaw Case. In *The Forgotten Centuries: Indians and Europeans in the American South, 1521–1704,* ed. C. M. Hudson and C. C. Tesser, 393–420. University of Georgia Press, Athens.

———. 1995. *Choctaw Genesis, 1500–1700.* University of Nebraska Press, Lincoln.

Green, T. J., and C. A. Munson. 1978. Mississippian Settlement Pattern in Southwestern Indiana. In *Mississippian Settlement Patterns,* ed. B. D. Smith, 293–330. Academic Press, New York.

Henning, D .R. 1993. The Adaptive Patterning of the Dhegiha Sioux. *Plains Anthropologist* 38(146):253–64.

Hoffman, M. P. 1986. The Protohistoric Period in the Lower and Central Arkansas River Valley in Arkansas. In *The Protohistoric Period in the Mid-South: 1500–1700,* ed. D. H. Dye and R. C. Brister, 24–37. Proceedings of the 1983 Mid-South Archaeological Conference. Mississippi Department of Archives and History, Archaeological Report 18, Jackson.

———. 1990. The Terminal Mississippian Period in the Arkansas River Valley and Quapaw Ethnogenesis. In *Towns and Temples along the Mississippi,* ed. D. H. Dye and C. A. Cox, 208–26. University of Alabama Press, Tuscaloosa.

———. 1995. Protohistoric Tunican Indians in Arkansas. In *Cultural Encounters in the Early South: Indians and Europeans in Arkansas,* comp. J. Whayne, 61–75. University of Arkansas Press, Fayetteville.

Hoffman, P. E. 1990. *A New Andalucia, and a Way to the Orient.* Louisiana State University Press, Baton Rouge.

House, J. H. 1990. Powell Canal: Baytown Period Adaptation on Bayou Macon, Southeast Arkansas. In *The Mississippian Emergence,* ed. B. D. Smith, 9–26. Smithsonian Institution Press, Washington, D.C.

———. 1991. The Mississippian Sequence in the Menard Locality, Eastern Arkansas. In *Arkansas Before the Americans,* ed. H. A. Davis, 6–39. Arkansas Archeological Survey Research Series 40, Fayetteville.

———. 1997. Noble Lake: A Protohistoric Archeological Site on the Lower Arkansas River. *The Arkansas Archeologist* 36:47–93.

Hudson, C. M. 1985. De Soto in Arkansas: A Brief Synopsis. *Arkansas Archeological Society Field Notes* 205:3–12.

———. 1987. An Unknown South: Spanish Explorers and Southeastern Chiefdoms. In *Visions and Revisions, Ethnohistoric Perspectives on Southern Cultures,* ed. George Sabo III and William Schneider, 6–24. Southern Anthropological Society Proceedings 20, University of Georgia Press, Athens.

———. 1988. A Spanish-Coosa Alliance in Sixteenth-Century North Georgia. *Georgia Historical Quarterly* 72(4):599–626.

———. 1992. *The Juan Pardo Expeditions: Exploration of the Carolinas and Tennessee, 1566–1568.* Smithsonian Institution Press, Washington, D.C.

———. 1993. Reconstructing the de Soto Expedition Route West of the Mississippi River: Summary and Contents. In *The Expedition of Hernando de Soto West of the Mississippi, 1541–1543,* ed. G. A. Young and M. P. Hoffman, 143–54. University of Arkansas Press, Fayetteville.

Jeter, M. D. 1986. Tunicans West of the Mississippi: A Summary of Early Historic and Archaeological Evidence. In *The Protohistoric Period in the Mid-South: 1500–1700,* ed. D. H. Dye and R. C. Brister, 38–63. Proceedings of the 1983 Mid-South Archaeological Conference. Mississippi Department of Archives and History, Archaeological Report 18, Jackson.

———. 1990a. Ethnohistorical and Archeological Backgrounds. In *Goldsmith Oliver 2 (3PU306): A Protohistoric Archeological Site Near Little Rock, Arkansas,* vols. 1–3, ed. M. D. Jeter, K. H. Cande, and J. J. Mintz, 32–96. Arkansas Archeological Survey, Fayetteville.

———. 1990b. Summary, Conclusions, and Alternative Interpretations. In *Goldsmith Oliver 2 (3PU306): A Protohistoric Archeological Site Near Little Rock, Arkansas,* vols. 1–3, ed. M. D. Jeter, K. H. Cande and J. J. Mintz, 507–37. Arkansas Archeological Survey, Fayetteville.

Jones, L. C. 1997. 1698–1707 Conversion of the Tamaroas and the Quapaws: An Unlikely Outcome in the Missions of the Seminary of Quebec. M.A. thesis, University of Arkansas, Fayetteville.

Kellogg, L. P., ed. 1917. *Early Narratives of the Northwest, 1634–1699.* Barnes and Noble, New York.

Knight, V. J., Jr. 1986. The Institutional Organization of Mississippian Religion. *American Antiquity* 51:675–87.

———. 1990. Social Organization and the Evolution of Hierarchy in Southeastern Chiefdoms. *Journal of Anthropological Research* 46(1):1–23.

McKivergan, D. A., Jr. 1995. Balanced Reciprocity and Peer Polity Interaction in the Late Prehistoric Southeastern United States. In *Native American Interac-*

tions: Multiscalar Analyses and Interpretations in the Eastern Woodlands, ed. M. S. Nassaney and K. E. Sassaman, 229–46. University of Tennessee Press, Knoxville.

Morse, D. F., and P. A. Morse. 1983. *Archaeology of the Central Mississippi Valley.* Academic Press, New York.

———. 1990. The Spanish Exploration of Arkansas. In *Columbian Consequences,* vol. 2, *Archeological and Historical Perspective on the Spanish Borderlands East,* ed. D. H. Thomas, 197–210. Smithsonian Institution Press, Washington, D.C.

Morse, P. A. 1993. The Parkin Archeological Site and Its Role in Determining the Route of the de Soto Expedition. In *The Expedition of Hernando de Soto West of the Mississippi, 1541–1543,* ed. G. A. Young and M. P. Hoffman, 58–67. University of Arkansas Press, Fayetteville.

Murray, K. A. 1989. Bioarchaeology of the Post Contact Mississippi and Arkansas River Valleys, A.D. 1500–1700. M.A. thesis, University of Arkansas, Fayetteville.

———. 1998. Bioanthropological Analysis of Parkin (3CS29). On file, Department of Anthropology, University of Arkansas, Fayetteville.

Nassaney, M. S. 1992a. Experiments in Social Ranking in Prehistoric Central Arkansas. Ph.D. diss., University of Massachusetts, Amherst. University Microfilms, Ann Arbor.

———. 1992b. The Influence of European Contact on Native American Ceramic Form and Design. Faculty Research and Creative Activities Support Fund Proposal. On file in the Department of Anthropology, Western Michigan University, Kalamazoo.

———. 1994. The Historical and Archaeological Context of Plum Bayou Culture in Central Arkansas. *Southeastern Archaeology* 13(1):36–55.

Nieberding, V. S. 1976. *The Quapaws.* Dixon's Inc., Miami, Oklahoma.

Phillips, P., J. A. Ford, and J. B. Griffin. 1951. *Archaeological Survey in the Lower Mississippi Alluvial Valley, 1940–1947.* Papers of The Peabody Museum of Archaeology and Ethnology 25. Harvard University, Cambridge.

Rankin, R. L. 1983. Language Affiliations of Some de Soto Place Names in Arkansas. In *The Expedition of Hernando de Soto West of the Mississippi, 1541–1543,* ed. G. A. Young and M. P. Hoffman, 210–21. University of Arkansas Press, Fayetteville.

Rappaport, R. A. 1971. Ritual, Sanctity, and Cybernetics. *American Anthropologist* 73:59–76.

Rose, J. C., and A. M. Harmon. 1999. Louisiana and South and Eastern Arkansas. In *Bioarcheology of the South Central United States,* ed. J. C. Rose, 35–82. Arkansas Archeological Survey Research Series 55, Fayetteville.

Sabo, G., III. 1991. Inconsistent Kin: French-Quapaw Relations at Arkansas Post. In *Arkansas before the Americans,* ed. H. A. Davis, 105–30. Arkansas Archeological Survey Research Series 40, Fayetteville.

———. 1993. Indians and Spaniards in Arkansas: Symbolic Action in the Sixteenth Century. In *The Expedition of Hernando de Soto West of the Mississippi, 1541–1543*, ed. G. A. Young and M. P. Hoffman, 192–209. University of Arkansas Press, Fayetteville.

———. 1995. Rituals of Encounter: Interpreting Native American Views of European Explorers. In *Cultural Encounters in the Early South: Indians and Europeans in Arkansas*, comp. Jeannie Whayne, 76–87. University of Arkansas Press, Fayetteville.

Schambach, F. F. 1993. The End of the Trail: Reconstruction of the Route of Hernando de Soto's Army through Southwest Arkansas and East Texas. In *The Expedition of Hernando de Soto West of the Mississippi, 1541–1543*, ed. G. A. Young and M. P. Hoffman, 78–105. University of Arkansas Press, Fayetteville.

Shea, J. G., ed. and trans. 1861. *Early Voyages Up and Down the Mississippi by Cavelier, St. Cosme, Le Sueur, Gravier, and Guignas.* Joel Munsell, Albany, N.Y.

Stahle, D. W., M. K. Cleaveland, and J. G. Hehr. 1985. A 450-Year Drought Reconstruction for Arkansas, United States. *Nature* 316:530–32.

Swanton, J. R. 1939. *Final Report of the United States De Soto Expedition Commission*, vol. 71. 76th Congress, 1st sess., House Document. Government Printing Office, Washington, D.C.

———. 1952. Hernando de Soto's Route Through Arkansas. *American Antiquity* 18:156–62.

Thomas, D. H. 1992. A Retrospective Look at *Columbian Consequences. American Antiquity* 57:613–16.

Whayne, Jeannie, comp. 1995. *Cultural Encounters in the Early South: Indians and Europeans in Arkansas.* University of Arkansas Press, Fayetteville.

Wylie, A. 1992. Rethinking the Quincentennial: Consequences for Past and Present. *American Antiquity* 57:591–94.

Young, G. A., and M. P. Hoffman, eds. 1993. *The Expedition of Hernando de Soto West of the Mississippi, 1541–1543.* University of Arkansas Press, Fayetteville.

2

The Identity of Stadacona and Hochelaga

Comprehension and Conflict

James F. Pendergast

In recent decades historians concerned with economic, social, and intellectual history have devoted increasing amounts of time to studying immigrants, the professions, women, labor, religious groups, and similar themes. Generally biography, archival, and narrative history, including the history of exploration, have fallen out of fashion. It is therefore not surprising that when the Columbian quincentenary drew the interests of a number of historians back to these long-neglected concerns, they took up the debate without fully taking into account recent developments in neighboring disciplines.

One remarkable result is that historians and anthropologists still do not agree on who it was that Jacques Cartier met in A.D. 1535 at Stadacona and Hochelaga, the palisaded villages that once stood where present-day Quebec City and Montreal now stand. They agree readily that the people Cartier and Roberval met were Iroquoian speakers, members of the large Iroquoian linguistic family whose several tribes and confederacies later so heavily influenced the European invasion in these latitudes. They also agree that these French encounters over the period 1534–1543 were the first recorded Iroquoian meetings with Europeans; the next recorded meeting did not occur until seventy-four years later, in 1607, when John Smith's English settlers met the Susquehannock Iroquoians at the head of Chesapeake Bay. But when it comes to attributing Stadaconans and Hochelagans to one or another of the historic Iroquoian tribes or confederacies, the historians and anthropologists part company. These are significant differences that extend beyond semantics and well into matters of substance. Although the *Huron-Iroquois, Mohawk, Laurentian Iroquois, Laurentian Iroquoian, St. Lawrence Iroquois,* and *St. Lawrence Iroquoian* identities that have been accorded Stadaconans and Hochelagans have become commonplace, the contradictions, inconsistencies, and anomalies on which these identities are founded are not so well known. These convolutions will be examined here.

Where once the significance of this polemic was largely confined to scholarly journals, recently the subject has attracted popular attention in the topical press. William Eccles's comments in the *Literary Review of Canada* regarding Ramsay Cook's (1993) introduction to his recent edition of *The Voyages of Jacques Cartier* and their spirited debate subsequently (Cook 1994; Eccles 1994a, 1994b) have breathed new life into the discussion that seeks to identify Stadaconans and Hochelagans. Not since the turn of this century, when Montreal lawyer William D. Lighthall's essays kept Hochelaga in the public eye for thirty-five years (1899:199–211; 1934:103–8), and again during the 1920s and 1930s, when antiquitarian Aristide Beaugrand-Champagne (1923:17–24) and historian Gustave Lanctot (1930:115–41) debated the "true" location of Hochelaga, has the subject enjoyed so high a public profile. Now we have the ethnohistoric record being examined in technical detail by two preeminent Canadian historians. Undoubtedly some of this new-found interest has been kindled by the emphasis placed on Native interests and perceptions revealed in the surge of Columbian quincentenary literature. No doubt, too, recent Mohawk activities in support of their land claims in the St. Lawrence Valley have given the identity of the Stadaconans and Hochelagans a new and urgent realpolitik significance for Canadians. Mark Abley's 1994 article "Where Was Hochelaga?" in the widely read *Canadian Geographic* magazine and Robert Fulford's (1993) perjorative assessment of Jacques Cartier in the *Toronto Globe and Mail* are reflections of popular interest in this facet of 16th-century Canadian history.

The disappearance of Iroquoians from the St. Lawrence Valley (circa A.D. 1580), including from their villages of Stadacona and Hochelaga, is beyond the scope of this chapter. This subject is treated in an extensive literature (see Pendergast 1993:9–48) that demonstrates a long, drawn-out, and complex sequence of events that began ca. A.D. 1400 in a wholly pre-Contact Native context and ended ca. A.D. 1580 under the influences of the European invasion (Pendergast 1982, 1993; Trigger 1985:144–48, 351; Trigger and Pendergast 1978:357–61).

The Iroquoian-Iroquois Convention

Before proceeding it might be worthwhile to note the longstanding convention that accords a particular meaning to the terms *Iroquoian* and *Iroquois,* by which all Iroquois are Iroquoians, but not all Iroquoians are Iroquois.[1] This is analagous to the fact that all Montrealers are Canadians, but not all Canadians are Montrealers. The convention has long been used (Fenton 1978:269–321; Hewitt 1907a; 1907b; Jenness 1932:290; White 1913:224–26) to enable Iroquoianist scholars to communicate readily and with precision to differentiate between the several 16th-century tribes and confederacies whose languages and dialects are attributable to the

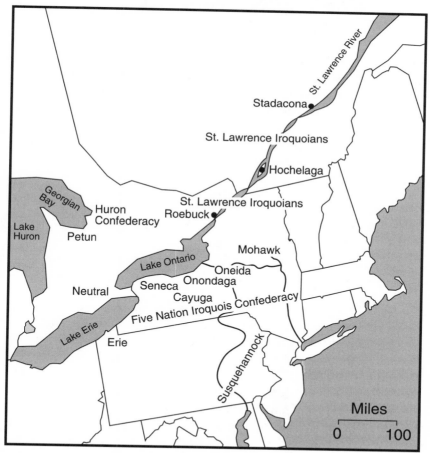

Fig. 2.1. Locations of Hochelaga and Stadacona relative to Iroquoian confederacies and tribes, ca. A.D 1500–1580

Iroquoian linguistic family. It separates the Cherokee in the southeastern United States; the Tuscarora, Nottaway, and Menherrin in the mid-Atlantic region; the Susquehannock on the Susquehanna River; the Huron, Neutral, Petun, Erie, and St. Lawrence Iroquoians in the Great Lakes–St. Lawrence River basin from the five (later six) Iroquoian-speaking, politically allied tribes of the Iroquois Confederacy. These are the Mohawk, Onondaga, Oneida, Cayuga, Seneca, and after A.D. 1722 the Tuscarora, all of whom lived in northern New York between present-day Albany and Rochester. It also permits differentiation between the large territory—bounded generally by a line stretching from Collingwood on Georgian Bay, to Quebec City on the lower St. Lawrence River, to Albany at the junction of the Hudson and Mohawk rivers, to Lancaster on the Susquehanna River, and back to Collingwood—occupied by the Iroquoian-speaking tribes and confederacies of the Northern Iroquoians from the much smaller territory in northern New York that was occupied by the five (later six) politically allied tribes that composed the five (later six) nation Iroquois Confederacy (see fig. 2.1). In a more general context it also serves to differentiate the socioeconomic and political patterning used to characterize all these Iroquoian-speaking peoples from the patterns that characterized the five (later six) tribes that composed the Iroquois League.

Scholars are under no compulsion to adopt this convention. Neither is there any suggestion that they be denied the right to introduce new nomenclature, or new meanings to replace old interpretations. However, to facilitate coherent dialogue it should be incumbent upon those who introduce new or alternative terms to define them relative to the existing taxonomy.

The Huron-Iroquois Identity Option

The presence of an Iroquois homeland on the St. Lawrence River was first noted by the Jesuit donné and French explorer Nicolas Perrot, who—possibly as early as 1680 and not later than 1717, when he died—recounted without elaboration how the Iroquois had once lived near present-day Montreal (Blair 1911; Perrault 1966; Perrot 1864).[2] In 1724 the Jesuit missionary Joseph-François Lafitau (1724:101; Fenton and Moore 1974:86) noted a Mohawk tradition that related how the Iroquois had once "camped" near present-day Quebec City.[3] Later, in 1727, the colonial English chronicler Governor Cadwallader Colden repeated Perrot's explanation without elaboration (Colden 1727). So too did the Jesuit historian Pierre-François-Xavier Charlevoix in his *Histoire et description générale de la Nouvelle France* (Charlevoix 1744; Shea 1866:127) and Claude-Charles LeRoy de la Potherie, Controller of the Marine at Quebec in the years 1698–1701, in his *Histoire de l'Amérique septentrionale* (Potherie 1753:288–90). Perrot's explanation was carried over into the 19th century by the Tuscarora Iroquois historian David Cusick in his 1825 *Sketches of Ancient History of the Six Nations* (Cusick 1848). This often-quoted but yet-to-be-demonstrated concept of an Iroquois homeland in Quebec has survived to become a basic tenet of Canadian history.

In 1851 the pioneer American ethnologist Lewis Henry Morgan made the first of many attempts to attribute Stadaconans and Hochelagans to a particular historic Iroquois tribe. In his classic *League of the Ho-de-ne-sau-nee or Iroquois,* he identified the Hochelagans as Iroquoian-speaking "Huron" farmers and the Stadaconans as Algonquian-speaking "Algonquin" hunters and gatherers (Morgan 1851:4–5). Apart from patently unlikely candidates—for instance, the Tuscarora, suggested by Beaugrand-Champagne (1937:93–114)—the three eastern tribes of the Five Nation Iroquois League (the Onondaga, Oneida, and Mohawk) were most often mentioned in this context. Lighthall (1899:199–211), for instance, held that the Stadaconans and Hochelagans were undifferentiated elements of the people who later would become the historic Onondaga, Oneida, and Mohawk tribes. All were claimed to have originated in the St. Lawrence Valley, particularly in the vicinity of Montreal, as a result of one or another of several west-to-east migration processes postulated by several 19th-century scholars to explain the presence of Iroquoians in the St. Lawrence Valley (Pendergast and Trigger 1972:48–60). Because Hochelagans and Stadaconans were alleged to have shared ancestors in this homeland, the perception was that they were all the same people. Essentially this concept prevailed as late as 1952, when it was proffered by Iroquoian archaeologist Richard MacNeish as part of his otherwise still largely valid, archaeologically oriented Iroquoian *in situ* hypothesis (MacNeish 1952).

Morgan's Huron identification for Hochelagans found favor with several scholars, while his identification of Stadaconans as "Algonquin" was largely ignored. Linguist Horatio Hale located the legend "Hurons 1535" at Montreal in the frontispiece map for his 1883 *Iroquois Book of Rites* (Hale 1883). Ethnohistorian Sir Daniel Wilson supported this Huron identity in 1884 (Wilson 1884). In 1870 and again in 1894, Wyandots on the Anderdon Reserve near Windsor, Ontario, recounted a Wyandot tradition that related how in the 16th century the Huron had lived with the Seneca near Montreal, where they had met Jacques Cartier (Clarke 1870; Hale 1894:1–4).

As a result of his examination of the Cartier vocabularies, Abbé Etienne-Michel Faillon, a philologist, advanced a Huron Iroquois identification in 1865 (Faillon 1865:14–15; Squair 1924:82). This correctly placed the Huron in the Iroquoian linguistic family but, because of the dual meaning of the Iroquois taxonomy then in use, this identity did not serve to differentiate between the several members of the *Iroquoian* linguistic family and the five tribes of the *Iroquois* League or Confederacy. Contrary to Morgan's suggestion, Faillon included Stadacona in his Huron-Iroquois identification in the belief that the Cartier vocabularies applied to both the Stadaconans and Hochelagans.

Many scholars adopted Faillon's 1865 Huron-Iroquois identification of the Cartier word lists (Hoffman 1961:156–60) as proof of identity for both Stadaconans and Hochelagans (see table 2.1). Nevertheless, there were dissenters. In 1869 Abbé Jean-André Cuoq, also a philologist, identified Cartier's vocabularies as "Iroquois, probably Mohawk" (Cuoq 1869:198–204). In 1936, in a largely sophistical discussion, Beaugrand-Champagne identified the Stadaconans as Huron while the Hochelagans remained an unidentified element of the Iroquois Confederacy (Beaugrand-Champagne 1936:34–192). As late as 1961, National Museum of Canada ethnologist Marius Barbeau vacillated between a Huron and Mohawk identity (Barbeau 1961:108–229). In 1952 MacNeish rejected the Mohawk identification. He identified Hochelagans as undifferentiated Onondaga-Oneida on the basis of archaeological similarities shared by material from the Dawson site in downtown Montreal, then presumed to be Hochelaga, with material excavated in Jefferson County, New York, then presumed to be Onondaga-Oneida (MacNeish 1952:73).

Possibly nothing has done more to perpetuate the erroneous Huron-Iroquois identity of Stadacona and Hochelaga than the thirteen unrevised printings of Diamond Jenness's *Indians of Canada* since 1932. In this widely circulated and still generally relevant classic, Jenness quotes Beauchamp's (1905:125, 146) and Hewitt's essays on the "Huron" (1907b: 584–91) to locate the Huron homeland between present-day Montreal and Quebec City. This aspect of the Beauchamp and Hewitt references, which largely repeat Morgan's 1851 identification, has been eclipsed by recent archaeological research. Unfortunately, the unrevised seventh printing of Jenness's work in 1977 by the University of Toronto Press (and six subsequent unrevised printings, the latest in 1993) have helped perpetuate the erroneous impression that Jenness's 1932 work still represents the state-of-the-art information regarding the location of pre-Contact Hurons and the identity of the Iroquoians indigenous to the St. Lawrence Valley.

Table 2.1. Some scholars who have used Faillon's identification of Cartier's word lists to identify Hochelaga and Stadacona as "Huron-Iroquois"

1. Faillon, E. M. (1865[1]:14)	11. Lighthall, W. D. (1924:91)
2. Shea, J. G. (1866[1]:118n6)	12. Innis, H. A. (1930:11)
3. Lloyd, H. M. (1901)	13. Bailey, A. G. (1933:97)
4. Beauchamp, W. M. (1905:125)	14. Beaugrand-Champagne, A. (1936:171)
5. Dawson, S. E. (1905)	15. Kroeber, A. L. (1939:map 1b)
6. Thomas, C. (1906:71)	16. Fenton, W. N. (1940:176)
7. Hewitt, J.N.B. (1907b[1]:584)	17. Hunt, G. T. (1940)
8. Grant, W. L. (1911[1]:98n1)	18. Robinson, P. J. (1948:127)
9. Orr, R. B. (1914:15)	19. Emerson, J. N. (1954)
10. Parker, A. C. (1916:479; 1922:136)	20. Driver, H. E. (1961)

Paradoxically, in view of the certainty with which most of these scholars have advanced a Huron-Iroquois identity, in no instance have they set out evidence to endow it with compelling credibility. To the contrary, credibility for the Huron Iroquois identity is left to emerge from repetition: repetition of Perrot's still-unsubstantiated account regarding Iroquois origins in the St. Lawrence Valley, repetition of Morgan's and Lloyd's yet-to-be demonstrated migration of undifferentiated Iroquois tribes from the Mississippi Valley into the Lake Ontario–St. Lawrence River basin, and repetition of Wilson's and Hale's still undemonstrated hypothesis regarding Huron origins in the St. Lawrence Valley.[4] Variations advanced by supporters of these scenarios frequently reflect a range of undemonstrated, often speculative elaborations to provide credibility for one identity or another. All these explanations derived from the documentary and cartographic sources available to 19th and early 20th century scholars contrast sharply with the conclusions derived from the large body of archaeological evidence excavated in Ontario, Quebec, Vermont, New York, and Pennsylvania by several scholars since the 1950s.

Commencing in the 1950s, the nature and quantity of the archaeological data available, coupled with the introduction of new, sophisticated archaeological analytical techniques (including settlement patterning, ceramic seriations, osteology, and funeral rites) have enhanced our perception of the Iroquoians when they first encountered Europeans. The conclusions obtained from the archaeological data are compelling when compared with the Huron-Iroquois identity derived from the documentary and cartographic sources available to 19th and early 20th century scholars. Current archaeological data wholly contradict any suggestion that any tribe of the Huron Confederacy originated in the St. Lawrence Valley, or in the vicinity of Montreal in particular (Heidenreich 1971; Latta 1976; Ramsden 1990:361; Tooker 1964; Trigger 1976). Indeed, there is now no doubt that pre-Contact Hurons developed in a distinct Huron homeland along the north shore of Lake Ontario (Ramsden 1993; Warrick 1990) and subsequently moved to their historic territory on Georgian Bay, where they were encountered by Champlain in 1615 (Biggar 1929:36, 1932:244). The archaeological data also demonstrates conclusively that the five historic tribes of the Iroquois League are the result of essentially parallel contemporary *in situ* developments in their widely separated historic homelands in New York State (Bradley 1987; Hosback and Gibson 1980; Lenig 1965; MacNeish 1952; Pratt 1976; Tuck 1971). This archaeological evidence wholly denies the perception that would have early undifferentiated or later discrete Onondaga, Oneida, and Mohawk tribes migrate from the Mississippi Valley into the St. Lawrence Valley, where they lived in the vicinity of present-day Montreal before moving south into New York State.[5] The identification of Stadaconans and Hochelagans as Huron-Iroquois is no longer credible in the light of this archaeological evidence.

What then are we to make of recent topical and scholarly works that continue to embrace a Huron-Iroquois identity for the Stadaconans and Hochelagans?[6] Examples that come to mind, for instance, are works by Morison (1971:375–455), Quinn (1977:5,11), Morton (1983:17), Kehoe (1992:243–4), and more recently Fagan (1996:89–93). Cartographic presentations too reflect this Huron-Iroquois identity, as evidenced in works by Allen (1992:500–521), Driver (1970: map), Force and Force (1990: 62), and Goetzmann and Williams (1992:26). Significantly, none of these authors takes into account post-1950 archaeological evidence. Little wonder the public perception of Stadaconan and Hochelagan identity is sometimes skewed.

The Mohawk Identity Option

The identification of Stadaconans and Hochelagans as Mohawk, a member tribe of the Iroquois Confederacy, is premised on one or another of the several hypotheses that claim tribally undifferentiated Iroquoians had once migrated from the Mississippi Valley into the Great Lakes–St. Lawrence River basin (Pendergast and Trigger 1972:48–60). In this scenario, Stadaconans and Hochelagans, and the three eastern tribes of the Five Nation Iroquois (the Onondaga, Oneida, and Mohawk), shared a common ancestry and homeland in the St. Lawrence Valley before some elements moved on to their Contact-period homeland in New York State. Joseph-François Lafitau identified the Mohawk in this context in 1724, when he recounted a Mohawk migration tradition that to this day remains the earliest documented evidence of a Mohawk claim of once having lived in the St. Lawrence Valley (Lafitau 1724:101; see also Fenton and Moore 1974:86). Lafitau related how the Mohawk claimed to have migrated from Asia "through the north of America . . . to a place where Quebec [City] is now situated" before they moved to their historic homeland in the Mohawk Valley. In 1869 Abbé Cuoq reinforced this explanation when, as a result of his studies of the Cartier vocabularies, he identified both Stadaconans and Hochelagans as members of the Five Nation Iroquois Confederacy,[7] "probably Mohawk" (Cuoq 1869: 198–204). However, it remained for William Beauchamp, a pioneer American anthropologist, to become the principal advocate for a Mohawk homeland in the St. Lawrence Valley. The several speculative hypotheses he proposed commencing in 1894 remain the still-undemonstrated documentary plinth on which the current Mohawk identity for Stadaconans and Hochelagans is constructed (Beauchamp 1894:61–69; 1905:125–46).

Beauchamp believed there were insufficient pre-Contact Mohawk archaeological sites in the Mohawk Valley to account for the long pre-Contact history claimed by the Mohawk in their oral traditions. This perceived discrepancy fueled his search for a Mohawk pre-Contact homeland elsewhere and eventually led him to equate a wide range of Mohawk artifacts excavated in the Mohawk Valley with the material Sir William Dawson, then principal of McGill University, had excavated on the archaeological site in present-day downtown Montreal. This location, now known as the Dawson site, was then believed to be the site of Hochelaga (Pendergast and Trigger 1972). As a result, Beauchamp concluded that the Mohawk had once lived in the vicinity of Montreal and had moved to the Mohawk Valley from Hochelaga shortly after Cartier's visit in 1535. Perforce, this perception located practically the whole of the Mohawk pre-Contact period in the St. Lawrence Valley. This is a surprising conclusion. In fact, at that time, apart from Dawson's collections from the archaeological site in downtown Montreal he called Hochelaga, and New York antiquarian Ephriam G. Squier's cursory examination of Iroquoian sites in Jefferson County, New York, and the Roebuck site nearby in eastern Ontario,[8] the St. Lawrence Valley was virtually unknown archaeologically. Indeed, to this day no archaeological site has been identified as the location of Stadacona. Beauchamp's hypothesis called for the other two tribes of the eastern Five Nation Iroquois, the Oneida and Onondaga, whether as a still-undifferentiated people or by then discrete tribes, to be relocated farther upstream between Montreal and Kingston, and particularly into Jefferson County, to make room for a traditional Mohawk homeland in the area of present-day Montreal. Paradoxically, having championed the identity of Hochelaga as Mohawk, Beauchamp and those who have supported his Mohawk identity have made no effort to demonstrate the role played by the minority Hochelagan (Montreal) Mohawk element in the genesis of the Five Nation Iroquois League, which by A.D. 1600 was so heavily influenced by the Mohawk majority located in New York State.

Beauchamp's hypothesis found support among most scholars of the day, and his model was carried well into the 20th century, often with detailed speculative elaborations and reservations (see table 2.2). However, where Beauchamp had focused his Mohawk hypothesis largely on Hochelagans, ethnologists Hewitt (1907a:548–91) and Bailey (1933:97–102) expanded it to include the Stadaconans and altered the Mohawk identification to reflect the presence of an undifferentiated Mohawk-Oneida people. National Museum of Canada archaeologist William J. Wintemberg (1936) adopted this Mohawk-Oneida identity when he examined the Roebuck archaeological site west of Montreal (see fig. 2.1). Paradoxically, in the light of earlier scholarly speculations attributing Iroquoians to this region, Wintemberg's excavations at Roebuck in 1912 and 1915 constituted the earliest comprehensive archaeological investigation of an Iroquoian archaeological village site in the St. Lawrence Valley. Later Beaugrand-Champagne (1937) expanded the Mohawk-Oneida identity unrealistically to include all five of the Iroquois tribes. Essentially, in one form or another Beauchamp's Mohawk-Oneida hypothesis prevailed until 1944, when William A. Ritchie (1944:316; 1969) rejected the Mohawk identity and substituted an Onondaga identification to reflect the then-current belief that the Onondaga had once lived in Jefferson County. In 1952 MacNeish identified the Iroquoians in the St. Lawrence Valley, including those in Jefferson County at the foot of Lake Ontario, as Onondaga-Oneida. Nevertheless, variants of Beauchamp's now-discredited hypothesis are being perpetuated to this day. For instance, Helen Allan in her *The Original People: Native Americans in the Champlain Valley* (Allan 1988:24) incorrectly relates how the "Mohawks occupied much of the upper St. Lawrence River previously occupied by the Laurentian Iroquois."

Table 2.2. Some scholars who have used Abbé Cuoq's identification of Hochelaga and Stadacona as "Mohawk"

1. Lloyd, H. M. (1901:188)	10. Symington, F. (1969:102)
2. Hewitt, J.N.B. (1907b:584)	11. Blanchard, D. (1980:86, 111)
3. Parker, A. C. (1922:106, 136)	12. Allan, H. (1988:24)
4. Orr, R. B. (1919:9–24)	13. Mitchell, M. (1989:107–8)
5. Lighthall, W. D. (1924)	14. Krotz, L. (1990:74, 81, 91)
6. Bailey, A. G. (1933: 97–102)	15. Trudel, P. (1991:53–58)
7. Wintemberg, W. J. (1936)	16. Morton, D. (1992)
8. Beaugrand-Champagne, A. (1937)	17. Wright, R. (1992)
9. Fenton, W.N. (1940:176–77)	

Not one of the claims for Stadaconans or Hochelagans to be Mohawk, Onondaga, or Oneida is borne out by the archaeological data. Since the 1950s a vast accumulation of archaeological evidence excavated in Ontario, Quebec, Vermont, Pennsylvania, and New York has consistently revealed compelling evidence demonstrating that neither the Mohawk, the Onondaga, nor the Oneida originated in the St. Lawrence Valley (Hosbach and Gibson 1980; Kuhn et al. 1993:76–86; Lenig 1965; MacNeish 1952:84–89; Pendergast 1991:47–74, 1993:9–48; Rumrill 1991:5–46; Tuck 1971). Indeed, the archaeological evidence excavated in the Mohawk Valley demonstrates conclusively that the historic Mohawk had developed from their pre-Contact ancestors in the Mohawk Valley over a long period (Lenig 1965; MacNeish 1952; Rumrill 1991). In short, all the archaeological evidence rejects a Mohawk identity for the Stadaconans and Hochelagans.

What then are we to make of the works of recent scholars who have embraced the Mohawk identity for Stadaconans and Hochelagans? These include Symington (1969:102), Krotz (1990:74, 81, 91), Trudel (1991: 53–58), and Morton (1992:2).[9] Not since Beauchamp and Parker has there been an advocate to match Ronald Wright's enthusiasm for the identification of Hochelaga as a Mohawk village, presumably in support of Mohawk land claims in the St. Lawrence Valley, which he had championed earlier in an article in the *Toronto Globe and Mail* (1990). In *Stolen Continents* Wright (1992: 112) explains how Jacques Cartier had visited "the important town of Hochelaga inhabited by several thousand Mohawks." His map titled "The Iroquois Confederacy" includes the legend "Mohawk Nation," a territory shown to encompass approximately the Ottawa Valley to Hawkesbury and the St. Lawrence Valley to Prescott. Although Wright does not indicate when this Mohawk occupancy prevailed, his captions suggest that the clusters of late pre-Contact St. Lawrence Iroquoian archaeological village sites in the Summerstown and Prescott areas can be equated with the Hochelagans as part of the "Mohawk Nation." Nevertheless, to his credit Wright is one of the few best-selling popular authors of Iroquoian Native history I know who have introduced post-1950 archaeological data in their works, another being Denys Delâge (1985). Ronald Wright's references to radiocarbon-dated archaeological features in the Howlett Hill Onondaga village site excavated by James Tuck are unique in this genre. Indeed, one might expect that Wright's familiarity with post-1950 archaeological data—evidenced by his use of Elisabeth Tooker's 1967 *Iroquois Culture, History and Prehistory*, in which Tuck's Howlett Hill Onondaga site paper appeared (Tuck 1967: 75–79)—would have led him to propose a more balanced discussion of Hochelaga identity. Nevertheless, in the end Wright embraced reality. In a footnote (1992:361, n18) he relates, "It has not been proved that these Indians were Mohawks, but Mohawks were living there when Montreal was founded in the 1640s, and they are living there today." (See my note 2 regarding Perrot's account of Native traditions and Jesuit evidence of a massive early historic Mohawk presence in the Montreal area circa A.D. 1676.)

Native Iroquois scholars support a Mohawk identity, particularly for Hochelaga (Anonymous 1986; Blanchard 1980:86, 111; Mitchell 1989: 107–8). Indeed, this identity for Hochelaga is fundamental to modern Mohawk land claims in the St. Lawrence River basin.

The Laurentian Iroquois and Laurentian Iroquoian Identity Option

The Laurentian *Iroquois* and Laurentian *Iroquoian* identity options are relatively recent. The Laurentian Iroquois designation arose in 1907, when J. N. B. Hewitt identified the Rock and the Deer tribes, the eastern tribes of the Huron Confederacy, as Laurentian Iroquois at a time when he suggested that they lived in the vicinity of present-day Montreal (Hewitt 1907b:583). This, it was alleged, was before they migrated from the St. Lawrence Valley to their historic homeland in Huronia, where Champlain encountered them in 1615. Several scholars supported this identification (Bailey 1933:98; Hewitt 1907a; Orr 1914:7–18; White 1913:206–7). This wholly Huron identification is the earliest of the several definitions currently still being accorded the term *Laurentian Iroquois*.

In 1916 (1916:483, 1922:106) Arthur C. Parker, then New York State archaeologist, proffered an Iroquois migration hypothesis akin to that proposed earlier by Beauchamp (1905:110, 134, 137, 147; Lloyd 1901). Parker speculated that a still tribally undifferentiated people, who were later to become the discrete three eastern tribes of the Five Nation Iroquois League (the Onondaga, Oneida, and Mohawk), had migrated from the Mississippi Valley eastward along the north side of Lakes Erie and Ontario into the St. Lawrence River basin. There, near Montreal, he alleged, they had shared a common homeland and a common ancestry with the Stadaconans and Hochelagans. When, as he put it, "the hive swarmed," elements moved southward to the Contact-period Iroquois tribal homelands in New York State.[10] However, the simultaneous presence of an element of Mohawk in their alleged Montreal-area homeland and another in their Contact-era Mohawk Valley homeland raised a problem. Parker solved it with a modified migration hypothesis that claimed only *some* Mohawk had migrated to the Mohawk Valley from their ancestral home in the vicinity of Montreal. Parker twice identified the main body who had moved to the Mohawk Valley as the *true* Mohawk. In separate works (Parker 1916, 1922) he twice named the minority that had remained behind in the St. Lawrence Valley at Hochelaga, "Laurentian Iroquois." There were claims that all this took place soon after Jacques Cartier's visit in 1535. Parker's wholly Mohawk identification is the second, and probably the most widely held, definition currently accorded the Laurentian Iroquois identity.

In his important 1940 monograph *Problems Arising from the Historic Northeastern Position of the Iroquois,* William Fenton (1940:176–77) examined the Huron-Iroquois and Mohawk identities advanced earlier by Morgan (1851:4–5) and Parker (1916:483, 1922:106). He went on to suggest that the Iroquoians in the St. Lawrence Valley may have been a discrete people who were not involved in the development of the Onondaga, or the Oneida, or the Mohawk. Fenton named this discrete Iroquoian population *Laurentian Iroquois.* This is the third still-current definition for the Laurentian Iroquois.

In 1961 Professor Floyd Lounsbury (1961:11–17, 1978:385; Mithun 1982), the eminent Iroquoian linguist, identified certain words in the Cartier vocabularies as being representative of a discrete Iroquoian language that he attributed to Stadaconans and Hochelagans. Lounsbury labeled this language *Laurentian,* the language of the Laurentian Iroquois who earlier had been identified by Parker and Fenton. This is the fourth definition for Laurentian Iroquois still current. Paradoxically, linguistic discrepancies between Laurentian Iroquois, the language of Parker's Mohawk who remained in their Montreal homeland area, and the Mohawk language spoken by the element of these same people who had moved to New York State from the Montreal area to become Parker's true Mohawk, remain unexplained.

In 1992 Professor Olive Dickason identified the Iroquoians involved in the 1534–43 Cartier/Roberval episodes as Laurentian *Iroquoians* in her erudite textbook, *Canada's First Nations: A History of Founding Peoples from the Earliest Times* (Dickason 1992:70, 98–102, 122, 435n27, 433n12).[11] Although Dickason conducts the burden of her discussion under the Laurentian *Iroquoian* rubric, she also uses the Laurentian *Iroquois* identity (Dickason 1992:82, 176). Professor Ramsay Cook (1993) also used the Laurentian Iroquoian identification in his *The Voyages of Jacques Cartier.* This Laurentian Iroquoian identity had not been accorded the Stadaconans and Hochelagans before. By identifying them as members of the Iroquoian linguistic family, Dickason and Cook distance themselves from the erroneous Five Nation Iroquois affiliation postulated by those who continue to support Parker's (1916, 1922) Mohawk hypothesis. Nevertheless, because Dickason and Cook have not defined their new term *Laurentian Iroquoians,* we are left to ponder which of the current Laurentian identities (Hewitt's Huron, Parker's Mohawk, or Fenton's discrete people who spoke Lounsbury's Laurentian language) they intended to adopt or adapt.

Dickason twice distinctly polarizes the discussion in favor of Hewitt's Huron identity. Following their defeat by the Iroquois in 1649, she suggests that Huron elements went "east in a return to their ancient territories along the north shore of the St. Lawrence" (Dickason: 1992:131). She speculates (1992:122) that it was the eastern tribe of the Huron Confederacy, the People of the Rock, the Arendarhonon, who "may have been Laurentian Iroquoians, refugees from the wars that swept the St. Lawrence Valley during the preceding century" (prior to 1600), who made this move from the St. Lawrence Valley to Huronia. The genesis for Dickason's suggestion appears to lie in part in her speculation (1992:435 n27) that "They [the Huron Rock tribe] may have been the most recent to join [the Huron Confederacy] about 1590 which raises the question whether they came from Stadacona." It is significant to note that apart from Dickason's having elected to include the Huron Rock tribe and to exclude the Huron Deer tribe from her discussion and her emphasis on Stadacona, her suggestion closely parallels Morgan's 1851 and J. N. B. Hewitt's 1907 hypothesis (Morgan 1851:4–5; Hewitt 1907b:583) that would have Hochelagans from the vicinity of present-day Montreal migrate westward to become the eastern Deer and Rock tribes of the Huron. It also resembles A. G. Bailey's 1933 suggestion by which he included both Hochelaga and Stadacona in his Laurentian Iroquois who had migrated westward from the St. Lawrence Valley to become the eastern Huron tribes (Bailey 1933: 97–108). At this juncture it is significant to note that Dickason's having equated the Huron Rock tribe with the Laurentian Iroquoians, and her having raised the possibility of their being Cartier's Stadaconans, is a wholly different proposition from the hypothesis proffered by Georges E. Sioui (1992: 82–89). Sioui suggests that after their defeat by the Iroquois in 1649, the Huron returned to their alleged homeland near Quebec City, where they enjoyed amicable relations with an adjacent group of St. Lawrence Iroquoians. The survival of a pocket of St. Lawrence Iroquoians in this region after circa 1580 has not been suggested before.

All this brings into sharp focus the fact that there is no archaeological evidence to equate any tribes of the Huron Confederacy with the Iroquoians indigenous to the St. Lawrence Valley, including Stadaconans and Hochelagans. Parenthetically, this situation should not be confused with the archaeological evidence that demonstrates the presence of St. Lawrence Iroquoians on indigenous Huron sites in Prince Edward County, on the axis of the Trent River, on the Humber River axis, and in Huronia during much of the period (ca. A.D. 1450–1630), long before and long after the Cartier-Roberval episodes (Ramsden 1993; Warrick 1990). This evidence dwarfs the incidence of Iroquoian artifacts from the St. Lawrence River basin on Mohawk, Onondaga, and Oneida sites in New York State over the same time period (Bradley 1987; Hosbach and Gibson 1980; Kuhn et al. 1993; Lenig 1965; MacNeish 1952; Pendergast 1993; Rumrill 1991; Tuck 1971). The distribution of Iroquoian archaeological material from the St. Lawrence Valley confirms the widespread and longstanding association of St. Lawrence Iroquoians with Iroquoians throughout much of Iroquoia without equating any of the several host Iroquoian groups with the Stadaconans or Hochelagans.

We are left to ponder which, if any, of the Laurentian Iroquoians that recent scholars have embraced (Cook 1993; Dickason 1992; Dobyns 1989:258–99; Eccles 1994b:19) best match the identities proposed by Hewitt, Parker, Fenton, and Lounsbury. We are still faced with the longstanding problems that arise when identities are attributed to Cartier's Iroquoians using the taxonomics and undemonstrated hypotheses derived from 19th and early 20th century documentary and cartographic sources.

The St. Lawrence Iroquoian and St. Lawrence Iroquois Identity Option

The term *St. Lawrence Iroquoian* was introduced in the mid-1960s to take cognizance of archaeological data that provides compelling evidence for a discrete and indigenous Iroquoian people in the St. Lawrence River basin in the late pre-Contact and early Contact eras. By that time Richard Mac-Neish, then an archaeologist with the National Museum of Canada, had used Iroquoian ceramic data to demonstrate that the Mohawk homeland was in the Mohawk Valley, not in the St. Lawrence Valley (MacNeish 1952). Subsequently, larger and more varied assemblages from more Mohawk archaeological sites examined by several archaeologists (Lenig 1965; Snow 1977, 1995b; Starna 1980; and Rumrill 1991) were used to confirm and expand upon MacNeish's in situ hypothesis, which had been derived from ceramic data alone. As a result neither Stadacona nor Hochelaga could any longer be identified as Mohawk villages. In 1965 archaeologist James Tuck (1971) demonstrated that the Onondaga had developed *in situ* in their historic homeland near present-day Syracuse, New York. In 1979 archaeologist James Bradley confirmed the unbroken Onondaga occupancy of this area in the Contact and historic period (Bradley 1987). In 1976 Peter Pratt demonstrated a continuous Oneida occupation of the area near Oneida Lake in the pre-Contact and Contact eras (Pratt 1976). Subsequently several scholars confirmed and expanded upon Pratt's Oneida findings (Hosbach and Gibson 1980). Clearly the archaeological data do not support there having been a Mohawk, Onondaga, or Oneida homeland in the St. Lawrence River basin at any time prior to their presence at the La Prairie and Sault St. Louis Jesuit missions near Montreal (ca. 1667–73). Concurrently these findings in New York State were supported by my work demonstrating an in situ development for an indigenous Iroquoian people in the St. Lawrence Valley (Pendergast 1975). This raised a compelling need to provide a discrete identity for the Iroquoians in the St. Lawrence Valley, one wholly free from the several long-standing and obfuscating identities then in use.

Commencing in 1962, with collateral papers in 1963, 1966, and 1968, Bruce Trigger recognized how misleading the then-current single designation *Laurentian Iroquois* could be for Iroquoian peoples as culturally diverse as the riverine-oriented Stadaconans and the Hochelagan farmers described by Jacques Cartier. This need for definition grew apace with the growing requirement to distinguish the indigenous Iroquoians in the St. Lawrence Valley from the remaining members of the Iroquoian linguistic family and the five tribes of the Iroquois Confederacy in particular. Trigger suggested that the Iroquoians in the Quebec City area be known as

Stadaconans and those on Montreal Island as Hochelagans. Until these people could be defined better, he suggested they be known collectively as St. Lawrence Iroquoians (Trigger 1962, 1963, 1966, 1968, 1972). This was the distinction drawn in 1972 when *Cartier's Hochelaga and the Dawson Site* was published and again in 1978 when the paper "Saint Lawrence Iroquoians" appeared in the *Handbook of North American Indians* (Pendergast and Trigger 1972; Trigger and Pendergast 1978).

Archaeological investigations over the past decade or more have supported the wisdom of this taxonomy. It is now clear that during the late pre-Contact and early Contact periods several discrete Iroquoian groups inhabited the nearly 690 km-long (approximately 425 mi) territory in the St. Lawrence Valley once discussed under the rubric "St. Lawrence Iroquoians." Indeed, current research now well advanced by a number of scholars working in several areas seeks to define these regional groups of Iroquoians.[12] Some seem likely to emerge as discrete Iroquoian tribes heretofore overlooked in the pre-1950 documentary sources. None of this archaeological evidence suggests that the now-discredited Huron-Iroquois or Laurentian identities will be revived.

In 1972, J. V. Wright, an archaeologist with the National Museum of Man, National Museums of Canada, published his widely read *Ontario Prehistory;* and in 1979 a companion volume, *Quebec Prehistory,* appeared (Wright 1972, 1979).[13] In both works Wright referred to the indigenous Iroquoians in the St. Lawrence Valley as St. Lawrence Iroquois. Because the terms *St. Lawrence Iroquois* and *St. Lawrence Iroquoians* are synonyms, wholly equivalent in every respect, several scholars have elected to use the term *St. Lawrence Iroquois.* As was noted earlier, all *Iroquoians* are not *Iroquois,* the latter being a term reserved for the Five Nations (tribes) in the Iroquois Confederacy (League). Neither are the *St. Lawrence Iroquois,* or the *St. Lawrence Iroquoians,* members of the Confederacy, through they belong to the *Iroquoian* linguistic family. The use of the adjective *St. Lawrence* makes them distinct from the Five Nations in the *Iroquois Confederacy* but includes them as members of the Iroquoian family.

Discussion

By now the nature and extent of the taxonomic and conceptual gulfs that separate many historians and Iroquoianist archaeologists regarding the identity of Stadaconans and Hochelagans will be apparent. Some historians have opted to continue to identify Stadaconans and Hochelagans using terminology and undemonstrated, sometimes speculative, interpretations derived from pre-1950 documentary and cartographic sources. By limiting their investigations to this largely derivative material they have perpetuated the now-erroneous logic on which the Huron-Iroquois, Mohawk, and Laurentian Iroquois identities for Stadaconans and Hochelagans are founded. On the other hand, anthropologists, particularly archaeologists, have introduced post-1950 archaeological, linguistic, and ethnohistorical conclusions into their deliberations. These sources deny the Huron-Iroquois, Mohawk, and Laurentian Iroquois identities in favor of the perception that a wholly indigenous and discrete Iroquoian people were present in the St. Lawrence Valley when Cartier arrived. The current anthropological convention is to designate these people St. Lawrence Iroquoians, in recognition of the fact that on-going archaeological research indicates that several discrete Iroquoian political entities were present in a number of widely dispersed geographical regions along the St. Lawrence River axis from Jefferson County at the foot of Lake Ontario to Quebec City and beyond.

The St. Lawrence Iroquoian identification has received a mixed reception. It is used by most Iroquoianist scholars and by elements of the topical and anthropologically oriented academic press. This acceptance can be attributed largely to the publication of *Cartier's Hochelaga and the Dawson Site* (Pendergast and Trigger 1972), and the paper "Saint Lawrence Iroquoians" in the *Handbook of North American Indians* (Trigger and Pendergast 1978). Subsequently the extensive coverage of the St. Lawrence Iroquoians in the 1987 *Historical Atlas of Canada* has enhanced this perception of early Canadian history (Harris 1987:5, 83, 84, plates 9, 12, 13). Later scholars—for instance, Allan D. McMillan in his 1988 *Native Peoples and Cultures of Canada,* James Axtell in his *After Columbus: Essays in the Ethnohistory of Colonial North America* (1988:152, 176), Ramsay Cook in his 1993 *Voyages of Jacques Cartier,* and Bruce Trigger in his 1994 paper "The Original Iroquoians: Huron, Petun and Neutral" (1994:42, 45–46)—have used the St. Lawrence Iroquoian identity to carry the burden of their discussion. The inclusion of the legend "St. Lawrence Iroquoians" on the maps "Northern Approaches," "Atlantic Gateways," and "New England" in the 1983–85 National Geographic cartographic series *The Making of America* (Garrett 1983, 1985, 1987) has endowed the St. Lawrence Iroquoian identity with credibility for a great number of nontechnical readers worldwide. Acceptance prospered when in 1988 the National Geographic Society published their *Historical Atlas of the United States* locating the St. Lawrence Iroquoians in the St. Lawrence River basin (Garrett 1988:34–35).

On the other hand some scholars have not embraced the St. Lawrence Iroquoian identity. In his widely read 1971 work, *The European Discovery of America: The Northern Voyages,* American historian Samuel E. Morison (1971: 375–455) repeatedly identified Stadacona and Hochelaga as Huron villages with no explanation for his having reached this conclusion. The English historian David B. Quinn (1977:5, 11, 476) examined the Huron-Iroquois identity option, weighed it against the documentation then available in support of the St. Lawrence Iroquoian option (which in 1962 he assessed as being "on the defensive"), and elected in his 1977 encyclopedic *North America from Earliest Discovery to First Settlement* to support a Huron identity for Stadaconans and Hochelagans. Olive P. Dickason in her 1992 work, *Canada's First Nations: A History of Founding Peoples from the Earliest Times* (1992:70, 98–102, 435 n27, 433 n7, 444 n18), has identified Stadaconans and Hochelagans as Laurentian Iroquoians. In 1966 Cornelius J. Jaenen used the Laurentian Iroquois identity in his Champlain Society work *The French Regime in the Upper Country of Canada during the Seventeenth Century.* Morison's and Quinn's preeminent international status, coupled with Dickason's and Jaenen's scholarly works, seem likely to perpetuate the Huron-Iroquois and Laurentian identifications well beyond the time when compelling evidence to the contrary might be expected to eclipse these yet-to-be-demonstrated options.[14] In his 1996 work *I Have Lived Here Since the World Began,* Arthur J. Ray (1996:7, 19, 48–52) identified Stadacona and Hochelaga as isolated Iroquoian villages in the St. Lawrence Valley with the explanation that they were discrete contemporaries of the Petun and several tribes of the Huron, Neutral, and Five Nation confederacies. Having commended the "intensive archaeological research since the late nineteenth century" in the St. Lawrence River basin that has "moved the history of the Native people of colonial Canada from the periphery, where historians had treated it as an aspect of European history, to centre stage, as a topic worthy of study in its own right" (1996:xv), Ray elects not to use this archaeological data to identify the Iroquoians indigenous to the St. Lawrence Valley.

Some recent works are inconsistent. The 1987 *Historical Atlas of Canada* records the presence of both St. Lawrence Iroquois and St. Lawrence Iroquoians (Harris 1987).[15] The 1988 edition of *The Canadian Encyclopedia* identifies Cartier's Iroquoians who disappeared from the St. Lawrence Valley. They can be St. Lawrence Iroquoians, Laurentian Iroquois and Iroquois.[16] The National Geographic map series *The Making of America,* published over the period 1983–87 (Garrett 1983, 1985, 1987), used the definitive "St. Lawrence Iroquoian" caption, while the map "Atlantic Canada" in the 1993 National Geographic series *The Making of Canada* (Graves 1993) uses the more general identification "Iroquoians." In 1996 John Warkentin and Grant Head adopted the St. Lawrence Iroquoian identity for the "Ontario" map later in the *The Making of Canada* series (W. Allen 1996). We are left to ponder whether the "Atlantic Canada" map represents an undocumented denial regarding the presence of a discrete St. Lawrence Iroquoian people, or a choice of the general over the particular for reasons left unexplained. There is no evidence to support an Iroquois, Iroquoian, and St. Lawrence Iroquoian equivalence.

It would be paradoxical if a polarization arose whereby American scholars adopted the definitive "St. Lawrence Iroquoian" identity, which was largely pioneered by Canadian anthropologists, while Canadian historians opted for the less definitive "Iroquoian" identity. If this polarization were to occur, the situation would resemble the chauvinistic dichotomy that prevailed earlier this century. At that time Canadian scholars identified the Laurentian Iroquois with some certainty as being ancestral to the Hurons located in Ontario, while contemporary scholars in the United States with at least as much conviction identified the Laurentian Iroquois as being the element of the Mohawk tribe of the Iroquois Confederacy that had remained behind near Montreal when the *true* Mohawk had migrated to the Mohawk Valley after about 1535.

Some current works with enticing, all-embracing titles make no reference to the St. Lawrence Iroquoians at all (Josephy and Limerick 1993; Ridington and Ridington 1993). Others mention them only in passing when they might be expected to note, at least, that the Hochelagans and Stadaconans were the earliest of all Iroquoians to encounter Europeans (Conrad et al. 1993; Delâge 1985).[17]

Conclusion

Some historians who seek to explain 16th-century events in the St. Lawrence Valley have not made use of the linguistic and archaeological knowledge available as a result of post-1950 research. Consequently, their perceptions are skewed by limitations inherent in pre-1950 sources. Claims for Stadaconans and Hochelagans to have been Huron-Iroquois, or Mohawk, or some element of the Mohawk designated Laurentian Iroquois, or its recent and more derivative Laurentian Iroquoians, are no longer credible in the light of the knowledge available from nearly fifty years of ongoing archaeological and linguistic research. On the other hand, the evidence for there having been an indigenous Iroquoian people in the St. Lawrence River basin, now known as St. Lawrence Iroquoians, is compelling. Unfortunately, reality has not kept pace with William J. Eccles's optimistic hope that "Indians as a major subject for investigation [had] at long last captured the serious attention of historians who were now willing to make use of the findings of scholars in other disciplines" (Eccles 1984:420). Would that this were so.

Possibly this confusion prevails because current archaeological publications do not serve the whole community of scholars interested in 16th-century New World history in these latitudes. If archaeological findings collateral to historical research were to be published in the appropriate historical journals, would the state of the art be perceived better? Norman Emerson's archaeological briefs, "New Pages of Prehistory," published in the late 1950s in *Ontario History* (Emerson 1956:183–96, 1958:39–59, 1959:49–72, 1961:121–48; Garrad 1992) come to mind as early attempts to bridge this gap. It might be useful if the *Canadian Historical Review* were to list certain archaeological and linguistic works in its "Recent Publications Relative to Canada." Possibly *Ethnohistory* too could list cogent archaeological publications that impinge upon the Contact and late pre-Contact eras. Reciprocal advantages might accrue if archaeological journals were to publish a list of recent historical and ethnohistorical papers that bear upon archaeological research. Be this as it may, joint sessions appear to provide the best forum for the discussion of emerging hypotheses that bear on more than one discipline. In these settings scholars from collateral disciplines can exchange viewpoints in person and in the intimate detail necessary to be able to comprehend fully the problem at hand. The symposia at the annual meeting of the American Society for Ethnohistory that led to this volume demonstrated once again the value of these joint meetings as clearinghouses for the exchange of ideas that overlap several disciplines.

Notes

1. William J. Eccles's (1994b:19) letter to the editor of the *Literary Review of Canada* chiding Cook over his particularized use of *Iroquois* and *Iroquoian*, and Eccles's pejorative comment that these are but terms "conjured up by latter day anthropologists and ethnohistorians," may be more tongue-in-cheek than might at first be apparent. Eccles himself used these terms in a conventional context to good avail in his *France in America* (1972:20), as did Ronald Wright more recently in his widely read *Stolen Continents* (1992:115).

2. In this context the "Iroquois" are the eastern three tribes of the Five Nation Iroquois League or Confederacy (the Onondaga, Oneida, and Mohawk) located between present-day Albany and Syracuse, New York. The western tribes of the League in the Rochester area, the Seneca, Cayuga, and later the Tuscarora, were not involved in the context of this discussion. Perrot's account of a tradition locating an Iroquois homeland on the St. Lawrence River may reflect the Oneida presence at the La Prairie mission opposite Montreal that dates from 1667. By 1676 the Mohawk dominated this mission, particularly after it moved from La Prairie to Sault St. Louis, the Lachine Rapids. Indeed, the Mohawks named the new mission location at the Lachine Rapids Caughnawaga, after the "lower Mohawk castle" in their Mohawk Valley homeland. The Jesuits noted that by 1673 there were more Mohawk warriors at La Prairie near Montreal than were left in their homeland in the Mohawk Valley (see Thwaites's *Jesuit Relations* 1900, vol. 63:179; Fenton and Tooker 1978:469; Delâge 1991:1–2; Snow 1995b).

3. Lafitau related: "They say that they came from afar from the direction of the west, that is to say from Asia. The Angé [Mohawk] Iroquois assure us that they wandered a long time under the leadership of a woman. . . . This woman led them all through the north of America. She made them go to the place where the City of Quebec is now situated" (Fenton and Moore 1974:86).

4. The hypothesis that would have the Iroquois migrate from the Great Plains and the Mississippi Valley into their homelands-to-be in the Great Lakes–St. Lawrence River basin continues to find support among some Native Iroquois scholars. For instance, it is the core of the concept put forward by Tehanetorens in his 1976 illustrated pamphlet, "Migration of the Iroquois," published by *Akwesasne Notes* as the "official publication" of the Mohawk Nation. On the other hand, an anonymous paper, "A Basic Call to Consciousness: The Haudenosaunee Address to the Western World," in *Akwesasne Notes* (1986:49, 54) relates how, "Since the beginning of 'human time' the Iroquoians have continuously occupied the 'homelands' in which they were first encountered by Europeans." In his paper "An Unbroken Assertion of Sovereignty," Chief Michael Mitchell asserts that the Mohawk have occupied their homeland "since time immemorial" (Mitchell 1989:107–8). These claims could be interpreted to support the discrete nature of the Hochelagans and Stadaconans proffered in this discussion.

5. This scenario has not been negated by a recent hypothesis advanced by Dean Snow (1995a). Snow postulates a late Middle Woodland proto-Iroquoian migration over the period A.D. 800–1100 from a common homeland in the Clemson's Island area of Pennsylvania to the several locations where Europeans first encountered Iroquoian tribes in the 16th and 17th centuries. The hypothesis suggested by Snow would have taken place long before the 16th-century events under discussion here.

6. What might appear to be Cook's identification of the "Huron-Iroquois family" in his *Voyages of Jacques Cartier* (Cook 1993:25 n139)—as indeed Eccles has taken to be the case in his reviews of Cook's work in the *Literary Review of*

Canada (1994a:21, 1994b:19)—is in fact Cook's direct quote of Biggar's note in his *Voyages of Jacques Cartier* (Biggar 1924:63 n16). Cook's inclusion of information from modern works sometimes blurs the source of some of his footnotes. For instance, his note 117 (p. 62) includes material from Lynn Ceci (1982:96–107); and his note 166 (p. 80) includes material from Jacques Rousseau (1954:171–201).

7. In 1882 linguist Horatio Hale suggested that, because Mohawk and Huron were the oldest of the Iroquoian languages, the Mohawk would be the last to leave their homeland in the St. Lawrence Valley (see Pendergast and Trigger 1972:50).

8. In 1848 Ephriam G. Squier published "Aboriginal Monuments of the State of New York, Comprising the Results of Original Surveys and Explorations," in which he located many Iroquoian archaeological sites in Jefferson County, New York. At the time these sites were attributed to the Onondaga Iroquois. It was alleged they later migrated to their 17th-century homeland near present-day Syracuse. In 1936 William J. Wintemberg published *The Roebuck Prehistoric Village Site, Grenville County, Ontario,* the first comprehensive account of the Iroquoians in the St. Lawrence Valley. He identified the Iroquoians in the St. Lawrence Valley as undifferentiated Onondaga-Mohawk Iroquois, thereby perpetuating, in part, Lafitau's, Abbé Cuoq's, and Beauchamp's Mohawk lineage.

9. In his *Military History of Canada: From Champlain to Gulf War,* Desmond Morton (1992:2) explains that the Indians Champlain fought on Lake Champlain in 1609 "were the heirs to the people Jacques Cartier had met along the St. Lawrence River in the 1540's [*sic*]. In the interim [over the period 1543–1609] they had retreated to their ancient homeland in what is now up-state New York." This erroneously resurrects Parker's 1916 now-discredited Laurentian origin for the Mohawk in the Montreal area.

10. To accommodate Parker's Laurentian Iroquois "Mohawk" identity, the Onondaga and Oneida, regardless of whether they were at the time undifferentiated or discrete tribes, were relocated from the Montreal area to the regions farther up-river between Montreal and Kingston. The Onondaga were assigned to Jefferson County, New York, at the foot of Lake Ontario, from whence, it was alleged, they later migrated to their historic homeland in the hills near Syracuse (see Pendergast 1993).

11. In a reference to Bruce G. Trigger's 1985 *Natives and Newcomers,* Dickason (1992:443 n12) states, "In general, I am following Trigger who discusses the question of the *Laurentian Iroquoians* in detail pp. 144–48." This text in Trigger's *Native and Newcomers* is entitled "The Disappearance of the St. Lawrence Iroquoians," and like the remainder of Trigger's book, it makes no mention of a Laurentian Iroquoian identity for Stadacona and Hochelaga. Indeed, Trigger pioneered their identity as St. Lawrence Iroquoians.

12. An insight into the orientation and intensity of this research may be obtained from Claude Chapdelaine (1980, 1989). Chapdelaine's "Eastern Saint Lawrence Iroquoian in the Cap Tourmente Area" (1993), Michel Plourde's "Iro-

quoians in the Estuary of the Saint Lawrence River" (1993), and Pendergast's "The St. Lawrence Iroquoians: Their Past, Present and Immediate Future" (1991) are more recent examples of this research.

13. In his essay "The Archaeology of Southern Ontario to A.D. 1650: A Critique," J. V. Wright (1990: 501) explains how his use of the term *St. Lawrence Iroquois* is in keeping with the earliest conventions, when the term *Iroquois* encompassed all Iroquoian speakers, not simply the Iroquois Confederacy tribes alone. Nevertheless, by 1907 J. N. B. Hewitt had drawn attention to the distinction between Iroquoian and Iroquois (Hewitt 1907a). In 1954 pioneer University of Toronto archaeologist Norman Emerson had made this distinction in his work "The Archaeology of the Ontario Iroquois" (1954:92, 96–97, 236–37, 239), the first Canadian doctoral dissertation to examine Iroquoian archaeology. In 1966 Wright used the Iroquois nomenclature in his seminal monograph *The Ontario Iroquois Tradition.* Subsequently several scholars adopted Wright's Iroquois nomenclature (e.g., Girouard 1972; Marois 1978; Clermont 1990; McGhee 1991). In Wright's 1987 contributions to the *Historical Atlas of Canada,* both the St. Lawrence Iroquois and the St. Lawrence Iroquoians are mentioned (see note 15 infra). In his 1994 paper "Before European Contact" in *Aboriginal Ontario* (1994), Wright used the St. Lawrence Iroquois synonymy.

14. Kerry M. Able, commenting upon the value of Dickason's *Canada's First Nations* in his 1994 review, remarked it was likely to "serve as a standard in Native history for some time to come."

15. Consistency is strained in the *Historical Atlas of Canada,* vol. 1, *From the Beginning to 1800* (Harris 1987). On one hand, the unattributed essay "Prehistory" (Anonymous 1987a:5), and plate 12, "Iroquoian Agricultural Settlement" by J. V. Wright and Rudolph Fecteau, use the St. Lawrence Iroquois identity. On the other hand, the unsigned essays "The Atlantic Realm" (Anonymous 1987b: 48) and "Inland Expansion" (Anonymous 1987c:83, 84); and J. V. Wright's "The St. Lawrence Settlements" (p. 113) and his plate 9, "Cultural Sequences, A.D. 500–European Contact"; and B. G. Trigger's plate 33, "The St. Lawrence Valley, 16th Century" and his plate 47, "Native Resettlement, 1635–1800," all use the St. Lawrence Iroquoian identity.

16. *The Canadian Encyclopedia,* 2d ed., contributes to the confusion when it seeks to explain which Iroquoians had disappeared from the St. Lawrence Valley. James Marsh's St. Lawrence Iroquois identification (1988:2066) is contradicted by Cornelius J. Jaenen's advice that it was the Laurentian Iroquois who had disappeared (1988:1435). Marsh's identification of Hochelaga as Iroquois (1988a:998) and Stadacona as St. Lawrence Iroquois adds to the confusion. The St. Lawrence Iroquois are not included in the encyclopedia's index.

17. Denys Delâge's 1985 book *Le pays renversé,* an interdisciplinary analysis of French, Dutch, and English intrusions into the New World over the period 1600–1664, notes the "Iroquoians also occupied the St. Lawrence valley from the mouth [*sic*] of Lake Ontario to the Ile d'Orléans." Cogently, Delâge excludes the St.

Lawrence Iroquoians from his definitive list of the Iroquoian confederations extant during the period 1600–64 (p. 46), in recognition of their having been destroyed circa A.D. 1580. However, when Delâge examines the Cartier-Roberval episodes over the period 1534–43, at a time when a St. Lawrence Iroquoian presence is well documented in the ethnohistorical and archaeological literature, he elects to use the generality "Iroquoian" to identify Stadacona, Hochelaga, and the Stadaconan chief Donnacona at Gaspé (1985:44, 84). Later, when Delâge explains why Cartier and Roberval were unable to found a French settlement on the St. Lawrence, he introduces the St. Lawrence Iroquoians (1985:84) but gives no indication as to who they might be. Delâge becomes a rare historian in this genre when he uses archaeological data from Barré and Girouard (1978:82) to demonstrate how the distribution of diagnostic St. Lawrence Iroquoian pottery can be used to delineate the extent of aboriginal trade before the European invasion. Delâge does not include the St. Lawrence Iroquoians in his index.

References Cited

Able, Kerry M. 1994. Review of Olive P. Dickason's 1992 *Canada's First Nations: A History of Founding Peoples from the Earliest Times. Canadian Historical Review* 75(4).

Abley, Mark. 1994. Where Was Hochelaga? *Canadian Geographic* 114(6):62–69.

Allan, Helen. 1988. *The Original People: Native Americans in the Champlain Valley.* Clinton County Museum, Plattsburgh, N.Y.

Allen, John L. 1992. From Cabot to Cartier: The Early Explorations of Eastern North America. In *America Before and After 1492: Current Geographical Research*, ed. K. W. Butzer. Annals for the Association of American Geographers 82(3):500–521.

Allen, William L., ed. 1996. Ontario. In *The Making of Canada* map series. *National Geographic* 189(6).

Anonymous. 1986. A Basic Call to Consciousness: The Haudenosaunee Address to the Western World. *Akwesasne Notes*, vol. 49, Rooseveltown, N.Y.

———. 1987a. Prehistory. In *Historical Atlas of Canada*, vol. 1, *From the Beginning to 1800*, ed. R. Cole Harris, 1–6. University of Toronto Press, Toronto.

———. 1987b. The Atlantic Realm. In *Historical Atlas of Canada*, vol. 1, *From the Beginning to 1800*, ed. R. Cole Harris, 47–51. University of Toronto Press, Toronto.

———. 1987c. Inland Expansion. In *Historical Atlas of Canada*, vol. 1, *From the Beginning to 1800*, ed. R. Cole Harris, 83–89. University of Toronto Press, Toronto.

Axtell, James. 1988. *After Columbus: Essays in the Ethnohistory of Colonial North America.* Oxford University Press, New York.

Bailey, Alfred G. 1933. The Significance of the Identity and Disappearance of the

Laurentian Iroquois. *Transactions of the Royal Society of Canada,* 3d ser., vol. 27, sec. 2: 97–108.

Barbeau, Marius. 1961. The Language of Canada in the Voyages of Jacques Cartier (1534–1538). In *Contributions to Anthropology 1959.* National Museum of Canada Bulletin 173: 108–229.

Barré, Georges, and Laurent Girouard. 1978. Les Iroquoiens: premiers Agriculteurs. In *Images de la préhistoire du Québec,* ed. Claude Chapdelain, 43–54. *Recherches amérindiennes au Québec* 7:1–2.

Beauchamp, William M. 1894. The Origin of the Iroquois. *American Antiquarian* 16:61–69.

———. 1905. *A History of the New York Iroquois: Now Commonly Called the Six Nations.* New York State Museum Bulletin 78, 125–461. Albany, N.Y.

Beaugrand-Champagne, Aristide. 1923. Le chemin d'Hochelaga. *Transactions of the Royal Society of Canada,* 3d ser., vol. 17, sec. 1, 17–24. Montreal.

———. 1936. Les anciens Iroquois de Québec. *Les Cahiers du Dix* 1:171–99. Montreal.

———. 1937. Le peuple d'Hochelaga. *Les Cahiers du Dix* 2:93–114. Montreal.

Biggar, H. P., ed. 1922–1936. *The Works of Samuel de Champlain,* 6 vols. Champlain Society, Toronto.

———. 1924. *Voyages of Jacques Cartier.* Publications of the Archives of Canada, no. 11, Ottawa.

Blair, E. H. 1911. Translation of Perrot's "Mémoire sur les moeurs." In *The Indian Tribes of the Upper Mississippi Valley and Region of the Great Lakes,* ed. Arthur H. Clark. Cleveland.

Blanchard, David. 1980. *Seven Generations: A History of the Kanienkahaka.* Kahnawake Survival School, Kahnawake, Quebec.

Bradley, James W. 1987. *Evolution of the Onondaga Iroquois: Accommodating Change, 1500–1655.* Syracuse University Press, Syracuse, N.Y.

Ceci, Lynn. 1982. The Value of Wampum among New York Iroquois: A Case Study of Artifact Analysis. *Journal of Anthropological Research* 38:96–107.

Chapdelaine, Claude. 1980. L'ascendance culturelle des Iroquoiens du Saint-Laurent. *Recherches amérindiennes au Québec* 10:145–52.

———. 1989. Le site Mandeville à Tracy: Variabilité culturelle des Iroquoiennes du Saint-Laurent. *Recherches amérindiennes au Québec* 7.

———. 1993. Eastern Saint Lawrence Iroquoian in the Cap Tormente Area. In *Essays in St. Lawrence Iroquoian Archaeology,* ed. James F. Pendergast and Claude Chapdelaine. Occasional Papers in Northeastern Archaeology no. 8, 87–100. Copetown Press, Dundas, Ontario.

Charlevoix, Pierre-François-Xavier de. 1744. *Histoire et description générale de la Nouvelle France.* 3 vols. Paris. Reprinted 1866 as *History and the General Description of New France,* 6 vols., ed. J. G. Shea. Loyola University Press, Chicago.

Clarke, Peter Dooyentate. 1870. *Origin and Traditional History of the Wyandots*

and Other Indian Tribes of North America; True Traditional Stories of Tecumseh and His League in the Years 1811 and 1812. Hunter, Rose, Toronto.

Clermont, Norman. 1990. Why Did the St. Lawrence Iroquois Become Agriculturalists? *Man in the Northeast* 40:75–79.

Colden, Cadwallader. [1727] 1750. *History of the Five Nations of Canada.* 2d ed., London. Reprinted 1958 as *The History of the Five Nations of the Province of New York in America.* Cornell University Press, Ithaca, N.Y.

Conrad, Margaret, Alvin Finkel, and Cornelius Jaenan. 1993. *History of the Canadian People.* Copp Clark Pittman, Toronto.

Cook, Ramsay. 1993. *Voyages of Jacques Cartier.* University of Toronto Press, Toronto.

———. 1994. Comments on William Eccles's review of Cook's *Voyages of Jacques Cartier. Literary Review of Canada* 19 (March).

Cuoq, Jean-André. 1869. Quels étaient les sauvages que recontra Jacq. Cartier sur les rives du Saint-Laurent? *Annales de philosophie chrétienne* 79:198–204. Quebec.

Cusick, David. 1848. *Sketches of Ancient History of the Six Nations.* Lockport, N.Y.

Dawson, Samuel E. 1905. *The St. Lawrence Basin and Its Border Lands: Being the Story of Their Discovery, Exploration and Occupation.* Lawrence and Bullen, London.

Delâge, Denys. 1985. *Le pays renversé: Amerindiens et européens en Amérique du nord-est, 1600–1664.* Boréal, Montreal. Trans. as *Bitter Feast,* 1993, by Jane Brierly. University of British Columbia Press, Vancouver.

———. 1991. Iroquois chrétiens des "reductions," 1667–1710: Imigration et rapports avec les français. *Recherches amérindiennes au Québec* 20:1–2.

Dickason, Olive P. 1992. *Canada's First Nations: A History of Founding Peoples from the Earliest Times.* McClelland Stewart, Toronto. (U.S. edition 1993, University of Oklahoma Press, Norman.)

Dobyns, Henry F. 1989. More Methodological Perspectives on Historical Demography. *Ethnohistory* 36(3):258–99.

Driver, Harold E. 1970. *Indians of North America.* University of Chicago Press, Chicago.

Eccles, William J. 1972. *France in America.* Fitzhenry and Whiteside, Vancouver.

———. 1984. Forty Years Back. *William and Mary Quarterly,* 3d ser. 40(3):410–21.

———. 1994a. Review of Ramsay Cook's 1993 *Voyages of Jacques Cartier. Literary Review of Canada,* February, 20–23.

———. 1994b. Letter to the editor. *Literary Review of Canada,* April.

Emerson, J. Norman. 1954. The Archaeology of the Ontario Iroquois. Ph.D. diss., University of Chicago.

———. 1956. New Pages of Prehistory. *Ontario History* 48(4).

———. 1957. New Pages of Prehistory. *Ontario History* 50(1).

———. 1958. New Pages of Prehistory. *Ontario History* 51(1).

———. 1959. New Pages of Prehistory. *Ontario History* 52(1).

———. 1961. New Pages of Prehistory. *Ontario History* 54(2).

Fagan, Brian. 1996. A Finite Iroquois Legacy. *Archaeology* September–October, 89–93.

Faillon, Etienne-Michel. 1865. *Histoire de la colonie française en Canada.* 3 vols. Montreal. Trans. John Squair, *Annual Archaeological Report for Ontario* 82(8) (1923).

Fenton, William N. 1940. Problems Arising from the Historic Northeastern Position of the Iroquois. In *Essays in Historical Anthropology of North America,* Smithsonian Miscellaneous Collections, vol. 100, 159–251. Smithsonian Institution, Washington, D.C.

———. 1978. Northern Iroquoian Culture Patterns. In *Handbook of North American Indians,* vol. 15, *Northeast,* ed. B. G. Trigger, 296–321. Smithsonian Institution, Washington, D.C.

Fenton, William N., and Elizabeth L. Moore. 1974. *Customs of the American Indians Compared with the Customs of Primitive Times.* 2 vols. Champlain Society, Toronto.

Fenton, William N., and Elisabeth Tooker. 1978. Mohawk. In *Handbook of North American Indians,* vol. 15, *Northeast,* ed. B. G. Trigger, 466–80. Smithsonian Institution, Washington, D.C.

Force, Roland W., and Marianne Tefft Force. 1990. *The American Indians: Peoples of North America.* Chelsea House, New York.

Fulford, Robert. 1993. The Voyages of a World-Class Bonehead. *Toronto Globe and Mail,* October 27.

Garrad, Charles, ed. 1992. *The Ontario Archaeological Society Index to Publication.* Ontario Archaeological Society Special Publication no. 7, Willowdale, Ontario.

Garrett, William E., ed. 1983. Atlantic Gateways. In *The Making of America* map series. *National Geographic* 163(3).

———. 1985. Northern Approaches. In *The Making of America* map series. *National Geographic* 167(2).

———. 1987. New England. In *The Making of America* map series. *National Geographic* 171(2).

Girouard, Laurent. 1972. Un site iroquoien sur la Rivière Richelieu. *Recherches Amérindiennes au Québec* 2(1):50–54.

Goetzmann, William H., and Glyndwr Williams. 1992. *The Atlas of North American Exploration: From Norse Voyages to the Race for the Pole.* Prentice Hall, New York.

Grant, William L., ed. 1911. *The History of New France* by Marc Lescarbot, 1618. 3 vols. Publication 7, Champlain Society, Toronto.

Graves, William, ed. 1993. Atlantic Canada. In *The Making of Canada* map series. *National Geographic* 184(4).

Hale, Horatio. 1883. *The Iroquois Book of Rites.* Brinton's Library of Aboriginal American Literature, no. 2. Reprinted 1972 by Coles Publishing Co., Toronto.

———. 1894. The Fall of Hochelaga. *Journal of American Folklore* 1:1–4.

Harris, R. Cole, ed. 1987. *Historical Atlas of Canada,* vol. 1, *From Beginning to 1800.* University of Toronto Press, Toronto.

Heidenreich, Conrad E. 1971. *Huronia: A History and Geography of the Huron Indians, 1600–1650.* McClelland and Stewart, Toronto.

———. 1990. History of the St. Lawrence–Great Lakes Area to A.D. 1650. In *Archaeology of Southern Ontario to a.d. 1650,* ed. C. J. Ellis and Neal Ferris, 475–92. Occasional Publication no. 5, London Chapter of the Ontario Archaeological Society.

Hewitt, J. N. B. 1907a. Iroquoian Family. In *Handbook of American Indians North of Mexico,* ed. F. W. Hodge, 224–26. Bureau of American Ethnology Bulletin 30, Washington, D.C.

———. 1907b. Huron. In *Handbook of American Indians North of Mexico,* ed. F. W. Hodge, 584–91. Bureau of American Ethnology Bulletin 30, Washington, D.C.

Hoffman, Bernard. 1961. *Cabot to Cartier: Sources for a Historical Ethnography of Northeastern North America.* University of Toronto Press, Toronto.

Hosbach, Richard E., and Stanford Gibson. 1980. *The Wilson Site (OND9): A Protohistoric Oneida Village.* Chenango Chapter, New York State Archaeological Association 18(4A).

Hoxie, Frederick E., ed. 1996. *Encyclopedia of North American Indians: Native American History, Culture, and Life from Paleo-Indians to the Present.* Houghton Mifflin, Boston.

Hunt, George T. 1940. *The Wars of the Iroquois: A Study in Intertribal Trade Relations.* University of Wisconsin Press, Madison.

Innis, Harold A. 1930. *The Fur Trade in Canada.* Yale University Press, New Haven, Conn.

Jaenen, Cornelius J. 1988. Laurentian Iroquois. *The Canadian Encyclopedia* (3):1435. Hurtig, Edmonton.

Jenness, Diamond. 1932. *Indians of Canada.* Bulletin 65, National Museum of Canada, Ottawa.

Josephy, Alvin, and Patrick Limerick. 1993. *The Native American: An Illustrative History.* Turner Publications, Atlanta.

Kehoe, Alice B. 1992. *North American Indians: A Comprehensive Account.* 2d ed. Prentice, Hall, Englewood Cliffs, N.J.

Kroeber, Alfred L. 1939. *Cultural and Natural Areas of Native North America.* University of California Publications in Archaeology and Ethnology 38.

Krotz, Larry. 1990. *Indian Country: Inside Another Canada.* McClelland and Stewart, Toronto.

Kuhn, Robert D., Robert E. Funk, and James F. Pendergast. 1993. The Evidence for a St. Lawrence Iroquoian Presence in Sixteenth Century Mohawk Sites. *Man in the Northeast* 45:77–86.

Lafitau, Joseph François. 1724. Moeurs des sauvages amériquains comparées aux moeurs des premiers temps. Paris. Reissued 1974 as *Customs of the American Indians Compared with the Customs of Primitive Times.* 2 vols. Trans. and ed. William N. Fenton and Elizabeth L. Moore. Champlain Society, Toronto.

Lanctot, Gustave. 1930. L'intinéraire de Cartier á Hochelagà. *Transactions of the Royal Society of Canada,* 3d ser., vol. 17, sec. 1, 115–41. Montreal.

Latta, Martha A. 1976. The Iroquoian Culture of Huronia: A Study in Acculturation through Archaeology. Ph.D. diss., University of Toronto.

Lenig, Donald. 1965. *The Oak Hill Horizon and Its Relation to the Development of the Five Nation Iroquois Culture.* Researches and Transactions of the New York State Archaeological Society, Rochester.

Lescarbot, Marc. 1911. *The History of New France.* 3 vols. Ed. William L. Grant. Champlain Society Publication 7.

Lighthall, William D. 1899. Hochelaga and the Mohawks: A Link in Iroquois History. *Transactions of the Royal Society of Canada,* 2d ser., vol. 5, sec. 2, 199–211. Montreal.

———. 1924. Hochelaga and the Hill of Hochelaga. *Transactions of the Royal Society of Canada,* 3d ser., vol. 18, sec. 2, 91–106. Montreal.

———1934. New Hochelaga Finds in 1933. *Transactions of the Royal Society of Canada,* 3d ser., vol. 28, sec. 2, 103–8. Montreal.

Lloyd, Herbert M., ed. 1901. *League of the Ho-de-no-sua-nee or Iroquois* by Lewis Henry Morgan. 2 vols. Dodd, Mead, New York. [*See also* Morgan, Lewis Henry.]

Lounsbury, Floyd. 1961. Iroquois-Cherokee Linguistic Relations. *Bureau of American Ethnology Bulletin* 180, 11–17, Washington, D.C.

———. 1978. Iroquoian Languages. In *Handbook of North American Indians,* vol. 15, *Northeast,* ed. B. G. Trigger, 334–43. Smithsonian Institution, Washington, D.C.

MacNeish, Richard S. 1952. *Iroquoian Pottery Types: A Technique for the Study of Iroquois Prehistory.* Bulletin 124, National Museum of Canada, Ottawa.

Marois, Roger. 1978. *Les gisement Beaumier: Essai sur l'évolution des décors de la céramique.* National Museum of Man, Mercury Series, Archaeological Society of Canada Paper No. 75, Ottawa.

Marsh, James. 1988a. Iroquois. *Canadian Encyclopedia* 2:998. Hurtig Publishers, Edmonton.

———. 1988b. St. Lawrence Iroquois. *Canadian Encyclopedia* 3:2066. Hurtig Publishers, Edmonton.

McGhee, Robert. 1991. *Canada Rediscovered.* Canadian Museum of Civilization, Hull, Quebec.

McMillan, Allan D. 1988. *Native Peoples and Cultures of Canada.* Douglas and McIntyre, Vancouver.

Mitchell, Michael. 1989. An Unbroken Assertion of Sovereignty. In *Drumbeat: Anger and Renewal in Indian Country,* ed. Boyce Richardson, 105–36. Summerhill Press, Toronto.

Mithun, Marianne. 1982. The Mystery of the Vanished Laurentians. In *Papers from the Fifth International Conference on Historical Linguistics,* ed. A. Ahlquist, 230–42. John Benjamin Publishing Co., Philadelphia.

Morgan, Lewis Henry. 1851. *League of the Ho-de-no-sua-nee or Iroquois.* Corinth Books, New York. [*See also* Lloyd, Herbert M.]

Morison, Samuel E. 1971. *The European Discovery of America: The Northern Voyages.* Oxford University Press, New York.

Morton, Desmond. 1983. *A Short History of Canada.* Hurtig Publishers, Edmonton.

———. 1992. *Military History of Canada: From Champlain to Gulf War.* McClelland and Stewart, Toronto.

Orr, Roland B. 1914. Tionnontates: The Petuns or Tobacco Nation of Notta-wasaga Lowlands. *1914 Annual Archaeological Report for Ontario* 7–18. Toronto.

———. 1919. The Iroquois in Canada. *1919 Annual Archaeological Report for Ontario* 9–55. Toronto.

Parker, Arthur C. 1916. Origins of the Iroquois as Suggested by their Archaeology. *American Anthropologist,* new ser., 18(4):479–507.

———. 1922. *The Archaeological History of New York.* Bulletin nos. 235, 236, New York State Museum, Albany.

Pendergast, James F. 1967. Iroquois Archaeology in Eastern Ontario and Southern Quebec. In *Iroquoian Culture, History and Prehistory,* ed. Elisabeth Tooker, 67–90. Proceedings of the 1965 Conference on Iroquois Research. New York State Museum and Science Service, Albany.

———. 1975. An In-Situ Hypothesis to Explain the Origins of the St. Lawrence Iroquoians. *Ontario Archaeology* 25:47–55.

———. 1982. The Significance of a Huron Presence in Jefferson County, New York. Paper presented at McMaster University Archaeological Symposium, February 20.

———. 1991. St. Lawrence Iroquoians, Their Past, Present and Immmediate Future. *New York State Archaeological Association Bulletin* 102: 47–74.

———. 1993. More on When and Why the St. Lawrence Iroquoians Disappeared. In *Essays in St. Lawrence Iroquoian Archaeology,* ed. J. F. Pendergast and Claude Chapdelaine, 9–48. Occasional Papers in Northeast Archaeology no. 8. Copetown Press, Dundas, Ontario.

Pendergast, James F., and Bruce G. Trigger. 1972. *Cartier's Hochelaga and the Dawson Site.* McGill-Queens University Press, Montreal.

Perrault, Claude. 1966. Nicolas Perrot. In *Dictionary of Canadian Biography,* vol. 2, 516–20. University of Toronto Press, Toronto.

Perrot, Nicholas. 1864. *Mémoire sur les moeurs, costumes et religion des sauvages de l'amérique septentrionale,* ed. J. Tailhan. Paris. Reprinted 1916 as *The Indian Tribes of the Upper Mississippi Valley and Region of the Great Lakes,* ed. Arthur H. Clark, trans. E. H. Blair. Cleveland.

Plourde, Michel. 1990. Un site iroquoien à la confluence du Saguenay et du Saint-Laurent au XIIIe siècle. *Recherches amérindiennes au Québec* 20(1):47–61. Minott Printing and Binding Co., Greenfield, Mass.

———. 1993. Iroquoians in the Estuary of the St. Lawrence River. In *Essays in St. Lawrence Iroquoian Archaeology,* ed. J. F. Pendergast and Claude Chapdelaine, 101–20. Occasional Papers in Northeastern Archaeology no. 8. Copetown Press, Dundas, Ontario.

Potherie, Claude-Charles Le Roy de La. 1753. *Histoire de l'amérique septentrionale,* 4 vols. Nyon fils, Paris.

Pratt, Peter P. 1976. *Archaeology of the Oneida Iroquois,* vol. 1. Occasional Publications in Northeastern Anthropology no. 1. Minott Printing and Binding Co., Greenfield, Mass.

Quinn, David B. 1977. *North America from Earliest Discovery to First Settlements: The Norse Voyages to 1612.* Harper and Row, New York.

Ramsden, Peter. 1990. The Huron: Archaeology and Culture History. In *The Archaeology of Southern Ontario to a.d. 1650,* ed. C. J. Ellis and Neal Ferris, 361–84. Occasional publications of the London Chapter, Ontario Archaeological Society, no. 5.

———. 1993. The Current State of Huron Archaeology. Paper presented at the Canadian Archaeological Association Annual Meeting, Montreal.

Ray, Arthur J. 1996. *I Have Lived Here Since the World Began: An Illustrated History of Canada's Native People.* Lester Publishing, Toronto.

Ridington, Jillian, and Robin Ridington. 1993. *People of the Longhouse: How the Iroquoians Lived.* Douglas and McIntyre, Vancouver.

Ritchie, William A. 1944. *Pre-Iroquoian Occupation of New York State.* Memoir 1, Research Records of the Rochester Museum of Arts and Sciences, Rochester, N.Y.

———. 1969. *The Archaeology of New York State.* Natural History Press, Garden City, N.Y.

Robinson, Percy J. 1948. The Huron Equivalents of Cartier's Second Vocabulary. *Transactions of the Royal Society of Canada,* 3d ser., vol. 42, sec. 2, 127–46. Montreal.

Rogers, Edward S., and Donald B. Smith, eds. 1994. *Aboriginal Ontario: Historical Perspectives on the First Nations.* Ontario Government Historical Series. Dundurn Press, Toronto.

Rousseau, Jacques. 1954. L'Annedda et l'arbe de vie. *Revue d'histoire de l'amérique française* 7(2):171–201.

Rumrill, Donald A. 1991. The Mohawk Glass Trade Bead Chronology ca. 1560–1785. *Beads: Journal of the Society of Bead Researchers* 3:5–46.

Shea, J. G., ed. 1866. *Charlevoix's History and General Description of New France.* 6 vols. Loyola University Press, Chicago.

Sioui, Georges E. 1992. *An American Autohistory: An Essay on the Foundation of a Social Ethic,* trans. Sheila Fischman. McGill-Queens University Press, Montreal.

Snow, Dean R. 1977. Archaeology and Ethnohistory in Eastern New York. *Researches and Transactions of the New York State Archaeological Association* 17:107–12.

———. 1995a. Migration in Prehistory: The Northern Iroquoian Case. *American Antiquity* 60(1):59–79.

———. 1995b. *Mohawk Valley Archaeology: The Sites*. Institute for Archaeological Studies, State University of New York at Albany.

Squair, John. 1924. Translation of Faillon's 1865 "Histoire de la colonie française en Canada" as "The Indian Tribes on the St. Lawrence at the Time of the Arrival of the French." In *1923 Annual Archaeological Report for Ontario*, 82–88.

Squier, Ephriam G. 1848. Aboriginal Monuments of the State of New York Comprising the Results of Original Surveys and Explorations. *Smithsonian Contributions to Knowledge* 2:9–188. Smithsonian Institution, Washington, D.C.

Starna, William A. 1980. Mohawk Iroquois Populations: A Revision. *Ethnohistory* 27:371–82.

Symington, Fraser. 1969. *The Canadian Indian: The Illustrated History of the Great Tribe of Canada*. McLean-Hunter Ltd., Toronto.

Tehanetorens. 1976. Migration of the Iroquois. *Akwesasne Notes* (unnumbered, unpaginated). Rooseveltown, N.Y.

Thomas, Cyrus. 1906. Ethnology of Canada and Newfoundland. Part 1: Historical Account. *Annual Archaeological Report for Ontario, 1905*, 71–83.

Thwaites, Reuben G. 1896–1901. *Jesuit Relations and Allied Documents*. 73 vols. Cleveland.

Tooker, Elisabeth. 1964. *An Ethnography of Huron Indians 1615–1649*. Bulletin 190, Bureau of American Ethnology, Washington, D.C.

———, ed. 1967. *Iroquois Culture, History, and Prehistory*. Proceedings of the 1965 Conference on Iroquois Research. New York State Museum and Science Service, Albany.

Trigger, Bruce G. 1962. Trade and Tribal Warfare on the St. Lawrence in the Sixteenth Century. *Ethnohistory* 9:240–56.

———. 1963. Settlement as an Aspect of Iroquoian Adaption at the Time of Contact. *American Anthropologist* 65:86–101.

———. 1966. Who Were the Laurentian Iroquois? *Canadian Review of Sociology and Anthropology* 3:201–13.

———. 1968. Archaeological and Other Evidence: A Fresh Look at the Laurentian Iroquois. *American Antiquity* 33:429–40.

———. 1972. Hochelaga: History and Ethnohistory. In *Cartier's Hochelaga and the Dawson Site*, ed. J. F. Pendergast and B. G. Trigger, 41–71. McGill-Queens University Press, Montreal.

———. 1976. *The Children of Aataentsic: A History of the Huron People to 1660*. 2 vols. McGill-Queens University Press, Montreal.

———. 1985. *Natives and Newcomers: Canada's "Heroic Age" Reconsidered*. McGill-Queens University Press, Montreal.

———. 1987a. Native Resettlement, 1635–1800. In *Historical Atlas of Canada,* vol. 1, *From Beginning to 1800,* ed. R. C. Harris, plate 47. University of Toronto Press, Toronto.

———. 1987b. The St. Lawrence Valley, 16th Century. In *Historical Atlas of Canada,* vol. 1, *From Beginning to 1800,* ed. R. C. Harris, plate 33. University of Toronto Press, Toronto.

———. 1994. The Original Iroquoians: Huron, Petun and Neutral. In *Aboriginal Ontario: Historical Perspectives on the First Nations,* ed. E. S. Rogers and D. B. Smith, 41–63. Ontario Government Historical Series. Dundurn Press, Toronto.

Trigger, Bruce G., and James F. Pendergast. 1978. Saint Lawrence Iroquoians. In *Handbook of North American Indians,* vol. 15, *Northeast,* ed. B. G. Trigger, 357–61. Smithsonian Institution, Washington, D.C.

Trudel, Pierre. 1991. Les Mohawks out-ils découvert Jacques Cartier. *Recherches amérindiennes du Québec* 21:53–58.

Tuck, James A. 1967. The Howlett Hill Site: An Early Iroquois Village in Central New York. In *Iroquoian Culture, History, and Prehistory,* ed. Elisabeth Tooker, 75–79. Proceedings of the 1965 Conference on Iroquois Research. New York Museum and Science Service, Albany.

———. 1971. *Onondaga Iroquois Prehistory: A Study in Settlement Archaeology.* Syracuse University Press, Syracuse.

Warrick, Garry A. 1990. A Population History of the Huron-Petun, A.D. 900–1650. Ph.D. diss., McGill University.

White, James, ed. 1913. *Handbook of Indians of Canada.* Geographic Board, Ottawa.

Wilson, Daniel. 1884. The Huron-Iroquois of Canada: A Typical Race of American Aborigines. *Transactions of the Royal Society of Canada,* 1st ser., vol. 81, sec. 2, 55–106.

Wintemberg, William J. 1936. *The Roebuck Prehistoric Village Site, Grenville County, Ontario.* Bulletin 83, National Museum of Canada, Ottawa.

Wright, J. V. 1966. *The Ontario Iroquois Tradition.* Bulletin 210, National Museum of Canada, Ottawa.

———. 1972. *Ontario Prehistory: An Eleven-Thousand-Year Archaeological Outline.* National Museum of Man, National Museum of Canada, Ottawa.

———. 1979. *Québec Prehistory.* National Museum of Man, National Museum of Canada. Van Nostrand Reinhold, Toronto.

———. 1987a. Cultural Sequences, A.D. 500–European Contact. In *Historical Atlas of Canada,* vol. 1, *From Beginning to 1800,* ed. R. Cole Harris, plate 9. University of Toronto Press, Toronto.

———. 1987b. The St. Lawrence Settlements. In *Historical Atlas of Canada,* vol. 1, *From Beginning to 1800,* ed. R. Cole Harris, 113. University of Toronto Press, Toronto.

———. 1990. The Archaeology of Southern Ontario to A.D. 1650: A Critique. In *The Archaeology of Southern Ontario to a.d. 1650,* ed. C. J. Ellis and Neal

Ferris, 493–503. Occasional Publication No. 5 of the London Chapter of the Ontario Archaeological Society.

———. 1994. Before European Contact. In *Aboriginal Ontario: Historical Perspectives on First Nations,* ed. E. S. Carpenter and D. B. Smith, 21–38. Ontario Government Historical Studies Series. Dundurn Press, Toronto.

Wright, J. V., and Rudolph Fecteau. 1987. Iroquoian Agricultural Settlement. In *Historical Atlas of Canada,* vol. 1, *From Beginning to 1800,* ed. R. C. Harris, 21–38 and plate 12. University of Toronto Press, Toronto.

Wright, Ronald. 1990. *Toronto Globe and Mail,* August 30, A17.

———. 1992. *Stolen Continents: The "New World" through Indian Eyes since 1492.* Houghton Mifflin, New York.

3

Echoing the Past

Reconciling Ethnohistorical and Archaeological Views of Ho-Chunk (Winnebago) Ethnogenesis

John P. Staeck

The Western Great Lakes region, composed of Wisconsin, the Upper Peninsula of Michigan, northern Illinois, northeastern Iowa, and eastern Minnesota (fig. 3.1), has been the stage for the emergence, zenith, and seeming decline of several late pre-Contact archaeological manifestations. For decades now scholars have speculated on the connections between these material remains and the Native American people who inhabited the region at the time when Europeans appeared. Although some researchers have sought to link certain extant peoples to various archaeological materials, such suggestions have remained largely unconfirmed and difficult, if not impossible, to test. This chapter discusses why this is so and then provides a synthesis of extant ethnohistorical and archaeological data. This work is offered as an example of the sort of research that might help resolve some of the complex issues noted above and as a provisional model to guide future investigations.

Archaeologically, the region is host to three major taxonomic groupings of material culture dating from the late pre-Contact (A.D. 300–1650) era. These groupings are: Upper Mississippian–Oneota, covering the era of approximately A.D. 1000–1650; Middle Mississippian, including approximately the period A.D. 1100–1250; and Late Woodland, including the distinctive Effigy Mound variant, spanning the period of approximately A.D. 300–1300, though in some areas similar materials persisted longer.

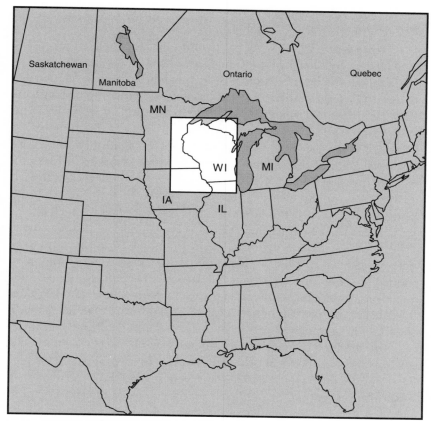

Fig. 3.1. The western Great Lakes region

At some point each of these three archaeological manifestations has been implicated as a founding population for the Ho-Chunk (Staeck 1994). Given archaeology's inability to identify a typical Ho-Chunk material signature that can be projected into the past according to direct historical methodologies, we are left with trying to prepare a goodness-of-fit model that links ethnohistoric documentation with interpretations of various archaeological signatures. It is important to stress that the resulting connections and assumptions must not be taken as representing unequivocal relations in the past but must instead be viewed as a model that warrants future testing and examination.

Against this background scholars have attempted to identify the origins of the Ho-Chunk and to reconstruct their past lifeways. Pivotal in this effort has been the research of Paul Radin (e.g., 1909, 1910, 1911, 1915a,

1915b, 1923, 1945), which was conducted principally during the first two decades of the 20th century, and Nancy Oestreich Lurie (e.g., 1952, 1960, 1961, 1972, 1978), whose work has spanned the latter half of the century. Based on data collected by Radin and Lurie, the Ho-Chunk of the Contact era are thought to have been more or less egalitarian, patrilocal, patrilineal, and to have primarily subsisted by hunting, gathering, fishing, and collecting in seasonal rounds (Jones et al. 1974; Lurie 1978; Radin 1923; see also Staeck 1992, 1994).

It was always accepted, though, that the Ho-Chunk had undergone substantial cultural change due both to the events associated with Euroamerican invasion (including disease, warfare, and land loss) and to their apparent catastrophic defeat at the hands of the Illini during the early Contact period. Indeed, this latter issue has been the focus of much discussion concerning the nature and timing of Ho-Chunk political decline in the Western Great Lakes region. The Ho-Chunk of 1634 were said to be numerous as well as militarily and politically strong, whereas they were reported to be essentially decimated later in the century. Thus, there seemed little choice but to infer that the war with the Illini had taken place after Nicolet's 1634 visit (or very near to it) and before the French established a more permanent presence in the region. Significantly, scholars paid little attention to questions regarding the nature of Ho-Chunk social structure and sociopolitical organization prior to their apparent decline. They often assumed that such questions were beyond the reach of anthropological investigation, or predicted that such structures and organizations were more or less similar to those recorded historically and ethnographically (see, for example, McKern 1945).

Three basic lines of investigation have been pursued in an effort to reconcile the apparent differences between the early and late 17th century, which I will summarize briefly. Overstreet, representing one line of research, has persisted in seeking sites in the eastern Wisconsin area that bridge the temporal gap defined above. He argues that sites such as McCauley, Astor, and Hanson may represent Ho-Chunk occupations immediately prior to face-to-face contact with the French (Overstreet 1993; cf. C. Mason 1976). He acknowledges the validity of criticisms that point out that his interpretations linking the Ho-Chunk with these sites rely on assumptions rather than on definitive evidence (e.g., R. Mason 1993), and he strongly encourages additional investigations. At this time, however, there is no demonstrable link between any of these three sites and any historically defined population.

The second line of investigation has been pursued by Hall (1993), who has argued that the pre-Contact and Contact-era Ho-Chunk in eastern Wisconsin are represented by ceramics typical of the more western Orr-Phase Oneota tradition as well as Lake Winnebago–Phase Oneota. Hall has suggested that following their defeat at the hands of the Illini, an event that he implicitly correlates with the decline of Lake Winnebago–Phase Oneota, at least some of the remaining Ho-Chunk moved west to live with the closely related Ioway. Some of these people eventually returned to eastern Wisconsin, bringing with them a ceramic style typical of their western relatives; hence the presence of Orr-Phase materials near Lake Michigan. R. J. Mason (1993) has questioned whether such a scenario can be demonstrated archaeologically and whether materials typical of the eastern Oneota Phase can be found on Orr-Phase sites. We might also question whether the Ho-Chunk population in eastern Wisconsin, especially if it is represented solely by Oneota material culture, could have recovered sufficiently from such a calamitous defeat in less than a hundred years. It is doubtful that they could have inhibited Ottawa and related traders from expanding into the region and so impressed Nicolet on the occasion of his visit.

The third line of investigation is characterized by the work of Salzer (1987, 1995) and Staeck (1994). Salzer's work at the Gottschall site, for example, strongly suggests a connection between Late Woodland, and in particular Effigy Mound, manifestations and Ho-Chunk oral traditions. While I concur with this view, my own work focuses on the formation of the historically defined Ho-Chunk identity.

We are left in a situation where it is necessary to begin reconciling the historic and ethnographic data pertaining to the Ho-Chunk with the archaeological record. The following alternative research strategies would seem plausible:

(1) To decrease the importance placed on the historical record on the grounds that it may be unreliable as a consequence of the biases and uneven coverage represented in the written sources.

(2) To deemphasize the limits of the current archaeological record on the grounds that important information may be missing or may have been destroyed by subsequent historic activities. (This perspective would encourage the continued investigation of late pre-Contact and early Contact sites in the region and is akin to the work undertaken by Overstreet.)

(3) To make the best-supported interpretations that we can given the available data, much as Hall has done.

(4) To make no interpretations regarding the questions at hand on the grounds that none can be adequately tested or supported given the data that we have in our possession (e.g., R. Mason 1993).

(5) To incorporate new data and paradigms in an attempt to bring additional information to bear on questions of identity and ethnogenesis. Such new data can then be used to formulate archaeologically testable hypotheses.

Of these possible options, it seems to me that the last may prove to be the most productive, especially in light of our current stalemate in identifying cultural identity markers in the archaeological record. What I am suggesting is that we turn to the Ho-Chunk sources in order to explore more fully questions of past identity. Such sources can be used to generate predictive models for past Ho-Chunk identity and material signatures that we can compare to the archaeological record. Such predictions can also be used to define the sorts of questions we seek to answer archaeologically, which in turn will help to determine the classes of data we seek to recover. Ultimately, this approach will improve our position to interpret the ethnogenesis of Ho-Chunk identity.

Conceptual Framework: Ethnicity and Salient Identity

A useful place to begin is with the concept of ethnogenesis. The term in its most basic form addresses the formation of a defined identity group, such as the Ho-Chunk. Barth (1969) has provided an influential anthropological definition of an ethnic identity group that centers on four criteria:

(1) The group is largely biologically self-perpetuating (endogamous).

(2) The members of the group "share fundamental cultural values, realized in *overt unity in cultural forms*" (Barth 1969:11, emphasis added).

(3) Group members define a range of communication and interactions that reinforce and help to structure their identity.

(4) The group "has a membership which identifies itself, and is identified by others, as constituting a category distinguishable from other categories of the same order" (Barth 1969:11).

This particular definition and those derived directly from it, however, can be criticized as inflexible and for portraying cultural interactions too simplistically (cf. Goffman 1959, 1963a, 1963b; Gonzalez 1989; Haaland

1969; S. Jones 1997; Nagata 1981). In response to such potential short-comings, Schortman (1989) proposed the concept of salient identity as a more accurate reflection of human identity marking processes.

Salient identity refers to those social identities that are most commonly operationalized and that generate affiliations that result in a strong feeling of common purpose and support (Schortman 1989:54). The social categories Schortman alludes to are culturally defined and accepted categories that guide interpersonal behaviors. Salient identity is adopted here because it is a broadly defined and flexible term that encompasses social differentiation both within a single population, such as class distinctions, and between multiple populations, such as ethnic, regional, and national distinctions. Similarly, the term recognizes that humans tend to define their identity fluidly (that is, with some variability), depending upon the social environment in which they find themselves at any given time (e.g., Haaland 1969; Nagata 1981; J. O'Brien 1986).

Given this, the concept of ethnogenesis needs to be expanded to incorporate a suite of salient identities that are more or less shared throughout a population. Significantly, such sharing need not compel all members of the population to adopt all salient identities present within their group. Indeed, the presence of ritual specialists, aggrandizers (cf. Hayden 1995), various clan and lineage roles, as well as any number of achieved statuses (such as a successful hunters, warriors, or the members of sodalities) makes it likely that there will be varying degrees of overlap in the salient identities individuals can adopt. The essential element in defining ethnogenesis, then, must lie in the recognition of identities that the members of a population accept as appropriate to their shared social values and structures.

An important component of this extension is the loss of apparent resolution in archaeological terminology. The fact that salient identities might be shared in decreasing amounts the farther away one travels from a core area of identity marking means that, at some point, people living at approximately equal social (and perhaps physical) distances from different identity cores may possess traits from both cores.

Conceptual Framework: Folklore and Interpretation

One means of examining identity is through the interpretation of folklore (see also Nassaney, chap. 15). It is important to note that the approach adopted in the following discussion is not new and utilizes notions developed and emphasized in part by pioneering researchers such as Boas

(1891, 1896, 1914, 1916, 1925), Malinowski (1926), and Propp (1968), among others. These approaches are essentially functional or psychological-functional (Doty 1986) and emphasize the importance of actions within tales rather than the plot of the tales. For instance, both Boas and Propp argued that tales included narrative activities with which both the raconteurs and the audience were familiar. Consequently, it has also been argued that the basic actions of the characters, although not necessarily the physical or temporal settings of these actions, reflect behaviors in existence at the time the tales originated, were collected, or that preceded such events (Boas 1916; Dundes 1984; Jacobs 1959; Radin 1915a, 1926).

In addition, it is argued that the tales were originally designed to be performed for the benefit and entertainment of audiences that were familiar with the expressed identity of the raconteur (Boas 1916; Braroe 1975; Dundes 1984; Propp 1968). The foundation of this position lies in the role that oral traditions play in defining and reinforcing social structure and in how identity derived from such structures is variably projected given different social environments (Braroe 1975; Gluckman 1962; Goffman 1956, 1959, 1963a, 1963b).

Criticisms of the suggestion that oral traditions and myth complexes can be analyzed in order to extract socially important information are not new. Radcliffe-Brown, for instance, notes that interpretations of lineality based on oral traditions are problematic since it is difficult for a modern researcher to ascertain the precise relationships between two people in the past. Hence, what might appear as a strong matrilineal relationship between a man and his sister's son may really be a reflection of the cordial relationship that such individuals develop in a strong patrilineal system. Such criticisms are apt but should not be construed to suggest that no models for social structure can be built. Indeed, Radcliffe-Brown's particular views on how societies function seem to articulate very strongly with interpretations of oral traditions, especially given substantial amounts of data such as we have in the case of the Ho-Chunk.

Similarly, structuralists have suggested that the relationships between individuals in oral traditions can often be reversed (e.g., Lévi-Strauss 1967). In such cases characters such as a disenfranchised male (common in several Ho-Chunk traditions) might not reflect male disempowerment but rather male empowerment, the disenfranchised status being the opposite of what would normally be expected in Ho-Chunk society. Yet, while this may be the case in some oral repertoires, such reversals are not inevitable and sometimes they are simply not present (see Lévi-Strauss 1960, 1967). In the case of the Ho-Chunk, though, we are fortunate in that we have a large corpus of traditions, including multiple versions of the same tradition provided by different raconteurs. Likewise, we have multiple lines of evidence that include extensive ethnographic observations (Lurie 1978; Radin 1923) and even some ethnomusicological data (Speck n.d.). In this case there is no good evidence for the structural reversal of roles that is sometimes present in the oral repertoires of other peoples.

Analysis and Interpretation

This brings us to the manner of examining the extant ethnohistoric data and how they may be interpreted. The primary body of literature analyzed for this project was the corpus of oral traditions recorded by Paul Radin during the first two decades of the 20th century and currently housed in the Library of the American Philosophical Society, Philadelphia. Although Radin published versions of a number of the oral traditions examined for this project, his published works demonstrate a strong editorial hand and a synthesis of different versions. In substantial part this is clearly attributable to publication constraints as well as to Radin's own philosophical and research biases.

The various oral traditions were collected principally from three Ho-Chunk informants over a period of five years. In many instances versions of the same traditions were recorded from each informant, sometimes over the span of several years. The consistency between the different versions of tales, as well as the time span over which they were collected, suggest that the informants provided Radin with reliable information and did not, as has been suggested by some modern Ho-Chunk, invent tales just to satisfy the anthropologist's requests for information. Significantly, the oral traditions written for Radin by the Ho-Chunk men do not show a great deal of variation in the details of events and, perhaps more significantly, in the social milieu against which the narrative events were described. Although it is impossible to eliminate completely the specter of misinformation or subconscious discrepancies between what the informants actually knew and what they provided Radin, the homogeneity of narrative details of the oral traditions suggest that the corpus of the data reflects a genuine attempt to convey real oral narratives as they were known among the Ho-Chunk of the early 20th century.

A total of thirty oral narratives were examined. The shortest of these were less than two thousand words in length, while the longest represent several tens of thousands of words. The narratives were examined for their overall content as well as for their portrayal of social relations between people, spirits, and different political groups. These behaviors were then organized into groups and compared one to another. The working assumption was that the accounts did not necessarily reflect historical events but that they would reflect conventions of social behavior common to both the raconteurs and their audiences. As noted above, it was recognized that structural inversions might be present among the narratives that might reverse real social structures in those instances when the narratives dealt with spirits and the spirit world. Special care was taken to seek such inversions as well as to identify narrative conventions (cf. Radin 1948). In the end, no narratives were identified in which structural inversions of behavior were evident, though several narrative motifs and conventions were identified (Staeck 1994). Included in the various motifs are complementary opposites in which one figure or image is symbolically set against a second image. Such structural manifestations include the opposition between Thunderers and Water Spirits as well as Ho-Chunk and non-Ho-Chunk.

The results of this segment of the research indicated that narratives of the sort known as *waikaan*, meaning that which is true, could be organized into three distinct groups (table 3.1). The first of these centered around human-spirit relations in which the spirits took the form of animals documented in Western natural histories, such as bears, snakes, and hawks. In these tales the culture heroes most often discussed were Sun, Turtle (in the form of a trickster), and Morning Star.

The second group of tales was organized around the presence of the spirits known as Thunderers (sometimes conceived of as Thunderbirds, *wakandja* after Radin [1923]) and Water Spirits (*waktexi* after Radin [1923] or *Wakjayxi-Hounk-ka* after Lurie [1988]), which are better understood as the terrestrial manifestation of spirits parallel to Thunderers rather than as menaces to humans (Staeck 1994). The significance of this lies in the possibility that Water Spirits, and not bear spirits, were once the primary beneath-sky beings. Certainly Lurie's (1988) gloss for Water Spirits as sacred animal chief warrants further consideration and suggests that the Ho-Chunk concept of the Water Spirit is significantly different from that possessed by their Algonquian neighbors. Given the very close relationship between the historic Ho-Chunk and Algonquian groups such as the Menominee, which emphasize the bear as a principal spirit, and given the strong similarities between the oral traditions of the Ho-Chunk and Menominee bear clans, a case can be made for the Water Spirit to have preceded the bear in the capacity as a foil for the Thunderer. Clearly, in the oral traditions examined for this research there is a strong and undeniable

Table 3.1. Seriation of Ho-Chunk narratives by common attributes

Oral narrative	Opposing forces	Primary cosmological characters	Settlement type	Ascribed status
Group 1				
Holy One	Animals	Holy One, Animal Spirits	N/A	N/A
Chief's Daughter and the Orphan	Underworld	Wolf Spirit	Small Village; Homesteads	Yes, male and female
Old Bear Clan Origin Myth	None	Bear Spirits	N/A	No
The Morning Star	Giants	Sun, Turtle	Homesteads	No
The Twins	Monsters	Cosmological Twins	Homesteads	No
Group 2				
The Blue Horn (all but the Twin Cycle, twins are nephews)	Thunderers	Water Spirits, Cosmological Twins, Thunderers	Multilineage Village	Yes, Females
The Thunderbird	Foreign People	Thunderers	Multilineage Village	N/A
The Woman Who Married a Snake	Foreign People	Water Spirits	Multilineage Village	Yes, Females
The Man Who Married a Thunderbird	N/A	Thunderers, Water Spirits	Unspecified Village	N/A
Red Horn (opening cycle)	Foreign People	Thunderers, Wolf Spirit, Turtle, Red Horn	Multilineage Village	Yes, Females
New Bear Clan Origin Myth	None	Thunderers, Bear Spirits	N/A	N/A

(continued)

Table 3.1. —*continued*

Oral narrative	Opposing forces	Primary cosmological characters	Settlement type	Ascribed status
Water Spirit Clan Origin Myth	None	Water Spirits	N/A	N/A
Buffalo Clan Origin Myth	None	Water Spirits, Youngest Buffalo	N/A	N/A
Group 3				
The Red Horn Cycle (all segments save opening cycle)	Giants, Water, and Water Spirits	Red Horn, Turtle, Wolf Spirit, Thunderers, Cosmological Twins	Multilineage Village	Yes, Males, Females
The Woman Who Loved Her Half-Brother	Foreign Male, Evil Bears	Brother	Multilineage Village	Yes, Males, Females
Daughters-in-Laws' Jealousy	Water Spirits	Thunderers	Multilineage Village	Yes, Females
The Man Who Visited the Thunderbirds	Foreign People	Thunderers	Multilineage Village	Yes, Males

structural balance between these two forces (Staeck 1994). This argument is strengthened when one considers that only two Ho-Chunk clans have identities marked by creatures or beings outside of a conventional, Western taxonomy and that these beings are the Thunderers and the Water Spirits.

Whatever the primary relationship between these beings and the forces they represent, in the segment of tales grouped together here, Water Spirits and Thunderers are both beneficial to humans and bestow significant visions upon Ho-Chunk deserving of such gifts. Significantly, Thunderers and Water Spirits are opposing forces and implacable rivals. The culture heroes most often discussed in this series of tales include Red Horn, who is closely associated with Thunderers, and figures such as Blue Horn, who is himself a Water Spirit.

The final group of tales also centers around Thunderers and Water Spirits, although in this series of tales Water Spirits are viewed as malevolent and are dominated by Thunderers. The culture heroes common to this segment of tales include Red Horn, Storms-as-He-Walks (a Thunderer), Wolf, and Turtle (again in the form of a trickster).

In order to evaluate the validity of this organization, the tales were also examined for descriptions of types of behavior that might be used as a basis for a second, independent seriation. The narratives were therefore reviewed for portrayals of marriage, residence patterns, settlement types, and warfare. These variables were selected because of their fundamental relationships to Ho-Chunk identity (Radin 1926) and to a culture's social structure. The results of the different seriations closely approximated the results of the analysis described above. Consequently, and for the sake of the model developed here, the variables were grouped together and assigned a relative chronological sequence.

The third group of tales represents ideas that closely approximate modern Ho-Chunk views of the nature of both Thunderers and Water Spirits. Likewise, the domination of the latter by the former because of the potential harm Water Spirits might do humans is a common motif among many modern Ho-Chunk. These tales feature descriptions of multilineal villages as well as dispersed settlements. Marriage centers on monogamy while postmarital residence tends to be associated with patrilocality, virilocality, or neolocality. Warfare is linked to non-Ho-Chunk people, including giants from the east, as well as with the historically known Illini. Like the Ho-Chunk views of Thunderers and Water Spirits, these behaviors match those described by Radin in the early 20th century. Consequently, the third group was fixed temporally at the most recent end of the spectrum.

The first group of tales, on the other hand, bears strong similarities to belief systems known for more westerly Siouan-speaking populations, especially the Lakota and Dhegiha speakers. Here culture heroes such as Sun and Morning Star still figure prominently in oral narratives and function as important actors in peoples' cosmologies. Settlement depicted in the narratives emphasizes dispersed homesteads, while marriage patterns, represented only tangentially in most traditions in this group, depict monogamy. Postmarital residence, however, is suggestive of matrilocality or uxorilocality. Warfare emphasizes small-scale conflict and competition with supernatural foreign groups such as giants and evil spirits. Given that linguists infer that the Ho-Chunk and Lakota dialects split at least two thousand years ago and that Dhegiha dialects and Ho-Chunk are separated by a thousand years (Grimm 1985; Springer and Witkowski 1982), the first group of traditions was placed at the early end of the sequence.

Through a process of elimination the final group was placed in the middle of the sequence. These traditions depict large, multilineal villages, hierarchical leadership in the form of village chiefs, both sororal and nonsororal polygyny, and large-scale conflict with foreign groups. Such conflicts include raids on villages and the taking of trophies, and are associated with supernatural enemies such as giants. Postmarital residence appears to be uxorilocal within the Ho-Chunk population, although marriages between Ho-Chunk and outsiders emphasize the need for residence within the Ho-Chunk village. The exception to this is that mortals who marry spirits eventually move to the village of the spirits. Such descriptions, though, reflect less of a structural reversal of behaviors and more of a prohibition against spirits living openly with mortals (Staeck 1994).

Ho-Chunk Ethnogenesis: A Provisional Model

The following model is a hypothetical construct. The purpose of this presentation is to stimulate exploration of new avenues of research into human lifeways in the past, that is, doing anthropology through archaeological techniques and strategies. The sequence of events hypothesized for the development of Ho-Chunk ethnic identity may be narrated as follows:

Stage 1: Prior to ca. A.D. 900, the western Great Lakes region was populated by people residing in dispersed homesteads. These residential units were probably based on kinship principles and, at least in the case of the Chiwere–Ho-Chunk speakers, may have been organized matrilocally or uxorilocally (see also Hollinger 1993). Descent *may* have been calculated matrilineally. Subsistence focused on hunting and gathering, although some horticulture appears to have been present. Social integration was likely achieved through intermarriage and participation in both kinship events (such as clan ceremonies) as well as sodalities that cut across kinship boundaries (Radin 1948).

Stage 2: Beginning about A.D. 900, villages appeared, some perhaps stockaded, and behaviors developed suggestive of increasing territorial control or more demarcated social identities. Among some populations that were dependent upon access to resource-rich and environmentally diverse ecological zones (e.g., those areas utilized by people employing Oneota and Effigy Mound material culture), villages probably reflect an aggregation of kinship-based units. These units reflect extended families that previously resided in neighboring residential units that aggregated together to effect increased subsistence efficiency. Allied kinship groups, those groups that habitually exchanged mates and perhaps pooled resources for economic and ritual purposes, formed networks of villages that probably tended to cluster spatially. The range of salient identities would have increased as more social roles were created and defined within the aggregating populations. In turn, these would find their way into the archaeological record in the form of stylistic elements of material culture and reflections of community organization, such as are present in village layouts. In general, local and regional stylistic elements would tend to group together as potters began living in increasingly close proximity to one another (e.g., Hill 1965, 1966, 1968, 1970, 1977; Hodder 1977, 1978, 1979, 1982; Johnson, chap. 4; Whallon 1968, among others).

Stage 3: By ca. A.D. 1000, some of these clustered villages began regular and increasingly frequent interactions with one another, to the exclusion of some other villages. Such interaction probably reflects increased pressure to maintain control over desired territories and may also reflect the increasing localization of allied networks of exchange, particularly of marriage partners. At about this time Mississippian material begins to appear in increasing amounts throughout the western Great Lakes region, and this may reflect the migration of peoples or diffusion of ideas from the south. Such ideas may have been adopted or, in fact, imported as means through which to express salient identities and to manipulate social roles.

Stage 4: By A.D. 1300, environmentally rich areas of the western Great Lakes region came under the control of closely allied networks of villages. Such alliances and the expanding cooperation between these villages probably increased their social and political integration. Interchange between different clusters of allied villages may have occurred regularly, especially between clusters that traditionally spoke the same dialects and

exchanged marriage partners. With the increased competition for resources in the western Great Lakes region, however, some groups had
already begun moving westward and perhaps southward. The Chiwere–
Ho-Chunk split is likely to have arisen as some elements of the language
group elected to move farther onto the Prairie Peninsula and Eastern
Plains while other elements opted to remain in their environmentally productive areas in the western Great Lakes region. Contact between the
groups undoubtedly continued (Grimm 1985; Hall 1962; Springer and
Witkowski 1982), but the increased geographic separation of the various
elements resulted in increasing divergence of language and identity
through time. This process marks the initial trend toward delineating the
broadly defined population that eventually developed Ho-Chunk identity.

Stage 5: By ca. A.D. 1500, intense pressure existed between various
aggregations of villages and other allied populations migrating into the
region for resource-rich environments capable of supporting increasing
population levels. The aggregation of villages had by this time responded,
or were in the process of responding, to pressure through further integration and geographic isolation (recall the previously discussed oral traditions). Territorial control and group identity presumably became key elements in survival and control strategies, and were the mechanism through
which strongly bounded social identities developed in the region. It is at
about this time that the people known as the Ho-Chunk, as well as perhaps Fox, Kaskaskia, Shawnee, and other groupwide salient identities
became well-defined populations.

Stage 6: By A.D. 1670, the aggregated group representing the Ho-
Chunk had lost its hold on its environmental base and was forced to adopt
radically new subsistence strategies. This loss of territory was accompanied by drastic population loss through both warfare and epidemic disease. The matter was further complicated by the distance that now separated the Ho-Chunk from their Chiwere-speaking relatives, making it
difficult for the Ho-Chunk to replace lost population through intermarriage or to be reassimilated into the Chiwere-speaking populations. As a
consequence of these events, Ho-Chunk subsistence and its associated
material culture were adapted for survival in less desirable environments
and for supporting more dispersed and smaller populations. The social
structure that defines current social identity also began to adapt to the new
survival strategies, although such cultural elements remained resilient
whenever possible. It is at this point that the culture of the Ho-Chunk
became frozen in the ethnographic present of the region.

Evaluating the Model

To move from this model to a means of archaeological testing requires consideration of the corollaries implicit in the model's structure. Price's (1981) arguments concerning the development of complexity among non-intensive food producers offer a systematic list of behaviors that can be tied to archaeological data. These behaviors are: overall population growth, larger coresident populations in settlements (i.e., larger populations in villages as well as across the territory inhabited by the population), reduction in residential mobility, increased structuring of space, increased intergroup exchange, exploitation of previously unused floral and faunal species, technical innovations to increase productivity, increased ritual activity designed to unify and identify individual populations, formalization of lineages and sodalities to increase the efficiency of social and political integration, increased status differentiation as the result of the development of a privileged managerial class, and increased identity signaling between and within coresident populations.

To what extent can these patterns be observed in the archaeological record of the western Great Lakes? Overall population growth is reflected both archaeologically and in oral traditions. Although we lack good estimates for Late Woodland era settlements, sites such as Statz (Meinholz and Kolb 1997), Bigelow, and Sanders (Hurley 1975), coupled with surveys of sites such as Bahr Village in the Muscoda, Wisconsin, region (Staeck n.d.), suggest multifamily aggregations ranging approximately between fifty and a few hundred people for at least part of the year. Additional excavations at the Red House Landing and F-T-D sites, both adjacent to the Mississippi River in northeastern Iowa, suggest that some of these aggregation localities may have been even larger, perhaps supporting many hundreds of people for substantial parts of the year. Additional aggregation is clearly present on Oneota settlements in the region, such as those near La Crosse (O'Gorman 1994) and Lake Winnebago, Wisconsin (Overstreet 1976, 1978, 1993), as well as those in and around modern Chicago, Illinois (Brown and O'Brien 1990).

Likewise, specific references to large villages are made in the Red Horn tales and "Blue Horn's Nephews." In these tales the characters function within large, multifamily villages. Red Horn and his companions, for instance, each marry into a village and become embroiled in large-scale conflicts with giants from the east (see Radin n.d., 1948). Similarly, Blue Horn arranges marriages for his adopted sisters with a prestigious and powerful warrior. In arranging the marriages, however, Blue Horn persuades the warrior to return all of his previous wives to their families; this suggests that multiple families were resident within or in the immediate vicinity of the village since this task was accomplished quickly. Similar depictions occur in "The woman who loved her half-brother," "The woman who married a snake," and "The chief's daughter and the orphan."

The overall trend of tales, however, suggests that the presence of relatively large, multilineage villages represents a late settlement organization among the people possessing the oral traditions examined here. As discussed previously, table 3.1 presents a seriation of traditions, and those traditions representing large populations and villages are inferred to be near the most recent end of the continuum. According to this proposed model, prior to this era settlements are portrayed as smaller and as being organized around members of a single lineage. For example, in the tale "The Morning Star," settlements include only the members of a single lineage and are small. The residential structures of the characters are separated from other, similarly sized residential units.

In terms of historical development, the tales suggest a transition from dispersed family residences to aggregated settlements consisting of multiple lineage groups. The trend from dispersed settlements toward population aggregation tends to coincide with other trends discussed below. In particular, these link with trends toward intensified use of land and the advent of horticultural fields, and to increasingly large-scale conflicts. These changes would plausibly also link to increased social and political pressure, factors envisioned as likely to have led to increased identity signaling and boundary-marking in the region (cf. Hodder 1982; Nagata 1981; Nassaney 1992; Schortman 1989). In general, such changes are reflected archaeologically in the increasing size of villages, their fortification, and the elaboration of decorative motifs on the ceramics of both Late Woodland and Oneota peoples (Benn 1995; Sampson 1988).

This same trend addresses issues of larger coresident populations within settlements, the reduction of residential mobility, and increased structuring of space. As noted above, the transition from dispersed homesteads to villages is accompanied by increasing numbers of people residing within the confines of a single settlement. Although this does not necessarily reflect finite population growth throughout the region, it does reflect localized population aggregation and, in terms of archaeological visibility, such settlements are more easily identified than isolated homesteads.

These arguments articulate with Price's (1981) thresholds for increasing complexity among hunter-gatherers, especially for the increased structuring of space. The construction of palisaded villages and earthworks are two manners in which space is demarcated both for members of a population and for outsiders (Charles and Buikstra 1983; Dragoo 1976; Gramly 1988; Staeck 1996, 1998). On one hand, such large and visible structures serve as outward representations of control and, in the case of palisades, military potential. Foreign groups moving into an area and encountering such structures would recognize that other people live in the region and that any utilization of the demarcated territory might be contested.

On the other hand, the construction of palisades, earthworks, and other forms of distinctive architecture has been argued to serve as a structuring element within the population of builders (see, e.g., Donley 1982; Donley-Reid 1990; Harré 1978; Leach 1976; Lévi-Strauss 1953). In North America, Mallam (1976) has argued that the construction of effigy mounds served as a unifying activity that bound elements of a population together. According to Mallam's arguments, Effigy Mound groups dispersed across a large range during the winter and aggregated during the spring, summer, and fall. Mounds were constructed in the spring as a symbolic rebirth of the population and in order to bury those members who may have died during the winter. More recently, I (Staeck 1998) have argued that there are multiple dimensions to mound construction and that no single purpose or meaning can be identified for their construction and maintenance.

While it is unknown if the construction of palisades may have served similar symbolic functions, researchers interested in community patterns have argued that the bounding of a community serves to structure both community and personal space (e.g., Kent 1990). The fact that an exterior wall surrounds a settlement requires those living within the settlement to arrange their residential structures according to the bounded space (Eco 1980; Kent 1990). Further, such organization extends both to the patterns of residential structures and to the symbolic representation of power, identity, and cosmology through architecture (e.g., Ashmore 1991; Kent 1990; Kus 1983; Lipe and Hegmon 1989).

To return to Ho-Chunk oral traditions, specific traditions reflect precisely this sort of symbolic structuring of space. In the Red Horn tales (Radin n.d., 1948), the daughter of a village chief is allowed to watch a footrace from a raised platform. This privilege is not afforded to other members of the population, and the construction of the platform for this purpose suggests that space was allocated to socially or politically important individuals at community gatherings.

Intergroup exchange, exploitation of previously unused resources, and technological innovation are areas where the Ho-Chunk traditions do not strongly bear on the kinds of customs suggested by models of the sort offered by Price (1981). Such models typically refer to the transfer of rare or desired goods between distinct populations. The traditions examined and discussed only mention the exchange of marriage partners between groups. Archaeological research in the western Great Lakes region has produced numerous sites and site components that contain material remains from different archaeological traditions. Certainly it would be desirable for the traditions to recount some form of trading behavior or strategy. It has become commonplace for archaeologists in the region to suggest that the appearance of exotic goods reflect trade (e.g., Stoltman 1991) or the presence of visiting groups (e.g., Hall 1962, 1993; C. Mason 1976).

Such a position, however, ignores the potential for archaeologists to uncover data about other meaningful exchange patterns, particularly those involving marriage partners (e.g., Fox 1967; Lévi-Strauss 1969: 233–55; Radcliffe-Brown 1950; see also Gero and Conkey 1991). Tales such as "The woman who married a snake," "The Red Horn," "The man who married a Thunderbird," and "The woman who loved her halfbrother," to name but a few, provide information on marriage customs and the exchange of mates between settlements. Given that this type of behavior is recorded in the oral traditions and that trade is not featured prominently, archaeologists need to evaluate the implications that exchange of marriage partners might hold for the archaeological record (see Kehoe, chap. 6).

In spite of the potential difficulties associated with predictions regarding the exchange and residence patterns of marriage partners, this sort of research has significant potential for identifying social structure and ethnic identity. As defined above, ethnic groups tend to be biologically self-perpetuating (Barth 1969). The identification of marriage networks, therefore, may be one avenue into identifying and mapping elements of pre-Contact and early Contact ethnic identity. As noted previously, ethnographic evidence from eastern North America generally suggests females were the primary potters among Native populations. Therefore, stylistic attributes might be used to map the distribution of ceramics across the western Great Lakes region given increased attention to other limiting factors (Plog 1983; Washburn 1977, 1978, 1983, 1989; Washburn and Crowe 1988).

Activities that might reflect increased ritual activity, formalization of lineages and sodalities, status differentiation, and increased identity signaling are strongly represented in Ho-Chunk oral tradition. The traditions examined for this paper included numerous, repeated, and consistent references to status differentiation, clan identity, and the use of material symbols to represent these identities. Differentiation occurs both horizontally (that is, between different clans and moieties) and vertically (between elite or privileged clans and nonprivileged clans). The symbolic placement of the lodges of important clans as well as the symbolic association of these clans with particular ideological and cosmological concepts reflects the interrelatedness of the formalization of lineages, the advent of status differentiation, and the increased signaling of identity.

There is good evidence for intensified ritual organization and behavior during the late pre-Contact era in the western Great Lakes region, particularly from the Muscoda region of Wisconsin. Here, Salzer (1987) has been able to document a sequence of human-produced sediments (anthroseds) with ritual implications along with pictographs. The latter, which may postdate the bulk of anthrosed production, are clearly attributable to oral traditions closely associated with the Ho-Chunk. Likewise, Hall (1993) has argued for a symbolic link between effigy-mound form and Ho-Chunk clan names. Of particular interest to this discussion is the fact that the pottery associated with effigy mounds and the Gottschall site vary in type and form, suggesting that people using a variety of different material cultural forms participated in ritual activities. In turn, this suggests that identity marking was flexible, with pottery reflecting one set of signals, and ritual at mounds or shrines reflecting another set of symbols, each present in a variety of social groups.

Turning to the oral traditions, increased ritual activity is most clearly represented in Radin's (1945) discussion of the origin of the Medicine Rite. Radin argues that the Medicine Rite was borrowed by the Ho-Chunk from neighboring Algonquian-speaking peoples. The ceremony and its corresponding suite of beliefs and lore, however, were not simply adopted in completed form by the Ho-Chunk but rather represented a reinterpretation of existing ceremonialism. In particular, Radin cites the Night-Spirit society and the Snake Clan feast as being identified by some Ho-Chunk as the precursors to the Medicine Rite: "It is only superficially that its organization is really unique, for both in the snake clan feast and the Night-spirit ritual society there are four positions just as in the Medicine Rite. The resemblance between the latter two are, in fact, so marked that we can well understand why some Ho-Chunk regarded the Night-spirit society as the model for the Medicine Rite" (Radin 1945:70).

As Radin notes later in the same discussion, the Ho-Chunk internalized the Medicine Rite and adapted it to their particular views and beliefs rather than vice versa. This is significant because, as argued previously in this chapter, such adaptation is one mechanism for the definition and perpetuation of ethnic identity. Thus, in this sense, the sequence of ritual performances and the intensification of belief systems through the shift from one ritual complex to the next reflect the sort of intensification Price (1981) predicts.

Also of significance are the emphases placed on war bundles and the Victory Dance, *Hok'ixe're* (Lurie 1978; Radin 1923). Although the war bundles and Victory Dance are distinct elements of Ho-Chunk identity, both reflect an emphasis on warfare and conflict. As Lurie (1978) notes, war bundles and the powers associated with them are among the most important possessions of the Ho-Chunk. The creation of new bundles involves a series of ritual offerings to supernatural forces associated with warfare and can be undertaken only as a consequence of direction from the supernatural. Hence, the creation of war bundles is a symbol of Ho-Chunk interaction with the supernatural and, as such, becomes an important point of identity marking.

In sum, phenomena such as population increase, increased definition of space, and the reduction of residential mobility should be examined archaeologically since these events are inferred from Ho-Chunk traditions. This suite of traits may be reflected in the process of intensifying land use around Lake Winnebago and Lake Koshkonong during the later pre-Contact era. Similarly, they may also be reflected in changes within more westerly archaeological manifestations, such as the origin and spread of village- and mound-building traditions in and around Red Wing, Minnesota, and Apple River, Illinois, and the area around Effigy Mounds National Monument in northeastern Iowa. Interestingly, all the areas contain substantial Oneota occupations, and both the Red Wing and Apple River areas are associated with Mississippian archaeological manifestations prior to Oneota florescence. The implications of this are discussed below.

A second suite of behaviors reflected in oral traditions is less archaeologically visible but potentially more important. Behaviors surrounding the formalization of lineages, increased ritual activity, the emergence of status differentiation, and increased identity signaling are all key elements in the establishment of salient identities. Unfortunately, without data pertaining to the organization of archaeological sites, differentiation within households, and the identification of structures associated with rituals, it is impossible to undertake an investigation of such behaviors.

For the model presented above, the lack of such data is critical. The model must remain a hypothetical construction until data are collected that can be used to evaluate it. For now, the model is constructed solely upon the limited archaeological information we have, most of which pertains to the first data set outlined above, and upon data derived from analysis of the oral traditions. Consequently, what is presented here represents the first step in a large-scale program that will require comprehensive testing on multiple sites. There is likely to be no easy solution to the problems of identifying social structure and ethnic identity in the past, or to uncovering the social forces that led to the generation of such phenomena. Nonetheless, in order for researchers to better understand the past and to undertake anthropological interpretations of past behaviors, such issues need to be confronted. The alternative is to continue to pursue complicated customs and developments through less complex and integrative research programs, a practice that can only yield results commensurate with the level of our inquiries and is not likely to shed new light on the complexities of past human beings and communities.

Conclusion

Given this information, we can predict that we should see certain materials and material organization in the archaeological record. Primarily, we can anticipate the presence of status differentiation, perhaps in the forms of (a) ceramic decoration, (b) the possession and display of rare items, (c) residential structure size and internal organization, and (d) village layout. Significantly, we have undertaken little ceramic sociology in the region, and we have precious little information on either household or village organization in the archaeological or historical records. Yet such data are often sensitive identity markers (Eco 1980; Hodder 1982, 1984; Johnson, chap. 4; Kent 1984, 1990; Kus 1983; Kus and Raharijoana 1990). I would suggest that these data are critical if we are to make progress on questions of Ho-Chunk origin and archaeological identities.

Second, we need to revise the theories regarding identity in which we ground our interpretations. It is hardly necessary to remind researchers that an archaeologically defined culture, which is by definition an etic construct, does not, in all but the rarest cases, correlate directly with an emically defined social entity. Further, it is naïve to anticipate that people in the past possessed and utilized only a single social identity (e.g., Gluckman 1962; Goffman 1956, 1959; Gonzalez 1989; Haaland 1969). Consequently, rather than seeking to discuss ethnic identity, it may be more appropriate to discuss what Schortman (1989) has labeled salient identity. Salient identity is expressed both between groups, as we would expect with conventional conceptions of ethnicity, but also within groups to define such relations as social status and clan or lineage. Given that the historic and ethnographic records tell us that the Ho-Chunk were divided into moieties and clans, and that they may have at one time organized themselves hierarchically, such concerns should become paramount in archaeological and ethnohistorical discussions of these people.

Finally, we need to extend our consideration of the dynamic nature of identity marking to the concept of a Ho-Chunk sociopolitical unit. Without doubt these people exist today and form a functioning, definable unit. The question of whether this or a closely parallel unit existed prior to European contact is another matter. There seems little doubt that some sociopolitical system or series of systems existed during the late pre-Contact period and that the presence of these systems eventually prompted Nicolet's visit to Wisconsin. However, we need not envision this unit or sequence of units as possessing a single material culture, nor do we need to postulate the presence of typologically related material expressions within the unit or units. Furthermore, there is no a priori reason that we should limit our search for the predecessors to the ethnographically defined Ho-Chunk to Oneota or similar sites. Indeed, the Ho-Chunk may be represented by multiple material culture traditions, including Effigy Mound.

In short, we simply may have missed the forest for the trees. Indeed, we may have become so fascinated with identifying the presence of certain sorts of trees that we have forgotten that there are dynamic relationships at work within the forest that we should become concerned with. So where might we find the archaeological materials of the predecessors to the Ho-Chunk? Perhaps we have been looking at them all along, in Effigy Mound, in Oneota, and in countless local variants of material culture that represent the myriad material responses that people make on individual and familial levels.

Acknowledgments

The author gratefully acknowledges the editors for their patience and skill. My thanks also go to the anonymous reviewers who made many helpful suggestions for improving this paper. Finally, I extend heartfelt thanks to Wendy Ashmore, Bob Hall, Uli Linke, Robin Fox, and Bob Salzer for their help in developing the ideas presented here. As always, any errors are mine alone.

References Cited

Ashmore, Wendy. 1991. Site-Planning Principles and Concepts of Directionality among the Ancient Maya. *Latin American Antiquity* 2:199–226.

Barth, Frederick. 1969. Introduction. In *Ethnic Groups and Boundaries,* ed. F. Barth, 9–38. Little, Brown, Boston.

Benn, David. 1995. Woodland People and the Roots of Oneota. In *Oneota Archaeology: Past, Present, and Future,* ed. W. Green. Report 20, Office of the State Archaeologist of Iowa, Iowa City.

Boas, Franz. 1891. Dissemination of Tales among the Natives of North America. *Journal of American Folk-Lore* 4:13–20.

———. 1896. The Growth of Indian Mythologies. *Journal of American Folk-Lore* 9:1–11.

———. 1914. Mythology and Folk-tales of the North American Indians. *Journal of American Folk-Lore* 27:374–410.

———. 1916. *Tsimshian Mythology.* Bureau of American Ethnology 31st Annual Report, Washington, D.C.

———. 1925. Stylistic Aspects of Primitive Literature. *Journal of American Folk-Lore* 38:329–39.

Braroe, N. W. 1975. *Indian and White: Self-Image and Interaction in a Canadian Plains Community.* Stanford University Press, Palo Alto, Calif.

Brown, J. A., and P. J. O'Brien, eds. 1990. *At the Edge of Prehistory: Huber Phase Archaeology in the Chicago Area.* Illinois Department of Transportation, Kampsville.

Charles, D. K., and Jane Buikstra. 1983. Archaic Mortuary Sites in the Central Mississippi Drainage: Distribution, Structure, and Implications. In *Archaic Hunters and Gatherers,* ed. J. L. Phillips and J. A. Brown, 117–45. Academic Press, New York.

Donley, L. W. 1982. House Power: Swahili Space and Symbolic Markers. In *Symbolic and Structural Archaeology,* ed. Ian Hodder, 63–73. Cambridge University Press, Cambridge.

Donley-Reid, L. W. 1990. A Structuring Structure: The Swahili House. In *Domestic Architecture and the Use of Space: An Interdisciplinary Cross-Cultural Study,* ed. Susan Kent, 114–26. Cambridge University Press, Cambridge.

Doty, W. G. 1986. *Mythography: The Study of Myth and Rituals.* University of Alabama Press, Tuscaloosa.

Dragoo, D. W. 1976. Some Aspects of Eastern North American Prehistory: A Review, 1975. *American Antiquity* 41:3–27.

Dundes, Alan, ed. 1984. *Sacred Narrative: Readings in the Theory of Myth*. University of California Press, Berkeley.

Eco, Umberto. 1980. Function and Sign: The Semiotics of Architecture. In *Signs, Symbols, and Architecture*, ed. G. Broadbent et al., 213–32. Wiley, New York.

Fox, Robin. 1967. *Kinship and Marriage: An Anthropological Perspective*. Penguin Books, New York.

Gero, Joan, and Margaret Conkey, eds. 1991. *Engendering Archaeology*. Basil Blackwell, Oxford.

Gluckman, Max, ed. 1962. *Essays on the Ritual of Social Relations*. Manchester University Press, Manchester.

Goffman, Erving. 1956. On the Nature of Deference and Demeanor. *American Anthropologist* 58:473–502.

———. 1959. *Encounters: Two Studies in the Sociology of Interaction*. Bobbs-Merrill, Indianapolis.

———. 1963a. *Behavior in Public Places: Notes on the Social Organization of Gatherings*. Free Press, New York.

———. 1963b. *Stigma: Notes on the Management of Spoiled Identity*. Prentice-Hall, Englewood Cliffs, N.J.

Gonzalez, N. L. 1989. Introduction. In *Conflict, Migration, and the Expression of Ethnicity*, ed. N. L. Gonzalez, 1–10. Westview Press, Boulder, Colo.

Gramly, R. M. 1988. Conflict and Defense in the Eastern Woodlands. In *Interpretations of Culture Change in the Eastern Woodlands during the Late Woodland Period*, ed. Richard Yerkes, 85–97. Occasional Papers in Anthropology 3. Ohio State University, Columbus.

Grimm, T. C. 1985. Time-Depth Analysis of Fifteen Siouan Languages. *Siouan and Caddoan Linguistics* (June).

Haaland, Gunaar. 1969. Economic Determinants in Ethnic Processes. In *Ethnic Groups and Boundaries*, ed. Frederick Barth, 39–52. Little, Brown, Boston.

Hall, R. L. 1962. *The Archaeology of Carcajou Point*. 2 vols. University of Wisconsin Press, Madison.

———. 1993. Red Banks, Oneota, and the Winnebago: Views from a Distant Rock. *Wisconsin Archaeologist* 74:10–79.

Harré, R. 1978. Architectonic Man: On the Structure of Lived Experience. In *Structure, Consciousness, and History*, ed. R. H. Brown and S. Lyman, 139–72. Cambridge University Press, Cambridge.

Hayden, Brian. 1995. Pathways to Power: Principles for Creating Socioeconomic Inequalities. In *Foundations of Social Inequality*, ed. T. D. Price and G. M. Feinman, 15–86. Plenum, New York.

Hill, J. N. 1965. Broken K: A Prehistoric Society in Eastern Arizona. Ph.D. diss., University of Chicago.

———. 1966. A Prehistoric Community in Eastern Arizona. *Southwestern Journal of Anthropology* 22:9–30.

———. 1968. Broken K Pueblo: Patterns of Form and Function. In *New Perspec-*

tives in Archaeology, ed. Sally Binford and Lewis Binford, 103–42. Aldine, Chicago.

———. 1970. *Broken K Pueblo: Prehistoric Social Organization in the American Southwest*. Anthropological Papers of the University of Arizona 18.

———. 1977. Individual Variability in Ceramics and the Study of Prehistoric Social Organization. In *The Individual in Prehistory: Studies in Variability in Style in Prehistoric Technologies*, ed. James Hill and Joel Gunn, 55–108. Academic Press, New York.

Hodder, Ian. 1977. The Distribution of Material Culture Items in the Baringo District, Western Kenya. *Man* 12:239–69.

———. 1978. *The Spatial Organisation of Culture*. University of Pittsburgh Press, Pittsburgh.

———. 1979. Economic and Social Stress and Material Culture Patterning. *American Antiquity* 44:446–54.

———. 1982. *Symbols in Action*. New York: Academic Press.

———. 1984. Burials, Houses, Women and Men in the European Neolithic. In *Ideology, Power, and Prehistory*, ed. Daniel Miller and Christopher Tilley, 51–68. Cambridge University Press, Cambridge.

Hollinger, R. E. 1993. Investigating Oneota Residence through Domestic Architecture. Master's thesis, Department of Anthropology, University of Missouri, Columbia.

Hurley, W. M. 1975. *An Analysis of Effigy Mound Complexes in Wisconsin*. Anthropological Papers no. 59, Museum of Anthropology, University of Michigan, Ann Arbor.

Jacobs, M. 1959. Folklore. In *The Anthropology of Franz Boas*, ed. Walter Goldschmidt, 119–38. Memoir 89. American Anthropological Association, Menesha, Wisc.

Jones, J. A., E. A. Smith, and V. Carstense, eds. 1974. *Winnebago Indians*. Garland Publishing, New York.

Jones, Sian. 1997. *The Archaeology of Ethnicity: Constructing Identities Past and Present*. Routledge, London.

Kent, Susan, ed. 1984. *Analyzing Activity Areas: An Ethnoarchaeological Study of the Use of Space*. University of New Mexico Press, Albuquerque.

———. 1990. *Domestic Architecture and the Use of Space: An Interdisciplinary Cross-Cultural Study*. Cambridge University Press, Cambridge.

Kus, Susan. 1983. The Social Representation of Space: Dimensioning the Cosmological and the Quotidian. In *Archaeological Hammers and Theories*, ed. J. A. Moore and A. S. Keene, 277–98. Academic Press, New York.

Kus, Susan, and Raharijaona, Vistor. 1990. Domestic Space and the Tenacity of Tradition among Some Betsileo of Madagascar. In *Domestic Architecture and the Use of Space: An Interdisciplinary Cross-Cultural Study*, ed. Susan Kent, 21–33. Cambridge University Press, Cambridge.

Leach, Edward. 1976. *Culture and Communication*. Cambridge University Press, Cambridge.

Lévi-Strauss, Claude. 1953. Social Structure. In *Anthropology Today: An Encyclopedic Inventory*, ed. A. Kroeber, 524–53. University of Chicago Press, Chicago.

———. 1960. Four Winnebago Myths: A Structural Sketch. In *Culture in History*, ed. Stanley Diamond, 358–78. Columbia University Press, New York.

———. *Structural Anthropology*. Anchor Books, Garden City, N.Y.

———. 1969. *The Elementary Structures of Kinship*. Trans. J. Belle, J. von Sturmer, and R. Needham. Beacon Press, Boston. (Originally published as *Les structures élémentaires de la parenté*, 1949.)

Lipe, W. D., and Michelle Hegmon, eds. 1989. *The Architecture of Social Integration in Prehistoric Pueblos*. Occasional Paper no. 1. Crow Canyon Archaeological Center, Cortez, Colo.

Lurie, N. O. 1952. The Winnebago Indians: A Study in Cultural Change. Ph.D. diss., Department of Anthropology, Northwestern University, Evanston, Ill.

———. 1960. Winnebago Protohistory. In *Culture in History: Essays in Honor of Paul Radin*, ed. Stanley Diamond, 790–808. Columbia University Press, New York.

———. 1961. *Mountain Wolf Woman: The Autobiography of a Winnebago Indian*. University of Michigan Press, Ann Arbor.

———. 1972. An Aztalan-Winnebago Hypothesis. Ms. on file, Anthropology Program, Luther College, Decorah, Iowa.

———. 1978. Winnebago. In *Handbook of North American Indians*, vol. 15, *Northeast*, ed. Bruce Trigger, 690–707. Smithsonian Institution Press, Washington, D.C.

———. 1988. In Search of Cheatar: New Findings on Black Hawk's Surrender. *Wisconsin Magazine of History* 71:162–83.

Malinowski, Bronislaw. 1926. The Role of Myth in Life. *Psyche* 24:29–39. Reprinted in *Magic, Science and Religion and Other Essays*, ed. Robert Redfield, 1948. Free Press, Glencoe, Ill.

Mallam, R. C. 1976. *The Iowa Effigy Mound Manifestation: An Interpretive Model*. Report no. 9, Office of the State Archaeologist, Iowa City.

Mason, C. I. 1976. Historic Identification of Lake Winnebago Focus Oneota. In *Cultural Change and Continuity: Essays in Honor of James Bennett Griffin*, ed. C. E. Cleland, 335–48. Academic Press, New York.

Mason, R. J. 1993. Oneota and Winnebago Ethnogenesis: An Overview. *Wisconsin Archaeologist* 74:400–421.

McKern, W. C. 1929. Regarding the Origin of Wisconsin Effigy Mounds. *American Anthropologist* 31:562–64.

———. 1945. Preliminary Report on the Upper Mississippi Phase in Wisconsin. *Bulletin of the Public Museum of the City of Milwaukee* 16:111–78.

Meinholz, N. M., and J. L. Kolb. 1997. *The Statz Site: A Late Woodland Community and Archaic Lithic Workshop in Dane County, Wisconsin*. Archaeology Research Series no. 5. Museum Archaeology Program, State Historical Society of Wisconsin, Madison.

Nagata, Judith. 1981. In Defense of Ethnic Boundaries: The Changing Myths and Charters of Malay Identity. In *Ethnic Change,* ed. Charles F. Keyes, 88–116. University of Washington Press, Seattle.

Nassaney, M. S. 1992. Communal Societies and the Emergence of Elites in the Prehistoric American Southeast. In *Lords of the Southeast: Social Inequality and the Native Elites of Southeastern North America,* ed. A. W. Barker and T. R. Pauketat, 111–43. Archaeological Paper no. 3. American Anthropological Association, Washington, D.C.

O'Brien, P. J. 1986. Evidence for Prehistoric Pawnee Cosmology. *American Anthropologist* 88:939–46.

O'Gorman, Judy. 1994. *The Tremaine Site Complex: Oneota Occupation in the La Crosse Locality, Wisconsin.* Archaeological Research Series no. 3. Museum Archaeology Program, State Historical Society of Wisconsin, Madison.

Overstreet, D. F. 1976. The Grand River, Lake Koshkonong, Green Bay and Lake Winnebago Phases: Eight Hundred Years of Oneota Prehistory in Eastern Wisconsin. Ph.D. diss., Department of Anthropology, University of Wisconsin-Madison.

———. 1978. Oneota Settlement Patterns in Eastern Wisconsin. In *Mississippian Settlement Patterns,* ed. B. D. Smith, 21–49. Academic Press, New York.

———. 1993. McCauley, Astor, and Hanson—Candidates for the Provisional Dandy Phase. *Wisconsin Archaeologist* 74:120–96.

Plog, Stephen. 1983. Analysis of Style in Artifacts. *Annual Review of Anthropology* 12:125–42.

Price, T. D. 1981. Complexity in "Non-Complex" Societies. In *Archaeological Approaches to the Study of Complexity,* ed. S. E. van der Leeuw, 54–97. University of Amsterdam, Amsterdam, The Netherlands.

Propp, Vladimir. 1968. *Morphology of the Folktale.* 2d ed. Trans. L. Scott. University of Texas Press, Austin.

Radcliffe-Brown, A. R. 1950. Introduction. In *African Systems of Kinship and Marriage,* ed. A. R. Radcliffe-Brown and D. Forde, 1–85. Oxford University Press, London.

Radin, Paul. n.d. Notes on file in the Library of the American Philosophical Society, Philadelphia, Pa.

———. 1909. Winnebago Tales. *Journal of American Folk-Lore* 22:288–313.

———. 1910. The Clan Organization of the Winnebago. *American Anthropologist,* n.s. 12:209–19.

———. 1911. Some Aspects of Winnebago Archaeology. *American Anthropologist,* n.s. 13:517–38.

———. 1915a. *Literary Aspects of North American Mythology.* Anthropological Series of the Canada Geological Survey 6. Canadian National Museum Bulletin 16. Ottawa.

———. 1915b. *The Social Organization of the Winnebago Indians, an Interpretation.* Anthropological Series of the Canada Geological Survey 6. Canadian National Museum Bulletin 16. Ottawa.

————. 1923. *The Winnebago Tribe.* Bureau of American Ethnology Annual Report, 1915–1916, 35–560. Washington, D.C.

————. 1926. Literary Aspects of Winnebago Mythology. *Journal of American Folk-Lore* 39:18–52.

————. 1945. *The Road of Life and Death.* Bollingen Series 5. Pantheon Books, New York.

————. 1948. *Winnebago Hero Cycles: A Study in Aboriginal Literature.* Indiana University Publications in Anthropology and Linguistics 1. Waverly Press, Baltimore.

————. 1956. *The Trickster: A Study in American Indian Mythology.* Routledge, London.

Salzer, R. J. 1987. Preliminary Report on the Gottschall Site (47Ia80). *Wisconsin Archaeologist* 68:419–72.

————. 1995. Ancient Ethnicity: The Archaeology of Ideology. Paper presented at the annual meeting of the American Society for Ethnohistory, Kalamazoo, Michigan.

Sampson, K. W. 1988. Conventionalized Figures on Late Woodland Ceramics. *Wisconsin Archaeologist* 69:163–88.

Schortman, Edward M. 1989. Interregional Interaction in Prehistory: The Need for a New Perspective. *American Antiquity* 54:52–65.

Speck, Frank. n.d. Notes on file in the Library of the American Philosophical Society, Philadelphia, Pa.

Springer, W. J., and S. R. Witkowski. 1982. Siouan Historical Linguistics and Oneota Archaeology. In *Oneota Studies,* ed. G. E. Gibbon, 69–84. University of Minnesota Publications in Anthropology 1. University of Minnesota, Minneapolis.

Staeck, J. P. n.d. Bahr Village Survey. Notes on file with the author.

————. 1992. Ethnicity and the Prehistoric Era of the Western Great Lakes Region. Paper presented at the 91st annual meeting of the American Anthropological Association, San Francisco.

————. 1994. Archaeology, Identity, and Oral Traditions: A Reconsideration of Late Prehistoric and Early Historic Winnebago Social Structure and Identity as Seen through Oral Traditions. Ph.D. diss., Rutgers University, New Brunswick, N.J.

————. 1996. Ranking, Marriage, and Power: Reflections of Ho-Chunk (Winnebago) Oral Traditions on Effigy Mound Transegalitarian Strategies for Developing Power and Prestige. Paper presented at the Midwest Archaeological Conference, Beloit, Wisc.

————. 1998. Mounds, Monuments, and the Politics of Power: Dimensions of Effigy Mound Function. Paper presented at the annual meeting of the Society for American Archaeology, Seattle.

Stoltman, James B. 1991. Ceramic Petrography as a Technique for Documenting Cultural Interaction: An Example from the Upper Mississippi Valley. *American Antiquity* 56:103–20.

Washburn, Dorothy K. 1977. A Symmetry Analysis of Upper Gila Area Ceramic Design. *Papers of the Peabody Museum of Archaeology and Ethnology,* vol. 68. Cambridge, Mass.

———. 1978. A Symmetry Classification of Pueblo Ceramic Design. In *Discovering Past Behavior: Experiments in the Archaeology of the American Southwest,* ed. P. Grebinger, 102–21. Gordon and Breach, New York.

———. 1983. Toward a Theory of Structural Style in Art. In *Structure and Cognition in Art,* ed. D. K. Washburn, 1–7. Cambridge University Press, Cambridge.

———. 1989. The Property of Symmetry and the Concept of Ethnic Style. In *Archaeological Approaches to Cultural Identity,* ed. S. J. Shennan, 157–73. Unwin Hyman, London.

Washburn, D. K., and D. W. Crowe. 1988. *Symmetries of Culture: Theory and Practice of Plane Pattern Analysis.* University of Washington Press, Seattle.

Whallon, Robert, Jr. 1968. Investigations of Late Prehistoric Social Organization in New York State. In *New Perspectives in Archaeology,* ed. Sally Binford and Lewis Binford, 223–44. Aldine, Chicago.

4

The Politics of Pottery

Material Culture and Political Process among Algonquians
of Seventeenth-Century Southern New England

Eric S. Johnson

Native American communities of 17th-century southern New England
were egalitarian societies characterized by open social networks among
communities, with individuals able to change their community affiliation.
Variation in form and decoration observed in pottery from that time is
consistent with the political characteristics of these communities. Where
political circumstances underwent unique changes, as they did among the
Mohegan community of southern Connecticut, pottery changed in ways
that reflected these new conditions. Specifically, the Mohegans responded
to the social and political pressures they experienced after the Pequot War
by intensified signaling of group identity.

In this chapter I explore the relationships between material culture
(pots) and politics among the Native American communities of southern
New England in the 17th century. The political landscape of the region
was characterized by fluctuating patterns of alliance, confederation, and
affiliation among communities (see Burton 1976; Burton and Lowenthal
1974; Johnson 1993, 1999; Robinson 1990; Salisbury 1982; Thomas
1979; cf. Bragdon 1996). As contact with Europeans intensified, epidemic
diseases struck parts of the region, and Native communities shifted their
political alliances and affiliations, sometimes rapidly. For at least one
community—the Mohegans of eastern Connecticut—the changes were
particularly rapid, dramatic, and unusual. Through timely alliances, military victories, and diplomatic successes, the Mohegan community's political status increased substantially. At the same time the community grew in

size and changed in composition as refugees from other communities joined the group, sometimes eagerly, sometimes reluctantly. The Mohegans also became isolated from at least some of their former allies as they experienced a prolonged conflict with the Narragansetts and other groups (Burton 1976; De Forest 1964; Johnson 1993; L. Williams 1972).

Within and between Native communities and confederations, political organization, alliance, allegiance, and identity could be varied and dynamic. New ties between communities were forged, and old ones were strengthened, weakened, or ruptured under the pressures, constraints, and opportunities that arose in the wake of epidemics as well as from the fur and wampum trade, from European settlement, and from conflicts. The basic geopolitical unit was the autonomous community—a group of people sharing a homeland or territory. Communities were never isolated; individuals and families sought to create alliances and kinship ties with members of other communities. A group of communities linked by such ties could form the nucleus of a larger political entity, which I call the confederation. Around a relatively stable nucleus of between one and a handful of closely linked communities was a less stable margin. Here weaker ties to the nuclear communities conferred greater autonomy, permitting allies to follow their own interests, sometimes to the point of leaving one confederation for another. This was a complex and dynamic political environment of confederates, allies, subordinates, superiors, and adversaries at many levels (confederations, communities, interest groups, families, and individuals) (see Bragdon 1996; Cave 1996; Johnson 1999; Robinson 1990).

The community affiliation and political identity of individuals appears to have been relatively fluid. There are numerous instances of individuals leaving one community for another. Some made this change upon marriage (local exogamy appears to have been common), others upon changes in their political fortunes. Some changes were precipitated by epidemics, when survivors of stricken groups joined other communities. Perhaps the best documented of many examples of this fluidity is the absorption of many Pequots into the Mohegan and Narragansett communities after the Pequot War in 1637. The key to fluidity of identity was the kinship ties among different communities. Every individual had extensive networks of kin or other allies along which he or she could move relatively freely across the boundaries of communities and confederations, except perhaps in times of conflict (Burton 1976; Johnson 1993, 1999; Robinson 1990).

Archaeological evidence in the form of patterns of variation in material culture—particularly ceramics—is consistent with these conditions: the political primacy of the community, the ephemeral and highly variable nature of confederation, the fluidity of individual identity, and the general permeability of social boundaries. Although the ceramics of southern New England vary in form and decoration, there is little indication that these variations reflect social boundaries between either communities or confederations (Goodby 1992, 1994, 1998). However, there is an exception to this pattern—the pottery made and used at Fort Shantok, the fortified settlement on the Thames River in southern Connecticut that was the political core of the Mohegan community (fig. 4.1).

The Mohegan Community in the 17th Century

Before 1636 the Mohegans were close but subordinate allies of the communities that formed the nucleus of the Pequot confederation. Many kinship ties linked Mohegans and Pequots. For example, the Mohegan sachem Uncas was married to the sister of the Pequots' principal sachem, Sassacus. Although the Pequot confederation at one time included allied communities throughout the Long Island Sound region, the confederation began to disintegrate in the 1630s owing to epidemics, conflicts with other Native groups, and the death of their principal sachem (Sassacus's father) at the hands of the Dutch in 1634. Even Uncas, despite his kinship with Sassacus, had made several unsuccessful attempts to overturn his community's subordinate status. When the English attacked the weakened Pequots in 1636, Uncas and the Mohegans joined in eliminating their former allies as a regional power (Cave 1996; Johnson 1993, 1996; Salisbury 1982:208–10; Trumbull 1859:478–80).

After the war, Uncas and the Mohegans created a Mohegan confederation, centered around Fort Shantok, a fortified settlement on the Thames River in present-day Montville, Connecticut. The Mohegans attracted new members from other communities, especially Pequots, and before long were competing with the Narragansetts for the allegiance of former Pequot allies. The Mohegans soon found themselves at war with the Narragansetts and *their* Native allies. This conflict lasted more than twenty years and included several large battles, numerous raids, murders, assassination attempts, English intervention (always on the Mohegans' behalf), and incessant political maneuvering (Burton 1976; Burton and Lowenthal 1974; De Forest 1964; Johnson 1993, 1996).

This pattern of alliances and enmities constrained the fluidity of individual identity and created a social boundary between the Mohegans and many other Native groups. The Mohegans survived their partial isolation

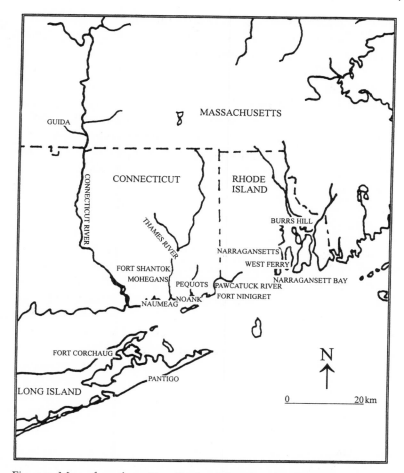

Fig. 4.1. Map of southern New England showing significant places mentioned in the chapter

through Uncas's deft manipulation of their English allies, alliance building with Native groups through marriages (he made at least seven marriages with women of influential families), and, on occasion, coercion (Burton 1976; Burton and Lowenthal 1974; Johnson 1993, 1996; R. Williams 1963:108, 109, 137).

The residents of Shantok were a diverse group. They faced unusually closed social boundaries because many of their Native neighbors were either committed enemies in a state of perpetual cold war (the Narragansetts and most of the Connecticut River communities) or reluctant allies (for example, the Naumeag Pequots). Although the Mohegans had English allies, there was certainly a social boundary between them. Under these conditions, group cohesion must have been under stress. In 1649 the Narragansetts attempted to exploit the Mohegans' diversity in order to split the community. They arranged a marriage between an influential Pequot woman and one of their close allies. This was intended to draw Pequots away from the Mohegans to the Narragansett side of the ongoing conflict (De Forest 1964; Pulsifer 1859:145). One strategy at least some of the Mohegans used to counter this pressure was the production of material culture with new, distinct design elements that expressed messages of community solidarity.

Pottery, Identity, and Style

That material culture played a role in political processes in 17th-century Native southern New England is abundantly clear. There was also a relationship between formal style in material culture and political process in 17th-century southern New England. Specifically, the political and social strains experienced within the Mohegan community after the Pequot War were expressed and responded to through intensified signaling of group identity. This affirmation of Mohegan identity was reflected in the inception of a new and distinctive Mohegan ceramic style, characterized by relative internal homogeneity and external differentiation.

Archaeologists have examined cultural variation and change in time and space through the record of stylistic variation in material culture, including ceramic form and decoration. These variations have been studied as they relate to information exchange (Wobst 1977:321), social interaction, and the learning and communication of style (Deetz 1965; Engelbrecht 1974; Longacre 1970; Whallon 1968). Although social interaction can indeed influence the spatial distribution of styles, this alone is insufficient to explain all stylistic patterning (Conkey 1990; Hodder 1978, 1979; Weissner 1983). Other factors that may influence patterning and variation in ceramics include technological and environmental variables (Arnold 1985; Chilton 1996, 1998), social boundaries (Stark 1998), inter-group competition (Hodder 1979), or intergender tensions (Handsman 1988a, 1990; Wright 1991). Since many potential factors influence stylistic variability in complex ways, and none can be consistently applied cross-culturally, stylistic variability must, ultimately, be explained with reference to particular historical circumstances (Braun 1991). Recent studies of style and social boundaries in northeastern North America (e.g., Brumbach

1975; Chilton 1996, 1998; Goodby 1994, 1998) have emphasized this particularist approach (Stark 1998). These studies of ceramic style suggest that a diversity of factors contribute to ceramic design. The messages encoded in ceramics or any other item of material culture may include a wide variety of diverse statements. Rarely do they send an unambiguous signal of group identity.

Native material culture in southern New England contained many items whose form and decoration had meaning. Among these were wampum belts (R. Williams 1973:213–14); effigy pestles (Volmar 1992); baskets (McMullen and Handsman 1987; Wood 1977:114); wooden and bark bowls, utensils, and mortars (Speck 1915); and clothing and the embroidered mats that lined the inner walls of wigwams (Josselyn 1833: 295, 297, 307; R. Williams 1973:118). The human body itself was often decorated with paint or tattoos (Wood 1977:85). The designs of 19th-century baskets and other, older items contain recurring elements (Speck 1915) that have symbolic meanings relating to community, cosmology, spiritual force, and the journey through life (Tantaquidgeon and Fawcett 1987). Some 17th-century ceramic designs have also been interpreted as affirming women's traditional social roles in the face of social changes (Handsman 1988a, 1990).

Of the several types of information transmitted through material culture, one of the most important is personal and social identity, which, according to Weissner (1983:256–57), is expressed in two ways. One is distinction from others; the other is identification with a group. The former is expressed through what Weissner (1983:258) calls "assertive style." This is personally based and transmits a message of individual distinctiveness. The distributions of assertive styles may be sensitive to factors affecting social interaction such as interpersonal contact, trade, marriage and residency patterns, contact within or across boundaries, or individual participation in political struggles or social conflicts.

The expression of identity through association with a group is expressed through "emblemic style." Emblemic style, as defined by Weissner (1983:257), has a distinct referent, most commonly a social group and its norms, values, property, and other characteristics. It transmits a clear message to a defined target population about conscious affiliation or identity. It should be strikingly uniform and clear within the boundaries of the referent group. Emblemic style, argues Weissner (1983:272), is best suited for expressing group affiliation under stressful conditions because of its efficiency for transferring recurrent messages to a socially distant segment of a population (Wobst 1977).

Several factors suggest that such signaling of group affiliation is an important determinant of the form of the ceramics associated with the Mohegans of the mid to late 17th century. I argue that: (1) signaling through material culture would be expected under the social circumstances of the Mohegans of Shantok; (2) pottery would have been an effective vehicle for such messages; and (3) messages of group identity would have been a component of Fort Shantok ceramic style.

Wobst (1977:323–26) argues that material culture is most effective as a means of information exchange between groups of intermediate social distance. Family members and close friends can easily receive messages through other modes of communication, or already know the messages. Members of groups that are socially very distant will not encounter and cannot interpret the message. Members of intermediate groups, however, can interpret the message and are likely to encounter the object(s) on which it is encoded, which makes them the ideal "target group" for stylistic signaling. Most Native American communities would consist of relatives and close friends, although, since group affiliation was relatively fluid, there would always be some element of a target population within any given community. Target groups for Native stylistic signaling were other Native communities, especially those less closely tied through kinship and alliance. Members of other communities would be likely to encounter the message and be able to decode it.

When members of different, but not socially distant communities began to live together, such signaling increased, since interactions with members of target groups intensified. The kinds of artifacts that carry stylistic signals expanded to include items that may not previously have carried such information because they were less visible to members of the target group, but were becoming more frequently seen. Fort Shantok, with its large size and diverse population, represents just such a scenario. The pottery made by the people of Shantok began to carry an increased load of stylistic information.

Material objects that are efficient for transmitting messages, such as those that can be viewed from a distance, or are likely to be viewed by a target group, especially during significant events, are most likely to contain stylistic information. Those artifacts that undergo many transformational stages during which stylistic information can be added, and those that have a long use life and are thus seen by many, will also be ideal for transmitting stylistic information (Weissner 1983:259; Wobst 1977). The artifacts best suited for carrying information about groups and boundaries are those with widely shared social, economic, political, and symbolic importance (Weissner 1983:272). Although pots cannot be viewed from a great distance, they possess characteristics that suit them for a role as information media. They undergo enough transformational stages in their manufacture that they can be encoded with attributes of shape and decoration. Although the use life of southern New England Native ceramics has never been investigated, it seems likely that some pots might last for as long as several years. Finally, and most importantly, that stylistic attributes of pottery should communicate to an audience beyond the family domestic unit is suggested by the importance of feasting and visiting outside of the immediate domestic circle. It was in ceramic vessels that food was cooked and presented in meals associated with rituals, feasts, and political negotiations. The pots used in cooking would thus be seen by many members of the community, relatives living outside the settlement, other allies, and other individuals, at least occasionally in politically charged settings. The symbols encoded on or embodied in vessels interred with the dead may also be assumed to have meaning to the living during mortuary ritual.

There are some hints that the practice of using designs or symbols to signal group identity dates back to the 17th century. For example, during the Pequot War, Narragansetts used colored paint or cloth tied around the head to mark themselves as allies to the English (R. Williams 1963:30). This may have been an adaptation of a more subtle Native practice of symbolizing group identity. William Wood's description of tattoos suggests that symbols may have been used to signify ancestry—a form of group affiliation: "Others have certain round impressions down the outside of their arms and breasts in form of mullets or spur-rowels, which they imprint by searing irons. Whether these be foils to illustrate their unparalleled beauty (as they deem it) or arms to blazon their antique gentility, I cannot easily determine" (1977:85).

The residents of Shantok constituted a population of very diverse origins: Mohegans, Pequots, refugees from eastern Massachusetts, individuals from Long Island, and people from other southern New England Native communities. Under these conditions, if assertive style, expressing the potter's individual identity to the rest of the community, was predominant, we should expect a great variety and diversity of pottery styles, reflecting the great diversity of potters coming from different local traditions. However, although the ceramics at Shantok are certainly not homogeneous, they do show significant consistencies.

Out of a diversity of people, the Mohegans built a group identity. A pattern of alliances and enmities created a social boundary around the

Mohegans at this time. Like many other Native communities, they were engaged in intense competition with other Native communities for a dwindling land base, an unreliable fur trade, and increasingly belligerent and slippery English and other European allies. Many of the Mohegans, including the sachem Uncas and those who had an interest in maintaining his position, tried to encourage and affirm a unified community identity, and to practice or encourage any behavior that stressed unity within their diverse community. Such practices included pottery manufacture that incorporated new, distinct design elements in an emblemic style.

In a very different vein, Handsman (1988a, 1990) has argued that some of the designs on Mohegan ceramics reflect tensions between genders related to the stresses of European contact (see also Nassaney, chap. 15). That such tensions were real, and that their expression involved certain material items linked to women's work and women's power (e.g., mortars and pestles), are also suggested by oral tradition, specifically the story of Chahnameed (Simmons 1986:274–76; Speck 1903; cf. Handsman 1988b). Women potters' affirmation of traditional women's social roles and the power associated with those roles may indeed be expressed in a variety of material items. Such expression is not incompatible with my argument that Shantok pottery reflects emblemic style. In fact, potentially divisive social tensions may be denied or masked through emblemic style; alternatively, both group identity and factionalism may be expressed through the same object. Alongside the need for potters to express or comment on their identities as women was a need to express their identities as Mohegans. The former discourse was located within the community and was occurring within other contemporary Native communities; it should be evident in material culture (for example, effigy pestles [Volmar 1992]) distributed throughout southern New England. The latter discourse was located specifically within the Mohegan community, although it spoke to a wider social environment. Although both gender and community identity may have been expressed on the same pots, Mohegan identity should be expressed in ceramics distributed predominantly within the Mohegan homeland.

Pre- and Post-Contact Period Ceramics of Southern New England

Seventeenth-century documents tell us little about the production, use, or significance of indigenous ceramics. Pottery is rarely mentioned by English or other European chroniclers of early New England. Roger Williams (1973:215) observed that "the Women make all their earthen vessels." Since pottery was the purview of Native women, it should not be surprising that it, like other women's activities, was seldom reported by European men. From these few hints, it is generally assumed that pottery was produced by women for their households or other close kin, and that skill in ceramic production was widely distributed rather than restricted to a few specialists.

The ceramics from Fort Shantok are so distinct that they have defined one of the traditional archaeological pottery types of southern New England—Shantok ware. Shantok ware was originally defined by Rouse (1945, 1980) and Smith (1980). Salwen (1969:83–85) revised their descriptions on the basis of his analysis of a larger sample. Lorraine Williams (1972) contributed additional analysis of the Fort Shantok ceramics as well as a large assemblage from Fort Corchaug, Long Island, which she described as a local expression of Shantok ware. Taken together, these archaeologists describe Shantok pottery as consisting of large, globular pots with distinctive collars and neck treatments. Vessels are thin walled (average thickness 6 mm), and bodies are globular or elongate-globular in shape. There are round bottoms, pronounced shoulders, constricted necks, and thickened or applied high collars with up to four, often conspicuous, castellations (fig. 4.2), which occasionally terminate in modeled nodes. Collars (including lips, lobes, nodes, and castellations) are decorated with impressed, punctate, modeled, or extruded decoration. Bands or plats of horizontal, vertical, or diagonal impressed lines are common on collars. Williams (1972) notes that what appear to be incised lines are actually impressed and dragged lines. Bodies are plain, with smooth surfaces on both interior and exterior.

Salwen (1969:84–85) defined three subtypes of Shantok ware on the basis of decorative treatment of the vessel neck. Subtype A is characterized either by no decoration or by treatment limited to a single row of punctates or short impressed lines at the base of the neck. In pots of subtype B, the bases of the collars are marked with a series of prominent triangular lobes or "bosses," which are either carved out of the vessel wall or applied (fig. 4.3). These are decorated with a single vertical impressed line and crossed by horizontal impressed lines, a motif that is also frequently employed on castellations. Subtype C is characterized by extruded bands, usually four in number, encircling the neck of the vessel below the collar and decorated with diagonal impressed lines and notching at the base of each. Paste was characterized by Salwen (1969:84) as fairly hard (3–4 on the Mohs scale) and buff to black in color, with grays predominating. Temper is almost exclusively shell in large amounts.

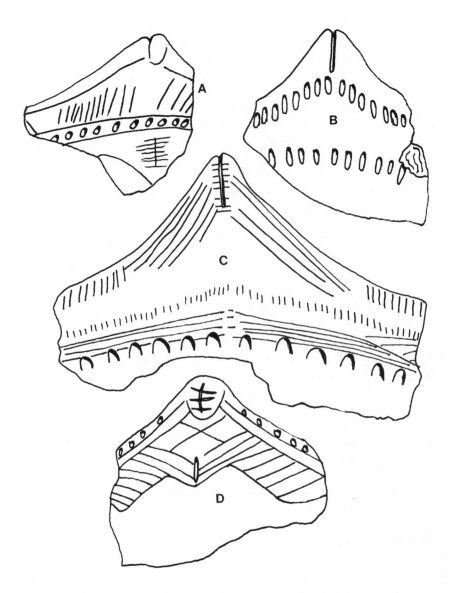

Fig. 4.2. Ceramic vessels from Fort Shantok showing castellations

Shantok pottery predominates at Fort Shantok and Noank in Connecticut, and at Fort Corchaug in eastern Long Island (Smith 1980:55; L. Williams 1972).

How does Shantok pottery compare with other contemporary ceramics from southern New England, specifically Niantic and Hackney Pond types? Descriptions of the latter two are necessary for such a comparison. Niantic pottery was, like Shantok, first defined by Rouse (1945). He characterized Niantic pottery as having thin and fine-grained paste with either shell or grit temper (the former predominating). Vessels have globular bodies, round bottoms, necks, and castellated collars. Interiors are entirely smooth and exteriors are decorated on the collars with impressed "Iroquois-like designs" (Rouse 1980:70). Incised and punctate designs are rare (Smith 1950:133). Decorative motifs include opposed diagonal, horizontal, or vertical lines bordered above and below by horizontal lines (Smith 1950; Lavin 1980), or a band of parallel horizontal lines bordered above and/or below by a row of short vertical or oblique lines (Lavin 1980:26).

Hackney Pond ceramics were defined by McBride (1984:154-65) as an identifiable pottery type within the Windsor ceramic tradition, associated with the Hackney Pond phase (A.D. 1600-1700) in the lower Connecticut Valley and contemporary with the Shantok tradition. Hackney Pond is an internally diverse type that includes both "Guida tradition" pottery, as defined by Byers and Rouse (1960) in their analysis of the Guida site in Westfield, Massachusetts, and elements (including Guida) ascribed to the Niantic phase of the Windsor tradition by Lavin (1980). Hackney Pond ceramics share many similarities with Shantok ware, but also differ in significant ways. The most important differences are in paste characteristics and decorative technique. Temper on Hackney Pond ceramics is fine mineral, described by Byers and Rouse (1960) at the Guida site as "fine micaceous." Paste is softer than that of Shantok ware and tends to flake. Decoration consists of incised lines, generally similar to those of Shantok ware but differing somewhat in arrangement and placement of design elements. In contrast to Shantok pottery, Hackney Pond does not exhibit nodes, bosses, or modeled figures. Although lobes are sometimes present, they are less prominent, never applied, and "consist of deep, wide incisions rather than distinct spaces" (McBride 1984:162-63).

In summary, although Shantok shares many decorative attributes with contemporary wares, such as the range of decorative motifs including opposed oblique lines, it can be distinguished by certain decorative characteristics. Specifically, the applied or extruded lobes or notched rings along the base of the collars (Rouse 1980; L. Williams 1972:346–55) are considered to be almost entirely unique to Shantok ware. The prominent castellations and their occasional modeling are also most often associated with Shantok ware, although Niantic ware and other Northeastern pottery styles occasionally exhibit these attributes.

Archaeologists initially hypothesized that Shantok was an intrusive tradition, not rooted in the Late Woodland Windsor-tradition ceramics that preceded it, and that culminated in the 17th-century Niantic ceramics of eastern Connecticut and Long Island (Smith 1980:50). In part, this was the result of the persistence of explanatory mechanisms such as migration, invasion, and diffusion that dominated the discipline (e.g., Rouse 1980:73), as well as the distinctive formal characteristics of the pottery. More recently, the origin of Shantok and its relationship to contemporary southern New England ceramics has been reinterpreted and debated. Salwen (1969:83) writes that while Shantok pottery "does, indeed, have some striking characteristics of its own, it at the same time shares many others with pottery attributable to the historic groups that were neighbors of the Mohegan-Pequot." These shared characteristics include collars with occasional castellations, smooth surfaces, and globular to semi-globular bodies. Differences are confined to paste composition and decorative technique. Archaeologists continue to discuss the significance and meaning of Shantok ware. Lavin (1986) affords Shantok a separate status, outside of the Windsor tradition. McBride (1984:161–62) argues that although Shantok is distinct in some ways, it "may in fact be better defined as a [17th-century] horizon style with various local and regional expressions." He further notes that the Late Woodland–Contact period "traditions" share many characteristics and appear to be closely related. Lizee (1989a, 1989b) places Shantok within the Windsor tradition, contemporary with Hackney Pond and Niantic ceramics.

The distribution of the various pottery types within southern New England indicates that Shantok ware is associated with the 17th-century Mohegans and their allies. Shantok ware is largely restricted to southern Connecticut, west of the Thames River, within the historic Mohegan homeland, including Fort Shantok. A sizeable sample has been recovered from Fort Corchaug, Long Island (Smith 1980; Solecki 1950; L. Williams 1972). East of the Thames and west of the Pawcatuck River—within the Pequot homeland—Hackney Pond and Niantic wares predominate at 17th-century sites, including the Mystic Fort (McBride 1990:99). Beyond these areas isolated pieces of Shantok or Shantok-like pottery have been reported from Narragansett Bay (Mrozowski 1980:86–87; Simmons

1970:89–91), eastern Massachusetts (Salwen 1969:86), and Pantigo Cemetery (Saville 1920:87–88) in eastern Long Island.

Lizee (1989a) analyzed small samples of Niantic, Hackney Pond, and Shantok ceramics. At least some, if not all, of the examples of the latter were from Fort Shantok. His purpose was to characterize the degree of stylistic (i.e., two-dimensional decorative treatment such as lines) and morphological (i.e., three-dimensional decorative treatment such as lobes or castellations) similarity within and among the types. His results suggest that the types contained similar variation in terms of both two- and three-dimensional decorative treatment. For example, line orientation was no more diverse within Niantic than within Shantok ware. All types exhibited similarly low degrees of internal morphological similarity, and even less similarity with one another (Lizee 1989a:7–10).

Lizee's data also affirm that the presence of lobes and modeling are strongly associated with Shantok ware. In his study sample, which consisted of 29 rim sherds representing 20 Niantic vessels and 7 Shantock vessels, but only 2 Hackney Pond vessels, *only* Shantok pots exhibited these decorative treatments. More than half of the Shantok vessels sampled contained lobes (4 of 7, or 57 percent) and/or modeling (5 of 7, or 71 percent). Several other attributes were strongly, although not exclusively, associated with Shantok ware. For example, castellations were present on 5 of 7 (71 percent) Shantok vessels, on neither of the Hackney Pond sherds, and on only 6 of 20 (30 percent) of the Niantic examples. Everted rims were present on 3 of 7 (42 percent) Shantok pots, on neither of the Hackney Pond pots, and on only 2 of the 20 (10 percent) Niantic vessels, which tended to have inverted rims (11 of 20, or 55 percent). Notching was also most often associated with Shantok (4 of 7, or 57 percent), and less often associated with Niantic (1 of 20, or 5 percent), although it was present on 1 of the 2 Hackney Pond sherds (50 percent) (Lizee 1989a:Tables 2,3). The results of this study suggest that the ceramics made at Fort Shantok were distinct, in important and highly visible ways, from the pottery made at roughly contemporary sites in other parts of southern Connecticut. The Shantok pottery was characterized by highly visible lobes, castellations, and notches, which were rare or absent on the ceramics made at other sites.

Fort Shantok Ceramics

Comparing samples defined typologically can yield suggestive information, as Lizee's study shows, but it should not be the only analytical undertaking. It is equally important to compare samples defined by provenience, in order to compare behaviors among different communities or even larger social units. In these cases, the significant unit is the site, representing the community, or the region, representing the confederation, rather than the type, which represents archaeologists' sometimes inchoate interpretations of a complex of technological, morphological, and stylistic variables. Of particular interest in this case is the ceramic assemblage from Fort Shantok, the primary settlement of the Mohegan community.

The assemblage from Fort Shantok is perhaps the largest and most thoroughly studied assemblage of Contact-period ceramics in southern New England (see, for example, Handsman 1989; Johnson 1993; Lizee 1989a, 1989b; Lizee et al. 1995; Salwen 1966, 1969; L. Williams 1972). The site's location and its association with the Mohegan community have been widely known since the 17th century. It has been subjected to looting and surface collecting for many years. Among the largest amateur collections from the site is that of Edward H. Rodgers. His collection is presently curated by the Institute for American Indian Studies in Washington, Connecticut. Professional archaeologists began excavating at Shantok in the 1960s. From 1962 to 1970 Bert Salwen directed excavations at the site. The results of these excavations are summarized in a doctoral dissertation by Williams (1972), who worked at the site along with Salwen. More recently, ceramic material from Shantok has been reanalyzed by Lizee (1989a, 1989b; Lizee et al. 1995) and the author (Johnson 1993). The following summary and discussion focuses on two questions. First, is the diversity of the Fort Shantok ceramics significantly greater or less than that from other contemporary sites? Second, are there recurring motifs associated with the Fort Shantok pottery that are rare or absent elsewhere? Such motifs may represent emblemic style.

Williams analyzed thirty-five vessels from Fort Shantok. Her analysis focused on attributes of vessel shape (especially profile) and decoration. She characterized the assemblage as exhibiting a "wide range of variation" (1972:347), and identified six separate subtypes or classes based on correlations of attributes (particularly profile shapes and decorative motifs). Williams's analysis does show that the Shantok assemblage contains considerable variation in such decorative elements as technique of decoration, the numbers of lobes or notched rings, and the presence or absence of applied collars. It thus demonstrates the value of going beyond a simple reliance on typological description, in which all the ceramics would be simply characterized as Shantok ware.

The significance of the various classes she defines is not readily explained. She suggests that some of the classes may have represented the pottery of "surrounding Indian groups" (L. Williams 1972:135). It is also possible that the classes represent variations on a single motif. The notched rings and lobes, while somewhat different, do share important similarities. Both produce the effect of protrusions of decorated surface around the upper portion of the vessel. In this respect they may be considered similar decorative motifs. Moreover, the two techniques are not always readily distinguishable. A notched ring can closely resemble a ring of lobes. My own analysis, which documents considerable variation in the size, shape, and technique of the lobes, further suggests that lobes and notched rings may simply represent a variety of techniques for producing a motif that encompasses considerable variation.

My analysis of a sample of sherds from twenty-five vessels from Fort Shantok (see Johnson 1993:289–94, 322–23) yielded results similar to those of Lizee in terms of recurrent decorative motifs. Because I did not select my sample based on types, but on site provenience, it may be expected that my sample might exhibit greater variation, since aberrant forms will not have been excluded through the classification process.

The ceramics I analyzed were from the Rodgers collection, curated at the Institute for American Indian Studies. This small sample was not included in Williams's analysis of the Fort Shantok ceramics. Since my goal in examining the Shantok pottery was to identify signaling, I analyzed only visible decorative attributes—design elements and motifs and their placement on the vessel. For each vessel, the motifs present and their arrangement on the vessel's collar and neck were recorded using a system similar in many respects to that used by Williams (1972:135–39, 345–63), although I did not use the six classes defined in her analysis. These data were then analyzed in order to identify recurring elements, as well as elements that were less pervasive within the site assemblage.

As was the case in Lizee's sample, castellations and lobes were common decorative elements. However, modeling beyond that employed in creating some of the castellations and lobes was not present on any of the sherds. Castellations (fig. 4.2) were present on at least nine of the twenty-five vessels (36 percent). Two others were probably castellated, judged on the basis of rim thickness and angle, and the others were too fragmentary to determine whether castellations were present or absent. All complete castellations were decorated with a single vertical line, which was sometimes accompanied by horizontal lines to form a design variously referred to as a "corncob," "caterpillar," or "skeleton." Lobes were also common. Of the twenty-one vessels for which the presence or absence of lobes could be determined, fifteen (71 percent) exhibited lobes at the base of the collar. These lobes generally took the form of an inverted triangle, but varied considerably in the manner of their creation, their size, prominence, and decorative treatment. Some lobes were made by pushing clay out from inside the vessel (extrusion), leaving a hollow impression behind the lobe. Others were created by applying clay to the vessel's outer surface (application); others were fashioned by cutting or carving the vessel surface before firing, and some vessels showed evidence of two or more of these techniques. Lobe shape and size exhibited considerable variation (fig. 4.3). Some protruded more than 18 mm from the collar and even farther from the neck; others were almost even with the surrounding vessel surface. Maximum width of the lobes varied from 5 to 75 mm, and maximum height varied from 8 to 70 mm. Lobes were decorated with a variety of linear or notched designs; most common among these were oblique or horizontal lines cut by a single vertical line similar to the decoration on many of the castellations, but sometimes so short and deep as to resemble a punctate.

The variation in method of manufacture, size, and shape suggests that it is not any specific aspect of the lobes, but the lobes themselves, that are the common signal in these vessels. Of the many decorative treatments, the presence of inverted triangular lobes or notched rings around the base of the collar is one that appears to be common, if not pervasive, at Fort Shantok. Other decorative elements, including the treatment of the spaces created by the lobes or rings themselves, appear to be more variable. This pattern suggests that the various arrays of lines, punctates, notches, and impressions may reflect either assertive style, stylistic ideas common throughout the Northeast, or emblemic style representing a subgroup within the Mohegan community such as lineage, gender, or political faction. The highly visible lobes or rings themselves may represent emblemic style: a mark of Mohegan identity.

Contemporary Ceramics from Other Sites

How do contemporary assemblages from other sites compare to that of Fort Shantok? This question is difficult to answer conclusively because there are few contemporary assemblages that are comparable in size and context. Moreover, the use of typological analysis, which has predominated until very recently, makes it difficult to characterize assemblage variability. However, analysis of ceramic assemblages from eastern Long Is-

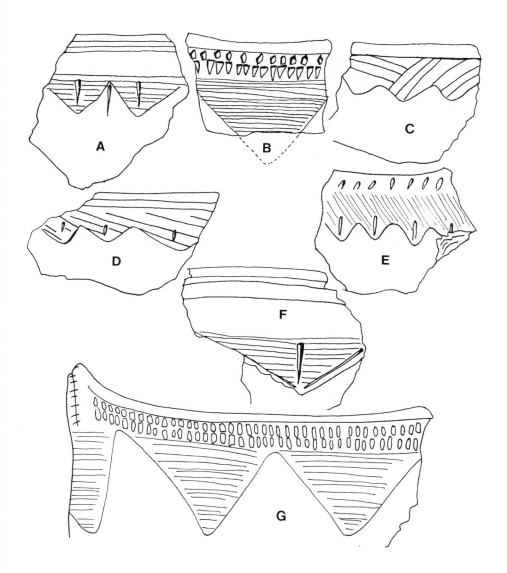

Fig. 4.3. Ceramic vessels from Fort Shantok showing lobes

land, the Narragansett Bay area, and the Fort Ninigret site, do provide some suggestive comparisons with Fort Shantok.

One 17th-century site on Long Island appears to share many ceramic attributes with Fort Shantok. This is Fort Corchaug, a fortified settlement, smaller than Shantok, which was associated with the Corchaug community of eastern Long Island. The site was excavated between 1936 and 1948 by Solecki (1950), and tested again in 1968 by Williams (1972). On the basis of the dates of European goods found at the site, the fort is thought to have been occupied during the first half of the 17th century (Solecki and Williams 1998).

From Solecki's and Williams's excavations, Williams analyzed a combined sample of 1,529 sherds of which 194 were decorated. All decorated sherds were similar to those from Fort Shantok; all of the decorative techniques and motifs encountered at Corchaug (including castellations, notched rings, and triangular nodes) were also represented at Shantok, although the reverse was not true (L. Williams 1972:370). An explanation for these similarities may be sought in the political environment of the inhabitants of Fort Corchaug.

The Corchaugs appear to have been part of a confederation of at least four eastern Long Island communities, sometimes called the Montauk Confederacy, whose sachems were referred to as brothers during at least part of the 17th century. Prior to the Pequot War, the Corchaugs and the other eastern Long Island communities were part of the Pequot Confederation. After the war, these groups became embroiled in the complex of alliances, land sales, tribute payments, threats, and acts of coercion among the Mohegans, Narragansetts, Niantics, English, and Dutch. Their uncertain status and their position as primary sources of wampum made them occasional targets of demands for and extortion of wampum on the part of both the Niantics and the Narragansetts (Ales 1979:49–61; L. Williams 1972:36; Winthrop 1944:43). At other times they were treated as allies, or at least potential allies, by, for example, Miantonomi in 1642 (Gardener 1897:142). Their relations with the Mohegans are even less well documented. However, at times both shared important English allies and Native enemies, both had been members of the Pequot Confederation, and both were apparently linked by kinship. Ales (1979:29) states that the two groups "were in close political, social and commercial contact." Fidelia Fielding, the renowned keeper of many Mohegan traditions, told Speck (1909:197) that "the old time Mohegans used to go down the Thames River and across Long Island Sound in dug out canoes. They were fond of visiting the Indians over there."

Simmons (1986:83) dates the events in Fielding's story to about 1740, but it likely reflects a relationship that predates the 18th century. In any case, it is certain that at least some of the inhabitants of Corchaug shared both kinship ties and political and economic interests with the inhabitants of Shantok. The ceramic evidence suggests that some of the Corchaugs attempted to signal an alliance or even identity with the Mohegans of Shantok through their material surroundings (e.g., ceramics).

Although the relationship between the Mohegans and the Corchaugs appears to have been generally close and cooperative, the opposite is certainly true for the Mohegans and the Narragansetts and Niantics. It should be unlikely that members of these communities would be signaling Mohegan identity. However, Shantok-tradition pottery, or at least pottery with some similarities to Shantok ware, has been recovered from several Contact-period sites within the historic territories of the Narragansett and Pokanoket-Wampanoag Confederations in what is now Rhode Island. A vessel from burial 6 at the West Ferry site in Jamestown contained a pot similar in decorative technique to those from Shantok; its short collar features a ring of inverted triangular lobes, each bisected by a vertical line. Unlike the pottery from Shantok, this vessel was not shell-tempered (Simmons 1970:89–93). Also from West Ferry, in the so-called "chief's" burial, was a shell-tempered pot with castellations and "vertically split [inverted triangular] nodes [lobes]" (Simmons 1970:156–58). The Burr's Hill cemetery in Warren contained an unusual double-collared pot that showed some similarities to Shantok pottery. It exhibited castellations with applied, deeply notched lobes, and coarse shell temper (Mrozowski 1980:86).

There are several possible explanations for the presence of these pots. They may have been acquired through exchange, discarded at the site by visiting Mohegans, or made at the site as local copies of Shantok pottery that borrow some of the motifs without the meanings. The latter is possible, especially if the target audience for Shantok pottery is the local community or immediate neighbors. Despite the frequent wars and tensions between the Mohegans and Narragansetts, there were undoubtedly genealogical ties between some members of the two groups, as Uncas himself claimed, and there must have been some contact, either directly or through intermediaries.

Is there any evidence for stylistic signaling of group identity through pottery among the Narragansetts, Pokanokets, or their member communities? At this point, it is unrecognized. Goodby's (1992, 1994, 1998) analysis of Late Woodland and Contact-period ceramics from the Narragansett Bay area uncovered significant diversity in stylistic attributes both within and among sites, along with evidence of an apparent intensification of decorative treatment in the Late Woodland and Contact periods. Goodby lists a variety of factors that may have been related to both the increasing volume of ceramic stylistic content and the specific meanings of ceramic decoration. These include (1) an apparent decline in long-distance interaction, (2) increased sedentism, (3) increasing reliance on horticulture, and (4) elaboration and differentiation of mortuary practices. Reasoning from this historical context, he further suggests three possible, nonexclusive, interpretations of ceramic style. It may express: (1) local social affiliation, such as residence unit or descent group, (2) "tribal" affiliation, or (3) gender categories that reflect a struggle over changing relations in production inherent in horticultural intensification and the growth of the fur trade (Goodby 1992). However, within the Narragansett Bay region, Goodby is unable to differentiate local decorative styles among communities or even to distinguish between Narragansett and Pokanoket ceramic styles. This pattern suggests that "no single ceramic design was being used to mark what some anthropologists [e.g., Speck 1928] have regarded as 'tribal' territories" (Goodby 1992:14).

Evidence from the Niantic site of Fort Ninigret also suggests that some Shantok or Shantok-like pottery was making its way into southern Rhode Island. However, although the ceramics from this site resemble Shantok ware technologically, they lack the distinctive decorative treatments of the pottery from Fort Shantok, and therefore are significantly different from Shantok ware in the most important ways. Fort Ninigret is located in present-day Charlestown, Rhode Island. It was used in the 17th century as a small, seasonally occupied, fortified habitation, possibly a trading center, associated with the Niantic community and their sachem Ninigret. Excavations conducted by Salwen and Mayer in 1976 and 1977 uncovered a small palisaded area that contained sheet midden, discrete refuse deposits, a large storage pit, and evidence for both Late Woodland and 17th-century occupation (Mayer 1985). The sample of 931 ceramic sherds was considered to be small compared to other contemporary sites, perhaps reflecting a limited presence of women there (Mayer 1985:19–20). The ceramic assemblage was analyzed by Mayer using the standard southern New England classification system based on the definitions and subsequent refinements of Rouse (1945), Smith (1950), Solecki (1950), Salwen (1969), Williams (1972), and Lavin (1980, 1984). Using this approach, Mayer classified 206 sherds as Shantok-tradition pottery, primarily on the basis of temper (large amounts of fine shell), color (buff, gray, and black surfaces with black interiors), thickness (3–7.5 mm with an average of 5 mm), and smooth, wiped, or scraped surfaces (Mayer 1985:5–6). Other classes of pottery based on similar kinds of attributes include several Windsor-tradition varieties, probably from a Late Woodland component.

Interestingly, although Mayer classifies the pottery as belonging to the Shantok tradition, she notes that the vessels "do not have the castellations, applied bosses, fillets and lobes which are found at the contemporary Long Island Sound–southern New England sites of related groups" (Mayer 1985:12). Significantly, although the ceramic assemblage at Fort Ninigret is technologically similar to the Fort Shantok assemblage, it lacks the most distinctive decorative attributes of the pottery from Fort Shantok. This disparity suggests that Shantok-tradition ceramics, as a classificatory construct, may represent a mixture of stylistic and technological attributes having overlapping but discontinuous distributions. It also exemplifies the difficulty in representing such complex variation using a typological approach to ceramic analysis, which can overlook important information on the significance of Shantok ware. Most importantly, it suggests that some of the spatially restricted, more distinctive decorative features of Shantok pottery are emblemic style, representing Mohegan identity.

Summary and Conclusions

During the Late Woodland and Contact periods, the Native peoples of southern New England began to decorate their ceramics more intensively. More pots were decorated and these pots contained more decorative treatments. Furthermore, this decoration became increasingly diverse, and the many different decorative elements had varying distributions. Undoubtedly this variation arose from a wide variety of sources. Women, who created the ceramics and gave them their form and decorations, were concerned with creating functional cookware and containers that also carried social information. Among the social issues or messages that may have been expressed through pottery were those most closely associated with women's status in the family or in the community. The importance of agriculture and agricultural land, one of the sources of women's economic power, was doubtless an important aspect of gender politics, as were the maintenance and transformation of traditional gender roles (hunting, gathering, farming, trading, politics, and ritual), obligations, and privileges (see Handsman 1990; Nassaney, chap. 15). Women were also participants in political struggles that crosscut gender lines—competition or cooperation among families, residential or descent groups, lineages, communities, or confederations.

One of these political processes was the development and elaboration of community or supra-community political identity. The nature of this identity appears to have been transformed at different times and places and in response to different pressures, constraints, and opportunities. I have argued that among the Mohegans and some of their allies on Long Island, the issue of group identity was of particular importance. In order to create a unified group comprising very disparate parts, and to maintain cohesion under a variety of pressures, the Mohegans developed a new kind of group identity, and both expressed and promoted this new ideal through material culture. The distinctive pottery of Fort Shantok was one expression of this new identity. Although the elaborately decorated vessels of Shantok, like most of the Native ceramics of 17th-century southern New England, certainly contained an abundance of messages, many of which are lost to us, one of the most important of these signals was Mohegan identity.

The distribution of Shantok ware suggests its association with the Mohegan people and their closest allies. It predominates at Fort Shantok and Fort Corchaug, is not uncommon in areas historically associated with Mohegan influence, and is not absent, but certainly much rarer, elsewhere in southern New England. The distinctive decorative treatments of the pottery from Forts Shantok and Corchaug further suggest that at least some decorative elements represent emblemic style: an assertion of group identity.

Assessing variation in ceramics, let alone its significance, is an uncertain and subjective task. This is especially true when one is confronted with typological studies that tend both to subsume the variation in ceramics and to ignore the importance of the people who made them. Future research should focus on attribute analysis, the comparison of site assemblages rather than typologically defined units, and consideration of the social context of the makers, users, and viewers of pottery, as well as other elements of material culture. Such research can give us a clearer picture of the patterns of variation in ceramics and may ultimately foster a greater understanding of the processes motivating the potters who were creating the ceramics.

In this study, a complex and dynamic picture of Native politics is complemented and enriched by a study of pottery, which is itself enriched by placing it in a social and political context. Pottery—and any form of material culture—is understood as the product of people with goals, concerns, identities, and histories. That understanding permits archaeologists to link the objects that we study with the objects of our study. The tie that binds pots and politics is people.

Acknowledgments

I thank Russell Handsman and the staff at the former American Indian Archaeological Institute (since renamed the Institute for American Indian Studies) in Washington, Connecticut, for access to the Rogers collection from Shantok. Many thanks to Michael Nassaney for his enthusiasm and insight. I would also like to thank Dena Dincauze, Arthur Keene, Barry O'Connell, Neal Salisbury, and Rita Reinke for their general encouragement and guidance in this research. Valuable comments and suggestions on earlier drafts of this chapter were offered by Michael Nassaney, Rita Reinke, and three anonymous reviewers. Any errors of fact and interpretation are strictly my own.

References Cited

Ales, Marion Fisher. 1979. A History of the Indians on Montauk, Long Island. In *The History and Archaeology of the Montauk Indians*, 13–124. Readings in Long Island Archaeology and Ethnohistory, vol. 3. Suffolk County Archaeological Association, Stony Brook, N.Y.

Arnold, Dean. 1985. *Ceramic Theory and Cultural Process*. Cambridge University Press, New York.

Bragdon, Kathleen J. 1996. *Native People of Southern New England, 1500–1650*. University of Oklahoma Press, Norman.

Braun, David P. 1991. Why Decorate a Pot? Midwestern Household Pottery, 200 B.C.–A.D. 600. *Journal of Anthropological Archaeology* 10:360–97.

Brumbach, Hetty Jo. 1975. "Iroquoian" Ceramics in "Algonkian" Territory. *Man in the Northeast* 10:17–28.

Burton, William John. 1976. Hellish Fiends and Brutish Men: Amerindian-Euroamerican Interaction in Southern New England, An Interdisciplinary Analysis, 1600–1750. Ph.D. diss., Kent State University, Kent, Ohio.

Burton, William J., and Richard Lowenthal. 1974. The First of the Mohegans. *American Ethnologist* 1:589–99.

Byers, Douglas S., and Irving Rouse. 1960. A Reexamination of the Guida Farm. *Bulletin of the Archaeological Society of Connecticut* 30:3–43.

Cave, Alfred A. 1996. *The Pequot War*. University of Massachusetts Press, Amherst.

Chilton, Elizabeth S. 1996. Embodiments of Choice: Native American Ceramic Diversity in the New England Interior. Ph.D. diss., University of Massachusetts, Amherst.

————. 1998. The Cultural Origins of Technical Choice: Unraveling Algonquian and Iroquoian Ceramic Traditions in the Northeast. In *The Archaeology of Social Boundaries,* ed. Miriam T. Stark, 132–60. Smithsonian Institution Press, Washington, D.C.

Conkey, Margaret. 1990. Experimenting with Style in Archaeology: Some Historical and Theoretical Issues. In *The Uses of Style in Archaeology,* ed. Margaret Conkey and Christine A. Hastorf, 5–17. Cambridge University Press, Cambridge

Deetz, James F. 1965. *The Dynamics of Stylistic Change in Arikara Ceramics.* Illinois Studies in Anthropology no. 4, University of Illinois Press, Urbana.

De Forest, John W. [1851] 1964. *History of the Indians of Connecticut: From the Earliest Known Period to 1850.* Archon Books, Hamden, Conn.

Engelbrecht, William. 1974. The Iroquois: Archaeological Patterning on the Tribal Level. *World Archaeology* 6:52–65.

Gardener, Lion. [1736] 1897. Leift Lion Gardener His Relation of the Pequot Warres. In *History of the Pequot War,* ed. C. Orr, 113–49. Helman-Taylor, Cleveland.

Goodby, Robert G. 1992. Diversity as a Typological Construct: Understanding Late Woodland Ceramics from Narragansett Bay. Paper presented at the annual meeting of the Northeastern Anthropological Association, Bridgewater, Mass.

————. 1994. Style, Meaning, and History: A Contextual Study of 17th Century Native American Ceramics from Southeastern New England. Ph.D. diss., Brown University, Providence, R.I.

————. 1998. Technological Patterning and Social Boundaries: Ceramic Variability in Southern New England, A.D. 1000–1675. In *The Archaeology of Social Boundaries,* ed. Miriam T. Stark, 161–82. Smithsonian Institution Press, Washington, D.C.

Handsman, Russell G. 1988a. Algonkian Women Resist Colonialism. *Artifacts* 16(3,4):29–31.

————. 1988b. Chahnameed and a Mohegan Woman's Mortars. *Artifacts* 16(3,4):11–27.

————. 1989. *The Fort Hill Project: Native Americans in Western Connecticut and an Archaeology of Living Traditions.* American Indian Archaeological Institute, Washington, Conn.

————. 1990. Corn and Culture, Pots and Politics: How to Listen to the Voices of Mohegan Women. Paper presented at the annual meeting of the Society for Historical Archaeology, Tucson, Ariz.

Hodder, Ian. 1978. Simple Correlations between Material Culture and Society: A Review. In *The Spatial Organization of Culture,* ed. Ian Hodder, 3–24. Duckworth, London.

————. 1979. Economic and Social Stress and Material Culture Patterning. *American Antiquity* 44:446–54.

Johnson, Eric S. 1993. "Some by Flatteries and Others by Threatenings": Political Strategies among Native Americans of Seventeenth-Century Southern New England. Ph.D. diss., University of Massachusetts, Amherst. University Microfilms, Ann Arbor.

———. 1996. Uncas and the Politics of Contact. In *Northeastern Indian Lives,* ed. Robert S. Grumet, 29–47. University of Massachusetts Press, Amherst.

———. 1999. Community and Confederation: A Political Geography of Contact Period Southern New England. In *The Archaeological Northeast,* ed. M. A. Levine, K. E. Sassaman, and M. S. Nassaney, 155–68. Bergin and Garvey, Westport, Conn.

Josselyn, John. [1675] 1833. *An Account of Two Voyages to New England.* Collections of the Massachusetts Historical Society, 3d ser., vol. 3, 211–354. E. W. Metcalf and Co., Boston.

Lavin, Lucianne. 1980. Analysis of Ceramic Vessels from the Ben Hollister Site. *Bulletin of the Archaeological Society of Connecticut* 43:3–4.

———. 1984. Connecticut Prehistory: A Synthesis of Current Archaeological Investigations. *Bulletin of the Archaeological Society of Connecticut* 43:3–41.

———. 1986. Pottery Classification and Cultural Models in Southern New England. *North American Archaeologist* 7(1):1–14.

Lizee, Jonathan M. 1989a. Niantic, Hackney Pond, and Shantok: An Examination of the Late Woodland and Contact Period Ceramic Typology in Southern New England. Paper presented at the annual meeting of the Northeastern Anthropological Association, Montreal.

———. 1989b. Stylistic Diversity and the Riddle of Shantok. Paper presented at the annual meeting of the Eastern States Archaeological Federation, East Windsor, Conn.

Lizee, Jonathan M., Hector Neff, and Michael Glascock. 1992. Clay Acquisition and Vessel Distribution Patterns: Neutron Activation Analysis of Late Windsor and Shantok Tradition Ceramics from Southern New England. *American Antiquity* 60(3):515–30.

Longacre, William A. 1970. *Archaeology as Anthropology: A Case Study.* Anthropological Papers of the University of Arizona no. 17, Tucson.

Mayer, Susan N. 1985. Ceramics at Fort Ninigret, Charlestown, Rhode Island. Paper presented at the annual meeting of the Society for American Archaeology, Denver.

McBride, Kevin A. 1984. Prehistory of the Lower Connecticut River Valley. Ph.D. diss., University of Connecticut, Storrs. University Microfilms, Ann Arbor.

———. 1990. Archaeology of the Mashantucket Pequots. In *The Pequots in Southern New England: The Fall and Rise of an American Indian Nation,* ed. L. M. Hauptman and J. D. Wherry, 96–116. University of Oklahoma Press, Norman.

McMullen, Ann, and Russell G. Handsman, eds. 1987. *A Key into the Language of Woodsplint Baskets.* American Indian Archaeological Institute, Washington, Conn.

Mrozowski, Stephen. 1980. Aboriginal Ceramics. In *Burr's Hill: A 17th Century Wampanoag Burial Ground in Warren, Rhode Island*, ed. S. G. Gibson, 84–87. Studies in Anthropology and Material Culture, vol. 2. Haffenreffer Museum of Anthropology, Brown University, Providence, R.I.

Pulsifer, David, ed. 1859. *Records of the Colony of New Plymouth in New England*, vol. 9, *Acts of the Commissioners of the United Colonies of New England*, pt. 1, *1643–1651*. William White, Boston.

Robinson, Paul A. 1990. The Struggle Within: The Indian Debate in Seventeenth Century Narragansett Country. Ph.D. diss., State University of New York at Binghamton. University Microfilms, Ann Arbor.

Rouse, Irving. 1945. Styles of Pottery in Connecticut. *Bulletin of the Massachusetts Archaeological Society* 7(1):1–8

———. [1947] 1980. Ceramic Traditions and Sequences in Connecticut. *Bulletin of the Archaeological Society of Connecticut* 43:57–75.

Salisbury, Neal. 1982. *Manitou and Providence: Indians, Europeans, and the Making of New England, 1500–1643*. Oxford University Press, New York.

Salwen, Bert. 1966. European Trade Goods and the Chronology of the Fort Shantock Site. *Bulletin of the Archaeological Society of Connecticut* 34:5–39.

———. 1969. A Tentative "in situ" Solution to the Mohegan-Pequot Problem. In *An Introduction to the Archaeology and History of the Connecticut Valley Indian*, ed. W. R. Young, 81–88. Springfield Museum of Science Publications n.s. 1 (1). Springfield, Mass.

Saville, Foster H. 1920. A Montauk Cemetery at Easthampton, Long Island. *Indian Notes and Monographs* 2(3):59–102. Museum of the American Indian, Heye Foundation, New York.

Simmons, William S. 1970. *Cautantowwit's House: An Indian Burial Ground on the Island of Conanicut in Narragansett Bay*. Brown University Press, Providence.

———. 1986. *Spirit of the New England Tribes: Indian History and Folklore, 1620–1984*. University Press of New England, Hanover, N.H.

Smith, Carlyle S. [1947] 1980. An Outline of the Archaeology of Coastal New York. *Bulletin of the Archaeological Society of Connecticut* 43:47–56.

———. 1950. *The Archaeology of Coastal New York*. Anthropological Papers of the American Museum of Natural History, vol. 43 (2), American Museum of Natural History, New York.

Solecki, Ralph S. 1950. The Archaeological Position of Historic Fort Corchaug, Long Island and Its Relation to Contemporary Forts. *Bulletin of the Archaeological Society of Connecticut* 24:3–40.

Solecki, Ralph S., and Lorraine E. Williams. 1998. Fort Corchaug Archaeological Site National Historic Landmark. *The Bulletin: Journal of the New York State Archaeological Association* 114:2–11.

Speck, Frank G. 1903. A Pequot-Mohegan Witchcraft Tale. *Journal of American Folklore*. 16(61):104–6.

———. 1909. Notes on the Mohegan and Niantic Indians. In *The Indians of*

Greater New York and the Lower Hudson, ed. C. Wissler, 181–210. Anthropological Papers of the American Museum of Natural History, vol. 3. American Museum of Natural History, New York.

———. 1915. Decorative Art of Indian Tribes of Connecticut. Canada Department of Mines Geological Survey Memoir 75, no. 10, Anthropological Series. Government Printing Bureau, Ottawa.

Stark, Miriam T. 1998. Technical Choices and Social Boundaries in Material Culture Patterning: An Introduction. In The Archaeology of Social Boundaries, ed. Miriam T. Stark, 1–11. Smithsonian Institution Press, Washington, D.C.

Tantaquidgeon, Gladys, and Jayne G. Fawcett. 1987. Symbolic Motifs on Painted Baskets of the Mohegan-Pequot. In A Key into the Language of Woodsplint Baskets, ed. Ann McMullen and R. G. Handsman, 94–101. American Indian Archaeological Institute, Washington, Conn.

Thomas, Peter A. 1979. In the Maelstrom of Change: The Indian Trade and Cultural Process in the Middle Connecticut River Valley: 1635–1665. Ph.D. diss., University of Massachusetts, Amherst. University Microfilms, Ann Arbor.

Trumbull, James Hammond, ed. 1859. The Public Records of the Colony of Connecticut: May 1678–June 1689. Case, Lockwood and Co., Hartford.

Volmar, Michael. 1992. The Conundrum of Effigy Pestles. Master's thesis, Department of Anthropology, University of Massachusetts, Amherst.

Weissner, Polly. 1983. Style and Social Information in Kalahari San Projectile Points. American Antiquity 48(2):253–76.

Whallon, Robert. 1968. Investigations of Late Prehistoric Social Organization in New York State. In New Perspectives in Archaeology, ed. S. R. Binford and L. R. Binford, 223–44. Aldine, Chicago.

Williams, Lorraine E. 1972. Fort Shantock and Fort Corchaug: A Comparative Study of Seventeenth Century Culture Change in the Long Island Sound Area. Ph.D. diss., New York University. University Microfilms, Ann Arbor.

Williams, Roger. 1963. The Complete Writings of Roger Williams, vol. 6, ed. J. R. Bartlett. Russell and Russell, New York.

———. [1643] 1973. A Key into the Language of America, ed. J. J. Teunissen and E. J. Hinz. Wayne State University Press, Detroit.

Winthrop, John. 1944. Winthrop Papers, vol. 4, 1638–44, ed. A. B. Forbes. Massachusetts Historical Society, Boston.

Wobst, H. Martin. 1977. Stylistic Behavior and Information Exchange. In Papers for the Director: Research Essays in Honor of James B. Griffin, ed. C. E. Cleland, 317–42. Anthropology Papers, vol. 61. Museum of Anthropology, University of Michigan, Ann Arbor.

Wood, William. [1634] 1977. New England's Prospect, ed. A. T. Vaughan. University of Massachusetts Press, Amherst.

Wright, Rita P. 1991. Women's Labor and Pottery Production in Prehistory. In Engendering Archaeology: Women and Prehistory, ed. Joan Gero and Margaret Conkey, 194–223. Basil Blackwell, Oxford.

5

Emblems of Ethnicity

Ribbonwork Garments from the Great Lakes Region

Susan M. Neill

For me, the most powerful moments of learning usually emerge from mundane encounters. Once in a while, when I find myself working with a collection in a dim museum basement, something about the object in my hands strikes a chord in me. A piece may not be markedly different from the last five or even fifty objects I've handled, and yet it is. I feel a profound sense of connection with the user of this spoon, or the dancer who brought this skirt to life, or the potter who held this bowl in much the way I am holding it now. These visceral perceptions are fleeting but unforgettable, akin to Stephen Greenblatt's (1991) "resonance" and "wonder" collapsed into a single experience.[1] Encountering objects is a powerful way of knowing them. As art historian Jules Prown points out, experience with objects is something we can share with people living in other places and time periods (1982).

Intuition is, of course, only one way of comprehending an item's significance. Inherent in every object is an observable set of qualities that convey information about the culture in which it was produced. Some facts are obvious, like the availability of materials or technology, while information about individual and cultural values may be more subtle. In order to recognize significant differences among similar objects, it may be necessary to measure and draw, tabulate, and tally the objects and their attributes. Additional sources, including written and pictographic records and interviews with makers and users of similar objects, can provide additional contextual information about production, meaning, and use.

This material culture study of ribbonwork originated in the examination of historic examples in the collection of the Milwaukee Public Museum. Ribbonwork is a unique art form used to adorn clothing and other personal items. It was developed by American Indian women in the Great Lakes region after the introduction of European, commercially woven goods. The term *ribbonwork* refers to specific cutting and sewing techniques that emphasize the shape, color, and texture of long, woven bands of silk called "ribbons." Ribbonwork panels are usually sewn onto a lightweight cotton backing and then attached to wool trade cloth. Designs are often bilaterally symmetrical, and some intricate panels incorporate more than twenty layers of ribbon. Ribbonwork is a syncretic tradition—a composite of European materials and Indian style. Although new designs, techniques, and materials have been introduced throughout the history of ribbonwork, contemporary ribbon appliqué bears strong resemblance to its early antecedents. The persistence of ribbonwork-adorned clothing for more than two hundred years suggests that it is both an important tradition and a significant marker of ethnic identity.

Based primarily on the date and the location where each object was collected, donors and collectors have attributed the forty-three pieces in the Milwaukee Public Museum collection to ten tribes, including several examples of Fox, Menominee, Potawatomi, Sauk, and Winnebago ribbonwork (see table 5.1). Additional data was collected in Chicago at the Field Museum of Natural History, which contains thirty-three examples attributed to seven tribes. This method of identification, by no means unique to these museums, is simplistic in that it ignores the complexities of American Indian life, including intermarriage, gift giving, and intertribal collecting. It is possible that some of these cultural attributions are incorrect. Therefore, an ascription system based on other criteria, such as stylistic attributes, may prove to be useful.

The immediate goal of this study is to determine which criteria, such as use of color, motifs, construction techniques, and garment design, are associated with the ribbonwork of various North American Indian tribes or ethnic groups. These observations can be used to construct a model based on visual characteristics that can be tested and further refined by applying it to additional specimens. Developing a system for attributing specific ribbonwork decorated objects to particular tribes is deemed useful because information about objects in museum collections is often incomplete.

Beyond developing a system of attribution, the larger goal of this preliminary investigation of ribbonwork is to probe the significance of this

Table 5.1. Cultural attributions and techniques of ribbonwork in collections in the Milwaukee Public Museum and the Field Museum of Natural History, Chicago

Cultural attribution	Count	Ribbonwork style				
		Developmental	Shingled	Positive	Negative	Appliqué
Ioway	1	0	1	0	0	0
Kickapoo	1	1	1	0	0	0
Menominee	11	2	4	6	0	3
Mesquakie[a]	24	3	7	9	2	6
Miami	2	0	2	0	0	0
Ojibwe	2	0	2	1	0	0
Omaha	2	2	0	0	0	1
Osage	5	1	2	1	2	0
Potawatomi	17	3	10	5	0	4
Winnebago	11	5	0	5	0	6
Totals	76	17	29	27	4	20

a. Includes Fox, Sauk and Fox, Sauk.

unique textile tradition. Due to the fragile nature of textiles and their general absence from the archaeological record, it is important to consider textiles as part of the larger material repertoire. In this chapter I attempt to convey the historic and contemporary meanings of ribbonwork. The first section introduces the roots and development of the tradition. The middle segment draws on a variety of visual, ethnographic, and primary sources that inform our understanding of the tradition. The final section presents some conclusions about the significance of ribbonwork, offers hypotheses toward establishing a system of attribution, and considers the implications of this study for additional research.

Historical and Technical Development

The Emerging Ribbonwork Tradition

The strong contemporary tradition of ribbon appliqué practiced by American Indian women in the Great Lakes region and in the southern Plains has its roots in the fur trade in the late 18th and 19th centuries. Through participation in this trade, Native Americans acquired a host of European materials, including metal cooking pots, guns, and wool cloth, that dramatically altered their ways of life (e.g., Quimby 1966; Rogers 1990). During this period, French and British traders often found themselves competing for Indians' favor, reflected in their preference for superior trade goods.

Indians obtained silk ribbons as gifts and through trade, but when, where, and how they were first acquired is unknown. Rachel Pannabecker (1986) conducted extensive research on the distribution of ribbons for her dissertation, which focuses on the development, diffusion, and endurance of ribbonwork within a cultural context fostering change. Pannabecker (1986) noted that Delaware Indians received silk ribbons as partial payment for some land in Pennsylvania in 1732. Further, her research into journals, traders' logs, and inventories in the United States, Canada, and France has demonstrated that between 1754 and 1779 traders in New York, Indiana, Illinois, and Pennsylvania stocked silk ribbons for the fur trade (Pannabecker 1986:109–11). Thus, we know that by the late 1770s ribbons were available throughout the Great Lakes region via trade networks. Textiles, including the wool cloth known as stroud, and printed cotton, called calico, had been mentioned in traders' lists for some time. According to Pannabecker, the addition of ribbon to traders' lists beginning in the 1740s suggests an increase in the value of silk ribbon in the Great Lakes region (1986:140).

Indians used the imported ribbons to adorn their robes, leggings, breechcloths, skirts, shawls, and other garments in much the same manner they were employed on fashionable European clothing. Beyond attaching ribbons as simple loops and borders, American Indian women invented new techniques for utilizing this trade material. The simplest and most widespread form of ribbonwork appeared as a sawtooth pattern. Ribbonwork panels in this basic form are almost always used in conjunction with more elaborate motifs.

The earliest dated example of ribbonwork is displayed on a mannequin at the Neville Museum in Green Bay, Wisconsin. This Menominee outfit includes the elaborate ribbonwork-decorated skirt and shawl of red stroud and blue woolen leggings worn by Sophie Therese Rankin at her wedding in 1802 (Conn 1980:12). Several advanced ribbonwork techniques and more than a hundred yards of blue, red, black, yellow, and green ribbon were used to create the ensemble. Based on this example, researchers agree that ribbonwork was a fully developed art form by the beginning of the 19th century.

While the specifics are unknowable concerning where ribbonwork was developed and by whom, the distinctive geometric designs of this post-Contact art form clearly relate to earlier American Indian textile traditions, including twined bags and quillwork. Carleen Ann McPharlin-Coen

(1974) has explored the related motifs found in several Great Lakes textile traditions. She posits that the proliferation of diamond patterns in quillwork and ribbonwork are rooted in old and established craft traditions that include twined and woven bags (McPharlin-Coen 1974:7). It is likely that textile artisans experimenting with new materials would continue to explore traditional motifs that appeared on ceramics or other materials, for example. McPharlin-Coen (1974:2) has argued that "cross-stimulation" occurs when a pattern developed in one medium is introduced and elaborated in another. The antiquity of the diamond motif and the relative simplicity of creating such designs likely explain the proliferation of diamond patterns in ribbonwork, including the so-called "otter tail" and McPharlin-Coen's "diamond-wave."

The other main pattern type in Great Lakes ribbonwork is curvilinear. These motifs can often be described as stylized floral designs that commonly appear in conjunction with simple sawtooth patterns. The characteristic mirrored designs result from the use of patterns cut from folded paper. Stylized floral designs in ribbonwork and contemporary appliqué are akin to other craft traditions, including birch bark patterns, both bitten (Densmore 1974) and cut-out (Howard 1980). The nonfloral curvilinear designs are often best described with Frank Speck's classic term for Algonquian motifs—the "double-curve" (1982).

Although utilizing entirely new materials, the Great Lakes tradition of ribbonwork relates to earlier art forms in its use of traditional design motifs. The techniques American Indian women developed to produce ribbonwork were disseminated throughout the region and finally extended to the southern Plains in the mid-19th century, when tribes such as the Winnebago, Potawatomi, and Kickapoo were "removed" to reservations there. The Mesquakie, historically called the Fox or the Sauk and Fox, are another group who adopted the practice of ribbonwork. They came to reside in central Iowa after they purchased land there a decade after their removal to a reservation in northeastern Kansas. In sum, ribbonwork is a unique textile tradition, utilizing ribbon and wool cloth, that was never adopted by non-Indians. Ribbonwork-decorated garments remain, to this day, expressive material markers of Native American identity.

Ribbonwork Techniques

Like most needlework traditions, ribbonwork is a woman's art taught to the young by mothers, aunts, and grandmothers (Riley 1995; State Arts Council of Oklahoma 1990). American Indian women utilize several construction techniques in this art form. Likewise, researchers have proposed several systems for classifying types of ribbonwork (e.g., Abbass 1979; Conn 1980; Marriott 1958; Marriott and Rachlin 1980). Of these typologies, only Abbass's system approaches the medium from the artisan's perspective and thereby best serves to describe the intricate examples that combine techniques. Emic categories allow us to view the pieces as they are constructed and avoid many observers' biases. Abbass initially described the typology in her dissertation "Contemporary Oklahoma Ribbonwork: Styles and Economics" (1979), which presents four styles of ribbonwork called developmental, shingled, positive, and negative. This classification system is simple and clear and, unlike the others, avoids unnecessary speculation about the evolution of ribbonwork techniques.

The following descriptions of ribbonwork techniques are based on Abbass's (1979) typology. The basic technique of ribbonwork forms a sawtooth pattern that is called "developmental." It is formed by placing one length of ribbon on top of another, making a series of perpendicular cuts into one long edge of the upper layer, folding the raw edges under, and stitching the layers together (see fig. 5.1). The second style, known as

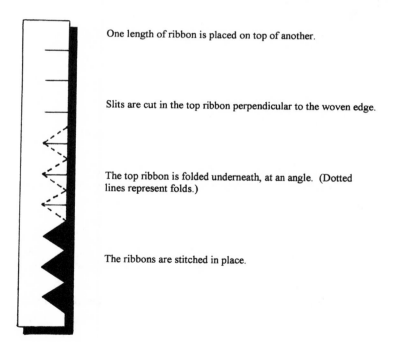

One length of ribbon is placed on top of another.

Slits are cut in the top ribbon perpendicular to the woven edge.

The top ribbon is folded underneath, at an angle. (Dotted lines represent folds.)

The ribbons are stitched in place.

Fig. 5.1. Construction of a simple "developmental" strip

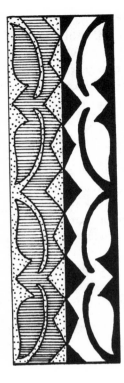

Fig. 5.2. Construction of a positive continuous strip with bilateral symmetry from a matched design, _Green_/Orange + Black_Yellow_. Based on Mesquakie skirt no. 17589/1471, Field Museum of Natural History, Chicago.

"shingled," is an elaboration on this basic technique repeated with several layers of ribbon. The other two ribbonwork techniques are formed with pairs of ribbons; when the top layer of ribbon forms the design it is "positive" (see fig. 5.2), and when the bottom layer makes the design it is referred to as "negative." Positive ribbonwork is frequently embroidered with herringbone stitches or secured with machine zigzag stitching.

Abbass's typology was developed to describe ribbonwork in Oklahoma. In order to establish a more universal system for describing ribbonwork in the Great Lakes region and continue to maintain what Abbass (1979:98) has called "ethnoscientific validity" (presumably observable characteristics significant within the culture studied), a fifth category must be added to represent contemporary ribbonworkers' term for their craft—ribbon appliqué (Carufel 1981; Riley 1995; Torrence and Hobbs 1989). This technique underscores a shift in design from cut and folded lengths of ribbon to cut out and sewn appliqués. Appliqué ribbonwork resembles positive ribbonwork insofar as designs in both techniques are formed by the top layer of ribbon (see fig. 5.3). All of the stitchers whom I consulted referred to their craft as ribbon appliqué. Thus, the term "ribbonwork" is used here to describe the tradition and techniques in general, but "ribbon appliqué" denotes the technique used almost exclusively in the Great Lakes region today.

In addition to her typology, Abbass has also formulated a system of notation to indicate which ribbon establishes the figure, as well as the order in which ribbons were applied to form the design. For example, the design in figure 5.2 can be described as a positive ribbon stripe with green and yellow figures and orange and black backgrounds, or it can be written as _Green_/Orange + Black_Yellow_. Underlining indicates the figure, "+" indicates a separate stripe, while the slashes and backslashes convey the arrangement of the layers. Thus, the notation can be used to differentiate between two visually identical but structurally different designs such as

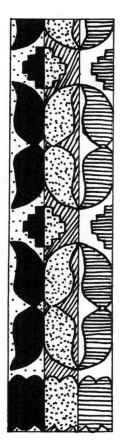

Fig. 5.3. Construction of an appliqué strip with bilateral symmetry, _Blue_/Yellow + Pink_Black_ + _Orange_/White. Based on Menominee appliqué strip no. 155875/1618-3, Field Museum of Natural History, Chicago.

Red/*White* and Red*White*. The notation system and five construction types described above are clearly descriptive of the Great Lakes ribbonwork tradition.

Later Technical Developments

No tradition, including ribbonwork, is static. Individuals express their creativity within the parameters of the tradition and are guided by the availability of materials. Discussing a particular skirt design, contemporary Mesquakie ribbonworker Adeline Wanatee explains, "This design is taken from a pattern of my Aunt Mary, but I have made changes in it" (Torrence and Hobbs 1989:49–50). Certain innovations are unique while others are taken up by the group and eventually alter the tradition. (See Johnson in chapter 4 on assertive and emblemic style.) Along with new materials, new tools are sometimes used in ribbonwork. Ribbonwork has seen many transitory innovations. In museum collections occasional ribbonwork-decorated garments are adorned with sequins, bells, and rickrack (a narrow zigzag braid), while numerous examples are ornamented with silver brooches or pins.

Other innovations have had a more enduring effect on the ribbonwork tradition. The introduction of the sewing machine, the use of appliqué designs, and the adoption of fabric widths for main design elements have had lasting influence on the tradition. While it is uncertain when Native American women began using sewing machines to produce ribbonwork, some women undoubtedly used them as soon as they were accessible (Feder 1956:13). Inventors contrived several sewing machine designs in the first half of the 19th century, but the first practical sewing machine was produced by Isaac M. Singer in 1851. This treadle sewing machine swiftly gained popularity with seamstresses. The sewing machine has been used to construct garments, to attach plain lengths of ribbon, and to sew simple ribbonwork designs. While it is possible that some ribbonwork was being machine sewn by the 1860s and 1870s, it is likely another decade or two passed before American Indian women had access to sewing machines. The earliest machine-sewn pieces I have encountered to date were collected in Wisconsin in 1917. Ribbonwork panels on both of these Potawatomi pieces were sewn by machine to a wool base. More accurate dates for early use of sewing machines in ribbonwork could be determined by conducting a comprehensive survey of ribbonwork in museum collections.

Such a survey would also reflect the transition from positive to appliqué designs in Great Lakes ribbonwork. True appliqué, created by cutting a design from one fabric and sewing it on top of another, emerges around the beginning of the 20th century. A Menominee robe accessioned by the Milwaukee Public Museum in 1922 (see figs. 5.4 and 5.5) combines both of these techniques and marks the transition between "old time" ribbonwork—which emphasizes continuous lengths of ribbon—and the contemporary tradition called "ribbon appliqué." It should be noted that museum objects were often made and sometimes used long before they were collected; thus an object's collection date is not its production date, but merely the most recent date it could have been made. Furthermore, the hearts and double-curve motifs on the Menominee robe shown in figures 5.4 and 5.5 are appliquéd onto the under layer. In contrast, the hearts on the Winnebago skirt in figure 5.6 are not sewn on top of the other ribbons, but placed under them to supply contrast where the hearts have been removed. The latter technique is known as reverse appliqué. Accessioned

Fig. 5.4. Front view of the vivid red Menominee robe no. 29969/7216, Milwaukee Public Museum. Note the combination of "positive" and "appliqué" techniques, as well as the figure/ground ambiguity in this sophisticated design. Dimensions as depicted: length 132 cm, width 88 cm.

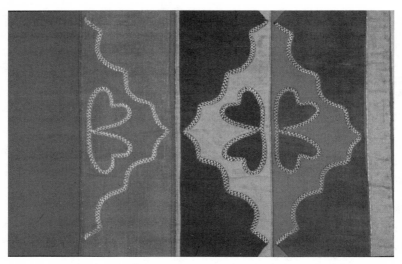

Fig. 5.5. Right detail of Menominee robe no. 29969/7216, Milwaukee Public Museum. Note the appliquéd hearts and fine herringbone hand stitching.

Fig. 5.6. Front detail of heart and flower motif on Winnebago skirt no. 3350/570, accessioned by the Milwaukee Public Museum in 1907. This stunning example of "positive" ribbonwork has contrasting reverse appliquéd hearts and herringbone hand stitching.

by the Milwaukee Public Museum in 1907, the Winnebago skirt supports the proposition that ribbonworkers were experimenting with appliqué techniques at the turn of the century.

In addition to adopting the sewing machine and developing appliqué techniques, ribbonworkers initiated another long-term change in their craft when they began utilizing widths of fabric in place of ribbons. According to anthropologist Alice Marriott (1958:54), the width of the ribbons used in the decorative panels increased from half an inch in early pieces to twelve inches in the early 20th century. While reflecting a trend, this statement is not wholly credible since the earliest example of ribbonwork, the 1802 Menominee wedding outfit mentioned above, includes many rows of ribbon several inches in width. A firm date for the shift to using fabrics instead of ribbon in the main design elements has not been established, although ribbons continue to be used for developmental borders and edgings. It appears that the development of appliqué and use of fabric occurred concurrently. Plausibly, silk ribbon became too scarce or costly to use in ribbonwork. However, the reverse may also be true; use of the cut-out appliqué technique may have prompted women to select fabric in order to create designs wider than available ribbons.

Apart from isolated instances of improvisation, it is clear that the ribbonwork tradition underwent significant changes during the late 19th and early 20th centuries. Use of sewing machines, the popularity of the appliqué technique, and the shift from ribbon to fabric all occur during this period. Because of their contemporaneity, it is currently unclear how each of these trends affected the others. For instance, did appliqué become popular because ribbons were unavailable? Or did it gain prevalence because it freed ribbonworkers from the confines of the relatively narrow ribbons? While these questions may remain unresolved, we do know that most contemporary ribbon appliqué is sewn by machine and the sewing machine's zigzag stitch has nearly replaced the herringbone hand-stitching common on earlier, positive designs (see figs. 5.5 and 5.6).

Other changes in ribbonwork are less design oriented and generally relate to materials and their availability. During the 1920s and 1930s, for instance, manufactured fibers such as rayon were created. Those, along with polyester, nylon, and other new materials available after World War II, eventually revolutionized the textile industry. An array of synthetic and synthetic-blend fabrics entered the market. While the standard wool cloth is still available in black, navy blue, and red, the traditional silk ribbon has been almost entirely replaced by cheaper polyester and acetate ribbons. Beyond changes in fabric technology and availability, contemporary ribbon appliqué bears strong resemblance to ribbonwork sewn by American Indian women generations ago.

Toward a System of Attribution

In order to evaluate attributions, I considered various visual characteristics including technique, design motif, color combinations, and cut of clothing, in the hope that these details would recur in combinations suggesting tribal or ethnic styles of ribbonwork. I designed a worksheet to record data for each piece and later devised a database to organize and compile the information. The database is a collection of searchable, sortable records that contain fields of data. Once the data set has been entered, the researcher can quickly search for a specific subset of objects that share particular formal characteristics, including techniques, colors, stitches, and materials, among others. New records can be added as the data set expands. The database is a powerful tool for testing hypotheses about which attributes constitute a tribal style of ribbonwork.

Equipped with a descriptive system based on Abbass's typology, a worksheet for recording specific attributes, and a computer to manipulate and analyze the data, I began examining the collection. It quickly became apparent that seemingly straightforward assessments such as object name were unclear. For example, what distinguishes the structurally and visually similar robe, shawl, and skirt? In order to answer this question I turned to historic photographs. Further, I explored available sources for clues about significant colors and the iconography of various tribes in order to formulate a testable model for ribbonwork attribution.

Sources of Context and Meaning

In addition to discerning the attributes of tribal styles of ribbonwork, I wanted to understand how ribbonwork-decorated garments were used, why they were made, and why they continue to be created and worn. To better grasp the significance of ribbonwork I turned to a variety of visual, ethnographic, and primary sources. In order to illustrate how ribbonwork serves as an emblem of American Indian identity, the next section of the chapter investigates auxiliary sources, including paintings, photography, ethnography, and American Indian written and oral accounts.

Visual Sources
Images such as sketches, paintings, and photographs can be useful in material culture studies for the evidence they provide about the people

who produced and used the objects under consideration. The earliest visual documents of ribbonwork-decorated garments are two oil paintings by George Catlin. Although scholars have challenged the accuracy of details in this celebrated artist's portraits and his depictions of American Indian life, much of the visual information he includes should not be dismissed (see Parker Miller, chap. 11). The people depicted in the paintings considered here are members of Indian tribes living just west and north of Lake Michigan at the time of European contact. Painted by Catlin in 1835–36, both of these depictions of ribbonwork have been reproduced in books in black and white. The first portrait depicts an unnamed "Wife of Keokuk," a Sauk and Fox woman, wearing a wraparound skirt decorated with shingled-style ribbonwork (Hassrick 1977:62). The other painting shows two unnamed Menominee men, one of whom carries a ribbonwork-decorated robe (Hassrick 1977:87). Catlin's paintings support several inferences. The depiction of the woman, whose husband was a prominent Sauk representative in council, suggests that ribbonwork was fashionable for people of high social ranking. Taken together the images indicate that during this era both genders wore ribbonwork. Finally, the prominence of ribbonwork in these formally posed compositions suggests that ribbonwork-decorated garments were important to both the artist and his subjects in conveying their identity.

Like painting, the photographic record reveals information about how ribbonwork garments were worn, by whom, and on what occasions. Based on the photo archive at the State of Wisconsin Historical Society, it is apparent that Native American men, women, and children in the Great Lakes region have worn ribbonwork-adorned clothing for at least 150 years. These garments were and are considered appropriate dress for powwows, public ceremonies, and studio portraits. In the exhibition catalog *Art of the American Indian Frontier,* David Penney (1992:39) indicates that wearing formal dress is a way that Native Americans living in the 19th century recognized the significance of an event, honored other participants, and proclaimed their identity. Ribbonwork is confined to women's skirts and robes in most photographs from the late 19th and early 20th centuries. The dearth of men's ribbonwork garments in the later photographs reflects the tendency for men to give up traditional dress more quickly than women; by the time photography was in wide use, many Native American men of the Great Lakes area had adopted European-style dress.

In addition to depicting the people who wear ribbonwork and on what garments, photographs also provide data about style and designs. In recording this information, I recognized the heart-and-flower design on the skirt worn by a woman in Paul Radin's 1923 ethnography called *The Winnebago Tribe* (1970) (see fig. 5.7). The same design appears on a skirt accessioned by the Milwaukee Public Museum in 1907 (see fig. 5.6). The appearance of this design on two skirts suggests that patterns may be used more than once, and that family or clan patterns may exist.

A color postcard promoting the 1981 Miss Indian America Pageant features Melanie Tallmadge, the twenty-sixth recipient of that title (Trumble Photography n.d.). Tallmadge, a young woman of Wisconsin Winnebago and Minnesota Sioux descent from Wisconsin Dells, Wisconsin, poses for the photograph wearing traditional dress, which includes beaded earrings and hair binding, a blouse ornamented with silver brooches, a ribbonwork skirt, and Winnebago-style moccasins. In addition, she carries a feather fan and a ribbonwork-ornamented shawl. This image, along with the limited text on its reverse, demonstrates that ribbonwork-embellished clothing is worn as an outward sign of pride in one's Indian heritage.

The available visual record, including portraits painted by George Catlin and the archives of a host of studio and amateur photographers, provides documentation of ribbonwork unavailable in written sources. From these representations it appears that ribbonwork was and continues to be part of the finery worn by American Indians to display ethnic identity and well-being. Most of the images reviewed for this study date to the late 19th and early 20th centuries. An obvious limitation of early photographs is their lack of color, which can be compensated for by examining ethnographic objects and accounts.

The Ethnographic Record

According to Pannabecker (1986:153), written descriptions of ribbon-decorated clothing appear as early as 1735. Descriptions of ribbonwork traditions, however, do not appear until the first part of the 20th century in publications such as the *Indian Notes and Monographs* series (e.g., Skinner 1921). The ethnographic record provides data pertaining to specific groups at specific periods in time; when considered collectively, these data can relate changes in the style and significance of ribbonwork. Some suggestive phrases in this literature propelled me in the search for diagnostic ribbonwork attributes.

In a 1921 article on Menominee material culture, Alanson Skinner (1921:268) suggested that ribbonwork was highly symbolic, although he provided only limited support for its symbolic meaning. Skinner indicated a connection with tribal mythology about eight Sky Women, four in the

Fig. 5.7. Undocumented photograph from Paul Radin, 1923. The woman on the left wears a skirt with a heart and flower design that also appears on a skirt in the collection of the Milwaukee Public Museum (see fig. 5.6).

south and four in the east, who are responsible for the destinies of women. Specific colors—red, black, white, yellow, and blue—are claimed to be associated with the Sky Sisters and the cardinal directions, although Skinner observed that the precise connections are unclear (1921:269). His most explicit statement about symbolism in Menominee ribbonwork relates to color: "The most that can be said, then, is that the colored ribbon work has a primary use which is purely ornamental, and a secondary use which is ceremonial, the colors being looked upon as protective emblems of the Sky Women" (1921:269). Although Skinner's work does not establish a clear connection between Menominee ribbonwork and mythology, it certainly provides information about auspicious colors for women. Thus, for Menominee women at least, the colors of ribbonwork-decorated garments can have sociocultural significance.

Similarly, Marriott and Rachlin (1980:27) indicate that earlier examples of ribbonwork were laden with meaning when they state that by the mid-1940s, "contrasting colored mirror images of tribal moiety symbols have lost their significance." This statement, part of a lament for the loss of traditional arts and crafts, suggests that mirrored ribbonwork carried tribal associations. The clouds, trees, and leaves in earlier patterns apparently represent a moietal division between earth and sky (Marriott and Rachlin 1980:27). Neither Marriott and Rachlin, nor Skinner provide keys for decoding ribbonwork, although all attest to its symbolic power. Skinner relates the significance of colors used in ribbonwork, while Marriott and Rachlin explicitly state the representation of moiety affiliations in ribbonwork. Both sources present lines of inquiry for evaluating tribal attributes.

Undoubtedly, the ethnography that best informed this study was *Mountain Wolf Woman: Sister of Crashing Thunder* (Lurie 1961). In recounting her life story for Nancy Lurie, Mountain Wolf Woman helped resolve my confusion with respect to skirts, shawls, and robes. The rectangular skirts, which were worn wrapped around the body and folded down over a belt, were the same size and shape as the shawls and robes, and were decorated in the same fashion. Photographs revealed that shawls worn about the shoulders were folded in the same manner as the skirts. The garments appeared to me to be identical. Mountain Wolf Woman, a self-described "old Winnebago lady" (Lurie 1961:xiv) who lived most of her life near Black River Falls, Wisconsin, described the clothing she wore to enter the home of her in-laws on her wedding day around the year 1900: "I had worn a blanket-shawl skirt and I had another one" (Lurie 1961: 89). Mountain Wolf Woman's comment about "blanket-shawl skirts" reveals that these garments were multi-purpose. Further, it suggests that collectors may have made distinctions about the function of garments beyond those made by Native Americans.[2] Mountain Wolf Woman's account also informs us about the propriety of formal dress. Again recalling the day of her wedding, she explained, "They dressed me. I wore a ribbon embroidery skirt and I wore one as a shawl. I wore a heavily beaded binding for the braid of hair down my back, and I had on earrings. It looked as if I were going to a dance" (Lurie 1961:29).

It should be noted that as a component of formal dress, ribbonwork represents a significant investment of time and accumulation of wealth. Pannabecker (1986:184) cites 19th-century sources that place the value of robes adorned with ribbonwork and silver brooches between $80 and $200. However, wearing valuable garments, including those made from ribbons and other trade goods, was more than a display of material wealth, as material culture analysts now frequently acknowledge. Penney writes, "Trade goods were valuable because Indians recognized in them attributes corresponding to their ideas of value—social and religious values as well as economic ones" (1992:35). He continues, "Wealth was understood traditionally as spiritual and social well-being and its material expression was valued only to the extent that it could be displayed in dress or dispersed through gift giving" (Penney 1992:35). Therefore, by appearing in formal dress, Native Americans convey their well-being, spiritually and otherwise. This value of balance and prosperity endures. The Miss Indian America postcard mentioned above states Melanie Tallmadge's belief that "physical well-being is as important as mental well-being" (Trumble Photography n.d.). In addition to mythical and moietal connotations, the ethnographic record shows that ribbonwork manifests economic and general well-being.

Primary Sources: Living Informants

As common sense suggests, the most informative sources about a contemporary art form are the people who make and, in this case, wear it. Diane Fraher, an Osage-Cherokee woman who works at the National Museum of the American Indian, sews traditional Osage ribbonwork and has written explicitly about its significance. "The ribbonwork pattern and colors worn on your clothes become outward symbols of your identity. Only you may wear your blanket. Ribbonwork is done in a variety of patterns. There are individual family patterns and clan patterns and even patterns from the two major divisions of the tribe" (Fraher 1994:32). She also notes that, "Traditionally, the wool broadcloth used to make a blanket denotes a child's place within the family: the eldest son or daughter wears red; the second son, a combination of red and blue; all other sons and daughters wear blue" (Fraher 1994:32). While the rules for traditional clothing among the Osage may not be applied directly to other tribes, Fraher's comments support the use of fabric, color, and design in ribbonwork to reflect its wearer's identity.

Like the Osage, the Mesquakie of Iowa have strong clothing traditions. In the exhibition catalog called *Art of the Red Earth People,* Gaylord Torrence claims that "ribbon appliqué is today the most important Mesquakie art form" (Torrence and Hobbs 1989:18). Garments decorated with ribbon appliqué are often highly symbolic. For example, Adeline Wanatee made a skirt for her granddaughter that "retains traditional elements of color symbolism within its modern design: red, the color of the Fox clan, is combined with black, the color associated with spiritual enlightenment and prayer" (Torrence and Hobbs 1989:18). The other original clan, the Bear clan, is represented by the color green. In order to decode Mesquakie symbolism one must know the visual vocabulary and grammar.

While it is probable that some Mesquakie ribbon appliqué is simply decorative, other specimens carry multiple meanings. Torrence quotes Wanatee, who observed, "You can see that our patterns are split—we Mesquakies are like that—half in this world and half in the spirit world. We are like the trees who have a visible form above the ground and an equal part which is out of sight beneath the surface. This is what my mother and aunt told me" (Torrence and Hobbs 1989:18). In this cogent statement Wanatee emphasizes two important values—spirituality and tradition. Ribbonwork reinforces the individual's place in the larger world and the connections to generations past and future. Later in the monograph Robert Hobbs writes, "Ribbonwork is not just decoration; it is a sacred collage that connects these people to natural forms, to abstract sacred meanings" (Torrence and Hobbs 1989:40). For the Mesquakie, ribbonwork is a metaphor for traditional life.

My limited discussions about ribbonwork with American Indians in Wisconsin have revealed a range of opinions about ribbon appliqué. While some say that colors and designs are merely a matter of personal preference, others choose ribbons and fabric in specific colors that represent their families. Patterns are chosen for their personal significance. Consensus indicates that ribbon appliqué is a traditional art, although what constitutes "traditional" is unclear. In this instance it appears that "traditional" includes things reminiscent of the old—albeit post-Contact—ways.

Numerous interpretations of ribbonwork designs exist among tribes in the southern Plains as well as in the Great Lakes region. A "child of both [Osage and Euro-American] cultures," Louis Francis Burns perhaps best articulates their various meanings when he writes, "The interpretations of these specific ribbon work designs are by no means universal. Each of the 24 Osage clans often had their own names and interpretations for the various designs. In fact, the designs themselves varied from clan to clan and even within the sub-clans" (Burns 1994:47). To ensure that the point is clear he adds, "it would be impossible to present all the divergent meanings" (Burns 1994:47). The significance of ribbonwork varies both within tribes and across tribes. Ultimately, the meaning of specific designs may vary with the viewer.

The difference of opinion about the meanings associated with ribbonwork seems to correspond with the multiplicity of tribal identities as well as individual opinions about what it means to be Indian. The thriving status of the ribbon appliqué tradition and its presence at public events such as pow-wows suggest that ribbonwork and its associated meanings merit further consideration. In any event, they clearly serve to create and reproduce Native American identities at multiple scales.

Summary and Conclusions

This investigation of visual, ethnographic, and primary sources shows that ribbonwork is a material symbol of American Indian identity. Garments decorated with ribbonwork carry a variety of meanings depending on the tribe and individual with whom they are associated. The specific combination of materials, colors, and designs in a ribbonwork-decorated garment can signify economic and spiritual well-being as well as family, clan, moiety, and tribal or ethnic associations. While these meanings vary between individuals, among tribes, and across regions, they are expressions of affiliation and belonging. The development of this syncretic art form signals dramatic changes in the lives of American Indians in the Great Lakes region. More than a vestige of the fur trade, however, the ribbonwork tradition reinforces traditional values. When wearing traditional clothing, Native Americans are literally embodied by their heritage; thus, these ribbonwork-decorated garments are truly emblems of ethnicity.

Further investigation of ribbonwork can provide additional information about the significance of traditional garments in American Indian cultures. Igor Kopytoff (1986) has proposed a concept that may prove useful in future examinations of formal dress. In "The Cultural Biography of Things: Commoditization as Process," Kopytoff recognizes the economic cycle of an object and emphasizes its periodic status as a commodity. He suggests, "A culturally informed economic biography of an object would look at it as a culturally constructed entity, endowed with culturally specific meanings, and classified and reclassified into culturally constituted categories" (Kopytoff 1986:68). This theory of the cultural biography of objects includes their economic, classificatory, and representative aspects. In considering the life of a ribbonwork garment, one would need to consider the bodies it has touched, the events it has witnessed, and the hands through which it has passed. Interviews with ribbonwork wearers and makers about specific garments would aid researchers in writing cultural biographies of objects.

In the study presented here, sources provide specific information about tribal designs in ribbonwork that may help to establish a system for attributing a specimen to a particular tribe based on its formal attributes. At least one study shows that the colors and styles of beadwork have been used to identify patterns of alliance and assimilation among 19th-century Plains Indian groups (Byers 1995). Let us consider several sources to explore whether similar patterns might be found in Great Lakes area ribbonwork. For the study of ribbonwork, Skinner's sources reported that the colors red, black, white, yellow, and blue were significant in Menominee culture (1921:268–69). The 1802 Rankin wedding ensemble also has red, black, yellow, and blue ribbons; and while no white is incorporated, it also includes green. This relatively favorable comparison led to an evaluation of the data to determine whether the five ribbon colors named by Skinner, the five on the Rankin outfit, or both, correlate with Menominee ribbonwork. Of the current data set of seventy-six pieces of ribbonwork, three included red, black, yellow, blue, and green, while twelve had white ribbon in addition to those colors. Of these fifteen pieces, only two were attributed to the Menominee compared with twelve specimens in the entire sample.

The apparent failure of this color test for Menominee ribbonwork raises an extremely important point. The current data set is too small to yield significant results. The seventy-six specimens are said to represent ten tribes. Even if these included an equal number from each tribe, it is not a large enough sample to represent the variety of techniques and materials used by ribbonworkers over the last two centuries. A valid test of this hypothesis of color in Menominee ribbonwork would require a much larger sample.

A similar analysis of the data was conducted based on the colors of the two original Mesquakie clans: red and green. Of the twenty-four specimens, four have red ribbon and five have green, while thirteen pieces incorporate both colors and two have neither. Without knowing more about color symbolism among the Mesquakie, it is not possible to associate examples of this tribe's ribbonwork with particular clans based on their color scheme.

Once a larger data set is collected, these and other hypotheses about ribbonwork attributes and tribal or clan affiliation may be tested. Some of these will undoubtedly be based on observation. For instance, the negative ribbonwork technique is found predominantly in the Plains and is essentially totally absent in the Great Lakes region. Also, certain combinations of details seem to recur in ribbon appliqué of specific tribes. For example, stepped triangles, leaf-like designs, and the color brown seem to characterize an early style of Winnebago ribbonwork. It would also be helpful to learn to recognize clouds, trees, leaves, and other stylized designs and to consider their clan and moiety associations. Ribbonworkers and other people familiar with the tradition would be prime sources for information about motifs.

This research indicates that more conservative tribes such as the Mesquakie and Winnebago have stronger traditions of ribbonwork. It might be fruitful to focus on the ribbonwork of a single tribe, perhaps even apprenticing with a master ribbonworker to learn the intricacies of the techniques. In order to explore the extent of tribal patterns, I would like to examine paper patterns in museums and private collections, particularly those retained by ribbonworkers. I also hope to consider the economic aspects of ribbonwork and utilize Kopytoff's model to create a cultural biography of a specific piece of ribbonwork. Finally, my future research will augment the data set in an ongoing attempt to develop a system of ribbonwork attribution. Ultimately, further research into the meanings embedded in ribbonwork can contribute to our understanding of Great Lakes region American Indian cultures from the time of contact with Europeans to the present, as well as enhance our understanding of the ways in which ribbonwork served and continues to serve as an emblem of ethnicity.

Notes

1. Greenblatt uses the terms *resonance* and *wonder* to describe two approaches to exhibition design that respectively emphasize the context or uniqueness of an object.

2. Recently I encountered the word "Wa-en-wa-wa-ja" as the Winnebago term for a blanket skirt acquired by a collector in 1927. Hopefully, future research will consider this and other emic terminology for ribbonwork-adorned clothing and objects.

Acknowledgments

Warmest thanks to Ann McMullen, Curator of North American Ethnology at the Milwaukee Public Museum, who recommended the initial investigation and provided ongoing encouragement and support; to the Anthropology staff at the Field Museum of Natural History for access to its holdings; to computer guru Brian Hassett, who was instrumental in designing the database; and to Lara Calloway for her gracious assistance with illustrations. Above all, I am grateful to the creative, talented, and generous stitchers—past and present—whose artistry forms the heart of this chapter and with whom I share the joy of process.

References Cited

Abbass, D. Kathleen. 1979. Contemporary Oklahoma Ribbonwork: Styles and Economics. Ph.D. diss., Southern Illinois University, Carbondale.

Burns, Louis Francis. 1994. Missionaries, Fur Traders and Osage Ribbon Work. In *The Artist and the Missionary: A Native-American and Euro-American Cultural Exchange,* ed. S. G. Tyler, 47–53. Buffalo Bill Historical Center, Cody, Wy.

Byers, Stan. 1995. Arapaho Assimilation and Distinction. Paper presented in the symposium Expressions of Ethnicity: Evolutionary and Historical Perspectives on Plains Indian Art, Southeastern Archaeological Conference, Knoxville, Tenn.

Carufel, Robin. 1981. *Winnebago Appliqué.* Wisconsin Department of Public Instruction, Madison.

Conn, Richard G. 1980. Native American Cloth Applique and Ribbonwork: Their Origin and Diffusion in the Plains. In *Native American Ribbonwork: A Rainbow Tradition,* ed. George P. Horse Capture, 9–22. Buffalo Bill Historical Center, Cody, Wy.

Densmore, Frances. [1928] 1974. *How Indians Use Wild Plants for Food, Medicine and Crafts.* Dover Publications, New York.

Feder, Norman. 1956. Ribbon Appliqué. *The American Indian Hobbyist* (2–3):12–23.

Fraher, Diane. 1994. Osage Childhood. In *Creation's Journey: Native American Identity and Belief,* ed. Tom Hill and Richard W. Hill, Sr., 32. Smithsonian Institution Press, Washington, D.C.

Greenblatt, Stephen. 1991. Resonance and Wonder. In *Exhibiting Cultures: The Poetics and Politics of Museum Display,* ed. Ivan Karp and Steven D. Lavine, 42–56. Smithsonian Institution Press, Washington, D.C.

Hassrick, Royal B. 1977. *The George Catlin Book of American Indians.* Watson-Guptill, New York.

Howard, James H. 1980. Birch Bark and Paper Cutouts: An Art Form of the Northern Woodlands and the Prairie Border. *American Indian Art* 5:55–61.

Kopytoff, Igor. 1986. The Cultural Biography of Things: Commoditization as Process. In *The Social Life of Things: Commodities in Cultural Perspective,* ed. Arjun Appadurai, 64–91. Cambridge University Press, New York.

Lurie, Nancy Oestreich. 1961. *Mountain Wolf Woman, Sister of Crashing Thunder: The Autobiography of a Winnebago Indian.* University of Michigan Press, Ann Arbor.

Marriott, Alice. 1958. Ribbon Applique Work of North American Indians, Part I. *Bulletin of the Oklahoma Anthropological Society* 6:49–59.

Marriott, Alice, and Carol K. Rachlin. 1980. Southern Plains Ribbonwork Development and Diffusion. In *Native American Ribbonwork: A Rainbow Tradition,* ed. George P. Horse Capture, 23–30. Buffalo Bill Historical Center, Cody, Wy.

McPharlin-Coen, Carleen Ann. 1974. Geometric Designs in Great Lakes Indian Art: Woven Goods, Quill Work, and Ribbon Work. M.A. thesis, University of Michigan, Ann Arbor.

Pannabecker, Rachel Karina. 1986. Ribbonwork of the Great Lakes Indians: The Material of Acculturation. Ph.D. diss., Ohio State University, Columbus.

Penney, David W. 1992. *Art of the American Indian Frontier: The Chandler-Pohrt Collection.* University of Washington Press, Seattle.

Prown, Jules. 1982. Mind in Matter: An Introduction to Material Culture Theory and Method. *Winterthur Portfolio* 17(1):1–16.

Quimby, George. 1966. *Indian Culture and European Trade Goods: The Archaeology of the Historic Period in the Western Great Lakes Region.* University of Wisconsin Press, Madison.

Radin, Paul. [1923] 1970. *The Winnebago Tribe.* University of Nebraska Press, Lincoln.

Riley, Jocelyn. [1992] 1995. *Her Mother Before Her: Winnebago Women's Stories of Their Mothers and Grandmothers, A Resource Guide.* Jocelyn Riley, Madison, Wis.

Rogers, J. Daniel. 1990. *Objects of Change: The Archaeology and History of Arikara Contact with Europeans.* Smithsonian Institution Press, Washington, D.C.

Skinner, Alanson. 1921. Material Culture of the Menomini. *Indian Notes and*

Monographs 20. Museum of the American Indian, Heye Foundation, New York.

Speck, Frank. [1914] 1982. The Double-Curve Motive in Northeastern Algonkian Art. In *Native North American Art History: Selected Readings,* ed. Zena Pearlstone Nathews and Aldona Jonaitis, 383–428. Peek Publications, Palo Alto, Calif.

State Arts Council of Oklahoma. 1990. *Ribbons of the Osage: The Art and Life of Georgeann Robinson.* Native American Master Artists Video Series 3. Full Circle Communications, Tulsa.

Torrence, Gaylord, and Robert Hobbs. 1989. *Art of the Red Earth People: The Mesquakie of Iowa.* University of Iowa Museum of Art, Iowa City.

Trumble Photography. n.d. Postcard of Melanie L. Tallmadge, Miss Indian America 26. Trumble Photography, Wisconsin Dells, Wis.

II

Change and Continuity in Daily Life

6

François' House, a Significant Pedlars' Post on the Saskatchewan

Alice Beck Kehoe

In 1768 James Finlay, a Scots merchant in Montreal, defied the Hudson's Bay Company monopoly on Rupert's Land—the huge drainage basin of Hudson's Bay—by building a trading post on the Saskatchewan River at the rendezvous Nipowiwinihk (present-day Codette, near Nipawin, Saskatchewan) (Meyer and Thistle 1995:419, 436). Finlay engaged an experienced middle-aged French-Canadian voyageur, François Le Blanc, as his partner. Called "Saswe" (said to be a Cree version of "François"), he was "a poor looking Small man about fifty years of age; . . . his dress was a ruffed Shirt, a Blanket Jacket, a pair of Long Trousers without stockings or Shoes, his own hair with a hatt bound about with green beinding . . . he Seemed to have a great Command over the men; he lay in the Middle of the Canoe with his wife and Son" (William Tomison, 1767, quoted in Morton 1939:277).

François' House, as the partners' post came to be called, was a significant historical entity, a successful challenge to the London-based "Company of Adventurers of England Trading into Hudson's Bay." To meet that challenge, the Company initiated its own inland posts, a radical turn that broke its century-long custom of demanding that Indians make the journey to the shores of Hudson's Bay, where the English seagoing ships docked. Important as François' House was, no records of its business survive: neither Finlay nor François was formally educated,[1] and it behooved them to keep their business secret, for the legality of their enterprise was disputed.

Matthew Cocking, a Hudson's Bay Company employee, scouted out these competitors in May 1773, reporting:

> The house is a long square; built log to log; half of it is appropriated to the use of a kitchen; the other half used as a trading room & Bedroom; with a loft above, the whole length of the building where He lays his furs; also three small log houses, the Men's apartments; the whole enclosed with ten feet Stockades, forming a Square about twenty yards. . . . I believe François hath about twenty men, all french Canadians. . . . He is an old ignorant Frenchman; I do not think he keeps a proper distance from his men; they coming into his apartment & talking with him as one of themselves. But what I am most surprised at, they keep no watch in the night; even when the Natives are lying on their plantation.
>
> On our arrival the Frenchman introduced the Natives unto his house, giving about 4 inches of tobacco. Afterwards they made a collection of furs, by the bulk about 100 Beaver, presenting them to the Pedler, who, in return, presented to them about 4 Gallons liquor, Rum adulterated; also cloathed 2 Leaders with a Coat & Hat. I endeavoured all in my power to prevent the Natives giving away their furs, but in vain; Liquor being above all persuasion with them. (Quoted in Morton 1939:285–86)

The "Pedler," as the Hudson's Bay Company termed their independent competitors, contrasted starkly with the Bay's factors. He was not only without formal education, he was openly of the same social status as the men he commanded; he exhibited neither fear nor distrust of his Indian visitors; and he had married into the country, publicly maintaining his Indian wife and their son. James Finlay also had a "country wife" and son, Jaco, who would grow up to work for his half-brother, James Finlay, Jr., in the North West Company.[2]

Tangible knowledge of François' House illuminates what a pedlars' post looked like, its wares and furnishings, and the manner in which the social contrasts noted between the Hudson's Bay Company and the pedlars played out on the ground. Beginning with Henry Kelsey in 1690, the Bay attempted to establish regular trade with inland groups (Russell 1993:74–75), but the independent traders were the first to build posts beyond Hudson's Bay and the Great Lakes. When Finlay and François constructed their house at the Nipowiwinihk portage, the Indian nations of the West had not yet suffered decimating epidemics (Ray 1974:105) nor declining resources; they were not resisting but exploiting foreign incursions. In this respect, archaeology at François' House examined a situation rather different from that described by, for example, Catherine Carlson for Kamloops (chap. 10).

The Saskatchewan Power Corporation allocated money to excavate François' House, threatened by potential erosion once the reservoir filled, when it built a dam at Squaw Rapids on the Saskatchewan River downstream from Nipawin. These excavations were carried out in 1963 and 1964, and reported in 1978 (Kehoe 1976, 1978). Later, a second dam on the river at Nipawin itself prompted extensive further archaeological work, reported in the Nipawin Reservoir Heritage Study series (Finnigan et al. 1983). The site of François' House is now destroyed.

The Nipawin area was homesteaded at the beginning of the twentieth century, and the trading post site was initially recognized by one of the colonists, William Bushfield, about 1912. Years later, Bushfield brought the historian Arthur S. Morton to the site, which he had preserved by allowing it to revert to bush after initial clearing. Morton identified the principal visible rectangle as the house Cocking had visited in 1773, but was puzzled by a second area of habitation thirty-six meters north along the river terrace. Morton guessed that perhaps Finlay had built a separate residence, and designated the southern sector François' House, subsequently given the official Canadian Borden system designation FhNa-3, and the northern sector "Finlay's," given FhNa-19. A third site, some forty meters north of FhNa-19, was designated FhNa-7 and identified by David Meyer (in Kehoe 1978:132) as James Bird's Hudson's Bay Company Fort Nipawi of 1794–95. (See fig. 6.1.) All three sites were excavated under my direction in 1963 and 1964.

FhNa-19 was the only one of the three sites with more than one stratum of occupation. It also had a peculiar pattern of wood, some logs excellently preserved and then inexplicable gaps. Based on these data, I interpreted FhNa-19 to have been the 1768–69 post referred to by William Pink and Edward Lutit in reports to their employer, the Hudson's Bay Company (Wallace 1954:7, 8). Neither Finlay nor François came into the country from 1770 to 1772. The odd pattern of log preservation in FhNa-19 can be postulated to indicate that when the partners returned to their lucrative location in 1773, they took logs from the cabins they had earlier built and used them in the construction of the house seen by Cocking.

The first cabin measured 6.5 × 3.4 m and was made of spruce logs laid horizontally upon sleepers between upright corner posts, with one upright post midway along each of the longer walls. A stone chimney and puddled-clay hearth were built in its south wall. West of this cabin, closer

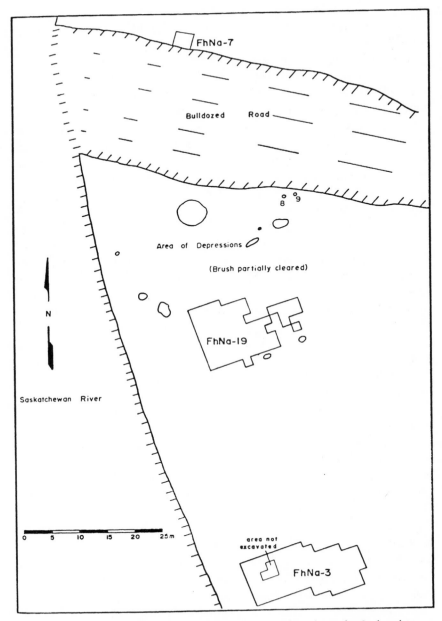

Fig. 6.1. The François-Finlay/Fort Nipawi site complex along the Saskatchewan River

to the riverbank, was a similar cabin 6.4 × 4.3 m, oriented at a right angle to the other, also with a fireplace on the south wall. Each cabin had a shallow storage cellar near its north wall. There was evidence of a log stockade wall extending north from the west cabin to enclose a narrow courtyard, with the east cabin's longer wall forming one end of the courtyard. The entire enclosed rectangular area measured 9.8 × 6.4 m. East of the enclosure was a small open smithy, and north of the stockade wall was an oval trash pit.

François' House, FhNa-3 (fig. 6.2), probably the post seen by Cocking in May 1773, required more labor than FhNa-19. Trenches were dug to make a rectangle 18.3 × 6.7 m (60 × 22 ft.), upright logs of spruce or jack pine about 15 cm (6 in.) in diameter were set in the trenches, and heavier wall-plate logs were laid horizontally on top of the upright-log walls. Cocking said the stockade was ten feet high. The roofs of the cabins were wooden shakes covered with a thick layer of mud chinking, over which were split logs half the length of the roof that may have formed a gable. The loft Cocking mentions was built of heavy planks, and at least one of the two doors was made of planking. As in FhNa-19, there were two stone chimneys with raised hearths surfaced with puddled clay, but as Cocking reported, there were more cabins. The "Master's house" closest to the riverbank formed the west end of the post rectangle, measured 6.7 × 4 m (22 × 13 ft.), and contained the planks from the loft but no hearth other than a shallow ash pit. Next to this house was a cabin 5.8 m (19 ft.) square, which allowed a narrow courtyard 1.2 meters wide between it and the south stockade wall. The plank door was in the stockade wall of the courtyard. The second cabin was 5.8 × 4.3 m (19 × 14 ft.), its longer west wall being also the second cabin's wall. The third cabin formed the east (inland) end of the post rectangle, and measured 6.7 × 4 m (22 × 13 ft.). Its east wall differed from the other walls in being built of horizontal logs on a sleeper beam. One stone chimney with a puddled hearth was in the north wall of the second building (first cabin); another was built between the two east-end cabins, and raised hearths extended from it into each (i.e., the two cabins shared a single chimney). Shallow ditches, presumably for drainage, ran outside the north and south walls of the post. Each of the four structures had a shallow cellar braced with logs dug into its dirt floor, and the cellar in the second structure had been plastered thinly with clay.

There was no evidence of a smithy close to François' House—the 1773 residents may have used the one at FhNa-19—nor of a large trash pit. A good deal of small trash was deposited in ash probably swept out of the hearths, but larger trash may have been tossed over the terrace edge. Arti-

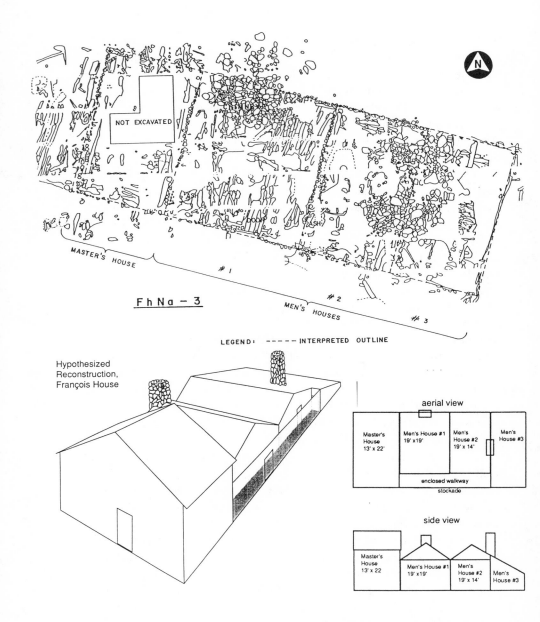

Fig. 6.2. Plan view of FhNa-3 and a hypothesized reconstruction of François' House as it may have appeared in ca. 1773

facts in both loci, François' House and FhNa-19, included many identical items. Some were identical, too, with items in FhNa-7, presumably Bird's HBC house of 1794–95. The trade items present in all three constructions demonstrated their near contemporaneity. Indigenous artifacts seem to have been absent from the probable Hudson's Bay Company house, although the much more limited excavation there—salvage work following unauthorized destruction of one edge of the house by a construction road—may be the reason for the apparent absence.

Nipowiwinihk, the Indian camping ground, was on the plateau over-looking the river terrace upon which François built his house, and there were also Indian camps on Bushfield's Flat, a tongue of land within the meander swinging out from the shallow rapids (Finlay's Falls) below the terrace. The portage path around the rapids came up to the terrace close to the post. From Cocking's observation, one would suppose Indians tented on the terrace beside the posts; our two seasons' work, limited to the immediate area of the fur trade buildings, did not reveal the indigenes' camps. Indigenous artifacts did cluster contiguous to the walls of François' House, especially along the outside of the sunny river-facing west wall. These Native domestic artifacts may have belonged to the pedlars' "country wives": we visualized the Indian women sitting beside the house, watching their toddlers and the life on the river as they carried on their everyday tasks.

Artifacts from FhNa-3 and FhNa-19 fall into three classes: European daily-life items, Indian daily-life items, and trade imports (table 6.1). What is striking about these classes is that they constitute a series of analogs. At this period of the fur trade, representing the first European penetration of the interior West, the First Nations maintained a fully viable indigenous technology (cf. Arkush, chap. 7; Carlson, chap. 10). The year 1773 was a generation before any attempt to colonize the prairies and nearly a decade before the first recorded major epidemic in the West decimated Native communities. François and his men could have learned from their Indian customers and in-laws how to live using the ways and artifacts of the country; conversely, their Indian wives and relatives in the post could have chosen to use the Canadians' metal tools exclusively.

The parallels shown in table 6.1 for sets of artifacts for daily life powerfully demonstrate the fundamental ethnic differentiation in Rupert's Land, a differentiation maintained even by an old voyageur such as François. The traders, both the Canadian and the European-born, eschewed Indian artifacts, whether utilitarian or ornamental. They appear committed to the technology familiar from their childhood—willing to paddle

Table 6.1. Comparison of indigenous and European artifacts, FhNa-3, -19, -7

European	Indigenous
brass kettles	ceramic pots
stoneware, tin-glazed earthenware	ceramic pots
guns, gunflints, gun repair tools	stone arrowpoint, bone harpoon
metal wire	bone thong softener
metal awls	bone awls
metal files, rasps, scrapers	bone and stone scrapers
metal knife blades	stone blades, beaver incisor
strike-a-light	[embers maintained]
whetstone	antler flaker
buttons	bone and shell beads
clay pipes (mold-made)	stone pipe bowls
Turlington's Balsom bottles	[perishable herbs]
razors	stone blades
log buildings	[tipis, not evidenced]
nails	thongs [+ fiber twine]
[metal drill bit, none recovered]	stone drill bit
[metal hammer, none recovered]	stone mauls

Trade items

   glass beads, mirrors
   sheet-metal for tinklers, spearpoints, arrowpoints
   metal rings, earrings, decorated buttons
   stroud cloth (evidenced from impressions on indigenous ceramics)
   double-pointed metal awls, gun worms
   [liquor, tobacco]

Note: Items in brackets are probable or text-documented but not recovered from the excavations. "Trade items" are identified through text documentation for the late 18th-century Canadian fur trade; in addition, they are evidenced by the numbers recovered in the excavations, suggesting quantities imported for trade.

and portage their clothes (Duckworth 1990:192, n41), metal tools, and even teacups and glass bottles of patent medicine,[3] and to labor at felling trees and constructing cabins and stockades rather than live in tipis. It is striking how these men maintained their own cultural inventory at great expense of energy, transporting their goods over immense distances and constructing their rectangular microcosmos on the bank of the Saskatchewan. Their Métis children living in the 19th century would combine elements from both European and Indian technologies and be viewed as a distinct third race.

At François' House none of the trade goods were necessities for daily life. Indians readily bought cloth, glass beads, metal awls, guns, rings, earrings, tinkling cones, liquor, and tobacco, enriching their repertoire of artifacts without eliminating their own manufactures. They exchanged their worn beaver coats (*castor gras,* preferred because the coarse outer hair had rubbed off) for ornaments, alternative tools (metal awls, kettles, knives, cloth), tobacco, and liquor. This contrasts strongly with the situation a century later, when "an Indian trader . . . to be successful . . . had to judiciously furnish in advance the outfit required by the Indian if he were to be successful in his winter and summer hunting. . . . [This included] the vital essentials—such as ammunition, guns, axes, and traps, and such luxuries as blankets, tea and tobacco" (Cowie [1913] 1993:272). It took two pandemics (1780–81, 1837–38) (Decker 1996; Russell 1982b:210) to break the independence of the First Nations and shift them into economic symbiosis with Euro-Canadian outfitters (Meyer and Thistle 1995:430). For a century and a half, Euro-Canadian entrepreneurs brought the inhabitants of the Saskatchewan Basin a variety of goods expanding upon their pre-Contact trade. (Obsidian and Knife River flint, and the Pacific molluscs *Dentalium* and *Trivia* were recovered from late pre-Contact occupations on Bushfield's Flat [Burley et al. 1982:60; Meyer and McKeand 1996:6].) Their basic way of life was not altered, nor were there the population shifts earlier historians had postulated (Russell 1982a:159). Not until the devastation of epidemics, and the subsequent development of the 19th-century Métis economy of subsistence agriculture with commercial hunting, were the First Nations of eastern Saskatchewan substantially affected by Euro-Canadian intrusion.

Fur trade historians have in recent years broached several stereotypes arising from their predecessors' standard general accounts. Van Kirk (1978, 1980; cf. Cox 1993, Payne 1994) focused on bringing to light the social history of the fur trade era, and Ray (1978) the actual economics, especially as these developed in response to negotiations between indigenous and foreign interests. These broadened views imbue the archaeological data with heightened significance. Sherds of indigenous-style ceramics lying against the southwest corner wall of François' House were impressed with European stroud cloth rather than the traditional indigenous twined fabric—mute testimony to selective amalgamation of imported and Native material objects. Since it is probable that women made the indigenous-style ceramics, the sherds' contiguity to the house, especially the ones directly associated with a quartz knife and a scrap of iron found against the sunny southwest corner, can be interpreted as physical evidence of "country wives" or Indian women slaves. Hudson's Bay Company observers recorded both classes of women here (Klimko 1982:119, 142). Van Kirk (1980:53) notes that Indian women in 18th-century posts were relied upon to process Native foods, make clothing, launder, and chop firewood. Nameless to Hudson's Bay Company inland travelers and to historians, these women creatively adapted the new circumstances along the Saskatchewan to their needs.

The "country wives'" procreative capacity mattered to the literate observers far more than their craft skills and ingenuity. Hudson's Bay Company policy forbade fraternization between Company men and Indian women, a rule increasingly breached. The Hudson's Bay Company refused to provide free provisions for country wives and children of its employees; its rival North West Company (1787–1821) did provision employees' families (Van Kirk 1978:166–169). Independent traders such as François Le Blanc and James Finlay were under no strictures. François had been married in 1733 to a Marie-Denise Deneau-Destaillis, presumably French-Canadian like himself, then "se serait allié à une Indienne, salon une habitude fréquente" (he married an Indian woman, according to a frequent custom) (quoted in Klimko 1982:119). Finlay acknowledged paternity of Jacques Raphael Finlay, called Jaco, whose mother is said to have been Saulteur (Ojibwe). Saswe's son and Jaco remained with their mothers when their fathers retired to the East. Jaco forged a name for himself by supervising a small North West Company trading post at Kootenai Plain, headwaters of the Saskatchewan River. In 1806 he blazed a trail through the Rockies to the Pacific watershed, ready for David Thompson's 1807 passage on his way to the Western Ocean (Bond 1970:60–63; Giraud 1986:348).

Cohabitation of Indian women with the Euro-Canadian traders can be read from the indigenous artifacts associated directly with the Master's House, cabins, and trash pits of FhNa-3 and FhNa-19. Artifacts are relevant also to the second theme of contemporary fur trade studies, the actual economics of the trade. Perhaps surprisingly, examination of records from Buckingham House, a Hudson's Bay Company post on the North Saskatchewan during the 1790s, and from Montreal merchants' accounts for 18th-century posts in the western Great Lakes reveals cloth and clothing to rank first in trade expenditures (Anderson 1994:108–11; Gullason 1994:130–36). Buckingham House employed a tailor who sewed, among other items, "Small Boys' coats," no doubt for the little sons of the country wives. Country wives wear Euro-Canadian style cloth dresses in their portraits, and early 19th-century sketches and paintings of Western Indian women, for example by Catlin and Kane, show women wearing cloth dresses in original styles—neither cut like hide clothing nor copying Euro-Canadian costumes (Karklins 1992:27). Indigenous women liked the greater comfort of cloth, compared to hides, and the increased variety of treatments possible with cloth's flexibility and range of bright colors and textures; they would also have appreciated the relative cheapness of cloth compared to the labor cost of preparing hides for clothing. Country wives' readiness to wear the foreign clothing did not indicate rejection of their Native culture but rather appropriation of generally desired innovations. Revised readings of fur trade economics, like the social histories of the trade era, reveal a populous sector of country wives and mixed-race sons and daughters between the conventionally opposed traders and Indians.

Interpretation based on historical documents fleshed out the archaeological data from François' House. Limitations imposed by the funds and time made available by the Saskatchewan Power Corporation in 1963 curtailed full exploration of the terrace. Our small test soundings beyond the visible walls of François' House and FhNa-19 did not produce artifacts or evidence of tipis (e.g., rings of rock lodge-cover weights), although later trenching yielded sparse data (Burley et al. 1982:117). Thus we do not have archaeological demonstration of Indian camping on the post plantation, as Cocking's description indicated (cf. Carlson, chap. 10). Indigenous artifacts (sherds, knife) immediately contiguous to the post walls and others within the walls or in the large FhNa-19 trash pit could have been discarded by the post's itinerant customers, but it is parsimonious to attribute them to the Indian women associated with the traders in the texts (cf. Gullason 1994:140). Glass beads and clay pipes, abundant in our excavations, were considered relatively minor components of trade inventories, according to documents. Frequency of these staples of the trade reflects their disposability rather than value (noted also at Fort Michilimackinac [Maxwell and Binford 1961:87]). Guns were evidenced archaeologically only by a cluster of gun parts in FhNa-19 that appears likely to have been a repair kit. Of liquor and tobacco no archaeological traces were observed, and only the impressions of cloth remained on ceramic sherds.

Conclusion

Archaeology has provided abundant documentation for a trading venture deliberately undocumented two centuries ago. In addition to revealing the structures and appurtenances of daily life in the trading post, archaeology exposed the strong ethnic differentiation maintained between the traders and their customers. The post itself, rectangular entrenched buildings forming a stockade on a cleared plantation, dramatically contrasted with the Native people's round movable tipis placed in natural openings in the Canadian parkland landscape. Artifacts carried in by the Canadians perpetuated their manner of living, visible even in details such as the European-style clay pipes for casual pleasure smoking beside the hearth. The quantities of small, cheap European ornaments and tools such as awls, rather than gun parts and metal traps, indicated that here in the Saskatchewan Basin around 1770, the intrusive traders were marginal to the economies of the First Nations, still in de facto possession of the country.

Archaeology also provided evidence of the genesis of Métis, the "mixed-race" frontier communities prominent in the 19th century. Close to the walls of François' House were household utensils of Indian manufacture—stone knife blades, scrapers, drill, maul, and pottery vessels. Contiguity of the Indian artifacts to the cabins implies they were used by the pedlars' country wives, the mothers of their children, who constituted the first generation of Métis in the prairie (Dickason 1992:263; Judd 1978).

François' House excavations illustrate the range and significance of ethnohistoric data mutely presented through archaeology: these data overlap the information in historical documents, confirming some statements, expanding upon others, while the documents partially fill the gaps left by the perishability of much material culture. Ethnohistory benefits from this marriage of research techniques, much as the traders' enterprises benefited from the country marriages common in the trading posts.

Notes

1. In 1769 Finlay was in London, where the Secretary of State for the Colonies interviewed him on his activities and found him to be "an illitterate person entirely unacquainted with Geography or perhaps the common points of ye Compass" (Wallace 1954:8–9).

2. Marriage *à la façon du pays* (after the custom of the country) was the term used for recognized unions between European traders and Indian women; hence these women were called "country wives." Many traders were also legally married

to Euro-Canadian women who remained in the colonized eastern section of Canada. Some Indian women, usually captured by enemy Indians, were held as slaves or concubines, lacking the respect afforded "country wives" who could expect support from their parents and other Indian relatives (Van Kirk 1980:4–5).

3. Life-saving properties were attributed to Turlington's Balsom of Life, at least by the Swiss trader Waden, a contemporary of François and Finlay, who when mortally wounded by his partner Peter Pond commanded his servant "de trouver la Boam Turleton et d'arretter le sang" (to find the Turlington's balm and to stop the bleeding), in that order (Innis 1930:94).

References Cited

Anderson, Dean L. 1994. The Flow of European Trade Goods into the Western Great Lakes Region, 1715–1760. In *The Fur Trade Revisited*, ed. J.S.H. Brown, W. J. Eccles, and D. P. Heldman, 93–115. Michigan State University Press, East Lansing.

Bond, Rowland. 1970. *The Original Northwester David Thompson*. Spokane House Enterprises, Nine Mile Falls, Wash.

Brown, Jennifer S. H. 1978. Linguistic Solitudes and Changing Social Categories. In *Old Trails and New Directions*, ed. C. M. Judd and A. J. Ray, 147–59. University of Toronto Press, Toronto.

Burley, David, James Finnigan, Olga Klimko, and Jean Prentice. 1982. *Nipawin Reservoir Heritage Study*, vol. 2, *Phase 1 Field Report and Datalog*. Saskatchewan Research Council Publication C-805-9-E-82, Saskatoon.

Cowie, Isaac. [1913] 1993. *The Company of Adventurers*. Reprint. University of Nebraska Press, Lincoln.

Cox, Bruce Alden. 1993. Natives and the Development of Mercantile Capitalism: A New Look at "Opposition" in the Eighteenth-Century Fur Trade. In *The Political Economy of North American Indians*, ed. J. H. Moore, 87–93. University of Oklahoma Press, Norman.

Decker, Jody F. 1996. Country Distempers: Deciphering Disease and Illness in Rupert's Land before 1870. In *Reading Beyond Words: Contexts for Native History*, ed. J.S.H. Brown and Elizabeth Vibert, 156–81. Broadview Press, Peterborough, Ontario.

Dickason, Olive Patricia. 1992. *Canada's First Nations*. University of Oklahoma Press, Norman.

Duckworth, Harry W., ed. 1990. *The English River Book: A North West Company Journal and Account Book of 1786*. McGill-Queen's University Press, Montreal.

Finnigan, James T., David Meyer, and Jean Prentice. 1983. *Nipawin Reservoir Heritage Study*, vol. 5, *Resource Inventory, Assessment, and Evaluation*. Saskatchewan Research Council Publication no. E-903-9-E-83, Saskatoon.

Giraud, Marcel. 1986. *The Métis in the Canadian West*. Trans. George Woodcock.

University of Nebraska Press, Lincoln. (Originally *Le Métis Canadien*. Museum National d'Histoire Naturelle, Paris, 1945.)

Gullason, Lynda. 1994. "No Less Than Seven Different Nations": Ethnicity and Culture Contact at Fort George–Buckingham House. In *The Fur Trade Revisited*, ed. J.S.H. Brown, W. J. Eccles, and D. P. Heldman, 117–42. Michigan State University Press, East Lansing.

Innis, Harold A. 1930. *Peter Pond*. Irwin and Gordon, Toronto.

Judd, Carol M. 1978. "Mixt Bands of Many Nations," 1821–70. In *Old Trails and New Directions*, ed. C. M. Judd and A. J. Ray, 127–46. University of Toronto Press, Toronto.

Karklins, Karlis. 1992. *Trade Ornament Usage among the Native Peoples of Canada: A Source Book*. Studies in Archaeology, Architecture and History, National Historic Sites, Parks Service, Environment Canada, Ottawa.

Kehoe, Alice B. 1976. Ethnicity at a Pedlar's Post in Saskatchewan. *Western Canadian Journal of Anthropology* 6(1):52–60.

———. 1978. *François' House: An Early Fur Trade Post on the Saskatchewan River*. Saskatchewan [Ministry of] Culture and Youth, Regina.

Klimko, Olga. 1982. Fur Trade History of the Saskatchewan River 1760–1850. In *Nipawin Reservoir Heritage Study*, vol. 3, *Regional Overview and Research Considerations*, ed. David Burley and David Meyer, 116–49. Saskatchewan Research Council Publication C-805-9-E-82, Saskatoon.

Maxwell, Moreau S., and Lewis H. Binford. 1961. *Excavation at Fort Michilimackinac, Mackinac City, Michigan, 1959 Season*. Michigan State University Museum Cultural Series 1 (1), East Lansing.

Meyer, David, and Peggy McKeand. 1996. The Municipal Camp Site (FhNa-119) Excavation Results: Selkirk and Middle Period Components. *Saskatchewan Archaeology* 15 (entire volume).

Meyer, David, and Paul C. Thistle. 1995. Saskatchewan River Rendezvous Centers and Trading Posts: Continuity in a Cree Social Geography. *Ethnohistory* 42(3):403–44.

Morton, Arthur S. 1939. *A History of the Canadian West to 1870–71*. Thomas Nelson and Sons, London.

Payne, Michael. 1994. Fur Trade Social History and the Public Historian: Some Other Recent Trends. In *The Fur Trade Revisited*, ed. J.S.H. Brown, W. J. Eccles, and D. P. Heldman, 481–99. Michigan State University Press, East Lansing.

Ray, Arthur J. 1974. *Indians in the Fur Trade*. University of Toronto Press, Toronto.

———. 1978. Indians as Consumers in the Eighteenth Century. In *Old Trails and New Directions*, ed. C. M. Judd and A. J. Ray, 255–71. University of Toronto Press, Toronto.

Russell, Dale. 1982a. The Ethnohistoric and Demographic Context of Central Saskatchewan to 1800. In *Nipawin Reservoir Heritage Study*, vol. 3, *Regional*

Overview and Research Considerations, ed. David Burley and David Meyer, 150–85. Saskatchewan Research Council Publication C-805-9-E-82, Saskatoon.

———. 1982b. The Eighteenth Century Parkland Cree. In *Nipawin Reservoir Heritage Study,* vol. 3, *Regional Overview and Research Considerations,* ed. David Burley and David Meyer, 186–210. Saskatchewan Research Council Publication C-805-9-E-82, Saskatoon.

———. 1993. The Puzzle of Henry Kelsey and His Journey to the West. In *Three Hundred Prairie Years: Henry Kelsey's "Inland Country of Good Report,"* ed. Henry Epp, 74–88. Canadian Plains Research Center, University of Regina, Regina, Saskatchewan.

Van Kirk, Sylvia. 1978. Fur Trade History: Some Recent Trends. In *Old Trails and New Directions,* ed. C. M. Judd and A. J. Ray, 160–73. University of Toronto Press, Toronto.

———. 1980. *Many Tender Ties.* University of Oklahoma Press, Norman.

Wallace, W. Stewart. 1954. *The Pedlars from Quebec.* Ryerson Press, Toronto.

7

Improving Our Understanding of Native American Acculturation through the Archaeological Record

An Example from the Mono Basin of Eastern California

Brooke S. Arkush

As students of both history and human behavior, ethnohistorians rely upon a variety of sources to reconstruct Native lifeways in post-Contact North America. Recently, a number of studies have used archaeologically recovered materials to improve our understanding of Native American cultural continuity and change at the regional level (e.g., Deagan 1990; Hester 1990; Hoover and Costello 1985; Lightfoot et al. 1991; J. D. Rogers 1990; Smith 1987; Wood 1986; see Nassaney and Johnson, Introduction), and these material remains have proven to be especially useful for interpreting changing economic practices and technological systems. Protohistoric and early historic objects associated with residential sites have provided some of the more comprehensive inventories of non-Native artifacts and foodstuffs that were adopted by Native populations because such sites typically resulted from intensive, multiseasonal occupation during which a variety of activities transpired.

This chapter focuses upon the post-Contact occupation of two residential camps within an extensive, multicomponent Native site complex (CA-Mno-2122) in the Mono Lake Basin of east-central California (fig. 7.1).[1] Site CA-Mno-2122, occupying over 300 ha, contains various late prehistoric, protohistoric, and historic Native encampments as well as three prehistoric pronghorn traps and one historic mustang trap (see fig. 7.2). In addition to providing important data regarding pre-Contact communal pronghorn hunting in the western Great Basin, the site yielded extensive information regarding cultural change and continuity among the Mono

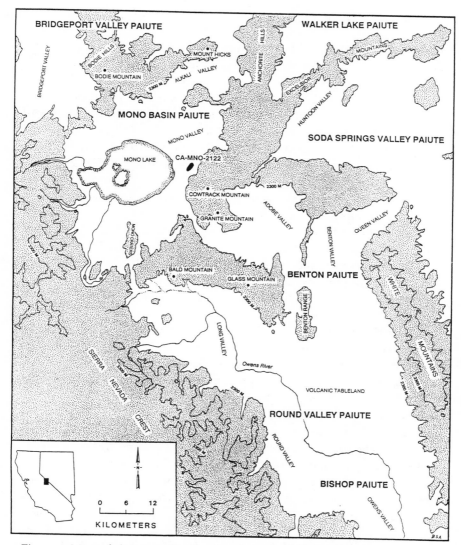

Fig. 7.1. Map of the natural and cultural geography of the east-central Sierra Nevada region, showing the location of archaeological site CA-Mno-2122

Basin Paiute during the late 19th and early 20th centuries. Site occupation commenced during Middle Archaic times (ca. 2000 B.C.), intensified during the succeeding Late Archaic and Protohistoric periods (A.D. 500–1800 and A.D. 1800–1850, respectively), and peaked during the early Historic period (A.D. 1850–1920) (Arkush 1995).

Ethnography and History

Historically, the Mono Basin was occupied primarily by the Northern Paiute–speaking *kucadikadi,* meaning "eaters of brine fly (*Hydropyrus hians*) pupae" (Fowler and Liljeblad 1986:464), a name that reflects the importance of the brine fly in the traditional Mono Basin Paiute diet. Brine fly pupae and larvae usually were harvested during the late summer, when large windrows were blown ashore at Mono Lake. These insects were then scooped up with baskets, sun-dried, husked by hand, and stored for the coming fall and winter (Brewer 1930:417; Davis 1965:33; Heizer 1950; Muir 1916:227; Steward 1933:256).

The aboriginal name applied to the Mono Basin Paiute was part of the Northern Paiute system of food- and area-named groups. Many areas in the western Great Basin were known to other Northern Paiute groups for the major food resources they contained. Therefore, the people who occupied these areas were the "eaters" of that resource. Maps of these areas and their corresponding names were produced by early ethnographers such as Julian Steward (1933:Map 1) and Omer Stewart (1939:Map 1; 1941:Map 1), and the possible functions of this terminological system have been discussed (Fowler 1982; Fowler and Liljeblad 1986:436–37). It appears that the primary function of such a system was to familiarize different Northern Paiute groups with the geography and resources of other regional areas, as these people were more or less free to move in and out of adjacent territories occupied by dialectically distinct Western Numic (Mono and Northern Paiute–speaking) groups.

The *kucadikadi* most likely consisted of some 200 (Davis 1965:36) to 250 (Bettinger 1982:22) individuals, distributed over an area of approximately 800 square miles. As with many Great Basin Numic groups, the bilaterally based nuclear family was the basis of pre-Contact *kucadikadi* economic and sociopolitical organization. Beyond the nuclear family was the camp group, whose size and composition was rather fluid. Such groups usually consisted of several related families, who camped and foraged together for much of the year and sometimes combined resources when necessary (Fowler and Liljeblad 1986:447).

The Mono Basin Paiute followed a pattern of residential movements in order to harvest various seasonally available food resources. During the late fall and winter, *kucadikadi* family units commonly gathered together to form large encampments. These camps probably represented the greatest annual social aggregation, and typically were located in the pinyon-juniper woodlands of the eastern and northern Mono Basin (Davis

1965:35). During this time, people subsisted primarily upon dried insects, pinyon nuts, and grass seeds harvested during the summer and early fall (Davis 1965:31).

In the early spring, winter encampments dispersed as individual families traveled into the lower canyons of the eastern Sierra Nevada and Bodie Hills in search of ripening greens and bulbs such as wild onion (*Allium* sp.), yellow cress (*Rorippa curvisiliqua*), wild hyacinth (*Dichelostemma pulchellum*), and sego lily (*Calochortus nuttallii*) (Bettinger 1982:30; Davis 1965:29). During the summer, meadows in the western and northern Mono Basin were the focus of activity, as temporary plant collecting and processing camps were established in order to exploit species such as Indian ricegrass (*Oryzopsis hymenoides*), wild rye (*Elymus cinereus*), and sunflower (*Helianthus* sp.). In addition to functioning as plant-processing sites, summer camps were often used as base camps for trans-Sierran trading expeditions (Bettinger 1982:30).

Summer probably also was a time when small groups of *kucadikadi* men hunted the high country for mule deer (*Odocoileus hemionus*) and mountain sheep (*Ovis canadensis*). Procurement of two major insect foods dominated the late summer. In July of alternate years, the larvae of the pandora moth (*Coloradia pandora lindseyi*), or *piagi*, were harvested in the Jeffrey pine groves (Aldrich 1921; Davis 1965:12, 29, 32; Eldredge 1923). Shallow trenches were dug around the bases of trees, and as the larvae migrated down the trunks, they were collected, dried, and stored in fiber bags inside small wood shelters. August was usually the time of the *kutsavi* harvest, when huge amounts of the larvae and pupae of the brine fly drifted ashore at Mono Lake (Aldrich 1912; Davis 1965:12, 33). As mentioned above, *kutsavi* was a seasonally important food item among the *kucadikadi*. It was also considered a delicacy, either eaten by itself, or added to a variety of foods. *Kutsavi* was much sought after by Native groups in central California, and was an important trade item offered by the Mono Basin Paiute.

Late summer and early fall was a time usually devoted to the harvesting of pinyon nuts, providing that the local stands of pinyon pine were productive (Davis 1965:33). This was when individual family camp groups gathered together for harvest festivals, rabbit drives, and, in some years, deer and pronghorn drives. Pinyon camps were sometimes used as winter encampments, but the majority of winter settlements were usually located at lower elevations, close to food caches (Davis 1965:35).

From their earliest contacts with Euro-Americans, the Mono Basin Paiute experienced dramatic changes that permanently altered their traditional culture. As with other Native groups throughout North America, these changes were manifested in modifications of both material and non-material culture. As elsewhere in the Great Basin, the Historic period of Mono Basin is characterized by sequential phases of Euro-American ex-ploration, early settlement associated with mining activities, and the es-tablishment of farms and ranches which spawned construction of perma-nent towns and transportation corridors and facilities. The latter developments were especially devastating for the Mono Basin Paiute, as they were displaced from optimal resource areas and forced to occupy the more marginal portions of their traditional home range.

Some regard the 1852 expedition of U.S. Army Lt. Tredwell Moore (Bunnell 1892) as the source of the earliest written account of the Mono Basin (e.g., Fletcher 1979, 1987), but it seems quite likely that the earliest historic account of the Mono Lake area was actually furnished by Zenas Leonard (1934:119–20) in 1833.[2] When Lieutenant Moore returned from Mono Basin in August 1852, he stopped in Mariposa, California, to dis-play samples of gold that his party had found just north of Mono Pass. These samples prompted Leroy Vining and several partners to settle in Mono Basin, where they began prospecting in the fall of 1852 (Bunnell 1892:278). Apparently, Vining never recovered much gold, as few people were attracted to the region until 1857, when the placer deposits at Dog-town were discovered by Mormon prospectors. The Dogtown placers were located just north of Mono Basin in the East Walker River drainage. These deposits created a great deal of excitement among miners working in the foothills of the western Sierra Nevada, where mining profits had been steadily declining.

In a short period of time, the rush to Dogtown was on, and men from various mining districts west of the Sierra Nevada came to the new dig-gings. As many as a hundred men worked the Dogtown placers from 1857 to 1859 during periods of good weather and stream flow (Kersten 1964: 495). Alarmed by early mining activities, the Mono Basin Paiute retreated into the more inaccessible portions of their home range, especially the remote canyons of the eastern Sierra Nevada Mountains (Davis 1965:7). After adjusting to the Anglo presence, they gradually returned to the newly settled areas of Mono Basin, where they began to practice a bicul-tural lifestyle in which their annual round of settlement and subsistence activities included seasonal wage labor and selling or trading traditional foods to white settlers.

In the fall of 1860, a new discovery at Esmerelda (soon to be renamed Aurora), in extreme western Nevada, marked the beginning of a substantial population increase throughout the region, and the subsequent degradation of the area's natural resources. In early 1863, the population of Aurora was over 3,000, and by summer it had risen to approximately 5,000 (Kersten 1964:497). This large influx of people spurred numerous developments in the Mono Basin, as roads were built, mills established, and ranches and farms created to provide meat and produce for the miners. Farming and stock raising came to dominate the Mono Basin economy after the Aurora mines started to fail in 1865.

Between 1865 and 1875, numerous farms and ranches were established at and near the springs, streams, and meadows of the western and northern Mono Basin (Browne 1869:396, 415, 443; Fletcher 1979:51–52; Le Conte 1875:114–15), areas that previously had been occupied by the *kucadikadi* during the spring and summer. These developments completely upset the aboriginal seasonal round, and forced local Natives to occupy the more marginal lands of the Mono Basin that had not been claimed by white settlers (Davis 1965:7; Fletcher 1979:53–54, 1987:40–41).

Euro-American activity in Mono Basin had a disastrous impact on the food resources of the *kucadikadi*. Settlers collected gull eggs by the thousands from the islands of Mono Lake, cut down entire tracts of pinyon pine, grazed their stock on the wild grasslands, and killed or drove away deer, pronghorn, and waterfowl. A transition slowly took place among the *kucadikadi* from an independent, aboriginally based lifeway to increasing dependence upon Euro-American employment, foods, and technology (Davis 1965:8), a familiar theme in the post-Contact settlement of North America (see Nassaney and Johnson, Introduction). *Kucadikadi* men and women earned between a dollar and a dollar and a half a day by performing menial tasks for local ranches, farms, mines, and the Bodie Railway and Lumber Company (Billeb 1968:128; Cain 1961:115; Calhoun 1984: 22; Fletcher 1979:55–57). Aspects of the aboriginal economy were quickly incorporated into the new one, as the Mono Basin Paiute sold or traded pine nuts, fish, waterfowl, gull eggs, and baskets to white inhabitants of the region (Cain 1961:120–21; Calhoun 1984:32–33). Participation in a system of wage labor formally marked the beginning of economic assimilation and social marginalization among the Mono Basin Paiute.

Historic developments in Mono Basin precipitated numerous changes in the cultural and physical landscape of the area. Euro-American settlement there had a wide range of effects upon the *kucadikadi,* forcing them to modify sociopolitical and economic practices that had prevailed in the region for at least a millennium. Materials and features present at the various Late Archaic, Protohistoric, and Historic period camps at CA-Mno-2122 have provided an extensive body of information from which aspects of the pre- and post-Contact Mono Basin Paiute lifeway can be extrapolated (Arkush 1995). A central strategy of this study was to augment archaeological data with ethnohistorical information to reconstruct processes of acculturative change that could not be extracted from the archaeological record alone. By carrying out such an exercise, one can document various aspects of the contact continuum as it occurred in the Mono Basin.

The historic component at CA-Mno-2122 is one of the more interesting aspects of the complex, and offers a great deal of empirical information concerning acculturation among the Mono Basin Paiute. As used here, the term *acculturation* is defined as major cultural changes that occur as the result of continuous, face-to-face contact between two distinct cultural traditions, with the Native population being the primary receptor culture, adopting cultural elements from the intrusive colonizing population (e.g., Foster 1960:6; Smith 1987:119; cf. Carlson, chap. 10; Kehoe, chap. 6). Use of the term *receptor culture* does not imply that Native peoples played a passive role in the acculturation process. Indeed, the vast majority of Native Americans in contact situations selectively adopted items of foreign material culture according to their own culturally distinct values and goals (e.g., E. Rogers 1983; Hugill and Dickson 1988). Not surprisingly, many nontraditional items and activities that were adopted by Native peoples provided them with distinct adaptive advantages in rapidly changing physical and social environments. The type of acculturation experienced by the Mono Basin Paiute was primarily nondirected, and whenever possible, new cultural elements were integrated into the preexisting Native lifeway so as not to entirely replace traditional practices.[3] For the most part, a Native worldview controlled which aspects of Euro-American culture were adopted, and these items were defined in a Native cultural context (e.g., J. D. Rogers 1990:11).

Various archaeological projects have documented Historic period Great Basin Native interaction with Euro-Americans by investigating Northern Paiute and Western Shoshone encampments associated with mining towns and ranches in western and central Nevada. Of these, the more notable studies include those in Grass Valley (Ambro 1972; Ambro and Wallof 1972), Virginia City (Hattori 1975), and Candelaria (Queen 1987). Artifact assemblages recovered from these sites reflect extensive material culture modification and are often dominated by Euro-American artifacts, including a wide variety of cans and bottles, nails, wire, spent

shotgun shells and cartridge casings, glass embroidery beads, and manufactured clothing remains. The presence of aboriginal artifacts such as
ground stone implements attests to the continued production of some traditional tool forms, as well as the consumption of traditional plant foods.
Faunal remains commonly recovered from historic Great Basin Native
sites include those of cattle, sheep, and pig, as well as jackrabbits and
waterfowl.

After 1850 most Great Basin peoples implemented three distinct adaptive strategies in response to Euro-American colonization of their homelands (e.g., Berry 1980:12). One was to withdraw altogether from contact
with whites, staying away from established roads and settlements in an
attempt to continue practicing a traditional lifestyle with a minimum of
interference (Malouf and Findlay 1986:513). Another strategy was to
consolidate several or many camp groups to form a raiding band. These
bands usually were well mounted and highly organized, and they as-
saulted emigrant wagon trains and ranches, appropriating livestock, foodstuffs, and material goods (Layton 1977:368). The third post-Contact
adaptive strategy was to coexist with white populations and exploit their
abundant resources. This often resulted in small groups attaching themselves to white settlements where they attempted to eke out a living
through a combination of traditional and nontraditional methods. One of
the more interesting aspects of the Mono Basin Paiutes' exploitation of
Hispanic- or Anglo-introduced resources represented at CA-Mno-2122
was the construction and use of wing traps for capturing wild horses that
roamed throughout the eastern Mono Basin region after about 1860 or
1870.

Mustang Trapping at CA-Mno-2122

Of the four V-wing traps at the site complex, three (Trap 1, 2, and 4) are
Late Prehistoric period pronghorn traps, and one (Trap 3) is a Historic
period mustang trap (fig. 7.2). All three pre-Contact wing traps consist
primarily of fire-felled juniper posts that are still in place but have burnt to
the ground, most likely in range fires. The vast majority of juniper posts at
Trap 3 were felled either with axes or saws; milled lumber, nails and wire
have been used to reinforce parts of the corral.

This extensive feature consists of some 1,100 juniper posts. Its drift
fences (or drive wings) were erected in an uneven "V" configuration, with
the west drift fence measuring 950 m and the east fence measuring 260 m
(fig. 7.3). Many of the drift fence posts at Trap 3 are still standing, and

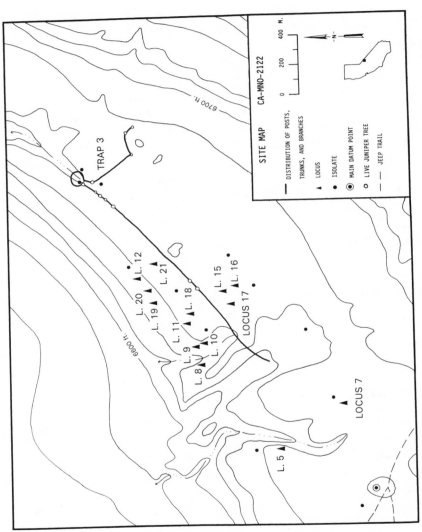

Fig. 7.2. Map of the central portion of archaeological site CA-Mno-2122, with locations of Historic period camps (loci) and mustang trap (Trap 3).

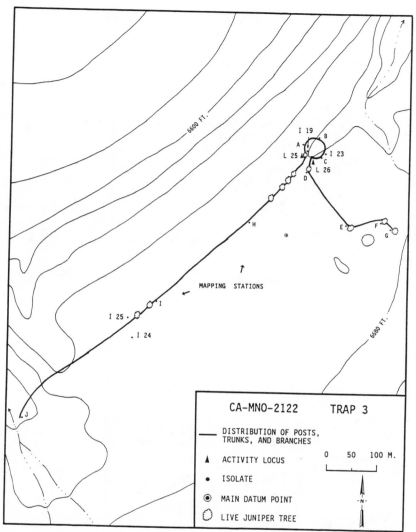

Fig. 7.3. Map of Trap 3

most range from 1.5 to 2.5 m in height (figs. 7.4 and 7.5). The two con-
verging fences end at a circular corral measuring 35 × 40 m; it consists of
numerous juniper posts ranging from 2.6 to 3.3 m in length and from 12
to 35 cm in diameter (fig. 7.6). Most of the corral posts have fallen over in
place, but their close spacing indicates that during its use, this corral was
quite sturdy. The catch pen was strategically placed at the head of a small

Fig. 7.4. Portion of west wing of Trap 3. View north.

Fig. 7.5. Portion of east wing of Trap 3. View east.

Fig. 7.6. Western portion of Trap 3 corral. View northeast.

gully, effectively concealing it from the horses' view as they were driven toward it. After entering the corral, the animals would have been confined to a relatively small area and surrounded by a network of large posts encircling the high ground of the drainage.

Two small sites (Locus 25 and 26) are associated with the Trap 3 corral (fig. 7.3), but it is uncertain whether they were formed as a result of mustang trapping activities there. Each one contained only small assemblages of ground stone tools (manos and/or metates) and fire-cracked rock, objects that are commonly found at both pre- and post-Contact Native sites throughout the region. One of the historic isolates found at the Trap 3 corral (Isolate 19) consists of a shovel with an 1878 patent date stamped onto its shank, and this artifact provides a reliable *terminus post quem* date for the trap's initial construction. The presence of cut nails in some of the Trap 3 timbers also supports a late 19th century date for the trap's inception. For the most part, cut nails were used in the American West until the very early 1900s, when they were replaced by wire nails between about 1905 and 1910 (e.g., Fontana et al. 1962:44–50). Wire nails also were used to reinforce portions of the Trap 3 corral, and their presence reflects early twentieth century use of this feature. Based upon the above-mentioned time sensitive artifacts, it seems likely that Trap 3 was constructed and used sometime between approximately 1880 and 1920.

The appearance of wild horses in Mono Basin apparently dates back to at least the 1870s (Fletcher 1987:88), because by the early 1880s, various feral herds ranged throughout the Bodie Hills and the upper reaches of Sierran canyons (Fletcher 1987:88), as well as on the east side of Mono Lake (Calhoun 1984:30–37; La Braque 1984:ii, 64, 69). George La Braque was a member of a Basque family that had settled in Mono Basin during the mid-1880s. His daughter, Lily Mathieu La Braque, wrote an account of the early history of Mono Basin and noted that, in 1911, her father was given a horse purchased from some *kucadikadi* men, who had captured it wild "back of Mono Lake" (La Braque 1984:64). La Braque (1984:69–71) also provided an interesting account of an attempt by a Paiute man named Scotty John and her father to drive a herd of feral horses into a corral on the east side of Mono Lake sometime around 1913; this incident may very well have occurred at Trap 3.

Various long-time residents of Mono Basin have heard of the mustang trap at CA-Mno-2122 (Wallace McPherson, personal communication 1987; Arlene Reveal, personal communication 1988; Tom Buckley, personal communication 1988). Tom Buckley, a *kucadikadi* elder who was born near Mono Lake in 1897, provided the most detailed information regarding the structure's history. During an interview at his home in Benton Station, California, he indicated that several Mono Basin Paiute men originally built this mustang trap, but that it had been used and maintained by both Paiutes and Anglos. According to Buckley, Jim Cline was one of the local white ranchers who captured mustangs at Trap 3, and most of these animals were used as rodeo horses. Tom Buckley apparently never drove mustangs at Trap 3, but he did participate in several mustang drives at a wing trap in Adobe Valley, located just southeast of Mono Lake. As he described the general design of a mustang trap, Tom Buckley drew a picture in the dirt of two wings ending in a corral, stating that "after we drove the horses into the corral, we'd close the gate with wire, then lasso 'em."

Perhaps the most interesting aspect of Trap 3 is that it demonstrates how the Mono Basin Paiute used a component of their aboriginal subsistence economy (big-game intercept hunting facilities) during historic times to exploit a new resource that had been introduced through Euro-American exploration and settlement of the region. Both archaeological and historical data indicate that Trap 3 was used solely to capture feral horses, and pronghorn were never driven there. For the most part, it seems that pronghorn had been extirpated from the Mono Basin by about 1880 (e.g., Billeb 1968:35; Wedertz 1978:172).

Domestic Architecture and Related Activities at CA-Mno-2122

Historic occupation of CA-Mno-2122 is represented by seventeen sites (referred to herein as "loci") dating between about 1880 and 1920.[4] Most historic loci appear to be base camps associated with fall and/or winter residence where a variety of traditional and semitraditional activities transpired. Eight historic loci are residential camps containing the remains of juniper-pole windbreaks and associated refuse scatters, and two historic loci (Locus 7 and 17; fig. 7.2) contain the remains of conical wood winter houses, or "wickiups," constructed of axe-cut juniper poles with circular-to-oval floor plans and having slightly excavated floors. Julian Steward (1933:264) described the typical Mono Basin winter house (*tomogani*) as being cone-shaped and "10 to 12 feet high and of equal diameter" with pole frames and coverings of sod, bark, wild rye, and pine or juniper needles. The wickiup sites experienced the most intensive use of all historic loci at CA-Mno-2122, and contained a wide array of Native and non-Native items. Therefore, these two residential bases best allow us to assess patterns of cultural continuity and change among the Mono Basin Paiute as portrayed at this site complex.

Locus 7

Locus 7 is situated along the west drift fence of Trap 2 (fig. 7.2), and surface features there include the remains of a burned winter house, a partial wickiup frame, a windbreak, and two woodcutting areas (fig. 7.7). The burned wickiup was completely excavated, and this effort resulted in the recovery of a substantial amount of material.

Burned Wickiup

The burned wickiup at Locus 7 was a traditional conical winter house (e.g., Steward 1933:264), composed of at least sixty-five juniper poles (fig. 7.8). The structure has a circular floor plan and a slightly excavated floor sloping inward toward the center. The superstructure of this house had been destroyed by fire, possibly as the result of traditional funerary practices (e.g., Ambro 1972:95); all that remained were the bases of posts, rising some 10 cm above the surface. The interior diameter of the structure measured 4.2 × 4.8 m. Both wire and nails may have been used to secure the structure, as these items were found in various parts of the wickiup

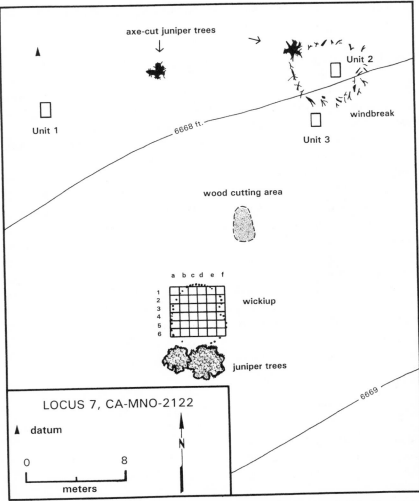

Fig. 7.7. Map of the southern and central portions of Locus 7, showing locations of surface features, wickiup excavation grid, and test units. (Surface artifacts not plotted.)

during its excavation. The doorway was 50 cm wide, faced due east, and was marked by an inward curving of the wall posts (fig. 7.8). When in use, a juniper bark door may have covered the east-facing entrance (e.g., Davis 1965:9). A section profile of the structure indicated that a shallow pit with a central depth of about 20 cm was dug prior to its construction.

Most recovered artifacts came from the living floor located beneath the roof fall stratum, including items of Anglo clothing and various foodstuff

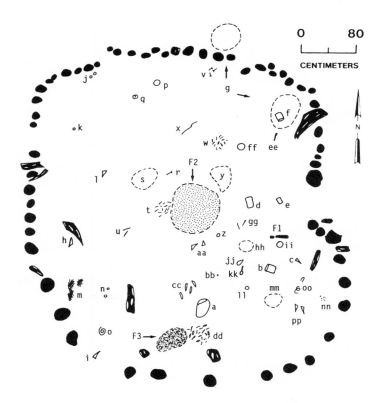

Fig. 7.8. Plan map of burned wickiup at Locus 7, showing locations of subsurface artifacts and features: *a*, fire-fractured basalt cobble; *b*, slip-lid can; *c*, bottle sherd; *d*, fire-fractured basalt cobble; *e*, spice can; *f*, slip-lid can; *g*, vandalized areas; *h*, window sherd; *i*, knife-cut large-mammal bone fragment; *j*, harness rivets; *k*, clothing rivet; *l*, bottle sherds; *m*, carbonized cotton fabric; *n*, metal buttons; *o*, coiled wire; *p*, can base; *q*, belt buckle; *r*, wire nail; *s*, glass beads (approx. 230); *t*, burnt bird bone fragments; *u*, cut nails; *v*, wire nails; *w*, burnt small-mammal bone fragments; *x*, wire strand; *y*, blasting-powder keg fragments; *z*, glass button; *aa*, window sherds; *bb*, clothing rivet; *cc–dd*, bottle sherds; *ee*, railroad spike fragment; *ff*, axle-grease can lid; *gg*, wire nail, cut nail; *hh*, glass sherds; *ii*, bottle base; *jj*, porcelain China doll's head fragment; *kk*, teaspoon; *ll*, bone button; *mm*, bottle sherds; *nn*, shell button fragments; *oo*, wire strands; *pp*, window sherds. *Features*: *F1*, wooden plank; *F2*, hearth area; *F3*, concentration of fire-fractured ground stone fragments.

containers. Numerous glass embroidery or "seed" beads suggested that one or more of the structure's occupants may have produced beaded craftwork, and ground stone artifacts indicated that some foods were prepared through traditional milling techniques. The metal artifact assemblage found within the wickiup is diverse, and one of these consists of a small stove that was fashioned from two blasting powder kegs that had been wired together and placed over a central hearth area.

Various window and bottle glass sherds were recovered from the wickiup, and many had melted as a result of the structure fire. Of special interest here is one complete aquamarine Chinese medicine vial recovered from the northern perimeter of the structure. These vials often are erroneously referred to as "opium bottles," and usually contained traditional types of Chinese medicine in either pill, powder, or liquid forms (Gilbert S. Lee, personal communication 1988). The presence of two Chinese medicine vials at Locus 7 (one was collected from the surface) suggests that the Paiutes there may have obtained this medication from Chinese migrant workers in the general region. Emil Billeb was the foreman of a lumber mill located in a jeffrey pine grove on the south side of Mono Lake who reported that the Chinese and Paiutes employed at Mono Mills were on friendly terms (Billeb 1968:127). This is not at all surprising, because both groups were relegated to low-status positions within the dominant Euro-American social system.

One of the three features that were identified within the burned wickiup consisted of the above-mentioned hearth, from which two flotation samples were collected. Results of floral and faunal analyses of these soil samples indicate that occupants of the structure processed and consumed pinyon nuts, jackrabbits and cottontails, various small birds, and possibly mule deer. Other animal remains recovered from the burned structure consisted of about 200 pieces of rabbit- and deer-sized bone, and additional macrobotanical remains collected during the screening process consisted of a burned peach pit fragment, several carbonized pinyon nuts, and various pinyon hulls.

Wickiup Frame

A partially standing historic wickiup frame is located northwest of the locus datum point (fig. 7.7). When intact, the basal diameter of this structure measured between 4.0 and 4.5 m, and it reached a maximum height of approximately 2.3 m (fig. 7.9). All poles are axe-cut, and most of them apparently were obtained from a juniper tree located immediately west of the structure. The apex of the frame has been secured with wire, and there

Fig. 7.9. Partially standing wickiup frame and completed Unit 4

is no evidence of a sod/bark covering over the frame, suggesting that its occupants may have used a tarp or some other type of mass-manufactured sheeting for a cover (e.g., Merriam 1955:Plate 19b).

A single 1 × 2 m test unit was excavated in the southern portion of the structure, and resulted in the recovery of an assemblage similar to that of the burned wickiup (i.e., metal, glass, leather, milled lumber, and ground stone). Metal specimens consisted of a slip-lid can, metal rod, shoe or boot eyelet, wire strand, square cut nails, and wire nails. Recovered glass artifacts consisted of several light green window glass sherds and over a hundred embroidery beads. Surface materials recovered from within the wickiup frame consisted of a piece of shoe leather, a basalt metate fragment, and several milled lumber fragments.

Locus 17

Located in the west portion of the Trap 2 corral (see fig. 7.2), Locus 17 contains the remains of a burned wickiup and an associated woodcutting area (fig. 7.10). The burned winter house was completely excavated and yielded an extensive historic artifact assemblage. Additionally, two 1 × 1 m test units were excavated in areas that contained numerous glass beads, from which over 1,750 specimens were recovered.

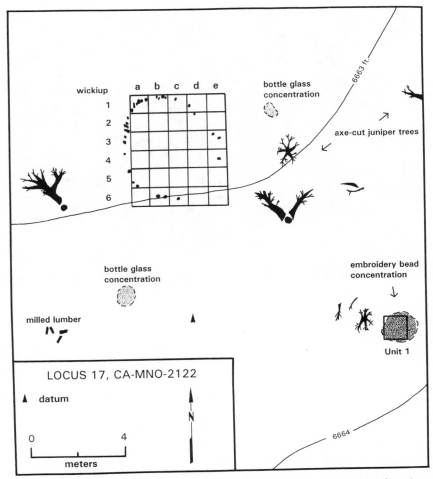

Fig. 7.10. Map of the western and central portions of Locus 17, showing locations of surface features, wickiup excavation grid, test unit, and selected surface artifacts.

Burned Wickiup

This winter house is ovate in plan, composed of at least sixty-three juniper posts, and measures 3 × 4 m in diameter (fig. 7.11). As with the wickiup at Locus 7, wire and nails appear to have been used in its construction because these artifacts were found throughout the upper portion of the house fill. This house also had been destroyed by fire, effectively sealing the living floor with a layer of charred wood and ashes. The east-facing doorway measured approximately 70 cm wide, and immediately outside the doorway was a one-meter-long vestibule (fig. 7.11). According to Steward (1933:264), this was the traditional orientation and design of winter house entrances at Mono Lake. A section profile of the wickiup interior indicated that it contained an inward sloping floor with a maximum depth of 35 cm.

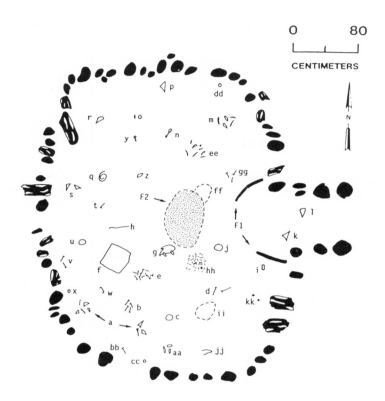

Fig. 7.11. Plan map of burned wickiup at Locus 17, showing locations of subsurface artifacts and features: *a*, window sherds; *b*, spike nails; *c*, slip-lid can lid; *d*, spike nails; *e*, wire nails; *f*, kerosene can base; *g*, portion of canvas raincoat; *h*, wire strand; *i*, spice can lid; *j*, can lid; *k*, window sherd; *l–m*, bottle sherds; *n*, teaspoon; *o*, obsidian arrow point; *p*, window sherd; *q*, wire strand; *r–s*, window sherds; *t*, cut nail; *u*, can lid; *v*, wire nails; *w*, metal handle; *x*, shotshell base; *y*, jackrabbit scapula; *z*, metal spout; *aa*, bottle sherds; *bb*, wire nail; *cc*, shotshell base; *dd*, metal button; *ee*, window sherds; *ff*, burnt small-mammal bones; *gg*, wire nails; *hh*, wire nails; *ii*, sheet metal fragments; *jj*, bottle sherd; *kk*, glass buttons. *Features*: *F1*, wooden planks; *F2*, hearth area.

Metal, glass, leather, shell, cloth, and flaked stone constituted the artifact assemblage recovered from within the wickiup. Metal objects were diverse and included several can bases, one of which is from a five-gallon kerosene can. The other can bases are from either slip-lid or hole-in-cap containers. One of these specimens exhibits approximately fifty 4-mm holes, indicating that it may have been used as a strainer, or else as a gauge to size the warp and weft materials used in producing basketry (e.g., Bates 1982:15). Two 10-gauge shotgun shell bases dating between about 1890 and 1900, one .44- or .45-caliber cartridge, and two ground-edge percussion caps also were recovered from within the wickiup.

The glass assemblage consisted of numerous aqua, amber, and light green bottle sherds, various window glass sherds, a large number of embroidery beads, several glass buttons, and a marble. Two obsidian arrow points (a fragmentary Desert Side-notched specimen and a complete, aberrant corner-notched specimen) and one obsidian flake also were found in the house fill.

Two features were identified within the Locus 17 wickiup, and one of them was a hearth area from which two ash samples were collected for flotation analysis. Not surprisingly, food remains recovered from the hearth area and living floor indicate that the inhabitants of Locus 17 consumed foods that were similar to those represented at Locus 7. Approximately 140 pieces of bone were collected from the Locus 17 wickiup deposit (some of which were burned), and most appeared to be those of rabbits, although some were large mammal elements, including domestic pig. Carbonized pinyon nuts and pinyon hull fragments, as well as part of a walnut shell, represent plant food debris recovered from the house fill.

General Surface Assemblage

The general surface assemblage of Locus 17 consists of metal, glass, leather, shell, cloth, ground stone, and flaked stone objects. One can lid or base exhibits numerous 4-mm holes (fig. 7.12) and may have been used to size the warp and weft materials used in making basketry (e.g., Bates 1982:15). An awl fashioned from a wire nail and a carved wooden handle (fig. 7.12) also may be associated with basket making at Locus 17. This awl closely resembles the Yuki specimen from northern California pictured by Meighan (1953:Plate 2, item 18). In pre-Contact times, various California Native groups used bone awls to manufacture coiled baskets, and after contact metal awls often replaced these tools. As noted by Bates (1982:15), metal awls were superior to those fashioned from artiodactyl

5 cm.

Fig. 7.12. Awl and modified can lid or base recovered from Locus 17. These implements were probably used to produce coiled basketry.

metapodials, as they stayed sharp longer, were more easily honed to a fine point, and did not break under rough handling.

A wide variety of glass artifacts were present on the surface of Locus 17. These included sherds of aqua, light green, clear, and amethyst bottles, pieces of window glass, and one button. Two drawn trade beads and over 1,800 embroidery beads also were recovered from the surface and subsurface deposit. The surface ground stone assemblage included several mano fragments, a metate fragment, pestle, and pumice abrader. Flaked stone objects included two Desert Side-notched arrow points, one of which is poorly made and produced by removing flakes from the margins of a thick triangular flake. Neither face exhibits pressure flaking, and seems to reflect historic devolution of the Mono Basin Paiute lithic industry (although a child may have produced it).

Discussion

Both Locus 7 and 17 are residential camps occupied over the course of perhaps several winters by family groups engaged in various traditional activities, the foremost being construction of aboriginal-style winter houses. Cross-dating of shotgun shell bases, embossed and labeled can lids, and other temporally diagnostic historic artifacts implies both loci were first occupied during the late 1880s or early 1890s, and abandoned sometime between 1910 and 1920. These two sites provide interesting information concerning cultural continuity among the Mono Basin Paiute. The burned wickiups demonstrate that traditional winter houses were built as late as 1920, and indicate the construction of aboriginal-style domestic structures was still an important aspect of post-Contact *kucadikadi* culture (Arkush 1987).

Further, the burned structures may represent the continued practice of traditional funerary rites (although lightning strikes or range fires may have destroyed them). It appears that both wickiups were intentionally burned, as there were still serviceable items within them at the time of their abandonment. Traditional Great Basin Native funerary practices typically included primary interment of the deceased in a crevice, cave, or hillside, and destruction of their dwelling and some of their belongings. The family or camp group then moved away from the camp where the death had occurred (Hultkrantz 1986:636; Scott 1966:65, 83; Steward 1941:257; Stewart 1941:412). Ghosts were feared because they were capable of taking the living with them to the land of the dead, and the practice of destroying a deceased person's home prevented the return of the dead person's spirit among her or his surviving relatives. Ambro (1972:95) has also identified a similar pattern at Ridge Village North, a historic Grass Valley Shoshone encampment in central Nevada.

Numerous items of Euro-American clothing at the wickiup loci indicate that the Mono Basin Paiute had adopted a wide variety of Anglo garments by 1900. Evidence from both sites attests to the use of leather boots and shoes, cotton shirts, bib overalls, cotton pants, and possibly socks. These archaeological data compare favorably with historical documentation provided by Billeb (1968), Cain (1961), and Calhoun (1984).

An interesting aspect of historic Mono Basin Paiute culture represented at Locus 7 was their possible use of traditional Chinese homeopathic medicines. The presence of two Chinese medicine vials there suggests that the *kucadikadi* consumed the contents of these vials, and did not simply collect empty medicine vials and other exotic Chinese artifacts, which were quite different from Euro-American artifacts. If the latter were true, one would expect to find other types of imported Chinese artifacts at Locus 7, but this is not the case. The *kucadikadi* may have adopted traditional Chinese medicines after livestock overgrazing reduced the availability of Native medicinal plants.

The presence of flaked stone and ground stone artifacts at Locus 7 and 17 also attests to the continued practice of some pre-Contact industries (e.g., Layton 1977:368), although the arrow points from Locus 17 are poorly made. Additionally, the occurrence of a wire nail awl, modified tin can bases or lids, and numerous glass seed beads suggests that one or more residents of Locus 17 may have produced beaded baskets. Historic basket-making among the Mono Basin Paiute is widely documented (Bates 1979, 1982; Merriam 1955:117–22), and represents post-Contact production of aboriginal textiles. Merriam also noted historic changes in the designs of Mono Basin Paiute baskets made for sale to white tourists:

> In the older ones the designs are usually simple but highly effective. In some of the modern ones they are more diffuse and much less artistic. Some of the small ones, now made to sell, are overloaded with design and the design is brought down over the bottom—a thing I have never seen in an old Paiute basket. . . . such baskets find a ready market and bring good prices, so that there is very little incentive for continuing the old styles. (Merriam 1955:121)

Most obsidian artifacts recovered from historic loci at CA-Mno-2122 and subjected to X-ray fluorescence analysis (including those from Locus 7 and 17) are from local source areas such as Mono Craters or Mono Glass Mountain. This may reflect the historic disruption of pre-Contact settlement and trade patterns, in which the *kucadikadi* covered an extensive home range and obtained exotic items through both local and distant trade networks.

Summary and Conclusions

Historically, CA-Mno-2122 was utilized by family groups for seasonal habitation during both fall and winter. At this time, the *kucadikadi* were living a bicultural existence, in which they had incorporated aspects of Anglo economics and behavior into their post-Contact lifeways. The traditional seasonal round had been extensively modified, and both *kucadikadi* men and women worked as wage laborers on farms and ranches, and in mills, mines, and towns during the spring and summer (figs. 7.13 and 7.14). With the coming of the pine nut harvest in early fall, they deserted white settlements to pursue traditional economic and social activities. Pinyon harvests functioned to maintain *kucadikadi* cultural identity, and probably allowed them to feel some sense of independence in spite of being surrounded by adversity. Many of the historic camps clus-

Fig. 7.13. Paiute man and woman and their dog in windbreak on Bodie Hill. Photograph by A. A. Forbes, ca. 1880. Photograph courtesy of Vickie C. Daniels.

Fig. 7.14. Northern Paiute woman, possibly Mono Basin Paiute, washing clothes at the Sentinel Hotel, Yosemite Valley, California. She is wearing a necklace of European glass trade beads. Photograph by John P. Soule, ca. 1870. Photograph courtesy of the Yosemite National Park Research Library.

tered within and north of the Trap 2 corral may have been occupied by multifamily task groups who established residential base camps there while harvesting pine nuts over a forty-year period during the late 1800s and early 1900s.

Historic site loci serve as gauges of cultural change among the Mono Basin Paiute. For example, artifact assemblages recovered from these areas demonstrate that various components of Euro-American material culture became increasingly common among them. Furthermore, numerous Anglo foods and beverages were adopted by the *kucadikadi* to supplement their traditional diet and replace foods that had been depleted by Anglo land-use activities. Both archaeological and ethnohistoric data indicate that the Mono Basin Paiute commonly ate the meat of pigs, cows, and sheep. Alcoholic beverages, evaporated milk, coffee, and tea also were consumed. Canned goods such as sardines, vegetables, and fruits, as well as flour, baking powder, and spices also were components of the historic Mono Basin Paiute diet. Many of the cans and bottles at the site could have been scavenged from refuse deposits, but the wages they earned probably enabled them to purchase food and beverages from the stores of Bodie, Lundy, and Mono Mills. In her Mono Basin Paiute ethnography, Emma Lou Davis (1965:35) reported that "the people drove to their winter camps in wagons loaded with potatoes, flour, and store goods." The *kucadikadi* desired a variety of Euro-American foods, beverages, tools, and clothing, and participated in a wage-labor system in order to obtain these goods.

Aspects of aboriginal culture that continued to be practiced by the *kucadikadi* included the production and use of ground and flaked stone implements and basketry, and the construction of traditional winter houses and V-wing traps. Ground stone artifacts recovered from historic loci consisted of manos, metates, pumice abraders, and mortars. Flaked stone objects recovered from historic activity areas consisted primarily of aberrant projectile points and cores and sparse amounts of lithic debitage.

The remains of conical wooden winter houses at Locus 7 and 17 indicate that the construction of traditional wickiups was still an important part of the post-Contact *kucadikadi* culture and worldview some three generations after Euro-American settlement of the Mono Basin (fig. 7.15). Additionally, Trap 3 illustrates how the *kucadikadi* utilized an aspect of their pre-Contact subsistence economy to exploit feral horses that roamed Mono Basin at the turn of this century. This historic mustang trap was built in the same fashion as many pre-Contact Great Basin pronghorn and deer traps.

Fig. 7.15. Two Bridgeport Valley Paiute girls in front of wickiup. Note the presence of lard buckets and manos in right foreground, and the Mono County courthouse in mid background. Photographer unknown, ca. 1890. Photograph courtesy of the Nevada Historical Society.

Ground stone artifacts were used at most historic site loci. Traditional plant foods, especially pinyon nuts, were consumed in historic times, and the *kucadikadi* used traditional ground stone implements to process these foods. Wells (1983:66) noted a similar pattern in the Grass Valley region of central Nevada, where manos and metates were found in association with historic artifacts at numerous historic Shoshone villages. Lowie (1924:204) also noted the widespread use of ground stone tools among the Northern Paiute of western Nevada during the early 1900s.

Although basketry was not recovered from Locus 17, this encampment yielded numerous artifacts that suggest coiled basketry was produced there. Historically, the Mono Basin Paiute were known throughout eastern California and western Nevada as excellent basket makers. Beginning in the early 1900s, whites began to purchase *kucadikadi* baskets, which provided an incentive for the continued production of these objects (Bates 1979). Not only was basketry a highly developed functional art form among the *kucadikadi*, it also became a major income source for some of them in the Historic period; various *kucadikadi* women continued to produce baskets well into the 1930s and 1940s (Bates 1979, 1982). This proud tradition continues today, as several members of the California Indian Basketweavers Association are of *kucadikadi* descent.

Components of aboriginal material culture were retained in historic times for several reasons. In some cases there were no readily available equivalent items of white material culture to replace such traditional implements as manos, metates, and pumice abraders. Other items (such as baskets) were associated with the core values of a viable cultural system, and the *kucadikadi* refused to abandon them. The Mono Basin Paiute also abandoned a number of pre-Contact cultural practices due to pressures from whites. For example, certain behaviors (such as nudity and consumption of raw animal foods) were looked upon with derision by settlers, and many Euro-American materials and customs may have been adopted in order to gain acceptance among the local non-Native population. Acceptance of Euro-American identity markers had survival value; the Mono Basin Paiute certainly were aware of this reality and exploited it to their benefit. By adopting various non-Native behaviors and materials, the Mono Basin Paiute were able to extend their socioeconomic support network beyond its traditional boundaries.

In spite of the fact that local whites economically exploited the *kucadikadi,* they also incorporated them into their social networks. In many cases, relationships between the Mono Basin Paiutes and their Anglo employers were much closer than those of typical wage laborers (e.g., Warren and Hearne 1974:28). This is evidenced by the practice of Paiutes adopting the surnames of their employers (Cain 1961:93; Calhoun 1984:32), attending white social functions (Calhoun 1984:60), and sending their children to local elementary schools (Calhoun 1984:60). Relationships of this kind certainly were more than just economically based, for they imply a degree of interdependence and social bonding.

During early contact between Native North Americans and Euro-Americans, all Native groups developed ways of dealing with a foreign and technologically powerful cultural system (e.g., J. D. Rogers 1990:3). In such situations, a major consideration governing the adoption of new cultural components is whether they threaten core values associated with traditional social organization, ideology, and aesthetics (Spicer 1961). For the most part, the *kucadikadi* quickly incorporated new types of tools that were technologically superior to portions of the aboriginal tool kit, but they were hesitant to adopt non-Native forms of social organization and religion (Davis 1965:6, 13). The high value placed upon Native aesthetics also partially explains the continued production of basketry, use of facial tattoos, and recitation of traditional myths and songs (e.g., Davis 1965:14; Merriam 1955:72, 117–22).

The acculturative milieu of the *kucadikadi* was primarily nondirected in that the element of force was not a significant factor in their post-Contact experience. Foreign cultural elements were accepted and integrated into Paiute culture in accordance with Native cultural interests and principles of integration. A classical functionalist model commonly associated with nondirected acculturation is that of incorporative integration (Spicer 1961:529–30), a process in which the transfer of elements from one cultural system and their integration into another system occur in such a way that they conform to the meaningful and functional relations within the accepting culture. Although this perspective is outdated and lacks interpretive power (e.g., Beaudry et al. 1991), it adequately describes an aspect of the *kucadikadi* post-Contact lifeway and their strategy of cultural accommodation. The concept of incorporative integration is similar to that of innovation acceptance (Hugill and Dickson 1988; E. Rogers 1983), in which aspects of foreign material culture are adopted selectively according to the values and goals of the receiving group. As J. D. Rogers (1990) noted, the single overriding aspect of all contact situations is that each culture operates according to its own set of expectations and attempts to maintain a viable cultural system.

The Mono Basin Paiute adopted some foreign material traits because they offered advantages over aboriginal implements, and were viewed as enhancing the existing organization of their culture. Obviously, the *kucadikadi* had some degree of freedom in choosing from an array of new material and behavioral possibilities, and adopted those that appealed to them or offered an adaptive advantage in a new cultural environment, and ignored those that were viewed as detrimental. It is quite clear that a Native worldview controlled which aspects of Euro-American culture were adopted by the Mono Basin Paiute, as it determined the value and role of an object or behavior in a Native context (e.g., J. D. Rogers 1990:11). This same type of strategy has been archaeologically documented throughout much of the Great Basin (Ambro 1972; Bettinger 1976, 1989; Clewlow and Pastron 1972; Delacorte and McGuire 1993; Hattori 1975; Queen 1987). Furthermore, some components of Euro-American material and nonmaterial culture probably were rejected by the Mono Basin Paiute as an expression of their dissatisfaction or contempt for the foreign socioeconomic system that had been imposed upon them (e.g., Rubertone 1989). In less than a generation, white colonization of the eastern Sierra Nevada region had upset the delicate ecology of the Mono

Basin and relegated its Native peoples to a marginal existence, a circumstance that surely evoked a good deal of anguish and confusion among the *kucadikadi*.

Historic site materials at CA-Mno-2122 indicate that the *kucadikadi* adopted various elements of Euro-American culture that either improved upon Native tools and practices or proved to be adequate substitutes for aboriginal resources that had been destroyed or monopolized by whites. The displacement of aboriginal material culture accelerated during the Euro-American settlement of the Mono Basin, as increased quantities of manufactured goods became available. Clothing styles, subsistence routines, and technological systems were modified as new materials were accepted.

Although Euro-American colonization of the eastern Sierra Nevada region forever altered local Native societies, most groups (including the Mono Basin Paiute) retained numerous pre-Contact sociopolitical and economic practices. By the early 20th century many groups had developed a distinctive bicultural system (e.g., Berndt and Berndt 1970:54) in which both the Northern Paiute and English languages were spoken, and Native children attended predominantly white schools. The continued production of Native artwork, use of traditional kinship terminology, and practice of Northern Paiute ceremonial and foraging activities were in part survival mechanisms that provided the *kucadikadi* with a sense of cultural identity and solidarity. Moreover, the retention of these traits may also have helped to mitigate the anomie that resulted from white settlement and Native disenfranchisement.

In a very general sense, much of the acculturative process experienced by the Mono Basin Paiute (as well as various other far western Native groups) was different from that of Native North American groups who practiced institutionalized warfare. With the exception of a segment of the Mono Basin Paiute participating in several small-scale battles that constituted the Owens Valley "War" during the early 1860s, the *kucadikadi* never engaged in organized military campaigns against Euro-American settlers. The lack of armed Native resistance to white encroachment appears to have been a major factor in the relatively nonviolent contact continuum experienced by the Mono Basin Paiute. This nonviolent response to white settlement and exploitation may have stemmed partly from the lack of a military organization that transcended local groups and would have allowed the Northern Paiute to field a relatively large force to attack a common enemy. Other factors that contributed to this situation included low Native and non-Native population density and abundant land, although the *kucadikadi* who attempted to practice a semitraditional lifeway certainly were forced onto the more marginal portions of the Mono Basin. Most white settlers also relied upon local Natives for wage laborers.

By implementing an adaptive strategy of coexistence with Euro-Americans, the Mono Basin Paiute were able to resist some unwanted change as well as such major cultural disruption as being forced from their traditional homeland and onto a marginal and distant reservation by federal troops. In an overall sense, acculturation of the Mono Basin Paiute was incomplete because they were able to preserve many of their core values well into the second half of the twentieth century. Clearly, many aspects of aboriginal culture were modified and partially or completely replaced by equivalent Euro-American elements. However, the continued practice of various traditional activities and behaviors such as jackrabbit drives, waterfowl hunting, *kutsavi*, *piagi*, and pinyon harvests, and round dances, allowed these people to maintain their ethnic identity and remain distinctly Paiute.

Interestingly, the continued practice of harvesting pine nuts allowed the *kucadikadi* to exercise some economic power over local white settlers. Historic pinyon harvests depleted the availability of Native labor, a workforce upon whom the merchants, townspeople, farmers, and ranchers of Mono Basin had grown dependent (Fletcher 1987:41). After winter supplies of pine nuts had been obtained, the *kucadikadi* enjoyed a position of increased bargaining power over their white employers. Because they could afford not to work, both Mono Basin Paiute men and women were able to demand higher wages from settlers, who often engaged in bidding battles to secure their services (Fletcher 1987:41). This scenario is yet another example of how, in many North American contact situations, power was not necessarily limited to colonizing Euro-Americans and should be viewed as a heterogeneous aspect of the domination/resistance dialectic (e.g., Paynter and McGuire 1991).

CA-Mno-2122 continued to be occupied during historic times because it was situated in an area removed from white settlement and control. There the Mono Basin Paiute could harvest foods such as brine fly larvae, waterfowl, grass seeds, and pine nuts, and sequester themselves away from Anglo interference for much of the fall and winter. Although the *kucadikadi* certainly desired a number of Euro-American materials and foodstuffs that enhanced their post-Contact lifeway, they actively resisted adopting non-Native sociopolitical organization, ideology, and aesthetics.

The well-preserved post-Contact archaeological record at CA-Mno-2122 supports and reinforces the above interpretations of Mono Basin Paiute acculturation.

Notes

1. Mono Basin is a triangular depression occupying an area of nearly 700 square miles immediately east of the Sierra Nevada's steep eastern escarpment. Mono Lake occupies the central basin floor and is the Holocene remnant of Pleistocene Lake Russell, a body of water that at times occupied a large portion of the hydrographic Mono Basin (Russell 1889:299–300, 329). The modern lake measures nine by thirteen miles. It has a maximum depth of about 150 feet and has no outlet, a circumstance that accounts for its high salinity.

2. Leonard was the historian of the Joseph R. Walker expedition to California, which departed from St. Louis, Missouri, in the spring of 1831. From a geographical standpoint, this journey was quite important because it included the first Euro-American crossing of the Sierra Nevada Mountains from east to west, and the earliest known written account of Yosemite Valley.

3. Nondirected acculturation refers to a process of cultural change that is not forced upon a group. Historic acculturation among the Mono Basin Paiute largely resulted from Euro-American land use practices that significantly reduced Native food resources and restricted access to those that remained. As a result, the Mono Basin Paiute were drawn into the local Euro-American socioeconomic system in order to survive a much changed social and physical environment.

4. Each site, or activity area, within CA-Mno-2122 was assigned a locus number according to the order of its discovery. The term *locus* denotes a spatially distinct area of human use or occupation, and all loci within CA-Mno-2122 are viewed as part of an extensive, multicomponent site complex.

Acknowledgments

Various people and institutions made important contributions to the Mono Basin Research Project, and I extend my thanks and appreciation to the following individuals and organizations. Personnel of the California Bureau of Land Management's Bakersfield District and Bishop Resource Area offices who assisted with project administration included Robert Bheeler, Linda Estrada, Eric Levy, James Morrison, and Marian Revitte. The efforts of former Bishop Resource Area Archaeologist Eric Levy are especially acknowledged, as his hard work and dedication were largely responsible for the success of my Mono Basin work. Much of the research reported herein was conducted under a cooperative agreement between the California Bureau of Land Management and the University of California at Riverside (UCR), and part of it was funded by several grants from the UCR Graduate Division.

Tom Buckley, Lily Mathieu La Braque, Wallace McPherson, Foster Murphy, and Helen, Herb, and Paul Williams provided invaluable information concerning the natural and cultural history of the Mono Basin region. Vickie Daniels, the Nevada Historical Society, and the Yosemite National Park Research Library kindly allowed me to publish several historical photographs from their collections. The organization and content of this chapter have benefited from the editorial guidance provided by Silvia Broadbent, Eric Johnson, Michael Nassaney, R. E. Taylor, Philip Wilke, and several anonymous reviewers.

References Cited

Aldrich, J. M. 1912. Flies of the Leptid Genus Atherix Used as Food by California Indians. *Entomological News* 23:159–63.

———. 1921. Coloradia Pandora Blake: A Moth of Which the Caterpillar is Used as Food by the Mono Lake Indians. *Annals of the Entomological Society of America* 14(1):36–38.

Ambro, Richard D. 1972. Preliminary Observations on the Surface Archaeology of Ridge Village North, an Historic Period Shoshone Village. In *The Grass Valley Archaeological Project: Collected Papers,* ed. C. W. Clewlow, Jr., and M. K. Rusco, 85–106. Nevada Archaeological Survey Research Papers no. 3, University of Nevada, Reno.

Ambro, Richard D., and Kurt Wallof. 1972. Preliminary Notes on Historic Period Shoshone House Types. In *The Grass Valley Archaeological Project: Collected Papers,* ed. C. W. Clewlow, Jr., and M. K. Rusco, 107–26. Nevada Archaeological Survey Research Papers no. 3, University of Nevada, Reno.

Arkush, Brooke S. 1987. Historic Northern Paiute Winter Houses in Mono Basin, California. *Journal of California and Great Basin Anthropology* 9(2):174–87.

———. 1995. *The Archaeology of CA-MNO-2122: A Study of Pre-Contact and Post-Contact Lifeways among the Mono Basin Paiute.* University of California Anthropological Records vol. 31. Berkeley.

Bates, Craig D. 1979. Miwok-Paiute Basketry 1920–1929: Genesis of an Art Form. *American Indian Art Magazine* 4(4):54–59.

———. 1982. Yosemite Miwok/Paiute Basketry: A Study in Cultural Change. *American Indian Basketry* 8:4–22.

Beaudry, Mary C., Lauren J. Cook, and Stephen A. Mrozowski. 1991. Artifacts and Active Voices: Material Culture as Social Discourse. In *The Archaeology of Inequality,* ed. Randall H. McGuire and Robert Paynter, 150–91. Basil Blackwell, Oxford.

Berndt, Ronald M., and Catherine H. Berndt. 1970. Some Points of Change in Western Australia. In *Diprotodon to Detribalization: Studies of Change among Australian Aborigines,* ed. A. R. Pilling and R. A. Waterman, 53–79. Michigan State University Press, East Lansing.

Berry, John W. 1980. Acculturation as Varieties of Adaptation. In *Acculturation: Theory, Models, and Some New Findings,* ed. A. M. Padilla, 9–25. Westview Press, Boulder, Colo.

Bettinger, Robert L. 1976. Flat Iron Ridge Site, 26-Ny-313 (D13). In *Prehistoric Pinon Ecotone Settlements of the Upper Reese River Valley, Central Nevada,* ed. D. H. Thomas and R. L. Bettinger, 313–27. Anthropological Papers of the American Museum of Natural History 53 (3), New York.

———. 1982. *Archaeology East of the Range of Light: Aboriginal Human Ecology of the Inyo-Mono Region, California.* Monographs in California and Great Basin Anthropology 1, Davis, California.

———. 1989. *The Archaeology of Pinyon House, Two Eagles, and Crater Middens: Three Residential Sites in Owens Valley, Eastern California.* Anthropological Papers of the American Museum of Natural History no. 67, New York.

Billeb, Emil W. 1968. *Mining Camp Days.* Howell North Books, Berkeley, Calif. (Reprinted: Nevada Publications, Las Vegas, Nev., 1986.)

Brewer, William H. 1930. *Up and Down California in 1860–1864.* Yale University Press, New Haven, Conn. (Reprinted: University of California Press, Berkeley, 1966.)

Browne, J. Ross. 1869. *Adventures in Apache Country: A Tour through Arizona and Sonora, With Notes on the Silver Regions of Nevada.* Harper and Brothers, New York.

Bunnell, Lafayette H. [1881] 1892. *Discovery of the Yosemite, and the Indian War of 1851 which Led to that Event.* 3d ed. rev. Fleming H. Revell Co., New York.

Cain, Ella M. 1961. *The Story of Early Mono County.* Fearon Publishers, San Francisco.

Calhoun, Margaret. 1984. *Pioneers of Mono Basin.* Artemisia Press, Lee Vining, Calif.

Clewlow, C. William, Jr., and Allen G. Pastron. 1972. Preliminary Archaeological Investigations in Grass Valley. In *The Grass Valley Archeological Project: Collected Papers,* ed. C. W. Clewlow, Jr., and M. K. Rusco, 11–32. Nevada Archaeological Survey Research Papers no. 3, University of Nevada, Reno.

Davis, Emma Lou. 1965. *An Ethnography of the Kuzedika Paiute of Mono Lake, Mono County, California.* University of Utah Anthropological Papers no. 75:1–55.

Deagan, Kathleen A. 1990. Accommodation and Resistance: The Process and Impact of Spanish Colonization in the Southeast. In *Columbian Consequences,* vol. 2, *Archaeological and Historical Perspectives on the Spanish Borderlands East,* ed. D. H. Thomas, 297–314. Smithsonian Institution Press, Washington, D.C.

Delacorte, Michael, and Kelly R. McGuire. 1993. Archaeological Test Evaluations at Twenty-three Sites Located along a Proposed Fiber-optic Telephone Cable Route in Owens Valley, California. Report on file, Eastern California Information Center, Archaeological Research Unit, University of California, Riverside.

Eldredge, I. F. 1923. Caterpillars a la Paiute. *American Forestry* 29(354):330–32.

Fletcher, Thomas C. 1979. The Mono Basin in the Nineteenth Century: Discovery, Settlement, Land Use. Master's thesis, University of California, Berkeley.

———. 1987. *Paiute, Prospector, Pioneer: A History of the Bodie–Mono Lake Area in the Nineteenth Century.* Artemisia Press, Lee Vining, Calif.

Fontana, B. L., J. C. Greenleaf, C. W. Ferguson, R. A. Wright, and D. Frederick. 1962. Johnny Ward's Ranch: A Study in Historic Archaeology. *The Kiva* 28(1–2).

Foster, George M. 1960. *Culture and Conquest.* Quadrangle Books, Chicago.

Fowler, Catherine S. 1982. Food-Named Groups among the Northern Paiute in North America's Great Basin. In *Resource Managers: North American and Australian Hunter-Gatherers,* ed. Nancy M. Williams and Eugene S. Hunn, 113–29. American Association for the Advancement of Science Selected Symposium 67. Westview Press, Boulder, Colo.

Fowler, Catherine S., and Sven Liljeblad. 1986. Northern Paiute. In *Handbook of North American Indians,* vol. 11, *Great Basin,* ed. W. L. d'Azevedo, 435–65. Smithsonian Institution, Washington, D.C.

Hattori, Eugene M. 1975. *Northern Paiutes on the Comstock: Archaeology and History of an American Indian Population in Virginia City, Nevada.* Nevada State Museum Occasional Papers no. 2. Carson City.

Heizer, Robert F. 1950. Kutsavi, A Great Basin Indian Food. *Kroeber Anthropological Society Papers* 2:35–41.

Hester, Thomas R. 1990. Perspectives on the Material Culture of the Mission Indians of the Texas–Northeastern Mexico Borderlands. In *Columbian Consequences,* vol. 1, *Archaeological and Historical Perspectives on the Spanish Borderlands West,* ed. D. H. Thomas, 213–29. Smithsonian Institution Press, Washington D.C.

Hoover, Robert L., and Julia G. Costello, eds. 1985. *Excavations at Mission San Antonio, 1976–1978.* Monograph 26, Institute of Archaeology, University of California, Los Angeles.

Hugill, Peter J., and D. Bruce Dickson, eds. 1988. *The Transfer and Transformation of Ideas and Material Culture.* Texas A & M University Press, College Station.

Hultkrantz, Åke. 1986. Mythology and Religious Concepts. In *Handbook of North American Indians,* vol. 11, *Great Basin,* ed. W. L. d'Azevedo, 630–40. Smithsonian Institution, Washington, D.C.

Kersten, Earl W. 1964. The Early Settlement of Aurora, Nevada, and Nearby Mining Camps. *Annals of the Association of American Geographers* 54:490–507.

La Braque, Lily Mathieu. 1984. *Man from Mono.* Nevada Academic Press, Reno.

Layton, Thomas N. 1977. Indian Rustlers of the High Rock. *Archaeology* 30(6):366–73.

Le Conte, Joseph. [1875] 1960. *A Journal of Ramblings through the High Sierra of California by the University Excursion Party.* Sierra Club, San Francisco.

Leonard, Zenas. 1934. *Narrative of the Adventures of Zenas Leonard,* ed. Milo M. Quaife. Lakeside Press, Chicago.

Lightfoot, Kent G., Thomas A. Wake, and Ann M. Schiff. 1991. *The Archaeology and Ethnohistory of Fort Ross, California,* vol. 1, *Introduction.* Contributions of the University of California Archaeological Research Facility no. 49. Berkeley.

Lowie, Robert H. 1924. Notes on Shoshonean Ethnography. *Anthropological Papers of the American Museum of Natural History* 20(3):185–314.

Malouf, Carling, and John M. Findlay. 1986. Euro-American Impact before 1870. In *Handbook of North American Indians,* vol. 11, *Great Basin,* ed. W. L. d'Azevedo, 499–516. Smithsonian Institution, Washington, D.C.

Meighan, Clement W. 1953. Acculturation in Californian Awl Forms. *Kroeber Anthropological Society Papers* 8–9:61–68.

Merriam, C. Hart. 1955. *Studies of California Indians.* University of California Press, Berkeley.

Muir, John. 1916. *The Mountains of California.* Houghton Mifflin, Boston.

Paynter, Robert, and Randall H. McGuire. 1991. The Archaeology of Inequality: Material Culture, Domination, and Resistance. In *The Archaeology of Inequality,* ed. Randall H. McGuire and Robert Paynter, 1–27. Basil Blackwell, Oxford.

Queen, Rolla L. 1987. Historical Archaeology and Historical Preservation at Candelaria and Metallic City, Nevada. M.A. thesis, University of Nevada, Reno.

Rogers, Everett M. 1983. *Diffusion of Innovations,* 3d ed. Free Press, New York.

Rogers, J. Daniel. 1990. *Objects of Change: The Archaeology and History of Arikara Contact with Europeans.* Smithsonian Institution Press, Washington, D.C.

Rubertone, Patricia E. 1989. Archaeology, Colonialism, and 17th-Century Native America: Towards an Alternative Interpretation. In *Conflict in the Archaeology of Living Traditions,* ed. Robert Layton, 32–45. Unwin Hyman, London.

Russell, Israel C. 1889. Quaternary History of the Mono Valley, California. *Eighth Annual Report,* 267–394. U.S. Geological Survey, Washington, D.C.

Scott, Lalla. 1966. *Karnee: A Paiute Narrative.* University of Nevada Press, Reno.

Smith, Marvin T. 1987. *Archaeology of Aboriginal Culture Change in the Interior Southeast: Depopulation during the Early Historic Period.* University Press of Florida, Gainesville.

Spicer, Edward H. 1961. Types of Contact and Processes of Change. In *Perspectives in American Indian Culture Change,* ed. E. H. Spicer, 517–44. University of Chicago Press, Chicago.

Steward, Julian H. 1933. *Ethnography of the Owens Valley Paiute*. University of California Publications in American Archaeology and Ethnology 33 (3), Berkeley.

———. 1941. *Culture Element Distributions: XIII, Nevada Shoshone*. University of California Anthropological Records 4 (2), Berkeley.

Stewart, Omer C. 1939. *The Northern Paiute Bands*. University of California Anthropological Records 2 (3), Berkeley.

———. 1941. *Culture Element Distributions: XIV, Northern Paiute*. University of California Anthropological Records 4 (3), Berkeley.

Warren, Claude N., and Thomas Hearne. 1974. Preliminary Report on Archaeological Investigations, Route 09-INY-395-118.3-129.4. Report on file, Eastern California Information Center, Archaeological Research Unit, University of California, Riverside.

Wedertz, Frank S. 1978. *Mono Diggings*. Chalfant Press, Bishop, Calif.

Wells, Helen F. 1983. Historic and Prehistoric Pinyon Exploitation in the Grass Valley Region, Central Nevada: A Case Study in Cultural Continuity and Change. Ph.D. diss., University of California, Riverside.

Wood, W. Raymond, ed. 1986. *Papers in Northern Plains Prehistory and Ethnohistory: Ice Glider (32OL110)*. Special Publication of the South Dakota Archaeological Society, no. 10. Sioux Printing, Inc., Sioux Falls, S.D.

8

Cache Pits

Ethnohistory, Archaeology, and the Continuity of Tradition

Sean B. Dunham

Clusters of very uniform shallow surface depressions (ca. 1 to 2 m diameter × 0.5 m deep) have been identified throughout the state of Michigan and have been described by Hinsdale (1931:12) as "the commonest type of earthwork found" in the state. He goes on to note that "they are often referred to as *Indian Pits* and occur singly and in groups numbering over a hundred. Sometimes the groups appear to be arranged according to plan, but usually they are dug regardless of any preconceived pattern." Despite the ubiquity of these features, they have proven somewhat problematic to interpret. When excavated, surface depression sites produce few associated artifacts, either from their contents or the sites at which they are found. At one such site "numbers of them were cleared out and carefully examined, but no clue was found to their possible use" (Hinsdale 1931:30).

A major goal of archaeology is the reconstruction of past lifeways through the examination and interpretation of patterned material remains. Archaeological data offer a unique source of information that directly links the creators of a site with its excavators. As such, archaeology provides a tangible, material approach to the study of the past. However, the process of transforming these physical remains into an understanding of the cultural activities that created them is not always a simple academic exercise. As a case in point, the surface depressions noted above have proven somewhat enigmatic to archaeologists in that they typically produce limited material evidence aside from the pits themselves. Lacking the remains required for purely archaeological interpretation, we require other approaches to aid in the understanding of these features. The most promising methodological approach involves model building based on data from the related fields of ethnoarchaeology, ethnohistory, and historical archaeology to derive material expectations that can be compared with the formal, spatial, and temporal dimensions of these archaeological features (cf. Binford 1983; Spector 1985). Such multidisciplinary research has the potential to illuminate the function of these surface depressions as well as their role within a given cultural context, allowing a greater anthropological understanding of these features than either archaeological or ethnohistorical research would allow by itself.

Fig. 8.1. Location of sites and places noted in the chapter: (1) Ne-con-ne-pe-wah-se site; (2) Spring Valley site; (3) Ranger Walker II site; (4) Porter Creek South site; (5) Missaukee Reserve; (6) Skegemog Point site; (7) 20GT59 and 20GT125; (8) Cross Village; (9) Colonial Point; (10) Nahma; (11) Black River Cache site/Alcona County; (12) Saginaw County/Saginaw Valley; (13) St. Joseph River.

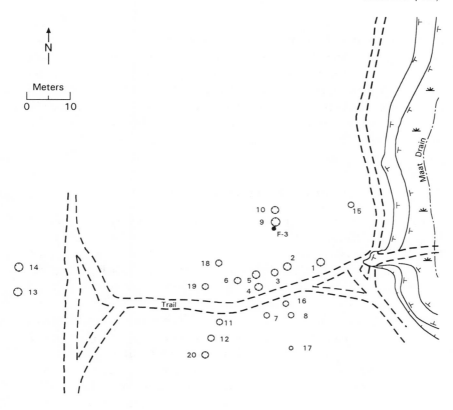

○ : Cache Pit
● : Subsurface Feature

Fig. 8.2. Plan view of site area

To demonstrate the utility of this approach to the archaeological record, I selected the Ne-con-ne-pe-wah-se site (fig. 8.1) as the focus of my analysis. It is a multicomponent site with diffuse scatters of Late Woodland and 19th-century artifacts. Moreover, the site exhibits no fewer than twenty surface depressions (fig. 8.2). Ethnographic and ethnohistoric sources relevant to the regional, cultural, and chronological contexts of the site offered several options for the function of the pits. The most likely interpretations of these features derived from the documentary sources include activities associated with food processing, preparation, and storage. These sources also indicate the significance of subsistence patterns as a basis of traditional culture among the region's Native American populations. Therefore, the site represents an ideal case study to explore the role that specific cultural processes play in the formation of an archaeological site, as well as an application of models derived from ethnohistoric sources concerning such activities in the interpretation of the site. Additionally, the surface depressions encountered at this site offer an excellent opportunity to explore the origin and function of these features in broader regional and temporal contexts.

Archaeology and Surface Depression Sites

During the first decades of the 20th century several surface depression locales were examined archaeologically in Michigan (Greenman 1927; Hinsdale 1925, 1931). Greenman (1927) excavated some surface depressions in the Missaukee Reserve in north-central lower Michigan and described them as averaging 5 feet (1.7 m) in diameter and about 2 feet (0.6 m) in depth at the surface, and extending from 3 to 6 feet (ca. 1 to 2 meters) in depth. Some of these pits produced charred or decayed wood, but, as noted above, typically they produced little or no cultural material. Other surface depression sites revealed similar results, although occasionally they produced greater amounts of charred wood, ash, and, in some cases, fire-cracked rock (Hinsdale 1928, 1931). These investigations led archaeologists to interpret some of the pits as earthen ovens, whereas other pits were assumed to have served for storage. The lack of remains contributed to this latter interpretation. It was assumed that the pits had been emptied of their contents prior to abandonment, which would explain the lack of cultural remains inside these features.

More recent excavations of surface depression features in Michigan have been carried out at the Ranger Walker II site (Branstner 1991), the Skegemog Point site (Hambacher 1992), and the Black River Cache site (O'Shea 1989). At least two sites have also been explored in Wisconsin: Oak Lake Site No. 2 (Overstreet and Brazeau 1982) and 47PK109 (Clark 1995). Each of these sites exhibited surface depression features like those described above. Like the pits examined earlier in this century, the more recently excavated features have produced relatively small and somewhat ambiguous assemblages. The ambiguity is largely the result of the low density of the pit contents—usually a few pieces of lithic debitage or fire-cracked rock, and the occasional sherd of pottery.[1] The areas surrounding the surface depressions typically provide little supporting data and are marked by a conspicuous lack of settlement debris (e.g., structural remains, living floors, refuse middens, and the like).

Surface depression complexes are often physically separated from the nearest known habitation (Hambacher and Holman 1995). For example, the surface depression features at the Porter Creek South site (Hambacher and Holman 1995) and the Black River Cache site (O'Shea 1989) are located at some distance from a known habitation site, and there is no evidence for intensive occupation of the surface depression locales themselves. This pattern is apparently repeated at the Missaukee Reserve surface depressions, which are located up to a quarter mile (400 m) from the Aetna I and Aetna II enclosures (Greenman 1927; Hinsdale 1931). Dustin (1936) also notes that the pits he described in Saginaw County are located at least 500 feet (150 m) from the nearest settlement. The Spring Valley site, in Newaygo County, is also physically separated from the nearest known Native American habitation (nearly a mile; 1.6 km), and is situated in an improbable settlement location (Branstner 1987).

The interpretation of the surface depression features at each of these sites is inconclusive at present. While we know they were created through conscious human activity, their function remains uncertain. When ascribed to a cultural period, these features, and most of the sites noted above, have been determined to date to the Late Woodland period (ca. A.D. 1000–1600) based on the associated ceramics.

The Ethnohistory and Ethnography of Surface Depressions

In addition to storage pits and earthen ovens, a variety of other functions can be posited, including wild rice hulling pits and maple sap processing and storage vats, based on ethnohistoric and ethnographic sources from the Great Lakes region.[2] In the following discussion I evaluate the various alternative interpretations from the perspective of the documentary sources. Certain archaeological considerations will also be presented based on the material expressions of such features, as described in the historical record.

Storage Pits

The act of storing food in pits is well documented in the ethnographic literature of the Great Lakes region (e.g., Densmore 1979; Hilger 1992; Waugh 1916), and there is evidence that the practice originated during pre-Contact times (Parker 1968). Ethnographic sources describe pits from 1 to 2 meters (ca. 3 to 6 ft) in diameter, and of similar depth, which were lined with bark (typically elm or birch), grasses, or hay. The food was stored in woven sacks, animal skins, baskets, bark containers, ceramic or metal vessels, or glass jars. Additional grass, straw, or bark was placed in the pit, and the top was covered with boughs, bark, wooden planks, or hay. Earth was often heaped on top for additional protection. A variety of foods are described as being stored in such pits, including maize, wild rice, squash, dried berries, and maple sugar (see Mason and Holman, chap. 9).

Storage pits were recorded in Michigan as early as 1721, when Charlevoix (1923:112–13) observed among the Miami of the St. Joseph Valley that "their corn and other fruits are preserved in receptories, which they dig into the ground and which are lined with large pieces of bark." The Ottawa at Cross Village used similar storage pits in the 19th century (Blackbird 1897). As recently as the 1930s, such pits were used by the Ojibwa in Wisconsin and Minnesota (Densmore 1979; Hilger 1992), as well as by a mixed Ojibwa and Ottawa community called *Sand Town* near Nahma in the central Upper Peninsula of Michigan (Winberg 1994). These sources uniformly praise the effectiveness of this storage method. Burying food in pits was a simple and efficient method of storage and preservation, as experimental research in the United States and Britain has confirmed (Morenon et al. 1986:28–30; Reynolds 1977).

Ethnohistoric and ethnographic sources indicate that storage pits are associated with two general locational contexts: settlements and specific activity areas (e.g., gardens, sugar bushes, wild rice camps, and along regular transportation routes). In both instances, storage pits are presumed to be situated in well-drained locales to protect their contents from decay (see also Reynolds 1977).

Storage pits appear to have been widely used throughout eastern North America. Such pits are described as being used by the Iroquois (Parker 1968) and the southeastern tribes (Swanton 1946), as well as by the Mandan in the Missouri River Basin (Coues 1897:360) and the Cree in the Hudson Bay region (Honigman 1956). Not only are they broadly distributed, storage pits have also worked their way into American mythology. The Pilgrims, for example, found buried stores of corn that sustained them over their first winter in the New World.

Storage pits would presumably be identifiable in the archaeological record based on their form and their contents. Depending on the level of preservation at a given site, one might expect to find evidence of bark lining. Similar expectations would apply to bark or fabric storage vessels, whereas ceramic, glass, or metal storage vessels would be more likely to be present. Additionally, some pits might contain evidence of the stored goods themselves, such as food or other items, depending on preservation and whether or not they were emptied prior to abandonment.

Pit Ovens

Pits serving as hearths or ovens are well represented in the ethnographic literature of the Great Lakes region. Among the Iroquois such ovens are described as being excavated into "the side of some convenient bank or clay deposit" (Waugh 1916:56). These pits were heated, the coals removed, and vegetable foods such as corn, squash, or beans were baked inside (Parker 1968; Waugh 1916). Large pits were also described that held a bed of embers over which corn was roasted in the husk (Parker 1968; Waugh 1916).

Similar ovens were described as being used at the Nahma Indian community of Michigan's Upper Peninsula in the early 20th century. One source describes bread being baked in holes near Lake Michigan (Moses 1994:36). Eighteenth-century sources concerning the Ottawa similarly recorded that bread was baked under the ashes or in hot sand (Kinietz 1965). A second source from Nahma recalls the roasting of a pig in a pit for a communal feast (Winberg 1994:24). Concerning the Ojibwa, Kohl (1985:300) recorded that "when the corn (maize) is still quite young and unripe, they cut it down, husk it, and boil or bake it in red hot pits. These pits are first filled with burning wood and hot stones, heated, and then cleaned out."

Based on the ethnohistoric and ethnographic descriptions, pit ovens would be expected to show evidence of burning, such as heat-altered soil horizons, fire-cracked rock, charcoal, or ash. If the pit were excavated in a clay ridge, as described by Waugh (1916), the clay perimeter of the pit should transform into a ceramic-like deposit around the feature. Carbonized botanical or faunal remains might also be found.

Wild Rice Threshing Pits

Some surface depressions similar to those described above in Minnesota (Jenks 1900; Johnson 1969a, 1969b) are thought to be wild rice processing pits. The processing of wild rice involves hulling the grain, which is in part carried out in pits referred to as stomping pits or rice jigs (Densmore 1974; Vennum 1988). After the grain has been hulled, it is separated from its chaff through a variety of methods. Pits were excavated for the purpose of stomping and were then lined with clay, animal hides, or a wooden vessel (Densmore 1974; Doty 1992; Vennum 1988). Rice was placed in the pit and either pounded with a mortar or treaded with the feet

(Densmore 1974, 1979). Wild rice was also stored in pits, as noted above, and wild rice camps would be likely to exhibit both types of pit feature (Spector 1985).

Wild rice has not been generally associated with Native American subsistence in the Lower Peninsula of Michigan. However, there is a growing body of archaeological data suggesting that this aquatic grain was utilized by the Native American inhabitants of Michigan, particularly in the Traverse Bay and Saginaw Valley regions (Branstner and Hambacher 1995; Ford and Brose 1975; Hambacher 1992; Lovis et al. 1994). The harvest and utilization of wild rice in the St. Joseph River Valley of southwestern Michigan is also described in 19th-century documentary accounts (Pokagon 1898; see also Jenks 1900). Although wild rice is currently a threatened species, it has recently been recorded in southwestern Lower Michigan and once had a wider distribution (Michigan Department of Natural Resources 1995; Voss 1972).

Stomping pits have been identified archaeologically and generally appear to be basin-shaped features of variable depth about a meter (3 ft) in diameter (Gibbon 1976; Jenks 1900; Johnson 1969a). Wild rice threshing pits are found on elevated, well drained locations along ricing lakes, often at inlets or outlets (Johnson 1969b). Based on the documentary sources, one type of ricing jig (stomping pit) would be represented by shallow basinlike features, possibly lined with clay, and exhibiting soil compaction in the surrounding matrix. Other wild rice hulling pits might be more narrow and cylindrical in form. These pits may include a wooden lining. Depending on preservation, stomping pits may include rice grains in their lining or surrounding matrix. Recent analysis suggests that phytoliths from wild rice might also be present in such contexts (Thompson et al. 1994).

Maple Sugaring

Eighteenth and 19th century sources (e.g., Henry 1969; Pond 1986; Schoolcraft 1851) concerning the practice of maple sugaring suggest that such activities were undertaken in small family camps, which were occupied for about a month each spring during the sap run (see also Mason and Holman, chap. 9). The camps were situated close to the resource, usually within a sugar grove. Maple sap was gathered in birch-bark containers. It was stored in wooden troughs or in shallow pits or trenches lined with moose or ox skins, and the sap was reduced in brass or iron kettles, which were arranged over a fire. When metal kettles were not available, heated rocks were used to boil the sap in skin-lined pits, or repeated freezing was used to promote the reduction. Maple sugar camps often included storage pits such as those described above. Likewise, the tools and equipment needed for sugaring were often cached in the sugar grove. Such pits would differ from food storage pits only in regard to content, which might include such items as iron or brass kettles, metal or bark pails or other containers, and tree taps.

Maple sap storage and processing pits would appear physically similar to the surface depressions. For example, Henry (1969:69) noted moose-skin vats (presumably a pit lined with the animal skin) holding 100 gallons of sap. A circular skin-lined pit 1 m in diameter and 1 m deep could hold approximately 155 gallons of liquid, suggesting that the scale of such storage vats would be similar to the surface depression features. Additionally, one would not expect to find many artifacts directly associated with these features, as they served solely as receptacles for the sap.

Archaeological Considerations

As noted above, storage pits are associated with two general locations—habitation sites and specific activity areas. Earthen ovens would be expected in or near habitation sites, while threshing pits and maple sap vats would be expected in direct relation to their respective resource procurement locales. Maple sugar and wild rice camps would also include storage pits. Thus, each of these feature types would be physically associated with some form of habitation, whether it was a logistical camp or a village. The exception to this observation would be storage pits that were associated with activity areas that would not necessarily include generalized settlement debris, such as transportation routes or agricultural fields. Therefore, it would appear that the surface depressions outlined above, and possibly those at the Ne-con-ne-pe-wah-se site, represent storage pits.

The physical separation between habitations and storage-pit locales appears to be of critical importance in the context of this discussion. Subterranean storage pits have been identified at habitation sites throughout North America. Storage pits are known from Late Archaic and Woodland contexts in western Michigan (e.g., Bettarel and Smith 1973; Garland 1990; Hambacher 1992). However, surface depression locales are typically not associated with evidence of intensive occupations. The separation of storage locales from habitation sites suggests an element of concealment. Concerning this theme, Hinsdale (1931:12) has observed that "the Indians and early hunters had the habit of secreting their stores in caches. Hence the term *cache pits* explains the use of many of these earth holes." (The term *cache* derives from the French verb *cacher,* to hide.) It has been suggested that concealed food stores may have resulted from subsistence strategies that relied on seasonally dense, abundant plant and animal resources, which in turn required a certain degree of settlement mobility (Binford 1980; DeBoer 1988; Kelly 1992). This type of settlement-subsistence pattern appears to have emerged in the Late Woodland period in Michigan (Cleland 1976, 1982), precisely the time when cache pits appear in the archaeological record.

Certain short-term logistical camps may also resemble caching locales. For example, neither the structures nor the associated processing tools at a maple sugar camp would have left a highly visible archaeological footprint, as most of the ethnographically documented materials used at such camps were made of wood, bark, or animal skins (cf. Loftus 1977). Additionally, sugar camps were physically placed to best exploit that resource and were not necessarily placed in a typical habitation site setting (Dunham et al. 1994; Holman 1984). Thus, a sugar camp occupied for a season or two might not include significant amounts of habitation debris, but might feature several surface depressions reflecting the use of sap storage and processing pits as well as cache pits. Similar considerations would also apply to wild rice, berrying, or other short-term, seasonal logistical camps (Holman 1984; Quimby 1962; Spector 1985).

Another rationale concerning the separation of habitation sites and cache pit locales may relate to their association with garden plots and agricultural fields. Several ethnographic sources note that storage pits are often placed near the fields (Hilger 1992; Parker 1968; Waugh 1916). This pattern has been observed at certain surface depression locales in northeastern Michigan as well (e.g., Colonial Point and Alcona County) (see Albert and Minc 1987; Hinsdale 1928, 1931). For example, Hinsdale (1931:14) writes "there are numerous groups of pit holes not far from the cornfield; some of them are arranged in rows with the pits in one row alternating with those upon the other side." Thus, surface depressions may appear to be separated from habitation sites because they represent a specific activity area (storage) associated with a specific task such as gardening or horticulture. Such locations would be physically distinct from habitation sites, but would not represent residential extractive encampments such as wild rice or maple sugar camps.

In sum, surface depressions may reflect several feature types, including storage pits, earthen ovens, wild rice threshing pits, or maple sap storage and processing pits. Each of these features would be present on habitation sites. Storage pits, on the other hand, may also appear in other locations separate from habitations. Thus, it may be possible to offer the working hypothesis that surface depressions that are not associated with a clear occupational component probably represent storage pits. With these considerations in mind, the Ne-con-ne-pe-wah-se site will be reexamined.

The Ne-con-ne-pe-wah-se Site

The Ne-con-ne-pe-wah-se site is located on the outskirts of the city of Fremont in Newaygo County, Michigan (see fig. 8.2). The major components of the site reflect Spring Creek Late Woodland (ca. A.D. 800–1100) and 19th-century historic Native American occupations (Dunham and Branstner 1995; Lockwood-Moore 1993). The Late Woodland component consists of lithic and ceramic artifacts sparsely scattered over a fairly wide area (approximately 0.64 ha) (Holman 1995). The 19th-century component was identified through an 1855 land patent awarded to a man named Ne-con-ne-pe-wah-se that included the entire project area. A small assemblage of historic artifacts, dating to the second half of the 19th century as well as the 20th century, was also recovered at the site. Neither component appears to represent an intensive occupation.

The site is situated within a beech-maple forest on a terrace overlooking a small stream that drains into nearby Fremont Lake. The soils at the site consist of well-drained sandy loams that are, in some areas, underlain by a natural layer of clay within 1 m of the surface. As noted above, the most visible component of the site was a series of twenty surface depressions (see fig. 8.2). The features were roughly circular, with diameters of 1–2.5 m (3 to 8 ft) and a mean diameter of 1.6 m (ca. 5 ft) (see fig. 8.3). The depth of the surface depressions ranged between about 15 and 40 cm (0.5–1.3 ft) below modern ground surface. Eight of these features were bisected and formally tested in 1994 (Cache Pits 1, 2, 5, 6, 7, 9, 11 and 17), and two were completely excavated (Cache Pits 12 and 14).

The surface depressions were cleared of debris (forest detritus), and the surrounding soil horizon was excavated to the base of the surface manifestation. At this interface the features appeared as dark circular stains in the lighter sandy soil and averaged about 1 m (3 ft) in diameter. The subsurface diameter of the features probably represents their original dimensions. The pit profiles ranged in depth from 40 to 130 cm below the modern ground surface with a mean feature depth of nearly 70 cm (table 8.1). A subsurface feature (Feature 3) was identified immediately south of Cache Pit 9 and appeared to represent a former pit as well. Each of the tested pits was circular in plan and generally cylindrical or basin-shaped in

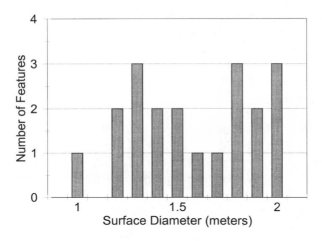

Fig. 8.3. Diameter of the surface depressions at 20NE331

profile. The surface manifestations appear to be the result of the former pits' slumping onto or into themselves.

Most of the pits had relatively simple stratigraphy represented by an upper zone of collapsed fill (leaf mat, detritus, and organic soils), and the subsurface soil stain. Some of the pits exhibited more complex stratigraphy, possibly reflecting multiple use stages or their post-use collapse. The profile of one of the tested features, Cache Pit 6, suggested that this surface depression represented a natural hollow in the landscape. In this instance, the depression did not appear to extend appreciably below the O/A horizon.

One of the larger pits tested at the site was Cache Pit 9, which also exhibited a somewhat more complex depositional sequence (fig. 8.4). While the pit was slightly disturbed by root activity, it retained a bell-shaped form to its base marked by four distinct fill zones. The upper zone corresponds to the current ground-surface zone of forest detritus and topsoil. The remaining three horizons may reflect different deposits associated with the pit's use or its post-use collapse. The base of the pit was defined by hard-packed sand. While it is possible that the soil was intentionally compacted by the pit's original excavators, this horizon appears to be natural.

The smallest of the surface features (Cache Pit 17) offered a more simple depositional sequence (fig. 8.5). The pit is quite regular in profile with a somewhat squared base that may have resulted when the original

Table 8.1. The surface and subsurface dimensions of the excavated cache pit features at 20NE331

Cache Pit	Surface diam. (cm)	Surface depth (cm)	Subsurface diam. (cm)	Subsurface depth (cm)
1	200	27	99	79
2	200	25	114	78
5	180	20	85	60
6	152	15	108	42
7	140	15	100	51
9	190	26	105	121
11	180	25	110	63
12	160	20	131	52
14	200	25	128	60
17	100	17	51	62
Feature 3	—	—	110	86
Mean	170.2	21.5	103.7	68.5

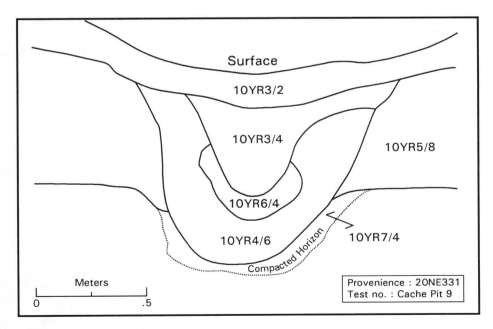

Fig. 8.4. Profile view of Cache Pit 9

Fig. 8.5. Profile and plan view of Cache Pit 17

excavators encountered the clay horizon. The fill in Cache Pit 17 appears to reflect a single depositional episode.

Each of the excavated pits contained very small numbers of artifacts dating to the Late Woodland or historic periods. However, a significant quantity of botanical material was recovered through flotation from three of the surface features (Cache Pits 5, 9, and 17) and the associated subsurface feature (Feature 3) (Egan 1995). The samples produced high proportions of uncarbonized edible nuts and fruit seeds, including beechnuts, cherry, sumac, raspberry, elderberry, and grape (table 8.2). In addition to the nuts and seeds, carbonized and uncarbonized bark was also recovered from the features. The form of the features, combined with the recovery of a high relative density of edible nuts and fruit seeds, appears to indicate that they were used to store food.

While the Ne-con-ne-pe-wah-se site as a whole is multicomponent, the cache pits themselves are associated with the historic component. This interpretation is supported by the recovery of historic artifacts from seven of the ten tested features (Cache Pits 1, 2, 5, 9, 12, 14 and 17), including fragments of solarized (amethyst) glass recovered from Cache Pits 1 and 17, a glass seed bead from Cache Pit 12, and a white clay pipe bowl from Cache Pit 1. All of these artifacts are mid to late 19th-century chronological markers, although none offer firm temporal parameters for dating the features. The orientation of the features along an extant trail, as opposed

Table 8.2. Floral remains (seeds) with potential cultural uses (after Egan 1995)

Cache Pit/Feature	CP 5	CP 5	CP 5	CP 9	CP 9	CP 9	CP 17	CP 17	F 3
Level[a]	5	6	7	8	10	11[b]	5	7[c]	9[d]
Flotation volume (liters)	10	10	10	-	10	10	7	5	10
cf. *Aronia arbutifolia* Chokeberry	-	-	-	-	-	-	3	-	-
Cornus canadensis Bunchberry	-	1	-	-	2	2	66	6	-
Cornus stolonifera Red-Osier Dogwood	-	-	-	-	-	-	-	-	3
Fagus grandifolia Beechnut	-	-	-	-	-	-	62[e]	-	-
cf. *Hamamelis virginiana* Witch-hazel	-	-	-	-	-	-	1	-	-
cf. *Lindera benzoin* Spicebush	-	-	-	-	-	-	2	-	-
Lonicera sp. Honeysuckle	-	-	-	-	-	-	1	-	-
Potentilla sp. Cinquefoil	-	-	-	-	-	-	7	-	-
Phytollaca americana Pokeweed	-	-	-	-	-	-	29	77	-
Prunus spp. Cherry	-	-	-	-	-	-	106	-	-
Prunus pennsylvanica Pin Cherry	2	5	-	-	-	-	70[f]	4	4
Prunus serotina Black Cherry	-	5	-	-	3	-	5	2	3
Rhus sp. Sumac	1	-	-	-	-	1	44	4	1
Rubus spp. Raspberry	11	3	-	-	-	-	30	6	-
Sambucus canadensis Elderberry	1	-	-	-	-	-	25	3	-
Solanaoeae Nightshade Family	3	2	-	-	-	-	-	7	-
cf. *Sorbus americana* Mountain Ash	-	-	-	-	-	-	1	-	-
Vitis sp. Grape	2	3	-	-	-	2	39	1	1
Zea mays[g] Maize	-	-	-	1	-	-	-	-	-

a. Level = arbitrary 10 cm excavation levels (e.g., level 5 = 40–50 cm below modern ground surface), unless specified.
b. Level 11 in Cache Pit 9 = 115–21 cm below modern ground surface.
c. Level 7 in Cache Pit 17 = 55–60 cm below modern ground surface.
d. Level 9 in Feature 3 = 80–86 cm below modern ground surface.
e. *Fagus grandifolia* in Cache Pit 17 includes three carbonized seeds.
f. *Prunus pennsylvanica* in Cache Pit 17 includes two carbonized seeds.
g. *Zea mays* in Cache Pit 9 was recovered with ¼" mesh hardware cloth.

to a natural land form such as the nearby ridge, may be further evidence of the pits' recent origin.[3]

Based on the archaeological data alone, the historic component of the site is quite intriguing. The site was a place where pits were dug and into which edible fruits and nuts were deposited. The surface features appear to represent the focus of 19th-century activity at the site; there is no other indication of contemporaneous occupation save a very sparse and diffuse scatter of historic artifacts. Thus, the site represents an activity area associated with a specific set of tasks involving the excavation of pits and the storage of fruits and nuts.

Historic and Cultural Context

A man named Ne-con-ne-pe-wah-se bought the site locale in 1857 (Dunham and Branstner 1995). This name identifies the man as a Native American, but the name cannot be confidently traced via census rolls to a specific tribal identity. The site is located in a region that has been linked with the Grand River Band of Ottawa Indians (McClurken 1994). While Ne-con-ne-pe-wah-se was most likely associated with this group, he may have been affiliated with another Ottawa or Ojibwa band. In any case, the land was acquired as a result of the 1855 Treaty of Detroit, which established eighty-acre farmsteads for Indians in northern Michigan (Cleland 1993; McClurken 1986a, 1994). One condition for keeping the land was that it had to be developed within five years of the patent's receipt. The definition of developed land was based on the 19th-century Euro-American ideal: cleared lands under cultivation and a permanent homestead (cf. Dunham 1993). If the land was not developed within the five-year period, it could be forfeited to white claimants. In this instance, however, the parcel was sold to a timber and land company in 1867 by Ne-con-ne-pe-wah-se's heirs, a man named Kentuckinim and his wife, Con-sog-ge-quah. Aside from these names, no other documentary evidence has been uncovered that directly identifies the former owners and, thus, the probable users of the 19th-century component of the site.

Ne-con-ne-pe-wah-se was one of fourteen Native Americans who filed for land patents near Fremont Lake in the 1850s (Dunham and Branstner 1995). Most of the other Native Americans who received land patents in the area lived nearly a mile to the east of the Ne-con-ne-pe-wah-se site. Many of the parcels were situated on what was known as Indian Town Road, and these claims may have been collectively referred to as Indian Town (Spooner 1954). Hinsdale (1931) notes the presence of a village in this general area, which may reflect use of the locale by this community prior to the 1850s land patents. The 1860 and 1870 censuses record the presence of a small Native American community in the area, listing all the household heads as farmers (U.S. Bureau of the Census 1860, 1870).

The Ottawa and Ojibwa are well represented in the ethnohistoric and ethnographic literature of the region (e.g., Densmore 1974, 1979; Hilger 1992; Landes 1938) as well as through the census, the records of regional Indian agents (Brooks 1877; Schoolcraft 1853), and contemporary Euro-American narratives (Henry 1969; Tanner 1956). A variety of Native American narratives are also available, including Blackbird (1897), Kawbawgam et al. (1994), and Broker (1983). These sources are valuable because they include the observations of men and women from inside and outside Ojibwa and Ottawa culture. Similar sets of culturally appropriate documentary sources have been used elsewhere to develop models or expectations concerning archaeological sites (Spector 1985).

Ojibwa and Ottawa Social Organization

It is difficult to separate social and economic spheres in Ojibwa or Ottawa society. The basis for both these cultural expressions is the extended family or band. The Ottawa and Ojibwa reckon kin patrilineally, through totemic clans. Thus, different families were related through clan affiliation. The familial analogy was extended to recognize the Ojibwa and Ottawa as elder and younger brothers respectively, and each acknowledged their close cultural affiliation as *Anishnabeg* or the True People. While the Ojibwa and Ottawa are considered separate "tribes," they have shared a long mutual history in the Great Lakes region and share similar language, customs, and traditions (Cleland 1993; Clifton et al. 1986). Furthermore, it was not uncommon for people of either heritage to be present at a given habitation during the historic period (Blackbird 1897; Henry 1969; Tanner 1956).

A typical Ottawa or Ojibwa family would include a mother, father, and their children, as well as grandparents and possibly the father's unmarried adult siblings. The family serves as the basic unit in Ojibwa and Ottawa society for the economic and social maintenance of the band. The tasks associated with these activities were assigned according to age and gender. With such cultural data, it should be possible to turn to traditional anthropological approaches to gain insights concerning the social and economic dynamics of these people, thereby clarifying the interpretation of the Necon-ne-pe-wah-se site and its place within the broader settlement and subsistence systems.

Settlement and Subsistence Round

Most Ottawa and Ojibwa families were highly mobile in the 19th century, as they pursued the seasonal settlement and subsistence patterns they had practiced prior to the treaties (Blackbird 1897; Cleland 1991; Fitting and Cleland 1969; McClurken 1994). The land patent filed by Ne-con-ne-pe-wah-se probably did not represent a permanent farm. E. J. Brooks (1877) wrote concerning the Ottawa and Chippewa Indians of northern Lower Michigan that "their idea of a homestead is a place on which to make sugar in the spring, raise a few potatoes and sufficient corn to supply their bread during the year, and to have a home upon which they may at any time return." This pattern is also described by Andrew Blackbird (1897: 32), who writes that "all the Indians of Arbor Croche (Cross Village) used only to stay there during the summertime, to plant their corn, potatoes, and other vegetables. As soon as their crops were put away in the ground, they would start all together towards the south . . . expressly to trap . . . all winter, and make sugar in the spring."[4] Among the Minnesota Ojibwa, Broker (1983) notes the existence of a sugar bush, blueberry place, ricing place, and a winter place, in addition to the band's summer place where gardens were maintained. Each place included a lodge or camp where the family lived for the season. Michigan Ojibwa and Ottawa followed a similar pattern, possibly with the exception of the rice camp and with the added presence of fishing villages (Blackbird 1897; Brooks 1877; Fitting and Cleland 1969).

Pre-Contact and historic Ottawa villages were typically nucleated settlements (Andrews 1995; Conway 1989; Feest and Feest 1978; McClurken 1986b) in which families resided for portions of the year as part of a seasonal round. Thus, it appears quite likely that Ne-con-ne-pe-wah-se and his family used the cache pit site locale for specific storage activities, but resided someplace else. The low density of occupational debris at the site and the lack of structural features, other than the pits, support such an interpretation. Ne-con-ne-pe-wah-se and his family may have lived at the Fremont Indian Town community, which is situated about a mile east of the cache pit site. The separation of habitation and caching locales has been observed in regard to Late Woodland cache pit sites, perhaps indicating continuity in traditional settlement and subsistence practices.

Cache Pits

For mobile people who practiced a seasonal subsistence round, cache pits would have served a practical purpose. Food not needed immediately could be stored against future need. Additionally, cached supplies did not need to be transported and would, presumably, be available upon return. Blackbird (1897), for example, noted that his parents would immediately assess the family's caches of corn and beans upon returning to their village (Cross Village) in the spring. As indicated earlier, one would expect cached provisions at primary habitations such as planting and fishing villages, as well as at task-specific locales, such as maple sugaring or berrying camps. Nodinens, for example, recalled that "a food cache was always near the sugar camp. We opened that and had all kinds of nice foods that we had stored in the fall. There were cedar-bark bags of rice and there were cranberries sewed in birch-bark makuks and long strings of dried potatoes and apples" (Densmore 1979:122).

The ethnohistoric literature suggests that Native American storage pits were often hidden, particularly among more mobile peoples such as the Dakota (e.g., Eastman 1971). Two explanations seem most germane to this discussion. Among mobile groups, pits were dug and used by individual households and extended family members, whereas sedentary folk like the Iroquois appear to have used them more communally along clan lines. In the latter case, a larger number of people would have been aware of a pit's location, limiting the effectiveness of concealment (see DeBoer 1988). Additionally, if the community was sedentary and used communal storage pits, any transgressions concerning these pits would probably be public knowledge. Public censure may have provided a better form of protection than concealment.

Untended food caches, on the other hand, are more vulnerable to human or animal disturbance. Many sources relate the necessity of caching for concealment as well as storage. To this end, the Dakota were described as being "very ingenious in covering up all traces of the hidden food" (Eastman 1971:203). Charlevoix (1923:112–13) explained that "when [the Miami] are obliged to be from home for any time or when they apprehend some interruption of the enemy, they make great concealments underground where these grains are exceedingly well preserved." Atwater (1831:102) similarly recorded that rice and maize were buried in the ground "to preserve it as well as to keep it from being stolen."

Stored food was not only at risk from outsiders. In some instances the greatest threat may have come from members of the same community. The Fox and Sac, for example, had strict traditions concerning the return to the planting village from the winter hunting grounds. One of the reasons for these social constraints was to prevent early arrivals from plundering their neighbors' corn cache (Marston 1912:163–64). An example from southeastern New England offers a gendered dynamic in regard to caching food. In this instance, the women expressly hid their corn caches from "the inquisitive search of their gurmandizing husbands, who would eate up both their allotted portion and reserved seed if they knew where to finde it" (Wood 1898:100). A final observation has suggested that Mississippian populations in the American Bottom hid their food in pits to avoid tribute demands of the societal elites (DeBoer 1988).

Cached food was not only hidden from human thieves; it was also cached against animal pilferers. In one account, wolves were blamed for the destruction of a northern Wisconsin wild rice cache (Curot 1911). To protect against such transgressions, measures were taken to protect as well as conceal food stores. For example, large logs were used to stop hogs from rooting out stored grain in New England (Wood 1898). Similarly, Hilger (1992:149) recorded a cache pit located in a grove of maple trees near her informant's garden. The pit was covered with cut saplings, old corn stalks, and dead leaves "to fool the deer."

Nineteenth and 20th-century accounts of the Ottawa record the use of cache pits. Atwater observed that the "Ottoways buried in ground granaries in birch boxes" (1831:102). Concerning the Ottawa at Cross Village, Blackbird (1897) recalled that some food was stored underground in large cylinders made of elm bark. Surface depressions have been recorded in the vicinity of Cross Village (Andrews 1995). Food caches were also described at the mixed Ottawa and Ojibwa community outside Nahma in the 20th century. Winberg (1994:20) recalled that "Sometimes we put them [potatoes, canned berries, squash, etc.] in the sand. We buried the carrots in the sand, those rutabagas and stuff." Surface depression sites have also been identified in the vicinity of Nahma but have not been formally tested to date (Dunham et al. 1994).

Nuts and Berries

The use of nuts and wild berries by Native Americans in the Great Lakes region is well documented in the ethnohistoric, ethnographic, and archaeological literature; these wild resources formed an important part of traditional foodways (Densmore 1974; Smith 1932; Waugh 1916; Yarnell 1964). The collection of fruit is an important part of the Ojibwa and Ottawa seasonal round, occupying much of the summer, which is often referred to as the *berrying* season (Densmore 1974, 1979; Winberg 1994).

The months of June, July, and August have been described as the Strawberry, Raspberry, and Blueberry moons respectively (Densmore 1979; Kawbawgam et al. 1994). In certain northern Michigan traditions the berry moons include September, differentiating the Little Blueberry Moon (August) and the Large Blueberry Moon (September) (Kawbawgam et al. 1994). This nomenclature refers to the economic and social importance of berries at that time of year.

Obtaining nuts and berries was principally the task of the women and children of a family band (Densmore 1974, 1979; Hilger 1992). Densmore (1979:127) notes that, "this was usually done by women and older children, and as the country of the Chippewa abounded in berries of many varieties it formed a summer industry of some importance." The berries and nuts were gathered by hand and placed in birch-bark containers or *mukuks*. The size and duration of a nutting or berrying expedition appears to have been variable. With the family as the basic economic unit, berrying parties would likely be composed of the women and children of a particular family or composite groups composed of two or more families. Nutting and berrying were undoubtedly conducted in conjunction with other tasks in the summer and early fall. The seasons of the various berries and nuts and their specific environments might require multiple short-term campsites throughout the region. In other words, different patches were likely to ripen at different times and places throughout a landscape, potentially necessitating multiple camps to procure these resources.

After the nuts or berries were collected, those that were not eaten immediately would be processed for later consumption, usually by drying or leaching before storage. Women processed and stored surplus nuts and fruits (Densmore 1974, 1979; Hilger 1992). Berries were typically dried, either on frames made of sticks or reeds or on birch-bark trays. Some berries, such as raspberries, were boiled down; then the concentrate was spread on birch-bark trays to dry. Nuts were similarly boiled, probably to leach toxins and to extract oils, and then dried. Cherries were generally dried for storage with the stone intact, then ground into a powdered form. It seems pertinent to note that cherry stones contain cyanide when the fruit is fresh, but do not when they have been dried, possibly explaining this method of processing (Kuhnlien and Turner 1991). The preferred method of drying fruits and nuts was in the sun; however, reference to drying by fire is also made (Robinson in Vennum 1988:140). Broker (1983:47) cites the role of young girls in monitoring the drying fruit by shooing away dogs and younger children.

Berries were collected in abundance in order to meet immediate needs as well as for winter storage, trade, and, in later times, commercial sale (Kinietz 1947; Kohl 1985; Winberg 1994). Dried berries were an integral component of the winter diet (Densmore 1974; Feest and Feest 1978; Kinietz 1965). Fleshy fruits, including cherries and berries, played an important nutritional role in the diets of pre-Contact as well as historic Native Americans (Kuhnlien and Turner 1991). Concerning the Ottawa in the vicinity of Newaygo County, it was recorded that one of the means of subsistence used by women and children in the late 19th century was the collecting and selling of berries (U.S. Bureau of the Census 1890). Regional Indian Agent E. J. Brooks (1877) observed that while embarked on summer hunting and fishing expeditions, "the wife and children subsist the family by picking and selling berries." This pattern continued into at least the 1930s in northern Michigan, as noted by Lucille Winberg (1994:5): "we did used to go back there years ago and pick blueberries. And that's how we survived." Likewise, preserved berries continued to be an important source of winter food in the early 20th century in northern Michigan as well. Winberg relates that "we eat that [hubbard squash] almost all winter and berries that we can[ned]" (1994:20).

Storage in the 19th century would have involved placing the dried berries into birch-bark *mukuks*. (It should be noted that the manufacture of *mukuks* was also a task conducted by women.) Later storage also involved canning in glass jars. Josephine Robinson recalled that, "when those berries [blueberries] got nice and dry that's where she'd pack them, in that birchbark muckok. She would sew it up and get it all filled up. It is amazing how many berries you can get into one of those things" (Vennum 1988:140). Densmore (1979) noted that four *mukuks* of fresh berries produced one *mukuk* of dried fruit. The dried nuts and berries were then stored, sometimes in cache pits. One such cache pit was described as follows: "she had deposited canned raspberries and Juneberries of the season [into a pit that] . . . was 22 inches in diameter and 12 inches deep. 'When I have my canning done, I'll tuck hay all around the jars and plenty of it on top, and then I'll cover both caches with earth, making a heap at least so high (18 inches) above the level of the ground'" (Hilger 1992:150). Nodinens recalled that "Grandmother had charge of all this, and made the young girls do the work" (Densmore 1979:122).

Nuts and berries are the most common plant remains to be recovered archaeologically on 15th- and 16th-century Ottawa sites in Ontario. These excavations have revealed the common presence of hazelnut, hickory nut, acorn, elderberry, brambleberry, cherry, hawthorn, and sumac (Fox 1990). Similar patterns are also present at Huron sites (Monckton 1992) and Late Woodland sites in Michigan (cf. Lovis et al. 1996; McPherron 1967; Yarnell 1964). The recovery of comparable species at the Ne-con-ne-pe-wah-se site, especially cherry, sumac, and elderberry, argues for the continuity of Native American foodways in the region from the Late Woodland period through the 19th century.

Several of the recovered plant species may reflect the conscious manipulation of the landscape through the use of fire by the site's users to facilitate the growth of wild fruits (e.g., pin cherry, raspberry, pokeweed [Egan 1995; Voss 1972]). Pin cherry, in particular, thrives in recently burned over areas, and its seeds often germinate after fire or other disturbance (Voss 1972). Native Americans used fire for the maintenance of berry patches in the Great Lakes region as well as for clearing garden plots and driving game (Albert and Minc 1987; Cleland 1993:268; Loope and Anderton 1998; Waugh 1916). Blackbird's (1897:10–11) description of Cross Village may reflect such practices: "My first recollection of the country of Arbor Croche, . . . there was nothing but small shrubbery here and there in small patches, such as wild cherry trees, but most of it was grassy plain: and such an abundance of wild strawberries, raspberries and blackberries that they fairly perfumed the air of the whole coast with the fragrant scent of ripe fruit."

The Cache Pits at the Ne-con-ne-pe-wah-se Site

Perhaps the most compelling archaeological evidence for the function of the pits at the Ne-con-ne-pe-wah-se site are the botanical remains. Beechnuts and fruit seeds, including cherry, sumac, raspberry, elderberry, and grape, were recovered from three formally sampled cache pits (Cache Pits 5, 9, and 17) and from Feature 3 (table 8.2). An uncarbonized maize cob was also recovered from Cache Pit 9. Aside from these edible nuts and berries, seeds from plants whose berries were used for medicinal, ceremonial, and other cultural purposes were also recovered from the pits (Egan 1995; Kuhnlien and Turner 1991; Meeker et al. 1993; Yarnell 1964). In fact, the nuts and fruits with documented cultural uses comprise approximately 97.5 percent of the botanical assemblage (see tables 8.2 and 8.3).

Not only do the recovered species include many possible cultural uses, but they also represent plants that are indigenous to a variety of ecological settings and that bear fruit at different times during the summer and fall. For example, most cherries and raspberries ripen in July or August, elderberry and grapes typically bear fruit in September or October, and beechnuts do not ripen until October or November (Voss 1972; Yarnell 1964).

Table 8.3. Floral remains (seeds) that do not appear to have cultural uses (after Egan 1995)

Cache Pit/Feature	CP 5	CP 5	CP 5	CP 9	CP 9	CP 9	CP 17	CP 17	F 3
Level[a]	5	6	7	8	10	11[b]	5	7[c]	9[d]
Flotation volume (liters)	10	10	10	-	10	10	7	5	10
Echinochloa sp. Wild Millet	-	-	-	-	-	-	1	-	-
cf. *Hippuris vulgaris* Marestail	-	-	-	-	-	-	-	-	1
Potamogeton sp. Pondweed	-	-	-	-	-	-	6	-	-
Rumex sp. Sorrel	-	-	-	-	-	-	-	1	-
Symphoricarpos sp. Snowberry	-	1	-	-	-	-	-	-	-
Umbelliferae Type I Parsley family	1	1	-	-	-	-	-	6	-
Umbelliferae Type II Parsley family	-	1	-	-	-	-	-	-	-
Unidentifiable	-	-	-	-	-	-	-	-	1

a. Level = arbitrary 10 cm excavation levels (e.g., level 5 = 40–50 cm. below modern ground surface), unless specified.
b. Level 11 in Cache Pit 9 = 115–21 cm below modern ground surface.
c. Level 7 in Cache Pit 17 = 55–60 cm below modern ground surface.
d. Level 9 in Feature 3 = 80–86 cm below modern ground surface.

In regard to ecological setting, bunchberry is found in lowland conifer forest settings, beechnuts come from northern mesic (beech) hardwood forests, and pin cherries from sandy, well-drained, open environments (Meeker et al. 1993; Voss 1972; Yarnell 1964). The seeds recovered from the pits provide evidence for the scheduled, seasonal collecting of nuts and berries from multiple environments and the intentional storage of surplus food at a specific location. This confirms the continued importance of the seasonal round in Ottawa subsistence during the 19th century.

The fact that most of the botanical assemblage is not carbonized is actually quite informative, both from the perspective of this study and in regard to caching behavior in general. First of all, the process of preserving dried fruit, as derived from the ethnographic sources, would be unlikely to produce carbonized remains. Therefore, one would not expect to find a significant amount of carbonized seeds in a cache pit. Secondly, the question of preservation becomes critical. The relatively recent, mid-19th century origin of the features made the preservation of uncarbonized seeds quite likely. However, an important implication of this relates to preservation of uncarbonized seeds from ancient contexts. While one would expect uncarbonized seeds to survive in a mid-19th-century Michigan site, one might not make this assumption concerning the region's pre-Contact sites.[5] The decomposition of uncarbonized seeds might explain the lack of such remains at other cache-pit sites, besides the standard interpretation that the pits were emptied and abandoned prior to post-use collapse.

Cache Pit 17 (50 cm in diameter × 60 cm deep) contained the widest variety of uncarbonized botanical material of any of the tested features at the site (table 8.2), including beechnuts, at least two varieties of cherry (pin and black), grape, raspberry, and elderberry. Berries that were used for dyes and medicinal purposes were well represented by the seeds of pokeweed and sumac. Medicinal plants include bunchberry as well as small samples of witch hazel, chokeberry, cinquefoil, and spicebush. More problematic taxa, such as those of the Nightshade family, were considered potentially cultural because many of the members of this family are edible or are used for other cultural purposes (Kuhnlien and Turner 1991; Meeker et al. 1993). The seeds from Cache Pit 17 were recovered from two samples representing two of seven arbitrary levels excavated from this feature. The number and variety of nuts and seeds recovered in Cache Pit 17 suggest that this pit was not emptied prior to the abandonment of the site.

The form of the features combined with the recovery of a high relative density of edible nuts and fruit seeds indicate that they represent cache pits. Further support for this contention can be derived from the recovery of a textile fragment from Cache Pit 14 and the presence of bark fragments in all of the excavated features. The cloth and bark may represent the disintegrated remains of boxes, baskets, or bags that once contained stored food, or possibly the bark lining of the pits themselves.

Based on the evidence derived from the archaeological and documentary data, the Ne-con-ne-pe-wah-se site represents a caching locale dating from the mid-late 19th century. As such, the site served as a specific activity area, one primarily devoted to the storage of food. While the site's function is clear, its utilization is not. For example, it is not known whether the site was used solely by Ne-con-ne-pe-wah-se's family or if it was a communal storage site used by the Fremont Native American community. Ethnographic data concerning the Ojibwa indicate that cache pits were used by individual households as well as by groups of women from two or three families (Densmore 1979; Hilger 1992). Thus, the site could reflect caching activities carried out by the Ne-con-ne-pe-wah-se family over several years (possibly decades) or the efforts of several families over a limited period.

Two possible lines of evidence suggest that the site was the location of multiple caching episodes. The first observation is the relationship of Cache Pit 9 and Feature 3. Feature 3 appears to represent a cache pit feature that was impacted by the construction and use of Cache Pit 9. Such a palimpsest of pits suggests multiple episodes of pit excavation and caching at the site. The second line of reasoning is more circumstantial and is based on the estimated volume of the features themselves. Quimby (1968:133) has estimated that a combination of five bushels of wild rice and five bushels of corn (about ten bushels of grain) were necessary to support a historic Indian family over the winter. A pit 1 meter in diameter by 0.7 meters deep, the mean pit dimensions from the site, would have an approximate volume of fifteen bushels. Assuming that as much as half of the pit was filled with insulation, seven to eight bushels of storage space remain. If a family's berry requirement, for food and medicine, was comparable to the grain requirement, then two cache pits would have been ample for the needs of a family. Further, if we assume that two pits were used per family per year, then the site reflects approximately ten years of use (twenty surface depressions and one subsurface pit). If the pits were used repeatedly, then a longer period of use is represented. Ne-con-ne-pe-wah-se and his heirs owned the property for a ten-year period between 1857 and 1867. While this discussion is highly conjectural, it provides a possible means for calculating the temporal duration of the site.

In sum, the Ne-con-ne-pe-wah-se site was formed as a result of the activities of 19th-century Native American women and children. This observation was greatly clarified through the interpolation of ethnohistoric and archaeological data that provided a cultural context or model to illuminate the archaeological data. Without such cultural context, the site would simply represent a storage site and not a locale reflecting gendered space and activity. Furthermore, the results of this study may clarify the function of other caching locales in the region, providing a baseline for interpretation and the design of testing strategies.

Conclusion

The cache pits at the Ne-con-ne-pe-wah-se site are noteworthy, as this class of features is a poorly understood phenomenon in Michigan archaeology. The recovery of a wide range of botanical materials representing a variety of food and other cultural taxa is compelling testimony that the features tested at 20NE331 were used for the storage of dried nuts and fruits in the late 19th century. However, it should be noted that 20NE331 represents a single site. Surface depressions like those at the Ne-con-ne-pe-wah-se site are known throughout Michigan and may represent a variety of specific activities (e.g., cache pits, earth ovens, rice hulling pits, maple sap vats, etc.). In this regard, the Ne-con-ne-pe-wah-se site offers a single interpretation of these features within a broader cultural expression.

The recovery of historic artifacts from several of the cache pits was critical to their interpretation and temporal placement. The presence of the uncarbonized cultural floral assemblage, partially the result of the recent origin of the features, provides physical evidence of food storage at the Ne-con-ne-pe-wah-se site that may not be preserved on older sites. The archaeological evidence, particularly the pit features and the botanical remains, presents a strong case for the continuity of a simple and efficient storage technology (caching) from the pre-Contact period to recent times. The cache pits and their contents also indicate the maintenance of traditional foodways, particularly the use of certain wild nuts and berries. Additionally, evidence derived from the site suggests the continuity of traditional settlement and subsistence systems based on seasonal rounds. The excavation and analysis of the cache pits at the Ne-con-ne-pe-wah-se site have provided tangible evidence for the continuity and persistence of the caching tradition in Michigan through the 19th century.

Notes

1. Botanical samples have been collected from some of these sites, but have produced little data (cf. Hambacher 1992) or have yielded problematic data (cf. Arzigian 1982). A surface depression at the Skegemog Point site, a later Late Woodland site, produced a single carbonized wild rice seed. While the recovery of wild rice is intriguing, the single grain provides little insight into the function of the feature. Flotation samples recovered from a surface depression at the Black River Cache site, also a later Late Woodland site, produced a problematic assemblage of 1,185 *Rubus* seeds (Arzigian 1982). The fact that over a thousand of these seeds were not carbonized and many of the other seeds were only partly charred led the investigator to determine that the seeds were modern and the feature exhibited a high degree of disturbance.

2. The attentive reader will note that smudge pits (cf. Binford 1967) were not considered an alternative in this discussion. While smudge pit features have been identified in Michigan (Bettarel and Smith 1973), these pits are typically much smaller than those observed at the Ne-con-ne-pe-wah-se site, and they contained much carbonized organic material such as corncobs (Binford 1967). (Smudge pits

were used to produce dense smoke for the tanning of hides.) The surface depressions at the Ne-con-ne-pe-wah-se site contained little or no carbonized materials and, as noted above, were significantly larger than the smudge pits. Despite the differences in the pits, the role of analogy in determining the function of the features at the Ne-con-ne-pe-wah-se site is indebted to such earlier research.

3. The uncarbonized seeds recovered from the pits also tend to support a recent origin for the features. While it has been suggested that uncarbonized seeds might survive for at least a millennium in certain mesic environments (Kaplan and Maina 1977), additional study of this topic has demonstrated that such preservation is unlikely over such a long period of time (Lopinot and Brussell 1982; Miksicek 1987; Miller 1989; Minnis 1981). Uncarbonized seeds from the mid-19th century, however, have a high probability of surviving to the present. Their survival was probably enhanced, in this instance, through burial in a soil that is slightly to moderately acidic (5.6–7.8 pH; Purkey 1995). The potential for preservation of plant material is considered better in acidic environments (Miksicek 1987).

4. When Blackbird (1897) refers to putting the crops away in the ground, he is referring to the storage of food in pits.

5. The author has recently investigated two other surface depression sites in northern Lower Michigan (Dunham et al. 1999). The preliminary results of these investigations appear to support the observations presented above. For example, a surface depression associated with a large Late Woodland site (20GT59) yielded a small number of carbonized seeds ($n = 6$) in flotation samples, including beechnut and blackberry (Egan 1999). Few uncarbonized seeds were observed in the samples. Based on the evidence presented above, one would expect to find low densities of carbonized floral material from a Late Woodland cache pit.

Another surface depression was tested at 20GT125. Flotation samples collected from the base of the feature contained a wide variety of carbonized and uncarbonized fruit seeds (Egan 1999). The species represented were similar to those recovered from the cache pits at the Ne-con-ne-pe-wah-se site, including blackberry, elderberry, pin cherry, and blueberry, round-leaved dogwood, honeysuckle, orchid, and snowberry. In addition to the seeds, the carbonized remains of beechnuts and acorn were also recovered. It should be noted that 93 percent of the uncarbonized remains were fruit seeds representing species with known cultural uses. Unfortunately, no other artifacts were recovered in association with these features, so no dates or cultural affiliations can be offered. (However, the site is located within a mile of Old Mission, which was the location of a ca. 1840–1852 mission to the local Ottawa and Ojibwa community.) Based on the recovery of uncarbonized seeds and the diversity of species, it seems reasonable that the site represents a historic cache pit locale.

Acknowledgments

The data presented in this paper were, in part, a result of a contract between Great Lakes Research Associates (GLRA) and the city of Fremont, Michigan. I would like to acknowledge the staff at GLRA for their assistance in all phases of the 20NE331 project. Particular thanks go to Mark Branstner, who served as the project's Principal Investigator; to Michael Hambacher, who provided much useful information and commented on an earlier draft of this chapter; and to Robert Karr, who drafted the maps that appear in this chapter. Likewise, I would like to thank the GLRA field crews who worked on the project: Scott Riley, Jeff Owens, Rebecca Osterland, Cindy Flannery, Eric Janulis, Dan O'Rourke, and Jordan Herron. I would also like to recognize the contributions of Margaret Holman, who conducted the analysis of the site's prehistoric assemblage and who commented on an earlier version of this chapter; and Kathryn Egan, who carried out the botanical analysis. Additionally, my gratitude to Caven Clark, who provided the preliminary results from his recent work at a possible cache pit site in Wisconsin; James McClurken, who shared recent research concerning the Little River Ottawa; Christine Hastorf, who commented on an earlier draft of this chapter; the four anonymous reviewers who provided additional comments; and Tina Dunham. Finally, I would like to thank Michael Nassaney and Eric Johnson for organizing the sessions at the 1995 annual meeting of the American Society for Ethnohistory (Kalamazoo, Michigan) that ultimately led to this volume.

References Cited

Albert, Dennis A., and Leah D. Minc. 1987. *The Natural Ecology and Culture History of the Colonial Point Red Oak Stands.* Michigan Department of Natural Resources and the University of Michigan Biological Station, Lansing.

Andrews, Wesley. 1995. *The Middle Village Archaeological Survey and Properties of Traditional Cultural Value Project, Emmet County, Michigan.* Andrews Cultural Resources, East Lansing.

Arzigian, Constance. 1982. Processing of Flotation Samples (20AA54). Manuscript on file at the U.S. Department of Agriculture, Forest Service, Huron-Manistee National Forests, Cadillac, Mich.

Atwater, Caleb. 1831. *Indians of the Northwest, Their Manners, Customs etc., or Remarks Made in a Tour to Prairie du Chien and then to Washington City in 1829.* Jenkins and Grover, Columbus.

Bettarel, Robert L., and Hale G. Smith. 1973. *The Moccasin Bluff Site and the Woodland Cultures of Southwestern Michigan.* Anthropological Papers no. 49, Museum of Anthropology, University of Michigan, Ann Arbor.

Binford, Lewis R. 1967. Smudge Pits and Hide Smoking: The Use of Analogy in Archaeological Reasoning. *American Antiquity* 32(1):1–12.

———. 1980. Willow Smoke and Dogs' Tails: Hunter-Gatherer Settlement Systems and Archaeological Site Formation. *American Antiquity* 45(1):4–20.

———. 1983. *In Pursuit of the Past: Decoding the Archaeological Record.* Thames and Hudson, New York.

Blackbird, Andrew J. 1897. *Complete Both Early and Late History of the Ottawa and Chippewa Indians of Michigan.* Rev. ed. Babcock and Darling, Harbor Springs, Mich.

Branstner, Mark C. 1987. *1987 Cultural Resource Inventory Survey: Manistee National Forest (Bid Item 2).* Great Lakes Research Associates, Williamston, Mich.

———. 1991. *National Register of Historic Places Evaluation of Selected Cultural Resource Properties, Oceana and Alcona Counties, Michigan.* Great Lakes Research Associates, Williamston, Mich.

Branstner, Mark C., and Michael J. Hambacher. 1995. *1991 Great Lakes Gas Transmission Limited Partnership Pipeline Expansion Projects: Phase III Investigations at the Cassassa Site (20SA1021), Saginaw County, Michigan.* Great Lakes Research Associates, Williamston, Mich.

Broker, Ignatia. 1983. *Night Flying Woman: An Ojibwa Narrative.* Minnesota Historical Society Press, St. Paul.

Brooks, Edwin J. 1877. Letter, E. J. Brooks to J. A. Williamson, Commissioner General Land Office (December 27, 1877). National Archive Series Microcopy, Series M234, Roll 413, Frames 64–103. Washington, D.C.

Charlevoix, Pierre François Xavier de. 1923. *Journal of a Voyage to North America,* ed. Louise P. Kellogg. 2 vols. The Caxton Club, Chicago.

Clark, Caven P. 1995. Parkwide Archaeological Survey of the Lower St. Croix National Scenic River, Minnesota and Wisconsin (47PK109). Draft ms. on file at the Midwest Archaeological Center, U.S. Department of the Interior, National Park Service, Lincoln, Neb.

Cleland, Charles E. 1976. The Focal-Diffuse Model: An Evolutionary Perspective on the Prehistoric Cultural Adaptations of the Eastern United States. *Midcontinental Journal of Archaeology* 1:59–76.

———. 1982. Indians in a Changing Environment. In *The Great Lakes Forests: An Environmental and Social History,* ed. Susan Flader, 83–95. University of Minnesota Press, Minneapolis.

———. 1991. From Ethnohistory to Archaeology: Ottawa and Ojibwa Band Territories of the Northern Great Lakes. In *Text-Aided Archaeology,* ed. Barbara Little, 97–102. The Telford Press, Caldwell, N.J.

———. 1993. *Rites of Conquest: The History and Culture of Michigan's Native Americans.* University of Michigan Press, Ann Arbor.

Clifton, James, George Cornell, and James McClurken, eds. 1986. *Peoples of the Three Fires: The Ottawa, Potawatomi, and Ojibwa of Michigan.* Grand Rapids Inter-Tribal Council, Grand Rapids, Mich.

Conway, Thor. 1989. *An Archaeological and Historical Study of Nineteenth-Century Manitoulin Island Ottawa Settlements*. Ontario Ministry of Culture and Communications, Archaeological License Report 88–82. Sault Ste. Marie, Ont.

Coues, Elliott, ed. 1897. *New Light on the Early History of the Greater Northwest: The Manuscript Journals of Alexander Henry, Fur Trader of the Northwest Company and David Thompson, Official Geographer and Explorer of the Same Company, 1799–1814.* 3 vols. Francis P. Harper, New York.

Curot, Michel. 1911. *A Wisconsin Fur-Trader's Journal, 1803–1804*, ed. Reuben G. Thwaites. Collections of the State Historical Society of Wisconsin 20:367–471. Madison.

DeBoer, Warren R. 1988. Subterranean Storage and the Organization of Surplus: The View from Eastern North America. *Southeastern Archaeology* 7(1):1–20.

Densmore, Frances. 1974. *How Indians Use Wild Plants for Food, Medicine and Crafts*. Dover Publications, New York. Original publication 1928, original title *Uses of Plants by the Chippewa Indians*. Forty-fourth Annual Report of the Bureau of American Ethnology to the Secretary of the Smithsonian Institution, 1926–1927. U.S. Government Printing Office, Washington, D.C.

———. 1979. *Chippewa Customs*. Minnesota Historical Society Press, St. Paul.

Doty, James D. 1992. Report on Indians, Communications, and Trade: James D. Doty to Lewis Cass, Detroit, September 20, 1820. In *Schoolcraft's Narrative Journal of Travels,* ed. Mentor L. Williams, 436–45. Michigan State University Press, East Lansing.

Dunham, Sean B. 1993. Thomas Jefferson and the Three Sisters: Agriculture as Culture in the Early American Republic. In *Survival and Renewal: Native American Values*, ed. Thomas Shirer and Susan Branstner, 265–76. Lake Superior State University, Sault Ste. Marie, Mich.

Dunham, Sean B., and Mark C. Branstner, eds. 1995. *Phase II Testing and Phase III Cultural Resource Investigations: The Ne-con-ne-pe-wa-se Site (20NE331), City of Fremont, Newaygo County, Michigan*. Great Lakes Research Associates, Williamston, Mich.

Dunham, Sean B., Michael J. Hambacher, and Mark C. Branstner. 1994. *1993 Cultural Resource Surveys: Hiawatha National Forest*. Great Lakes Research Associates, Williamston, Mich.

Dustin, Fred. 1936. Prehistoric Storage Pits in Saginaw County, Michigan. *Papers of the Michigan Academy of Science, Arts and Letters* 21:7–11.

Eastman, Charles A. 1971. *Indian Boyhood*. Dover Publications, New York.

Egan, Kathryn. 1995. Floral Analysis. In *Phase II Testing and Phase III Cultural Resource Investigations: The Ne-con-ne-pe-wa-se Site (20NE331), City of Fremont, Newaygo County, Michigan*, ed. Sean Dunham and Mark Branstner, 58–61. Great Lakes Research Associates, Williamston, Mich.

———. 1999. Floral Analysis. In *Cultural Resource Management Surveys: Old Mission State Park, Grand Traverse County, Michigan,* ed. Sean Dunham, Michael Hambacher, and Mark Branstner. Great Lakes Research Associates, Williamston, Mich.

Feest, Johanna, and Christian Feest. 1978. Ottawa. In *Handbook of North American Indians,* vol. 15, *Northeast,* ed. Bruce Trigger, 772–86. Smithsonian Institution Press, Washington, D.C.

Fitting, James E., and Charles E. Cleland. 1969. Late Prehistoric Settlement Patterns in the Upper Great Lakes. *Ethnohistory* 16:289–302.

Ford, Richard I., and David S. Brose. 1975. Prehistoric Wild Rice from the Dunn Farm Lake Site, Leelanau County, Michigan. *Wisconsin Archeologist* 56:9–15.

Fox, William A. 1990. The Odawa. In *The Archaeology of Southern Ontario to A.D. 1650,* ed. Chris Ellis and Neal Ferris, 457–73. Occasional Publication no. 5, London Chapter, Ontario Archaeological Society, London, Ont.

Garland, Elizabeth B., ed. 1990. *Late Archaic and Early Woodland Adaptation in the Lower St. Joseph River Valley, Berrien County, Michigan.* Michigan Cultural Resource Investigation Series vol. 2, Lansing, Mich.

Gibbon, Guy E. 1976. The Old Shakopee Bridge Site: A Late Woodland Ricing Site on Shakopee Lake, Mille Lacs County, Minnesota. *Minnesota Archaeologist* 35:2–56.

Greenman, Emerson F. 1927. The Earthwork Inclosures of Michigan. Ph.D. diss., University of Michigan, Ann Arbor.

Hambacher, Michael J. 1992. The Skegemog Point Site: Continuing Studies in the Cultural Dynamics of the Carolinian-Canadian Transition Zone. Ph.D. diss., Michigan State University, East Lansing.

Hambacher, Michael J., and Margaret Holman. 1995. Camp, Cache and Carry: The Porter Creek South Site (20MN100) and Cache Pits at 20MN31 in the Manistee National Forest. *Michigan Archaeologist* 41(2, 3):47–94.

Henry, Alexander. 1969. *Alexander Henry, Travels and Adventures in Canada and the Indian Territories between the years 1760 and 1776,* ed. James Bain. Burt Franklin Publisher, New York.

Hilger, M. Inez. 1992. *Chippewa Child Life and Its Cultural Background.* Minnesota Historical Society Press, St. Paul.

Hinsdale, Wilbert B. 1925. *Primitive Man in Michigan.* Michigan Handbook Series, Ann Arbor.

———. 1928. Indian Corn Culture in Michigan. *Papers of the Michigan Academy of Science, Arts and Letters* 8:31–49.

———. 1931. *Archaeological Atlas of Michigan.* Michigan Handbook Series 4, University of Michigan Press, Ann Arbor.

Holman, Margaret. 1984. The Identification of Late Woodland Sugaring Sites in the Upper Great Lakes. *Midcontinental Journal of Archaeology* 9(1):63–89.

———. 1995. Prehistoric Artifacts. In *Phase II Testing and Phase III Cultural Resource Investigations: The Ne-con-ne-pe-wa-se Site (20NE331), City of Fremont, Newaygo County, Michigan,* ed. Sean Dunham and Mark Branstner, 35–55. Great Lakes Research Associates, Williamston, Mich.

Honigman, J. J. 1956. The Attawapiskat Swampy Cree: An Ethnographic Reconstruction. *Anthropological Papers of the University of Alaska* 5:23–82.

Jenks, Albert E. 1900. The Wild Rice Gatherers of the Upper Great Lakes: A Study in American Primitive Economics. *Nineteenth Annual Report of the Bureau of American Ethnography, 1897–1898*, 2:1013–1137. U.S. Government Printing Office, Washington, D.C.

Johnson, Elden. 1969a. Archaeological Evidence for the Utilization of Wild Rice. *Science* 163(1):276–77.

———. 1969b. Preliminary Notes on the Prehistoric Use of Wild Rice. *Minnesota Archaeologist* 30(2):31–43.

Kaplan, Lawrence, and Shirley Maina. 1977. Archaeological Botany of the Apple Creek Site, Illinois. *Journal of Seed Technology* 2:40–53.

Kawbawgam, Charles, Charlotte Kawbawgam, and Jacques LePique. 1994. *Ojibwa Narratives of Charles and Charlotte Kawbawgam and Jaques LePique, 1893–1895*, recorded by Homer H. Kidder, ed. Arthur Bourgeois. Wayne State University Press, Detroit, Mich.

Kelly, Robert L. 1992. Mobility/Sedentism: Concepts, Archaeological Measures, and Effects. *Annual Review of Anthropology* 21:43–66.

Kinietz, W. Vernon. 1947. *Chippewa Village: The Story of Katikitegon*. Cranbrook Institute of Science Bulletin 25. Bloomfield Hills, Mich.

———. 1965. *The Indians of the Western Great Lakes*. University of Michigan Press, Ann Arbor.

Kohl, Johann, G. 1985. *Kitchi Gammi, Life among the Lake Superior Ojibwa*, trans. Lascelles Wraxall. Minnesota Historical Society Press, St. Paul.

Kuhnlien, Harriet V., and Nancy J. Turner. 1991. *Traditional Plant Foods of Canadian Indigenous Peoples: Nutrition, Botany, and Use*. Gordon and Breach Science Publishers, Philadelphia, Pa.

Landes, Ruth. 1938. *The Ojibwa Woman*. Columbia University Press, New York.

Lockwood-Moore, Rose. 1993. *A Cultural Resource Survey of the Proposed Industrial Park for the City of Fremont*. Rose Lockwood-Moore, Mio, Mich.

Loftus, Michael K. 1977. A Late Historic Period Chippewa Sugar Maple Camp. *Wisconsin Archeologist* 58(1):71–76.

Loope, Walter L., and John B. Anderton. 1998. Human vs. Lightning Ignition of Presettlement Surface Fires in Coastal Pine Forests of the Upper Great Lakes. *American Midland Naturalist* 140(2):206–18.

Lopinot, Neal H., and David E. Brussell. 1982. Assessing Uncarbonized Seeds from Open-air Sites in Mesic Environments: An Example from Southern Illinois. *Journal of Archaeological Science* 9:95–108.

Lovis, William, Kathryn Egan, Beverley Smith, and G. William Monaghan. 1994. Muskrat and Fish, Wild Rice and Goosefoot: Changing Subsistence Strategies and the Origins of Indigenous Horticulture at the Schultz Site. Draft ms. on file, Department of Anthropology, Michigan State University, East Lansing.

Lovis, William, Kathryn Egan, G. William Monaghan, Beverley Smith, and Earl J. Prahl. 1996. Environment and Subsistence at the Marquette Viaduct Locale of the Fletcher Site. In *Investigating the Archaeological Record of the Great Lakes State: Essays in Honor of Elizabeth Baldwin Garland*, ed. M. B. Holman, J. G. Brashler, and K. E. Parker, 251–306. New Issues Press, Kalamazoo, Mich.

Marston, Morrell. 1912. Letter to Reverend Doctor Jedidiah Morse by Major Morrell Marston, U.S.A., Commanding at Fort Armstrong, Illinois, November 1820. In *Indian Tribes of the Upper Mississippi Valley and Region of the Great Lakes*, vol. 2, ed. Emma H. Blair, 139–82. Arthur H. Clark and Co., Cleveland, Ohio.

McClurken, James M. 1986a. Ottawa Adaptive Strategies to Indian Removal. *Michigan Historical Review* 12 (Spring):29–53.

———. 1986b. The Ottawa. In *Peoples of the Three Fires: The Ottawa, Potawatomi and Ojibwa of Michigan*, ed. James Clifton, George Cornell, and James McClurken, 1–38. Grand Rapids Inter-Tribal Council, Grand Rapids, Michigan.

———. 1994. *Ethnohistory Report on the Little River Band of Ottawa Indians*. Department of Anthropology, Michigan State University, East Lansing.

McPherron, Alan L. 1967. *The Juntunen Site and the Late Woodland Prehistory of the Upper Great Lakes Area*. Anthropological Papers no. 30, Museum of Anthropology, University of Michigan, Ann Arbor.

Meeker, James, Joan Elias, and John Heim. 1993. *Plants Used by the Great Lakes Ojibwa*. Great Lakes Indian Fish and Wildlife Commission, Odonah, Wis.

Michigan Department of Natural Resources. 1995. *Zizania aquatica* (Southern Wild Rice), State Threatened Species. Ms. on file at the Michigan Natural Features Inventory, Michigan Department of Natural Resources, Lansing.

Miksicek, Charles H. 1987. Formation Processes of the Archeobotanical Record. In *Advances in Archaeological Method and Theory*, vol. 10, ed. M. B. Schiffer, 211–47. Academic Press, New York.

Miller, Naomi F. 1989. What Mean These Seeds: A Comparative Approach to Archaeological Seed Analysis. *Historical Archaeology* 33(2):50–59.

Minnis, Paul E. 1981. Seeds in Archaeological Sites: Sources and Some Problems. *American Antiquity* 46(1):143–52.

Monckton, Stevan G. 1992. *Huron Paleoethnobotany*. Ontario Archaeological Reports 1. Ontario Heritage Foundation, Toronto.

Morenon, E. Pierre, Paige Newby, Anthony Zalucha, John Brown, John McDonough, and Thompson Webb. 1986. *Archaeological Sites at an Ecotone: Route 4 Extension, East Greenwich and North Kingstown, Rhode Island*. Vol. 3: *Data Recovery: Subsistence and Contact Period Documentation*. Occasional Papers in Archaeology no. 14. Public Archaeology Program, Rhode Island College, Providence.

Moses, Edna. 1994. *Oral History of Edna Moses: "Sand Town" Indian Community*. Hiawatha National Forest Oral History Series no. 49. U.S. West Research, LaCrosse, Wisc.

O'Shea, John. 1989. Black River Cache, 20AA54. Draft ms. on file, U.S. Department of Agriculture, Forest Service, Huron-Manistee National Forests, Cadillac, Mich.

Overstreet, David F., and Linda A. Brazeau. 1982. *Archaeological Inventory and Evaluation at Exxon Minerals Company Crandon Project Site in Forest County and Langlade County, Wisconsin.* Great Lakes Archaeological Research Center, Milwaukee, Wis.

Parker, Arthur C. 1968. Iroquois Uses of Maize and Other Food Plants. In *Parker on the Iroquois,* ed. William Fenton, 5–119. Syracuse University Press, Syracuse, N.Y.

Pearsall, Deborah M. 1989. *Paleoethnobotany: A Handbook of Procedures.* Academic Press, New York.

Pokagon, Simon. 1898. Letter, Simon Pokagon to Albert Jenks (December 16, 1898). Albert E. Jenks Papers, State Historical Society of Wisconsin, Archives Division, Madison.

Pond, Samuel. 1986. *The Dakota or Sioux in Minnesota as They Were in 1834.* Minnesota Historical Society Press, St. Paul.

Purkey, Thomas H. 1995. *Soil Survey of Newaygo County, Michigan.* U.S. Government Printing Office, Washington, D.C.

Quimby, George I. 1962. A Year with a Chippewa Family, 1763–1764. *Ethnohistory* 9(3):217–39.

———. 1968. *Indian Life in the Upper Great Lakes, 1100 b.c. to a.d. 1800.* University of Chicago Press, Chicago.

Reynolds, Peter J. 1977. Experimental Iron Age Storage Pits: An Interim Report. *Proceedings of the Prehistoric Society* 40:118–31.

Schoolcraft, Henry Rowe. 1851. *Personal Memoirs of a Residence of Thirty Years with the Indian Tribes on the American Frontier.* Lippincott, Grambo, and Company, Philadelphia, Pa.

———. 1853. *Information Respecting the History, Conditions, and Prospects of the Indian Tribes of the United States,* vol. 3. Lippincott, Grambo, and Company, Philadelphia, Pa.

Smith, Huron H. 1932. Ethnobotany of the Ojibwa Indians. *Bulletin of the Public Museum of Milwaukee* 4(3):327–525.

Spector, Janet. 1985. Ethnoarchaeology and Little Rapids: A New Approach to 19th Century Eastern Dakota Sites. In *Archaeology, Ecology, and Ethnohistory of the Prairie–Forest Border Zone of Minnesota and Manitoba,* ed. Janet Spector and Elden Johnson, 166–203. J&L Reprints in Anthropology, vol. 31, Lincoln, Neb.

Spooner, Harry L. 1954. The First White Pathfinders of Newaygo County, Michigan. Ms. on file at the Library of Michigan, Lansing.

Swanton, John R. 1946. *Indians of the Southeastern United States.* Bureau of American Ethnology Bulletin 137. Smithsonian Institution Press, Washington, D.C.

Tanner, John. 1956. *A Narrative of the Captivity and Adventures of John Tanner,* ed. Edward James. Ross and Haines, Minneapolis.

Thompson, Robert, Rose Kluth, and David Kluth. 1994. Tracing the Use of Brainard Ware Through Opal Phytolith Analysis of Food Residues. *Minnesota Archaeologist* 53:86–95.

U.S. Bureau of the Census (USBC). 1860. *Federal Population Census Schedules, Michigan. Newaygo County, Fremont Township.* Microfilm on file at the Library of Michigan, Lansing.

———. 1870. *Federal Population Census Schedules, Michigan. Newaygo County, Sheridan Township.* Microfilm on file at the Library of Michigan, Lansing.

———. 1890. *Report on Indians Taxed and Indians Not Taxed in the United States Except Alaska at the Eleventh Census.* U.S. Government Printing Office, Washington, D.C.

Vennum, Thomas, Jr. 1988. *Wild Rice and the Ojibwa People.* Minnesota Historical Society Press, St. Paul.

Voss, Edward, G. 1972. *Michigan Flora: A Guide to the Identification and Occurrence of the Native and Naturalized Seed-Plants of the State.* 3 vols. Cranbrook Institute of Science and the University of Michigan Herbarium, Bloomfield Hills, Mich.

Waugh, Fredrick W. 1916. *Iroquois Food and Food Preparation.* Canada Department of Mines, Geological Survey, Anthropological Series no. 12. Government Printing Bureau, Ottawa.

Winberg, Lucille. 1994. *Oral History of Lucille Winberg: History of "Sand Town" Outside of Nahma, Michigan.* Hiawatha National Forest Oral History Series no. 60. U.S. West Research, LaCrosse, Wisc.

Wood, William. 1898. *New England's Prospect.* E. M. Boynton, Boston.

Yarnell, Richard A. 1964. *Aboriginal Relationships between Culture and Plant Life in the Upper Great Lakes.* Anthropological Papers no. 23, Museum of Anthropology, University of Michigan, Ann Arbor.

9

Maple Sugaring in Prehistory

Tapping the Sources

Carol I. Mason and Margaret B. Holman

Archaeologists have used ethnohistorical data and methods in the same way that Molière's Bourgeois Gentilhomme used prose: he was amazed that he had been speaking it all of his life. Archaeologists have always used the data of history without thinking twice about it; they have never felt any diffidence whatsoever in behaving as if ethnohistorical work is their own province or ethnohistorical research is one of their necessary and proper functions. From work on trading houses, southern slave cabins, colonial plantations, and frontier forts to analyses of the political structure of the Coosa chiefdom or the settlement patterns of the historic Winnebago, archaeologists have treated ethnohistory as one of their ordinary but certainly critically important tools. Ethnohistorical research on a sophisticated level is a commonplace of archaeological practice as archaeologists have reached surely into the literature of history and felt quite at home there. Indeed, some archaeologists comfortably wear two hats and produce as much in one field as in the other. One has only to consider—in the Upper Midwest, for example—the work of Birmingham (1984), Cleland (1971), Hall (1962), R. J. Mason (1986), Quimby (1966), Wedel (1959) and others to realize that ethnohistorical research is no stranger to archaeologists.

The question of traffic in the other direction is more difficult to assess. Do ethnohistorians use archaeology as often as archaeologists use ethnohistory? Certainly ethnohistorians make use of archaeological data when they can (e.g., see Hudson 1990), but whether they routinely consider it an initial source of primary information is another question. Clearly, they do not themselves ordinarily include archaeological fieldwork in planning their research programs: ethnohistorians do not usually envision themselves as excavating their way to their conclusions. The nature of the problems determines what techniques are to be used, and ethnohistory is, after all, history, implying a dependence upon written records. Archaeological research is probably not a tool worth considering for ordinary use in most ethnohistorical work. However, archaeology's potential for dealing with questions not answerable from the usual historical materials makes it a resource of immense importance even when a documentary approach would seem to be the first mode of attack.

An example of the potential inherent in archaeological and ethnohistorical collaboration concerns the origins of maple sugaring—specifically, whether maple sugaring was an indigenous practice in North America or was introduced by Europeans. Sugaring was a regular early spring activity among both Indians and European settlers in the Northeast and Great Lakes regions. The debate about the origins of the practice began by the late 17th century, with different positions taken by a variety of Europeans such as Charlevoix (1966) and LaHontan (1905). Intensive Indian sugaring is well documented only for the 19th century, however (C. Mason 1990). In Europe, people tried making sugar from trees but did not do so regularly because there were cheaper sources for sugar (Deerr 1949). Maple products were an integral part of Indian culture: they were used as preservatives and seasonings, served on social occasions, given as gifts, and traded or sold (Holman 1984; C. Mason 1985). There are reports of maple sugar being used as a famine food in early spring, but the important features of syrup and sugar are that they preserve very well and can be easily transported, making them useful at any time of the year.

As distinguished an American scholar as Lewis H. Morgan provided a capsule impression of the problem when he wrote a description of an Iroquois bark tray in 1849 (Tooker 1994). His initial interpretation was that maple sugaring was a "very ancient" art, but he was troubled by the inability of anyone to tell him how the process was carried on without European tools. By the time he finished his formal description of the bark tray, his uncertainty took the form of trying to supply ethnographic data that might support pre-Contact sugaring and also confessing that he simply did not know "whether they learned the art from us, or we received it from them" (Tooker 1994:184). On the face of it, the question would seem simple to solve; arriving at a conclusive judgment would be a matter of chronological ordering of sources and an interpretation based on straightforward descriptive history. On the contrary, the way has been thorny, and 300 years' worth of assembled documents have not yielded a clear answer in spite of intensive scrutiny by numerous scholars. These efforts include a search for very early descriptions of Indian sugaring as well as inferential arguments based on Indian terminology for sap, sugar, and processing implements, Indian traditions and mythology concerning the origins of sugaring and its use in yearly rituals, and the place of sugar in economic cycles (e.g., Chamberlain 1891; Henshaw 1890; Munson 1989: Pendergast 1982). It is a comfort to those working with this relatively minor problem to realize that many of the really great outstanding issues in other fields relate to questions asked long ago by Aristotle and have proved similarly thorny. They, too, have been chewed over by generations of scholars retrieving bones of contention that one might have thought were exhausted long ago. "Actually most scientific problems are far better understood by studying their history than their logic," observed Mayr (1982:6), and the uncertain origins of maple sugaring is a modest part of this tradition.

Examining the history of this problem demonstrates the perceived power of ethnohistorical documentation and the eagerness of scholars to depend upon ethnohistorical data as the final word, even when that word is no more than a squeak. The earliest scholarly examination of the question by anthropologists using the ethnohistorical documents at their disposal was in the pages of the *American Anthropologist* at the close of the 19th century. H. W. Henshaw (1890) and A. F. Chamberlain (1891) considered the question in separate but linked papers, and both concluded that maple sugaring was certainly indigenous. They had only a small number of relevant sources available to them at the time, and both understood the critical importance of having very early reports of the practice rather than any from, say, the 18th century. Depending upon the very earliest sources has continued to be of central importance in all the subsequent discussions of maple sugaring. It is a simple and reasonable observation that only the earliest documents can be the basis of argument, but the accumulating weight of later materials has sometimes caused this point to be overlooked. Henshaw, at least, was additionally motivated by more than simple curiosity: he was anxious to demonstrate the usefulness of Indian contributions to the agricultural products industry of his time, pointing out the contemporary market value of maple sugar and weighing its contribution to modern economic life.

The next intensive scrutiny of the historical documents came in the 1930s, when anthropologists Felix Keesing and Regina Flannery both carefully examined what ethnohistoric sources they were able to find. The body of documents was indeed larger by this time, and consequently the search for a definitive answer might be expected to be easier. Keesing acknowledged that ethnographers generally considered the practice of maple sugar manufacture to be indigenous, but he came away from his examination of the data convinced that ethnographers were wrong (Keesing 1971:21). Flannery (1939:22) similarly examined a wide range of sources and felt that the evidence was not sufficient to establish the presence of maple sugaring prior to the European arrival.

Both Keesing and Flannery in the 1930s depended solely on documentary evidence, and by the 1930s that pool of evidence was beginning to have finite boundaries. Newly discovered records were fewer and fewer, and the same ones were examined over and over again in the hope that some nuance of meaning might leap from them. Such compendiums of sources as Schuette and Schuette (1935) and Schuette and Ihde (1946) assembled the basic materials and arranged them chronologically, enabling anyone to see at a glance what was and was not possible from the records. Probably the most detailed examination of those records in the following decades is the work of Darrell Henning (1965), who critically examined the whole matter and produced a carefully argued interpretation of the data. His conclusion was that Indians did not practice maple sugaring prior to the arrival of Europeans in the New World. Again, Henning's work was straightforward ethnohistorical practice; it depended upon the documents as he understood them, and his conclusions were based on those documents.

Subsequent examinations of the documentary sources have essentially sifted and winnowed the same materials. The most important and exhaustive reexamination took place as recently as 1982, when James F. Pendergast undertook to cast again into that pool of historic sources and reexamine the conclusions reached by scholars such as Keesing, Flannery, and Henning. In a careful and reasoned discussion, Pendergast came to a conclusion exactly opposite from that of his immediate predecessors—that maple sugar manufacture in North America did have indigenous origins. His conclusions did not go unchallenged by those who had examined the same sources and continued to support the position of Keesing, Flannery, and Henning (C. Mason 1987, 1990).

Methodologically, the goals of those seeking support for pre-Contact maple sugaring has been to find the documentary equivalent of the "smoking gun," a single source that can be construed as describing Indians making maple sugar early enough for the activity to have been unaffected by a European presence. The search for that single clear reference involves researchers in endlessly reinterpreting, retranslating, and reweighing the slightest documentary clues, producing what amounts to a cottage industry in documentary phrenology. It comes down to a kind of laying on of hands and "my interpretation is as good as yours." Clearly, at this point, the documentation is not sufficient to establish the origins of early maple sugaring; ethnohistorical research has reached a stalemate.

It is at this point that the independent voice of archaeological research holds out hope of an answer. What distinguishes Pendergast's work is that he is an archaeologist: he was always sensitive to the possibilities for archaeological understanding of a past pattern of life that included sugaring as part of the economic round. As early as 1974, he was willing to entertain the idea that archaeological remains might indicate the presence of pre-Contact maple sugaring (Pendergast 1974).

The only real proof that Native peoples made maple sugar prior to the arrival of Europeans must come from the archaeological record. Yet, like early documents, the archaeological record is enigmatic so far. Hard evidence such as implements to make sugar or sugar itself has never been found. The likelihood that implements will be found is very poor. Even in historic times, spiles, collecting buckets, gathering troughs, granulating bowls, and paddles were made of wood or bark materials that do not easily survive. At the moment, sugar residue is the only hope for definitively establishing prehistoric sugaring.

There is indirect support for sugaring in the archaeological record at sites where features and artifact assemblages suggest the sugaring process. Such characteristics include short-term use, intensive cooking activity, a limited range of activity, and use of dried or cached foods. For example, large amounts of fire-cracked rock mixed with lenses of charcoal along with relatively few artifacts—mainly ceramic containers—led Lovis (1978:44) to suggest that the Late Woodland McAlpin site (20CN9) in northern Lower Michigan was a sugaring site. Lovis (1978) drew his conclusions from the work of Quimby (1966) and Loftus (1977), who addressed the question, What would a sugar camp look like archaeologically? Quimby's (1966:178) material expectations of a sugaring site are derived from the account of Alexander Henry's year with a Chippewa family (1763–64); Loftus's (1977) come from his excavations of a known historic-period Chippewa sugar camp. Both of these, of course, derive from the intensive sugaring patterns of relatively recent times.

Like Lovis (1978), Kingsley and Garland (1980:27) drew on the work of Loftus (1977) to interpret their observations of the Late Woodland DeBoer site (20AE62) in southwest Michigan. Specific similarities between the historic-period sugar camp and DeBoer included proximity to maple trees, sparse artifacts, and a high frequency of containers for sap, coupled with a low frequency of tools and food remains. Because there was no evidence of extensive burning at DeBoer, Kingsley and Garland (1980:28) suggested that it may have been used for sap collecting rather than sap processing.

Distinguishing maple sugaring from other seasonal activities where one could expect a site with an absence of extensive living debris and an abundance of containers is clearly difficult. Kingsley and Garland (1980:20) offered an alternative hypothesis for their observations. DeBoer could have been used for collecting nuts and acorns during the autumn, though there was no specific evidence of this either.

Like Kingsley and Garland (1980), Pendergast (1974) addressed the problem of how to differentiate the archaeological evidence for one season (for example, spring) from another season (for example, fall or winter). Evidence from the Sugarbush site, an Iroquoian site in Ontario having relatively few artifacts spread over a large area with large numbers of ash deposits, indicated to Pendergast (1974:37) that the site was occupied by a relatively large group of people for perhaps one season. Pendergast (1974:37) suggested these characteristics pointed to the possibilities that the site was a spring sugar camp, a winter camp, or a "hamlet" that burned before a large amount of occupation debris could accumulate.

Holman (1984:79) used ethnohistoric and recent sources to develop criteria for identifying environments in which maple sugaring sites might be found. These include percentage of maple forest, the presence of topographic features that could be used to prolong the sap season, and relatively isolated locations in the vicinity of warm-season villages. These criteria were to be used in conjunction with site evidence to help discern an early spring sugaring occupation and to differentiate it from occupation in other seasons.

Thus far, archaeologists have tried to understand how sugaring would be evident in the pre-Contact archaeological record. The greatest difficulty with archaeological evidence for sugaring, however, is not preservation of implements, delineation of expectable site characteristics, or the development of micro-environmental criteria. These to some degree are always problems in trying to interpret an archaeological site. The biggest difficulty in discerning sugaring archaeologically relates to the argument expressed by C. Mason (1985, 1990)—that sugaring is not indigenous. If sugaring did not occur, it cannot be seen in the archaeological record. Thus, as is the case with historic sources, the archaeological record is subject to differing interpretations, and the burden of proof falls on the proponents of sugaring.

Despite the apparent impasse, the possibility of prehistoric sugaring is still alive because the argument raised by ethnohistorians regarding technological feasibility has been eliminated through a series of controlled, replicable experiments. Beyond documentation, one of the major objections ethnohistoric research placed in the path of establishing early sugaring was the perceived need for European equipment, most notably metal boiling kettles for sugar production. This perception, referred to informally as the "argument from technology," has been important to many scholars, for example, C. Mason (1985) and Morgan (Tooker 1994), who assert that without metal kettles Native Americans could not boil sap into sugar.

To test this proposition, Holman and Egan (1985) processed maple sap in ceramic and birch bark containers. Vessels of both materials would have been available to indigenous peoples and were reported to have been used for the purpose of "sugaring" (e.g., Armstrong 1892; H. Smith 1933). The various techniques used in these experiments were reported in the ethnohistoric literature and include freezing (J. Smith 1831), heating directly over the fire (H. Smith 1933), and stone boiling (Keating 1825). The experiments were photographed, and in each case, records were kept of the length of time it took to process the sap and the quantity of sap processed. The processed sap was analyzed at a Michigan Department of Agriculture laboratory and compared with national standards for maple syrup. Although some techniques and containers worked better than others, syrup approaching modern standards in sugar content was produced, and it was concluded that indigenous technology was adequate to process maple sap into syrup and probably sugar as well.

Subsequently, Munson (1989) pointed out that syrup and sugar are quite different. He argued that low-fired, earthenware containers could not withstand the more intense direct heat required to make sugar and that the only way sugar could have been made was by stone boiling. In an experimental attempt to make sugar, Munson stone boiled some syrup with notable lack of success. He concluded that prehistoric peoples might have made syrup but not sugar.

More recent efforts to make sugar have been successful. In 1993, Ettawaghezik and Cowan attempted to make sugar by directly boiling syrup in replicas of prehistoric pots and granulating the processed sap in a wooden trough with a wooden ladle. They carefully recorded quantities and processing times and photographed the experiments. Although their results have not yet been formally published, they were briefly reported by Holman (1993), who witnessed the experiments. Sugar was easily made. Chris French of the Michigan Archaeological Society also easily made sugar in replicas of pre-Contact ceramic vessels at the society's fall 1993 workshop. Taken together, these experiments have shown that both syrup and sugar can be made in bark or ceramic cooking containers in quantities sufficient to make sugaring worthwhile. The "argument from technology" is not supported.

The advantage of such experiments is that other observers can replicate them. No matter how many experiments are performed, however, they cannot confirm indigenous sugar making: demonstrating that something is possible is still a far cry from demonstrating that it is probable. Again, the only way to prove the case for ancient sugaring is to find archaeological evidence of sugar: syrup or sugar residue in pre-Contact vessels is the last hope for proving indigenous sugaring.

Might syrup or sugar be preserved in the interstices of porous ceramic vessels or as cooking char? In 1961 Clancy (at the Bronson Museum in Massachusetts) used microscopic analysis, spectographic analysis, and X-ray defraction on three samples of residue from a Late Woodland–period pot from the Indian Hill site in Middleboro, Massachusetts. He hoped to identify the components of the residue and thus determine the probable contents of the pot. Clancy (1961:45) found that the char was mainly carbon, and he could not identify organic materials indicative of particular foods having been in the pot. He did, however, observe that a portion of the char was very black, very glossy, and very frothy in appearance, so that it was probably, but not necessarily, derived from sugar (Clancy 1961:45). Clancy (1961:46) also noted that his spectographic analysis was certainly affected by the fact that the pot had been in the ground for many years, so that leaching might add minerals, such as calcium, and spalling might cause pieces of the pot to become embedded in the char. Thus Clancy (1961) observed quartz and silica in the residue.

The chemical and structural problems with finding sugar in residue are reflected in Clancy's (1961) analysis. Residue on a pot surface is mainly char, sugar may not be the only substance that looks "glossy and frothy," and residue that has been on pottery in the ground for hundreds of years is subject to leaching.

Residue from a 19th-century metal kettle (found by Don Simons of the Michigan Archaeological Society) known to have been used to make syrup was examined using scanning electron microscopy by Richard Bisbing (letter to Holman, 1993), who noted some of the difficulties in searching for maple residue. Maple syrup contains calcium, potassium, and residual materials. But other substances also contain calcium and potassium, so that if, for example, calcium were found, one could not be certain it came from maple syrup. Maple sugar is 99 percent sucrose, so that if any water-soluable sugar could survive leaching, any "signature" sugar unique to maple would remain in such small amounts as to be impossible to detect. Nonetheless, at the moment, residue is the only way to find prehistoric maple sugar.

If indigenous maple sugaring has not yet been proven archaeologically, what is the importance of archaeology for solving a question raised by ethnohistorians? Perhaps the answer lies in the approach to evidence taken by archaeologists—a conscious and explicitly scientific stance. For the first time in this 300-year-old controversy, hard evidence is being sought in the only place it really can be found—in the archaeological record. It may never be known if maple sugaring is indigenous to North America. Or perhaps scholars are in the position of the paleontologist Alfred Romer, who for many years argued about some aspect of the coela-canth/crossopterygian fishes, feeling sure that he would never know the truth about these long-extinct creatures. Then one day a fisherman from South Africa caught one.

References Cited

Armstrong, B. G. 1892. *Early Life among the Indians: Reminiscences from the Life of Benjamin G. Armstrong*. Dictated to and written by Thomas P. Wentworth. Press of A. W. Browion, Ashland, Wis.

Birmingham, Robert A. 1984. Dogtown: A Historical and Archaeological Study of a Late Historic St. Croix Chippewa Community. *Wisconsin Archeologist* 65(3):183–300.

Chamberlain, A. F. 1891. Maple Sugar and the Indians. *American Anthropologist* 4:381–83.

Charlevoix, Pierre D. 1966. *Journal of a Voyage to North America*. Originally published 1761 by R. and J. Dodsley, London. University Microfilms, Ann Arbor.

Clancy, J. J. 1961. Chemical Analysis of Residue from Indian Hill Ceramic Pot. *Bulletin of the Massachusetts Archaeological Society* 23:44–46.

Cleland, Charles E. 1971. *The Lasanen Site: An Historic Burial Locality in Mackinac County, Michigan*. Anthropological Series 1, no. 1. The Museum, Michigan State University, East Lansing.

Deerr, Noel. 1949. *The History of Sugar*, vol. 1. Chapman and Hall, London.

Flannery, Regina. 1939. *An Analysis of Coastal Algonquian Culture*. Catholic University of America Anthropological Series 7, Washington, D.C.

Hall, Robert L. 1962. *The Archaeology of Carcajou Point*. University of Wisconsin Press, Madison.

Henning, Darrell Davis. 1965. The Origins and History of the Maple Products Industry. Master's thesis, State University of New York, College of Oneonta, Cooperstown.

Henshaw, H. W. 1890. Indian Origins of Maple Sugar. *American Anthropologist* 3:341–51.

Holman, Margaret B. 1984. The Identification of Late Woodland Maple Sugaring Sites in the Upper Great Lakes. *Midcontinental Journal of Archaeology* 9(1):63–89.

———. 1993. Other Ways to Make Maple Sugar. *Journal of Ethnobiology* 13(2):283–306.

Holman, Margaret B., and Kathryn C. Egan. 1985. Processing Maple Sap with Prehistoric Techniques. *Journal of Ethnobiology* 5:61–75.

Hudson, Charles. 1990. *The Juan Pardo Expeditions: Spanish Explorers and the Indians of the Carolinas and Tennessee*. Smithsonian Institution Press, Washington, D.C.

Keating, William H. 1825. *An Expedition to the Source of the St. Peter's River*. Whittaker, London.

Keesing, Felix M. [1939] 1971. *The Menomini Indians of Wisconsin*. Johnson Reprint Corp., New York.

Kingsley, Robert G., and Elizabeth B. Garland. 1980. The DeBoer Site: A Late Allegan Phase Site in Allegan County, Michigan. *Michigan Archaeologist* 26(1):3–44.

LaHontan, Baron de. [1703] 1905. *New Voyages to North America*, ed. R. B. Thwaites. A. C. McClurg and Co., Chicago.

Loftus, M. K. 1977. A Late Prehistoric Chippewa Maple Sugar Camp. *Wisconsin Archeologist* 58(1):71–76.

Lovis, William A. 1978. A Numeric Taxonomic Analysis of Changing Woodland Site Location Strategies on an Interior Lake Chain. *Michigan Academician* 1(1):39–48.

Mason, Carol I. 1985. Prehistoric Maple Sugaring Sites? *Midcontinental Journal of Archaeology* 10(1):149–52.

———. 1987. Maple Sugaring Again; or the Dog That Did Nothing in the Night. *Canadian Journal of Archaeology* 11:97–107.

———. 1990. Indians, Maple Sugaring, and the Spread of Market Economies. In *The Woodland Tradition in the Western Great Lakes: Papers Presented to Elden Johnson*, ed. Guy Gibbon, 37–43. University of Minnesota Publications in Anthropology no. 4, Minneapolis.

Mason, Ronald J. 1986. *Rock Island: Historical Indian Archaeology in the Northern Lake Michigan Basin*. *Midcontinental Journal of Archaeology*, Special Paper no. 6. Kent State University Press, Kent, Ohio.

Mayr, Ernst. 1982. *The Growth of Biological Thought: Diversity, Evolution, and Inheritance.* Belknap Press, Cambridge.

Munson, Patrick J. 1989. Still More on the Antiquity of Maple Sugar and Syrup in Aboriginal Eastern North America. *Journal of Ethnobiology* 9:159–70.

Pendergast, James F. 1974. The Sugarbush Site: A Possible Iroquoian Maple Sugar Camp. *Ontario Archaeology* 23:31–61.

———. 1982. The Origin of Maple Sugar. *Syllogeus* 36. National Museum of Canada, Ottawa.

Quimby, George I. 1966. *Indian Culture and European Trade Goods: The Archaeology of the Historic Period in the Western Great Lakes Region.* University of Wisconsin Press, Madison.

Schuette, H. A., and A. J. Ihde. 1946. Maple Sugar: A Bibliography of Early Records II. *Transactions of the Wisconsin Academy of Sciences, Arts, and Letters* 38:89–184.

Schuette, H. A., and Sybil C. Schuette. 1935. Maple Sugar: A Bibliography of Early Records. *Transactions of the Wisconsin Academy of Sciences, Arts, and Letters* 29:209–36.

Smith, Huron H. 1933. Ethnobotany of the Forest Potawatomi Indians. *Bulletin of the Public Museum of Milwaukee* 7(1):1–230.

Smith, James. 1831. *An Account of Remarkable Occurences during Captivity with the Indians, 1755–59.* Grigg, Philadelphia.

Tooker, Elisabeth. 1994. *Lewis H. Morgan on Iroquois Material Culture.* University of Arizona Press, Tucson.

Wedel, Mildred Mott. 1959. Oneota Sites on the Upper Iowa River. *Missouri Archaeologist* 21 (204).

10

Archaeology of a Contact-Period Plateau Salishan Village at Thompson's River Post, Kamloops, British Columbia

Catherine C. Carlson

This chapter presents an overview of an archaeological study that has focused on the early 19th-century origins of Native and European contact in the Interior Salish region of British Columbia, specifically at the Thompson's River Post (Fort Kamloops). Culture contact between Native peoples and Europeans in North America has long interested anthropologists and ethnohistorians (see Nassaney and Johnson, Introduction). The arena of culture contact and colonialism raises intriguing questions about the cultural transformations that frequently brought new forms of economic production, political institutions, and domestic relations, in both aboriginal and nonaboriginal groups. More often than not, our preoccupation has been with how Europeans changed Native peoples' lives (see Arkush, chap. 7). Native people in western Canada, however, have significantly resisted European acculturation, beginning with their first contact with fur traders in the early 19th century. My particular interest in the Contact period is the history of Native response to European culture in the villages of the British Columbia Interior Plateau, particularly as expressed through archaeological material culture.

Some archaeologists working to define the effects of culture contact on Native North Americans have abandoned the concept of acculturation, or transculturation, in search of a more sophisticated understanding of the Native cultural change brought about by European contact. These scholars have come to appreciate that Native peoples used material objects, cultural practices, and a creative reworking of ideas to maintain their ethnic identities (e.g., Bragdon 1988; Brenner 1980; Carlson 2000; Nassaney and Johnson, Introduction; Pyszczyk 1997; Rubertone 1989). For example, Bragdon (1988:128) observed that, "we have become increasingly aware of the ways in which dominated or oppressed groups within a larger society, such as the Christian Indians, manipulate symbols, both tangible and intangible, in order to preserve and maintain distinctiveness as individuals and groups." Similarly, Rubertone (1989) argues for an "archaeology of native resistance" where studies of material culture in Native contexts reveal aspects of their cultural resistance. Thus, there has been a theoretical shift toward looking more closely at the adaptive relations established between Native groups, at the development of reciprocal obligations with Europeans, and at various other creative strategies to deal with European colonization (Smandych and Lee 1995:25).

Certainly there is considerable Canadian ethnohistorical literature that discusses Native culture as an integral component of the 19th-century fur trade (e.g., Cox 1993; Fisher 1977, 1996; Kehoe, chap. 6; Van Kirk 1980), when European traders began establishing trading posts on Indian land in the Canadian Plateau (fig. 10.1). In 1811 one early explorer and trader in the Kamloops locality, Alexander Ross, described meeting over 2,000 Native peoples who had come to engage his party in trade (Ross 1969:215), indicating a considerable indigenous interest in commercial trade. The Native peoples constituted the local population's majority in and around the Kamloops trading post until the smallpox epidemic of 1862 reduced their numbers by over two-thirds (Shuswap Nation Tribal Council 1989:9).

Despite their strong presence in the region and involvement during the fur trade, only limited archaeological documentation exists regarding Native peoples as active agents in this extensive commercial enterprise in British Columbia. Most of the archaeological studies of the Northwest fur trade have focused on the sites and structures of the Europeans at the fur trade posts. Numerous sites have been investigated in British Columbia and in Washington State (e.g., Fort d'Epinette [Bedard 1990; Burley et al. 1996; Williams 1978]; Rocky Mountain Fort [Hamilton et al. 1988]; Fort McLeod [Quackenbush 1990]; Fort Langley [Porter 1997; Porter and Steer 1987]; Fort Umpqua [Schlesser 1975]; Fort Vancouver [Caywood 1948; Ross 1977]; Fort Okanagan [Grabert 1973; Swanson 1962]; Spokane House [Combes 1964]; Fort Walla Walla [Garth 1952]; and Fort Colville [Pfeiffer 1981]). At most of these sites, however, emphasis has been placed on the areas where Europeans were living and working (e.g., the stockade, the officers' quarters, the factor's house, the storehouses, the

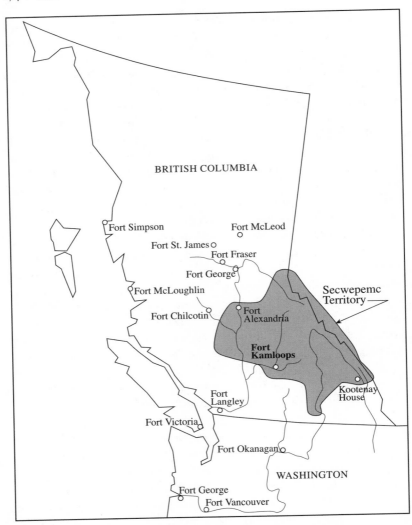

Fig. 10.1. Trading post locations of the mid-19th century in the Pacific Northwest shown in relation to the Secwepemc (Shuswap) First Nation traditional territory

blacksmith's area). Invariably, these excavations have focused on European material culture and the configuration of the fort buildings, especially for interpretive park reconstructions. While this work is useful for chronological comparison with the European material culture of Fort Kamloops, there is little with which to compare the aboriginal material culture, architectural features, or subsistence remains.

Despite the potential importance of these trading-post sites for under-standing Native-white cultural dynamics, investigation of aboriginal cul-ture, economy, and village life at trading post sites has not been a priority in the archaeology of the Canadian Plateau. The domestic structures and villages of the Native peoples in the vicinity of the trading posts at Euro-pean contact remain generally unstudied. Yet villages were the places where Native ethnic boundaries and material differences would have been maintained, and where "cultures of resistance" were enacted in the face of European expansion and the development of new economic relations. Aboriginal sites of the historic period have probably been ignored because much archaeology of the Northwest Pacific fur trade period has been con-ducted under a Eurocentric paradigm of historical archaeology, which was largely unconcerned with the role of Native culture in the development and maintenance of the British commercial centers. According to Patricia Rubertone (1989), until the 1980s historical archaeology of the colonial period in North America was dominated by two research themes. The first was colonial archaeology, which was concerned with reconstructing ev-eryday life in European settlements in the context of a culturally void wilderness. The second theme was acculturation archaeology, where "em-phasis is placed on investigating the effects of culture contact as mani-fested in the inter-change of cultural traits, and in emergence of European social and cultural dominance" (Rubertone 1989:34), such that Native culture is ultimately transformed and assimilated into the dominant soci-ety. It constructs a history that assumes the dependency of Native consum-ers without question, supporting the ideology of conquest. Yerbury (1986), for example, calls the time period from 1821 to 1890 in the west-ern Subarctic the "trading post dependency period," with the Native peoples cast as the dependents. Elise Brenner (1980:135) points out that "the colonists are invariably viewed as the decision-makers, the activists who 'do things *to*' the native groups; while the native communities are viewed as 'having things done *to them*.'"

In a recent article on culture-contact studies, Lightfoot (1995) dis-cussed how historical and prehistoric archaeology have separated, both in theory and practice, to the detriment of Native historic archaeology (see also Nassaney and Johnson, Introduction). He points out that the theo-retical and methodological barriers that presently exist between historic and prehistoric archaeology have hampered significantly our ability to understand and study the Native cultural components at historic archaeo-logical sites. This has certainly been true for the practice of historical ar-chaeology in British Columbia.

Given that the archaeological record is one that emphasizes material culture, it is also important to ask specifically how changes in the manipulation of material culture reflect underlying social processes in a time of intense cross-cultural interaction. Archaeology is unique in the social sciences and humanities in its focus on material culture and the relationship of material culture to behavior (Deetz 1977). Artifacts have been called "tangible incarnations of social relationships embodying the attitudes and behaviors of the past" (Beaudry et al. 1991:150). Material culture, modified in its use from that of its original context, can communicate subculture or "group definition and boundary maintenance," as for example in the "punk usage of safety pins as earrings rather than fasteners" (Beaudry et al. 1991:155; see also Nassaney and Johnson, Introduction). Thus, artifacts become the text and symbols of past behavior in the archaeological record; although not always easily interpreted, they add a Native voice to the record of the past.

One archaeological approach for defining cultural continuity or change has been to look at artifact trait lists and to quantify the relative proportions of Native and imported goods. The underlying assumption is that the greater the amount of non-Native material at an indigenous site, the greater the degree of assimilation or acculturation that has taken place. Critics have pointed out, however, that the adoption of European technologies or materials does not necessarily mean that social, economic, political, or ideological changes have concurrently taken place (Bragdon 1988; Wilson and Rogers 1993). In addition, this assumption often ignores the important fact that the European technology was most often adopted as a replacement for a preexisting Native technology or modified so as to be utilized within the context of Native cultural meanings, not European ones (Ferguson 1992; Kehoe, chap. 6). Issues of sample size and curation are also problematic (Pyszczyk 1997).

Another archaeological approach to understanding cultural maintenance has been to look at ethnicity (see also Johnson, chap. 4; Neill, chap. 5; Kehoe, chap. 6). Artifact trait lists have been used to define ethnic groups within and between multi-ethnic sites. For example, Pyszczyk (1989) examined the relationship between ethnicity (Native, French Canadian, and Orkney) and material culture patterning in six late 18th-century and 19th-century fur trade sites in northern Saskatchewan and Alberta. He argues that "distinct ethnic consumption patterns" can be observed in different sites with similar access to fur trade goods in terms of both the relative frequencies of specific types of artifacts and those defined as luxury versus utilitarian goods. He also points out that the historic records are limited to defining only that which was available for consumption, "but not entirely how those goods are used according to 'culturally dictated plans'" (1989:243), for which the archaeological records of consumption give meaning. Of interest here are the broader theoretical implications for defining ethnicity as a measure of cultural resistance in a dynamic Contact-period context where all groups have access to the same material culture items but use them in culturally different ways. In this way, ethnic boundary maintenance becomes a form of cultural resistance and expression of identity (see Johnson, chap. 4; Neill, chap. 5). The multi-ethnic use of space has also been studied (Lightfoot et al. 1998).

In the Thompson's River Post study, the focus is on interpreting how the archaeology of domestic artifacts and structures in a trading post setting can provide insight into Native identity and cultural maintenance during this Contact-period situation. More specifically, is it possible that Native peoples organized and used land, technology, architecture, and subsistence practices to maintain their ethnicity and autonomy, and if so, can these processes be interpreted from the archaeological record? In the following analysis I examine domestic architectural features, storage facilities, portable technological objects, and faunal remains to determine how this material evidence may reflect the maintenance and reproduction of Native social identity in the context of early post-Contact cultural interactions in the Canadian Plateau region.

The Geographic, Historic, and Ethnographic Context of Kamloops

The Thompson's River Post site is located in the small inland city of Kamloops, 350 km northeast of Vancouver. It is within the Canadian Plateau Culture Area, in the traditional territory of the Shuswap people (see fig. 10.1). Shuswap is the anglicized name for Secwepemc (or Sxwapmx), literally translated as "the widely distributed (or scattered) people" (Gibson 1973:v), who collectively are speakers of the Shuswap language, one of four languages of the Interior Salish language family. Ethnographer James Teit (1909) recorded a map of the traditional Shuswap territory as a vast area in south-central British Columbia extending from the Rockies west to the Fraser River, being the largest territory of all the Interior Salish people. Speakers of Shuswap within this widespread geographical territory refer to themselves today as the Shuswap or Secwepemc Nation.

Kamloops, the anglicized name for *k'mlupsy*, means "meeting of the rivers" or "confluence," a reference to the confluence of the North and South Thompson rivers (Kuipers 1974). These are major tributaries of the

Fraser River, and therefore support important spawning runs for spring (king/chinook), sockeye (red), and coho (silver) salmon. This strategic location was a meeting place, trading center, and permanent winter village location for at least 5,000 years prior to the arrival of the first Europeans, David Stuart and Alexander Ross, in 1811 (Richards and Rousseau 1987; Smith 1900; Wilson and Carlson 1980). It was the obvious site to set up business for two early rival fur-trade companies, the Pacific Fur Company and the North West Company. Access via river transportation to the Columbia and Fraser rivers, in addition to aboriginal trade routes throughout the locality, made it an ideal place for the fur traders to capitalize on the preexisting aboriginal trade.

Alexander MacKenzie was the first European to travel through Shuswap country in 1793, when he descended the Fraser River as far as Alexandria (central British Columbia) via an overland route from the northern Rockies. Here he met Shuswap people (called "Atnah") in the far northern region of Shuswap territory. He noted that they lived in "subterraneous recesses" (i.e., pithouses) and had in their possession "iron, arms, and utensils" which they had traded "from their neighbors to the Westward" — goods originating from the coastal maritime fur trade (Lamb 1970:314). In 1808 Simon Fraser traveled south along the Fraser River through the westernmost portions of Shuswap territory. In his journals, he made note of Shuswap summer houses ("shades") and underground winter houses, and commented on the people's subsistence practices, such as the eating of dried salmon, dog, and different kinds of roots, and the hunting of deer (Fraser 1960). He also passed the mouth of the Thompson River at its confluence with the Fraser River, naming it after his friend and fellow North West Company explorer, David Thompson; however, neither Fraser or Thompson traveled up the Thompson River, and neither visited Kamloops.

David Thompson, while working for the North West Company, built Kootanae House on the Columbia River to the east of Shuswap territory, where he traded with Shuswap who came there in the years 1807–11 (Glover 1962). In 1813–14, Thompson drafted a map for the North West Company; while apparently never having been to the Kamloops vicinity or the Thompson River, he marked the confluence of the North and South Thompson rivers, identifying both as the "Sheewap River." In addition, he marked the "N.W. Coy" (North West Company fort) at the confluence (Belyea 1994), which had been built there in 1812.

The first recorded European in the South Thompson River area was David Stuart of Astor's Pacific Fur Company, in November 1811. Traveling from Fort Okanagan to the east, Stuart was looking for a place to establish a new fur-trading post. Alexander Ross described Stuart's account of his journey to Kamloops:

> [C]rossing a height of land fell upon Thompson's River . . . after travelling for some time amongst a powerful nation called the She Whaps . . . the snows got so deep that we considered it hopeless to attempt getting back, and therefore passed some time with the She Whaps and other tribes in that quarter. The Indians were numerous and well-disposed, and the country throughout abounds in beavers and all other kinds of fur; and I have made arrangements to establish a trading post there the ensuing winter. (Ross 1969:163)

Stuart stayed in this area for almost four months (from November 1811 through February 1812), and presumably he camped in the Kamloops vicinity. Three months later, in May 1812, Alexander Ross, also of the Pacific Fur Company, retraced Stuart's route, reaching the "She Whaps on Thompson's River," at a place "called by the Indians Cumcloups [Kamloops], near the entrance of the north branch [confluence of North and South Thompson rivers]" (Ross 1969:215). Staying at Kamloops for ten days, Ross "sent messages to the different tribes around." He described how at least 2,000 Natives assembled there, bringing in furs and showing themselves to be "anxious" to trade (Ross 1969:215). Whether these "different tribes" were all Shuswap, or included other Salishan groups as well, was not noted.

Following up on Ross's success, David Stuart traveled to Kamloops later that year, where he apparently erected a building for seasonal trade. In addition, Joseph Larocque of the friendly rival company, the Canadian North West Company, built another trading post alongside that of Stuart's (Balf 1969; Favrholdt 1987), in what Yerbury (1986) refers to as the "competitive trade period: 1800–1821." Stuart described how "the country was everywhere rich in furs, and the native population very peaceable. The She Whaps will be one of the best beaver posts in the country" (Ross 1969:225). The seasonal trading posts of these two companies were probably located close to each other on the shore of the South Thompson River, but by the second year of operation (1813), the Astorians were bought out by the Nor'Westers. Unfortunately, any archaeological remains of these two early adjacent seasonal trading posts have been destroyed by modern city developments.

In 1821, when the Hudson's Bay Company (HBC) took over the North West Company, it erected a new, permanent post across the river at the northeast confluence of the North and South Thompson rivers, on the present Kamloops Indian Reserve. The post represented Kamloops' first permanent and year-round trading post. It was relocated to the west bank of the North Thompson River in 1842, following the murder of the old fort's factor, Samuel Black, by a local Native person. After the old fort's abandonment, it was left under the occupancy of Lolo St. Paul, a retired HBC servant and interpreter of mixed Iroquoian and European ancestry (Balf 1969).

The old fort was located on the east bank of the North Thompson River, approximately 500–1000 m north (upriver) of the confluence with the South Thompson River. A late 1862 map provides sketchy locational information, and supplements another unscaled 1862 map that marks the locations of both the "old" (1821–42) and "new" (1842–62) forts. No illustration or documentation pertaining to the size, layout, or configuration of the post and its surrounding community are known to exist. The only known description of the post is that of Chief Trader Donald Manson, who took over the fort in 1841 after the death of Samuel Black. Manson commented, "I found the Fort in a wretched state of defense, the houses and store being completely rotten . . . the Fort Pickets and Bastions are even worse than this" (cited in Favrholdt 1987:21). The post had apparently fallen into such disrepair that it was decided to build a new one across the North Thompson River on its west bank rather than renovate the old site.

Very little is noted in the historical records about the Native presence at the site. From Ross's comment that 2,000 Native people assembled in 1811, it is assumed that they came in considerable numbers to trade at the fort. Whether they traveled to the fort purely on a seasonal basis, or whether permanent or semipermanent villages were occupied adjacent to the fort, is not reported in the historic documents. There are numerous pre-Contact winter pithouse villages recorded in the vicinity of the confluence, but other than a few burials, no Contact-period assemblages had been documented archaeologically (Smith 1900; Wilson and Carlson 1980). Hudson's Bay factor John McLeod commented in 1822–23 on "the Shew-shapps which nation inhabit that part of the Country immediately in the vicinity of the post of Kemeloops" (Hudson's Bay Company 1822–23b), implying a local Native presence. Other brief references to "Kameloops Indians," to "those Indians who remain about the point," and to Indian people preparing their houses in order to winter about the fort are the only indications of Native people around Fort Kamloops in the historic accounts (HBC 1822–23a). None of the limited written documentation provides information about the Fort's exact location and architecture, the configuration and size of a possible associated Indian village, or whether an Indian community occupied the area year round or on a seasonal basis. Nevertheless, there is considerable documentation worth examining that describes Shuswap culture in its general outlines from the perspective of late 19th-century observers.

Ethnographic Baseline for Protohistoric Shuswap Culture

To understand more fully the cultural interactions of the 19th century, it is necessary to have a baseline understanding of pre-Contact Native culture with which to make comparisons with the historic archaeological record. Without such information, obtained through both archaeology and the careful analysis of ethnographic descriptions, there is no way to evaluate the nature, degree, and direction of cultural change. This point has been emphasized by Lightfoot et al. (1993).

Ethnographic sources are useful for providing information on traditional Shuswap social and political organization, material culture, economy, and subsistence. However, it must be recognized that all of these sources reflect Shuswap culture as it was in the late 19th century, several decades after initial Contact. They include the writings of anthropologist Franz Boas (1891), who briefly interviewed Kamloops Shuswap people, geologist and ethnographer George Dawson (1892), and ethnographer James Teit (1909). Teit lived in the Thompson Salishan village of Lytton at the mouth of the Thompson River, and was married to a Thompson Native woman. His close association with the Native peoples, and his ability as a speaker of their languages, enabled him to write (with assistance from Franz Boas) the most comprehensive of all the ethnographic accounts of the four Interior Salish cultures. These were published as part of Boas's Jesup North Pacific Expedition (Teit 1909). The bulk of our understanding of protohistoric Native "traditional" lifeways in the British Columbia Interior Plateau is based almost entirely on Teit's writings.

Teit's ethnographies have been relied upon heavily by archaeologists for ethnographic information, and have even been interpreted as representative of pre-Contact Shuswap traditional culture or "unaffected traditional cultures" (Hayden 1992:4). Teit was concerned (as was Boas) with recording traditional Salishan culture before Europeans radically transformed it. He largely ignored potential areas and processes of Native cultural change and adaptation. Another early writer, Charles Hill-Tout (1900), for example, pointed out that by the late 19th century, disease and missionaries had already substantially altered many aspects of Interior Salish culture, aspects that are not identified in Teit's ethnographies. Teit's writings reflect certain ethnographic biases because they are written from the viewpoint of recreating the "pristine" traditional culture by selectively filtering out cultural changes evident after several decades of European contact. Another limitation of Teit's ethnographies for Contact-period archaeology is that they tended to describe generalities of Shuswap culture without referring to specific villages, historical events, and cultural practices at individual villages. While we will never know how "pristine" Teit's descriptions are, with cautious use his ethnographies provide the only written baseline, or departure point, that allows for the direct historical approach to interpret change and stability in Native culture.

Teit has also been a departure point from which modern people refer to that which has been "lost" in Native society through acculturation. This is because Teit (1909) was not concerned with recognizing the adaptive processes by which Native people were redefining their identity in the 19th century through various forms of resistance to the economic and political imposition, and later domination, by outsiders. I am interested in documenting evidence of how Native peoples were redefining, as opposed to losing, their ethnicity in the hundred years following European contact. Thus, the archaeological record—in contrast to Teit's ethnographic record, which was focused solely on recording a static ethnographic culture—may have greater potential to expose these dynamic processes, albeit within the limitations of the archaeological record in general.

Shuswap Sociopolitical Organization and Trade Relations

According to Teit (1909), the major social units in Shuswap society were residential kinship groupings, such as camps, villages, bands, and possibly "divisions" (a larger social grouping identified by him [1909:457] and composed of several bands within a geographic area). The most important and basic social and residential unit was the domestic household, composed of an independent nuclear or polygynous family, or an extended bilateral and patrilocal family. This was a highly mobile hunting-and-gathering family group that traveled together to resource-harvesting stations (for hunting, fishing, and plant gathering), occasionally joining other family households at warm-season mat-lodge camps, and settling with other families in pithouse villages for the winter months. A principal winter village, along with a number of smaller villages in the immediate vicinity, constituted the band (Teit 1909:457). Band composition was not well defined, as band affiliation for small villages equidistant from the large principal villages was arbitrary and flexible, so village band composition was often in flux (Teit 1909:457). Winter villages had a riverine settlement orientation, and the main villages were located along the Thompson River and on the shores of Kamloops and Shuswap lakes.

It has been suggested that traditional Plateau political organization was "atomistic" (Ray 1939:4)—that is, each band was a politically autonomous unit. The HBC traders at Fort Kamloops recognized a chief and a council of principal men for each band, although ethnographers attribute only limited power to the chief, and the social organization is recognized as primarily egalitarian and nonhierarchical. The HBC journals of the 1820s name two chiefs of the Kamloops division (Savona and Kamloops bands) as being Joe Courty Pott and Tranquille, the former being recognized as the chief in charge of the fort vicinity (HBC 1822–23a).

Many of these villages and bands were linked by peaceful trade and intermarriage, and they participated in each other's pow-wows. However, Kroeber (1917:396) stated that they "were linked like nations of the civilized world, whose intercourse, however intimate, friendly, and long enduring, is always as it were in a condition of suspense," or social fluidity.

Traditionally, Shuswap peoples did considerable trading. The Kamloops and Shuswap Lake groups received roots, Indian-hemp bark, horses, saddles, buffalo robes, woven bark thread bags, painted hide bags, parfleches, and wampum beads from the neighboring Okanagan to the east. They exchanged these for dentalium (traded from the coast), copper, marmot robes, and occasionally snowshoes, and, in later days, glass beads and iron. From the Thompson and Bonapart Indians to the west, they received roots, dried salmon, salmon oil, Indian-hemp bark and thread, horses, woven bags and baskets, parfleches, and wampum beads, for which they gave dentalium, marmot and rabbit robes, occasionally snowshoes, dressed moose and caribou skins, and some paint (Teit 1909:536).

Once the trading post at Kamloops was built, the Shuswap people sold to the Hudson's Bay Company: "large quantities of furs of all kinds, dressed skins, moccasins, dried roots and berries, dried meat, fat, dried salmon, dogs and horses, receiving in exchange principally woollen blankets, cloth, glass beads, steel traps, flintlock muskets, powder, ball and shot, axes, tomahawks, steels and flints, knives, tobacco, iron, copper kettles, brass finger-rings, bracelets, etc." (Teit 1909:537). Feathers are an example of a traditional trade item (of particular value were golden eagle tail feathers and redheaded woodpecker scalps) that declined in value and importance after the HBC arrived, being replaced by the demand for beaver skins (Teit 1909:537).

Just as the value of certain commodities in Shuswap society changed, so too did trading relations between bands. It is not known how a fur-trade post, established in the political territory of an autonomous band, functioned as a commercial center linking many other autonomous bands. Did Native residency at the post coincide with the summer settlement pattern, with many mobile groups sharing the locality as a place to trade? Or did the Natives take up winter residency analogous to a winter village (in which case one would suspect that the traditional winter village inhabitants would lay sole claim to the trading site)? In either scenario, would the traditional village occupants have authority, perhaps as intermediaries or "hosts," in the trading relations between Natives and Europeans? The ethnographies describe how, traditionally, "territorial segmentation is highly specific along river courses, but hunting territory is invariably used in common by a number of villages" (Ray 1939:15). The territories along the river banks were delineated on the basis of fishing grounds (for warm-season camps), but winter villages were not necessarily located adjacent to fishing sites (since it was not the fishing season); instead they were situated relative to such factors as topography and winter warmth.

The Thompson's River Post was located along the riverbank, which would have been in the territory of an autonomous winter village: "The village with territorial rights over the station [i.e., river bank locale] is quite definitely the visitor's host" (Ray 1939:16). Did the trading post village "host" the Hudson's Bay Company as well as other Native traders? Teit (1909:536) mentions that, "After the establishment of a trading-post at Kamloops, the band there sold many articles of European manufacture to the other Shuswap bands and to the Thompson tribe, receiving furs in return; but this did not last long, as the various bands found it more advantageous to deal directly with the post, and the Thompson Indians commenced to repair there also." This suggests that the local and regional Shuswap who came to trade at the center were maintaining traditional egalitarian social structures and not adopting more European hierarchical trading relations with one another.

Traditionally, one of the largest regional trading centers in the Plateau was at The Fountain on the Fraser River to the west, where Kamloops people and others would travel to trade. Teit (1909:536) observed that, "This was a great trading place in early days. There were no restrictions, members from any part of the tribe trading where they liked." The impact of the HBC post at Kamloops on these traditional "trade fairs," and also its impact on the Kamloops locale itself, is not well documented, but clearly it is important for understanding changing interband relations. Teit (1909:535–36) also noted that after the establishment of the Thompson's River Post at Kamloops, the Shuswap "sometimes bought furs and moose-skins from the Iroquois band [people who had moved in with the traders], which they sold with their own furs when they repaired to the post."

Archaeological Investigations

Today the parcel of land that is the presumed location of the 1821–42 post is part of the Kamloops Indian Reserve. It is at the northeast confluence of the rivers, now called "Indian Point." Remarkably, despite the increasing commercial development of the Reserve lands, this property is largely undisturbed by modern development, unlike any of the later trading-post sites in Kamloops. While an earthen flood-dyke was built across the site in the summer of 1999, this construction had limited impact on the archaeological deposits.

Preliminary testing was first undertaken in 1993, during a six-week archaeological field school, to determine if material traces of a potential trading-post village might exist. Other researchers had previously surveyed and recorded surface depressions of cultural significance in the site locality in 1974 and 1979 (designated site EeRc 22). However, it was not known if they represented historic remains of the trading post and/or village, or if they were pre-Contact features. Sixteen such depressions or features had been mapped, one of which was a surficially indistinct rectangular depression (28 × 14 m in size), at the north end of the site. This was hypothesized on the EeRc 22 site form to represent the European settlement's "fort" location. Six other depressions were identified as historic, three of which are known to be very recent 20th-century features; the remainder, all circular depressions, were thought to be pre-Contact in age.

Preliminary field excavations were undertaken in 1993 at two small circular depressions, 5–6 m in diameter, at the south end of the site that had been relocated during a spring walkover of the area with Secwepemc elder Clarence Jules and long-term Kamloops resident Keith Gagne. In the 1995 field season (again run as a field school), a third circular cultural depression was excavated adjacent to the first two tested. In addition, two other areas north of the circular features in and adjacent to the "rectangular depression" were tested to locate potential remains of the European structures at the trading post, but no archaeological remains of the fort were discovered there.

In brief, the 1993 and 1995 excavations of the three clustered circular cultural depressions revealed the remains of 19th-century aboriginal pithouses (earthlodges), including a number of associated artifacts and faunal remains. Of the 185 artifacts recovered in the first season (1993), most date to the mid-to-late 19th century. These include household goods (bottle glass, metal basins, metal cans), raw materials (pounded copper, rolled birch bark), personal items (glass beads, clay pipe fragments), hunting implements (lead shot), and sewing items (brass pins and buttons).

In general, the artifact assemblage is impoverished compared to other historic archaeological assemblages from contemporaneous European sites. Interestingly, no lithic artifacts or European ceramics were recovered in the three pithouses, and only a very limited amount of fire-cracked rock was present. In addition, a varied faunal assemblage was recovered that included wild game, birds, and fish (both salmon and lake fishes), as well as domesticated horse. The stratigraphy of the cultural depressions, wooden roof posts, and associated features (including a bark-lined, bell-shaped storage pit), in addition to the artifacts, indicate that the depressions represent the remains of three 19th-century aboriginal domestic structures of traditional design (i.e., pithouses). These initial findings indicated that historic archaeological remains of a Native community at the trading post were present at the site, and that the preliminary goal of finding domestic structures related to an aboriginal community at a historic trading post had been accomplished.

In 1997 another field school was conducted that tested an area 125 m north of the three clustered historic house pits, where a pile of large stones was located. Testing here revealed the base of a dismantled chimney, wooden floorboards, a cellar hole, and a range of mid-19th-century European artifacts and faunal remains. This area represents the remnants of a European-style log structure, which has been interpreted as one of the buildings of the original trading post.

The 1999 field-school season focused on testing two very large circular depressions (17 m and 13 m in diameter), initially presumed to be pre-Contact house-pit features. They were located immediately adjacent to the North Thompson riverbank in the center of the site area. The largest of these was partially eroded by the river. Testing was conducted to determine if the site had been used as a village prior to the arrival of the fur traders. However, the work here has also revealed that there were two more historic-period house pits that appear to be slightly older than the previous ones investigated. The historic artifacts are more limited in number than in the three smaller houses, and include a cobalt blue faceted Russian trade bead, and two Kamloops side-notched projectile points (late pre-Contact to early historic in age).

The history that is slowly emerging from the four seasons of archaeological fieldwork at this site is that a new Native village was built at the northeast confluence of the two Thompson rivers after the trading post was constructed. Pre-Contact villages occur in the immediate vicinity of this historic village, up and down both banks of the rivers around Kamloops, but "Indian Point" probably originated as a village only after European contact. To date, no pre-European occupational evidence has been discovered at the site.

The material evidence recovered here through archaeological excavations demonstrates an overall persistence of Native culture in the early Contact period, particularly in terms of the architectural features, storage facilities, portable technology, and faunal remains. The five circular features investigated were all traditional Interior Salish–style pithouse dwellings, based on their stratigraphy and preserved wood structural remains. They were semi-subterranean and circular in shape, with interior upright log wall-shoring, wooden-post roof supports, and earth-covered roofs. The absence of wood planks indicates the structures had earthen floors. The complete absence of nails, window glass, and door hardware suggests traditional construction methods in the three smallest houses. A few nails were found in the two large houses, but no window glass or door hardware. A large subterranean storage-pit feature found between two of the small houses is of typical Native design, being almost a meter in depth, with a circular opening, an interior bell shape, and with indications that it was birch-bark lined. In the largest house, two interior cache pits of traditional bell-shaped design were found beneath the floor of the house.

Inside the dwellings, there was an array of traditional and adopted items. Of interest is the complete lack of chipped stone or European ceramics in the three smaller houses. In the two larger houses, there were few ceramic fragments, two stone points, and negligible lithic debitage. Native North Americans frequently abandoned lithic technology during the Contact period (see Arkush, chap. 7); once metal tools and firearms were introduced, stone cutting blades and hunting tools became obsolete. Likewise, groups that maintained a traditional lifestyle of relative mobility would have avoided ceramics, which are heavy, breakable, and generally nonportable; thin metal basins would be better suited to traditional mobile lifeways. The small amounts of fire-cracked rock may suggest an abandonment of boiling stones in baskets for cooking in favor of metal cooking basins placed over direct heat. The limited use of ceramics cannot be explained by the possibility that ceramics were not brought on the HBC brigade trails, because we find ceramic fragments in the European structure that probably represents part of the trading post north of the aboriginal houses. Further work is needed to determine if ceramics were in short supply and, therefore, would have been retained by the HBC traders for their own use.

The traditional subsistence economy remained relatively unchanged, as the fauna attest, with the exception of the incorporation of horse into the diet. The faunal remains are dominated by wild species of mammal (principally deer), bird, and fish (salmon and suckers), indicating that they continued to practice a varied, general, subsistence economy involving many traditional hunting and fishing skills. Spiral fracturing of long bones reveals a continuation of the traditional practice of bone marrow extraction. The presence of the butchered remains of horse suggests that European domesticates began to supplement the traditional food base. Fort Kamloops was a major staging ground and corral for the Hudson's Bay Company's horse brigade trails, and undoubtedly lame horses provided a convenient additional foodstuff to the local economy.

The record of material culture also appears to reveal that Native peoples were not particularly active consumers of European goods (cf. Arkush, chap. 7; Kehoe, chap. 6). Admittedly, short-term occupations produce limited refuse (there is only a twenty-year site occupation at Thompson River Post), and the far-inland location of the site put it at the end of the supply route (although it was also at the "front" of the trade). Nevertheless, the paucity of European goods may suggest that Native peoples were selective in obtaining items that could be used in traditional ways. Most of the typical European trade goods described by Teit (1909) in his ethnography of the Shuswap were not encountered in these three houses. In a similar archaeological study undertaken by Lightfoot et al. (1993) at Fort Ross, a 19th-century Russian trading post on the California coast, reference is made to the Russian manager of the post from 1830 to 1838 who was amazed at the disregard of Native Californians for European customs and goods: "Their inattention and indifference to everything goes to extremes. They look at our watches, burning-glasses, and mirrors, or listen to our music without attention and do not ask to know how and why all this is produced. Only such objects as might frighten them make some impression, but that probably more because of their timidity than thirst for knowledge" (Lightfoot et al. 1993:172).

In general, the Thompson's River Post artifact assemblage excavated from Native houses will ultimately be useful in defining discrete Native "ethnic consumption patterns" for material-culture assemblages from sites where comparable architectural features do not exist. Interestingly, no substantial differences in the amounts of material culture between the five houses are evident; this may suggest the maintenance of egalitarian social relations, despite the presence of European systems of social stratification at the trading post.

In summary, while the archaeological sample is small, it illustrates that the material remains are distinctly Native ones, colored by images of the preservation of their culture and the creative reworking of European technologies into Native practices. The archaeology in no way suggests the emergence of European social and cultural dominance at this time, but indicates instead an incorporation of European trinkets within a fundamentally independent Native social structure.

Conclusions

The research described in this paper concerns the beginnings of social and commercial interactions between aboriginal and nonaboriginal peoples in western Canada in the mid-19th century. The material record of the Native peoples associated with an early fur-trade post in Kamloops in the years 1821–42 indicates the persistence of traditional aboriginal households and villages, economic and trading practices, and natural resource utilization, while European technological items are incorporated where appropriate. Traditionally fluid village settlement patterns, flexible and opportunistic trading relations, and an egalitarian social organization enabled the Shuswap to accommodate the new fur traders into their economy and lives.

The archaeological site (EeRc 22) studied represents the only undisturbed fur-trade post on the Thompson River; three other trading-post sites in the modern Kamloops city limits have been destroyed by recent development. Further excavation and analysis of visible surface features of the EeRc 22 site will enable a fuller reconstruction of the spatial organization of the community in relation to the European-style buildings, clarify the nature of intercultural material transactions, and permit an evaluation of the subsistence economy and trade during this period.

Until the history of Native cultural autonomy is addressed more fully, we will continue to ignore aspects of the past that concern contemporary First Nation peoples in Canada. Ethnohistorical scholarship on the Canadian fur trade has largely treated "the Natives only as customers . . . never as active agents in their own right" (Cox 1993:87). Archaeology can play a role in more broadly illuminating the history of social control during the process of colonization that is directly relevant to the political processes attending modern aboriginal affairs in Canada. Greater comprehension of the ways in which aboriginal peoples both accommodated and resisted the intrusive European culture (see Nassaney 1989), through adaptation and persistence in their traditional lifeways, will promote intercultural understanding of political and social processes that continue today. Brenner (1980:137) has argued that, "As long as native strategies for survival and adjustment in colonial situations are ignored or misunderstood, colonial policy will continue to be characterized by the use of force, militaristic control, paternalism and neglect resulting in the devastation of Native groups."

Negative images of dependency and disintegration of Native society, beginning in the fur trade, are no longer acceptable. Archaeological studies can play an important role in demonstrating that Native peoples have a strong continuity with their past by showing that they have always employed strategies of autonomy and self-determination, and that this is not just a late-20th century phenomenon. This does not negate the fact that change has occurred in Native societies, but it is not the case that Native peoples had to remain the same in order to remain Native. Secwepemc political systems and leadership began to adapt early on in order to compete successfully in the changing climate of 19th-century commerce.

The excavation of this unique Contact-period site has had strong support from the Kamloops Indian Band Council, who are actively engaged in the promotion, preservation, and revitalization of their culture, land, and economic base, in addition to pursuing self-government. Interestingly, the Kamloops Band today maintains its cultural tradition of controlling commercial activities at "Cumcloops" by operating, and having sole control over the revenue of, their Mount Paul Industrial Park, where land and buildings surrounding the old fort are leased to local businesses.

Once analysis is complete, artifacts and records from this project will be housed at the Secwepemc Cultural Education Society's museum on the Kamloops Indian Reserve. The Secwepemc Museum is one of only a handful of Native-run museums in Canada, and one of the most successful and visible in the country. The project benefits greatly by working with the

Kamloops Indian Band and from their commitment to preserving Native culture and history through archaeology. As Jamie Morton (1992:15) put it, "Commemoration of native themes will only occur if it is important to the people responsible for commemoration, and native culture is most important to native people." In North American archaeology, Native culture has been most important in pre-Contact studies, but historical archaeology is increasingly contributing to an understanding of the many cultural and historical processes that are ongoing in western Canada today.

Acknowledgments

I would especially like to acknowledge the support that Chief Manny Jules and the Council of the Kamloops Indian Band have given this research over the last seven years. John Jules and Richard Jules have been particularly instrumental in facilitating this work, and I thank them for their commitment to the project. The archaeological fieldwork has been carried out under permit to the Kamloops Indian Band. I would also like to thank the administration at the University College of the Cariboo for their financial and logistical support for the archaeological field schools that enabled the excavations of the site. The field school students, too numerous to name, deserve huge applause for their unending humor, enthusiasm, and commitment, despite often grueling field conditions. My teaching assistants, Cindy Matthew, Kelly Martin, and Duncan McLaren, were essential to the success of the fieldwork; I could not have done it without them. I probably would not have completed this chapter without the encouragement, patience, and constructive criticism of Michael Nassaney and Eric Johnson. I thank Jean Hourston-Wright for the preliminary analysis of the faunal remains, and the University College of the Cariboo Scholarly Activity Committee for funding the faunal analysis. My partner in career and life, George Nicholas, as always was vital to the completion of this paper, and I thank him for his assistance with the fieldwork logistics, his sharing of field-school teaching ideas, and his substantial editorial improvements. Any errors in fact or interpretation are my own.

References Cited

Balf, Mary. 1969. *Kamloops: A History of the District up to 1914.* Kamloops Museum, Kamloops, B.C.

Beaudry, Mary C., Lauren J. Cook, and Stephen A. Mrozowski. 1991. Artifacts and Active Voices: Material Culture as Social Discourse. In *The Archaeology of*

Inequality, ed. Randall H. McGuire and Robert Paynter, 150–91. Basil Blackwell, Oxford.

Bedard, Elizabeth L. 1990. The Historic and Ethnographic Background of Fort d'Epinette (HaRc 27): Considerations for the Archaeological Determination of Ethnicity. M.A. thesis, Simon Fraser University, Burnaby, B.C.

Belyea, Barbara, ed. 1994. *Columbia Journals, David Thompson 1770–1857.* McGill-Queen's University Press, Montreal.

Boas, Franz. 1891. The Shuswap: Second General Report on the Indians of British Columbia. *Report of the Sixth Meeting of the British Association for the Advancement of Science, 1890,* pt. 4, 632–47. Newcastle-upon-Tyne.

Bragdon, Kathleen J. 1988. The Material Culture of the Christian Indians of New England, 1650–1775. In *Documentary Archaeology in the New World,* ed. M. C. Beaudry, pp. 126–31. Cambridge University Press, Cambridge.

Brenner, Elise M. 1980. To Pray or to Be Prey: That Is the Question: Strategies for Cultural Autonomy of Massachusetts Praying Town Indians. *Ethnohistory* 27(2):135–52.

Burley, David V., J. Scott Hamilton, and Knut R. Fladmark. 1996. *Prophecy of the Swan: The Upper Peace River Fur Trade of 1794–1823.* University of British Columbia Press, Vancouver.

Carlson, Catherine C. 2000. The Archaeology of Seventeenth and Eighteenth Century Praying Indians in Massachusetts. In *The Archaeology of Contact: Processes and Consequences.* Proceedings of the 25th Annual 1992 Chacmool Conference, 1992, ed. B. Kulle, K. Lesick, and A. Sponholdz. University of Calgary Press, Calgary, Alberta (in press).

Caywood, Louis R. 1948. The Archaeological Excavation at Fort Vancouver. *Oregon Historical Society* 49:99–116.

Combes, John D. 1964. Excavations at Spokane House–Fort Spokane Historic Site, 1962–63. *Reports of Investigations* 29, Laboratory of Anthropology and History, Washington State University, Pullman.

Cox, Bruce Alden. 1993. Natives and the Development of Mercantile Capitalism. In *The Political Economy of North American Indians,* ed. John H. Moore, 87–93. University of Oklahoma Press, Norman.

Dawson, George. 1892. Notes on the Shuswap People of British Columbia. *Proceedings and Transactions of the Royal Society of Canada for the Year 1891,* vol. 9, section 2:3–44. Dawson Brothers Publishers, Montreal.

Deetz, James F. 1977. Historical Archaeology as the Science of Material Culture. In *Historical Archaeology and the Importance of Material Things,* ed. Leland Ferguson, 9–12. Special Publication 2, Society for Historical Archaeology, Tucson, Ariz.

Favrholdt, Ken. 1987. "Cumcloups" and the River of Time. *The Beaver,* August–September, 19–22.

Ferguson, Leland. 1992. *Uncommon Ground: Archaeology and Early African America, 1650–1800.* Smithsonian Institution Press, Washington, D.C.

Fisher, Robin. 1977. *Contact and Conflict: Indian-European Relations in British Columbia, 1774–1890*. University of British Columbia Press, Vancouver.

———. 1996. Contact and Trade, 1774–1849. In *Pacific Province: History of British Columbia*, ed. Hugh J. M. Johnston, 48–67. Douglas and McIntyre Publishers, Vancouver, B.C.

Fraser, Simon. 1960. *Letters and Journals, 1806–1808*. Ed. W. K. Lamb. Macmillan Publishers, Toronto.

Garth, Thomas. 1952. Archaeological Excavations at Fort Walla Walla. *Northwest Quarterly* 43(1):27–50.

Gibson, James A. 1973. Shuswap Grammatical Structure. Ph.D. diss., University of Hawaii, Honolulu.

Glover, Richard, ed. 1962. *David Thompson's Narrative, 1784–1812*. Publications of the Champlain Society 40, Toronto.

Grabert, Gar F. 1973. Early Fort Okanagan Euro-American Impact on the Historic Okanagan Indians. In *Historical Archaeology in Northwestern North America*, ed. R. M. Getty and K. R. Fladmark, 109–25. Archaeological Association, University of Calgary, Alberta.

Hamilton, J. Scott, David V. Burke, and Heather Moon. 1988. Rocky Mountain Fort and the Land Based Fur Trade Research Project: The 1987 End of Season Report. Report to the British Columbia Heritage Trust, Vancouver.

Hayden, Brian, ed. 1992. *A Complex Culture of the British Columbia Plateau: Traditional Stl'atl'imx Resource Use*. University of British Columbia Press, Vancouver.

Hill-Tout, Charles. [1900] 1978. Notes on the N'tlaka'pamuQ of British Columbia, a Branch of the Great Salish Stock of North America. In *The Salish People*, vol. 1, *The Thompson and the Okanagan*, ed. Ralph Maud, 41–129. Talonbooks, Vancouver, B.C.

Hudson's Bay Company. 1822–1823a. Fort Kamloops Journal, August 1822–March 1823. Hudson's Bay Company Archives B.97/a/1, Winnipeg.

———. 1822–1823b. Spokan House Report, 1822–1823, and Columbia Report, 1823. Hudson's Bay Company Archives B.208/e/1, Winnipeg.

Kroeber, Alfred L. 1917. *The Tribes of the Pacific Coast of North America*. Proceedings of the 19th International Congress of Americanists, 385–410. Washington, D.C.

Kuipers, Aert. 1974. *The Shuswap Language: Grammar, Texts, Dictionary*. Mouton, The Hague.

Lamb, W. Kaye, ed. 1970. *The Journals and Letters of Sir Alexander Mackenzie*. Macmillan, Toronto.

Lightfoot, Kent G. 1995. Culture Contact Studies: Redefining the Relationship between Prehistoric and Historical Archaeology. *American Antiquity* 60(2):199–217.

Lightfoot, Kent G., Antoinette Martinez, and Ann M. Schiff. 1998. Daily Practice and Material Culture in Pluralistic Social Settings: An Archaeological Study of

Culture Change and Persistence from Fort Ross, California. *American Antiquity* 63(2):199–222.

Lightfoot, Kent G., Thomas A. Wake, and Ann M. Schiff. 1993. Native Responses to the Russian Mercantile Colony of Fort Ross, Northern California. *Journal of Field Archaeology* 20:159–75.

Morton, Jamie. 1992. "Worthy of Commemoration in the Usual Form": Native Culture in the Interpretation of Fort Langley National Historic Sites since 1924. Paper presented at the Chacmool Conference, University of Calgary.

Nassaney, Michael S. 1989. An Epistemological Inquiry into Some Archaeological and Historical Interpretations of 17th Century Native American–European Relations. In *Archaeological Approaches to Cultural Identity*, ed. Stephen J. Shennan, 76–93. Unwin Hyman, London.

Pfeiffer, M. A. 1981. Clay Tobaccco Pipes from Spokane House and Fort Colville. *Northwest Anthropological Research Notes* 15(2):221–35.

Porter, John. 1997. Fort Langley National Historic Site: A Review of Archaeological Investigations. *The Midden* 29(1):6–9.

Porter, John, and Don Steer. 1987. Archaeological Investigations at Fort Langley National Historic Park. *The Midden* 19(2):3–4.

Pyszczyk, Heinz W. 1989. Consumption and Ethnicity: An Example from the Fur Trade in Western Canada. *Journal of Anthropological Archaeology* 8:213–49.

———. 1997. The Use of Fur Trade Goods by the Plains Indians, Central and Southern Alberta, Canada. *Canadian Journal of Archaeology* 21:45–84.

Quackenbush, William. 1990. Tastes of Canadians and Dogs: The History and Archaeology of McLeods Lake Post, British Columbia. M.A. thesis, Simon Fraser University, Burnaby, B.C.

Ray, Vern F. 1939. *Cultural Relations in the Plateau of Northwestern America.* The Southwest Museum, Los Angeles.

Richards, Thomas, and Michael Rousseau. 1987. *Late Prehistoric Cultural Horizons on the Canadian Plateau.* Archaeology Press no. 16. Simon Fraser University, Burnaby, B.C.

Ross, Alexander. [1849] 1969. *Adventures of the First Settlers on the Oregon or Columbia River.* Edited by Milo Milton Quaife. The Citadel Press, New York.

Ross, Lester A. 1977. Transfer Printed Spodeware Imported by the Hudson's Bay Company: Temporal Markers for the Northwestern United States, ca. 1836–1853. *Northwest Anthropological Research Notes* 11(2):192–217.

Rubertone, Patricia E. 1989. Archaeology, Colonialism and 17th-century Native America: Towards an Alternative Interpretation. In *Conflict in the Archaeology of Living Traditions,* ed. Robert Layton, 32–45. Unwin Hyman, London.

Schlesser, Norman D. 1975. Hudson's Bay Company Fort Umpqua, 1836–1852. *Northwest Anthropological Research Notes* 9(1):70–86.

Shuswap Nation Tribal Council. 1989. *The Shuswap: "One People with One Mind, One Heart and One Spirit."* Shuswap Nation Tribal Council, Kamloops, B.C.

Smandych, Russell, and Gloria Lee. 1995. Women, Colonization and Resistance: Elements of an Amerindian Autohistorical Approach to the Study of Law and Colonialism. *Native Studies Review* 10(1):21–45.

Smith, Harlan I. 1900. The Archaeology of the Thompson River Region, British Columbia. *American Museum of Natural History Memoirs* 2(6):401–42.

Swanson, Earl H., Jr. 1962. Historic Archaeology at Fort Okanagan, Washington, 1957. *Tebiwa* 5(1):1–10.

Teit, James A. [1909] 1975. *The Shuswap.* AMS Press, New York.

Van Kirk, Sylvia. 1980. *Many Tender Ties: Women in Fur-Trade Society in Western Canada, 1670–1870.* Watson and Dwyer, Winnipeg.

Williams, Jean H. 1978. Fort D'Epinette: A Description of Faunal Remains from an Early Fur Trade Site in Northern British Columbia. M.A. thesis, Simon Fraser University, Burnaby, B.C.

Wilson, Robert, and Catherine Carlson. 1980. *The Archaeology of Kamloops.* Archaeology Press, Simon Fraser University, Burnaby, B.C.

Wilson, Samuel M., and J. Daniel Rogers. 1993. Historical Dynamics in the Contact Era. In *Ethnohistory and Archaeology: Approaches to Postcontact Change in the Americas,* ed. J. D. Rogers and S. M. Wilson, 3–15. Plenum Press, New York.

Wood, W. Raymond. 1993. Integrating Ethnohistory and Archaeology at Fort Clark State Historic Site, North Dakota. *American Antiquity* 58(3):544–59.

Yerbury, J. Colin. 1986. *The Subarctic Indians and the Fur Trade, 1680–1860.* University of British Columbia Press, Vancouver.

11

Obtaining Information via Defective Documents

A Search for the Mandan in George Catlin's Paintings

Mark S. Parker Miller

As a result of his 1832 visit to the Upper Missouri, American artist George Catlin produced over thirty paintings with Mandan subjects. Catlin stated that he created these works and other paintings of Native Americans "for the use and instruction of future ages" (Catlin 1841, 1:3). As documents, however, Catlin's images offer a manipulated reality. If we acknowledge this fact, then to what extent can we use these paintings as evidence for understanding the historical Mandan? This question is the focus of this study.

The Mandan

The Mandan had settled in the region long before Catlin's time. Their ancestors probably moved into the area of the upper Missouri River as early as the 13th century (Bruner 1961:192–93; Meyer 1977:5–6; Peters 1995:19; Wood 1995). (They were not the first people in the region, of course. Other populations lived there by the late Pleistocene, some 11,000 years earlier [Fagan 1995; Wood 1995].) On the high banks of the main river and its tributaries, the Mandan established towns where they resided in earth-covered log dwellings. In addition to hunting bison and other animals, fishing, and harvesting native plants for food, they cultivated corn, beans, squash, sunflowers, and tobacco in the fertile alluvial soil of the lowlands immediately adjacent to the river. Beginning long before their contact with Euro-Americans, the Mandan participated with other Native Americans in a trading network that reached both coasts of the continent, exchanging surplus produce and locally quarried flint for bison meat, hides, and a variety of other goods (see Metcalf 1992:6). By the early 18th century, the Mandan (and their neighbors, the Hidatsa) had secured a central position in the exchange system between Euro- and Native Americans, serving as intermediaries in the transfer of furs, horses, guns, and various objects made of metal. By the early 19th century, clashes with the Sioux and other nomadic neighbors of the Mandan—peoples displaced from areas to the east (see Nassaney and Johnson, Introduction)—had increased in frequency and intensity. These encounters hampered Mandan movement beyond their villages and made it difficult for them to obtain bison by hunting. In addition, the establishment of such permanent Euro-American trading posts as Fort Clark (ca. 1829) close to the Mandan towns significantly reduced trade between the Mandan and other Native American groups by enabling the latter to deal directly with agents at the posts. This combination of factors made it less and less feasible for the Mandan to live as they had in the past (Bowers 1950; Bruner 1961; Cash and Wolff 1974; Ewers 1967; Jennings 1993; Metcalf 1992; Meyer 1977; Peters 1995; Will and Spinden 1906; Wood and Thiessen 1985).

George Catlin

George Catlin arrived in the region in 1832. He was a thirty-five-year-old artist, a native of Wilkes-Barre, Pennsylvania. In the early years of his career, Catlin had worked in Philadelphia, New York, and Washington, D.C., executing miniatures and portraits in oils. His election to the Pennsylvania Academy of Fine Arts in 1824 and to the National Academy of Design in 1826 provides some indication of his success as a painter and of his ties to the contemporary fine-art establishment. In 1830 Catlin began traveling around the western territories of the United States to paint images of Native Americans. In 1832 he went from St. Louis up the Missouri River on the first steamboat to travel all the way to Fort Union, a trading post at the mouth of the Yellowstone River. In late July, on his trip back down the river, Catlin stopped to visit the Mandan (Dippie 1990; Ewers 1967; McCracken 1959; Truettner 1979).

Catlin spent about three weeks in the vicinity of the Mandan villages. During most of his stay he lodged at Fort Clark, a trading post of the American Fur Company (the same firm that operated Fort Union and the steamboat that had carried him upstream). Located within sight of one Mandan town and named after one-half of the Lewis and Clark duo (who had stayed with the Mandan during the winter of 1804–5), the "fort" was a one-story, log structure measuring 44 by 49 paces. James Kipp, the trader in charge of the post and the spouse of a Mandan woman, served as Catlin's translator during the visit (see Kehoe, chap. 6, on traders and "country wives"). While among the Mandan that summer (or later, in some cases, working from sketches), Catlin produced at least thirty oil paintings with Mandan subjects, including ten individual portraits and about twenty works depicting various aspects of Mandan life (Ewers 1967; McCracken 1959; Truettner 1979).

Catlin continued to travel and paint pictures of Native Americans through 1836. He also wrote about his experiences in letters that were published from 1832 to 1837 in the *New York Commercial Advertiser.* As early as 1833, Catlin exhibited his works, the Mandan canvases among them, at venues west of the Alleghenies. In the latter years of the decade, he presented his "Indian Gallery," consisting of hundreds of paintings and several tons of Native American artifacts, in a number of cities in the eastern United States. Catlin then toured Europe with the show, beginning in 1840 and continuing through much of the next decade. Nine years after his sojourn with the Mandan, while in London, he published a two-volume book, *Letters and Notes on the Manners, Customs, and Conditions of the North American Indians* (1841). This book revealed how strongly the Mandan had impressed him and how important they still were to his thinking; the portions of the publication that discuss the Mandan occupy about 200 pages, almost one-quarter of the total work. Catlin remained in Europe for many years. Despite public enthusiasm for his project, however, he failed to make a profit from the book or the exhibitions and by 1852 was deeply in debt. Joseph Harrison, an American locomotive manufacturer, aided him with a sizable loan and took Catlin's Indian Gallery (which by this time included over 550 paintings) as collateral, shipping it to Philadelphia, where he stored it at his boiler factories. Catlin had long hoped that the U.S. Congress would buy his Gallery, but it never did, and he never recovered the collection from Harrison. In 1878, however, Harrison's heirs donated it to the Smithsonian Institution, where the Catlin paintings are now administered by the National Museum of American Art. Catlin, following the crisis of 1852, traveled in South America and around the west coast of North America, producing paintings of Natives. In the 1860s he created (or re-created) works related to his experiences of thirty years earlier. He referred to this second series (at least as large in number as the original group, but these executed on paperboard) as the "Indian Cartoons."[1] In the early 1870s, Catlin exhibited the new collection briefly in Europe and in the United States, before he died in December of 1872 (Dippie 1990; Ewers 1967; McCracken 1959; Truettner 1979; Will and Spinden 1906).

Later Mandan History

In the upper Missouri River valley, the decades following Catlin's visit were difficult ones for the Mandan (as well as for other Native Americans). In 1837 an outbreak of smallpox devastated their communities. Individual epidemics in the 18th century had reduced the Mandan population by as much as 68 percent in one year, but this time there were only about 130 survivors out of a pre-epidemic population of approximately 1,700. Numerous attacks by the Sioux, occurring throughout the 19th century, also took a heavy toll on the village dwellers of the Upper Plains. By 1845 most of the remaining Mandan were living with the surviving Hidatsa in a single settlement. The Arikara joined them there in 1862, forming what eventually became known as the Three Affiliated Tribes. By the end of the 19th century, the United States government had designated an encompassing parcel of land as a reservation for them and had convinced the residents to abandon their town and live on individual farms. In the early 1950s, the construction of Garrison Dam again uprooted the Mandan and their neighbors. The project created a huge lake that filled the river valleys, submerging the best farmland and forcing most of the population to relocate. Nevertheless, in spite of the odds, descendants of the Mandan still live along the Missouri River, on Fort Berthold Reservation in North Dakota, and elsewhere in the United States (Bruner 1961; Cash and Wolff 1974; Meyer 1977; Will and Spinden 1906; Wood and Thiessen 1985).

Catlin's Goals

In his 1841 book, Catlin (1841, 1:3) identified some key objectives of his travels among Native Americans—including his 1832 visit with the Mandan—and of the paintings he produced:

> the history and customs of such a people, preserved by pictorial illustrations, are themes worthy the life-time of one man, and nothing short of the loss of my life shall prevent me from visiting their country, and becoming their historian. . . . I set out . . . with the determination of reaching, ultimately, every tribe of Indians on the Continent of North America, and of bringing home faithful portraits of their principal personages, both men and women . . . views of their

villages, games &c. and full notes on their character and history. I designed, also, to procure their costumes, and a complete collection of their manufactures and weapons, and to perpetuate them in a <u>Gallery unique</u>, for the use and instruction of future ages.

In other words, Catlin intended the paintings to have a documentary function, as components of a comprehensive, historical record that he desired to assemble. He hoped that people in "future ages," including our own, would be able to learn about the historical Mandan and other Native Americans through his images.

Criticism of Catlin's Work

Even in Catlin's own lifetime, however, some people questioned the value of his paintings as historical documents. For example, David D. Mitchell, superintendent of Indian affairs in St. Louis, writing for the extensive, federally sponsored compilation *Historical and Statistical Information Respecting the History, Condition and Prospects of the Indian Tribes of the United States* (1853), was particularly critical. In regard to Catlin's representations of the Mandan, he concluded, "The scenes described by Catlin, existed almost entirely in the fertile imagination of that gentleman" (Mitchell 1853:254). Mitchell apparently dismissed Catlin's work because he did not believe the artist's ostensibly eyewitness descriptions (verbal and pictorial) of the Mandan Okipa ceremony, a four-day religious observance that included ritual torture of some of the participants. Perhaps he could not accept Catlin's story because too few Euro-Americans had reported such an event. Since the 1850s, however, enough evidence has come to light confirming Catlin's account that this objection no longer has merit (Ewers 1967:25–33). On the other hand, with respect to two other stories disseminated by Catlin that attracted criticism from his contemporaries, it has become obvious that Catlin was mistaken. First, he erroneously reported that the Mandan became extinct following the smallpox epidemic of 1837. Second, he engaged in extraordinary efforts, particularly in his writings, to prove that the Mandan were descended from a Welsh prince named Madoc and his crew who, according to legend, sailed across the Atlantic in A.D. 1170. For most historians this notion is simply nonsense (Dippie 1990; Ewers 1967; Meyer 1977; Will and Spinden 1906). What effect, if any, this latter belief had on Catlin's paintings remains unclear.

By the third quarter of the 20th century, scholars were ready to salvage Catlin's reputation. Long-time Smithsonian anthropologist John Ewers

Fig. 11.1. George Catlin, *Bird's-eye view of the Mandan village, 1800 miles above St. Louis*, 1837–39. Oil on canvas, 24⅛ × 29". National Museum of American Art, Smithsonian Institution, Washington, D.C.; gift of Mrs. Joseph Harrison, Jr.

(1956), for example, carefully distinguished the artist's successes from his failures and, based on this analysis, celebrated Catlin's works as uniquely valuable records of life on the Great Plains in the early 19th century.

More recently, Catlin's work has drawn criticism from scholars focusing on other issues. Julie Schimmel, for example, writing for the catalog of the 1991 Smithsonian Institution exhibition "The West as America," called attention to ways that 19th-century Euro-American preconceptions about Native Americans might have determined the images Catlin produced as well as the audience's perceptions of them. Regarding Catlin's *Bird's-eye view of the Mandan village* (fig. 11.1), Schimmel (1991:157) observed:

> Indians at leisure . . . might . . . be scorned by a culture that valued industriousness. The "Bible-toting mountain man" Jedediah Smith, encountering a Sioux camp that must have appeared as inviting as

Catlin had found the Mandan village, commented in his journal that the scene would "almost persuade a man to renounce the world, take the lodge and live the careless, Lazy life of an indian." It is well to remember that . . . white audiences probably viewed paintings such as *Mandan Village* with mixed reactions. Indians might not suffer from the ills of progress and civilization, but neither did they exhibit the virtues admired by white society.

On a similar note, Kathryn S. Hight, in a 1990 *Art Journal* article, examined Catlin's belief in the concept of Indians as a vanishing race, doomed to perish as they came in contact with "civilization." According to Catlin, only in his art would they live on. Hight also investigated how Catlin manipulated the Mandan material in particular to express these attitudes while he toured with the Indian Gallery. According to her analysis, "some of his paintings and the way in which he used them . . . can be seen today as presenting the public not so much an ethnological report as a validation of the . . . theory behind the national Indian policy" (Hight 1990:119). Specifically, Catlin consistently presented Native Americans who lived beyond the frontier more favorably than he did those who lived farther east. Thus, his work served to reinforce the policy, adopted by Congress in 1830, of removing Native Americans to west of the Mississippi, away from "civilization," in order to postpone their inevitable demise.

As should be clear by now, Native Americans have not vanished, and extinction was never inevitable. This was only a myth among Euro-Americans, invoked to deny the element of choice in their own actions. Another myth to which Catlin subscribed, and that influenced his work, is a variation of primitivism; he viewed Native Americans, especially those beyond the "frontier," as existing in an "original state." On one hand, he represented them as living in a timeless world—one lacking change, rupture, history. On the other, he described them as peoples of the European past—ancient Romans or Britons, Europeans in their younger days, when life was simpler and they were more naive (Truettner 1979; see also Antliff and Leighten 1996). In fact, these Native Americans were, like Catlin, sophisticated participants in the complex American present.

Defining the Problem and Methodology

In light of these considerations, there is little doubt that the "documents" that Catlin produced representing the Mandan are fundamentally flawed. However, as historians have become increasingly aware, all documents are defective. They are not disinterested, objective conveyers of pure truth. Rather, documents are artifacts, fashioned and used by human agents for various purposes, and those purposes affect their content (see also Nassaney and Johnson, Introduction). Art historians, including myself, have become fairly comfortable with treating the content of paintings as fiction. A standard article of faith among us is that a work of art can provide much information about the artist and the artist's culture. A trickier task, after acknowledging that our documents are defective, that they are works of fiction, is to obtain information about the subject (of a portrait or village scene, for example) and the subject's culture (especially when it differs from that of the artist). The question is to what extent can we rely on the content of a painting as evidence in this task?

In the remainder of this chapter, I will examine a few of Catlin's Mandan paintings in relation to archaeological information, scenes by other artists, and surviving artifacts in order to evaluate to what degree certain details of Catlin's paintings are reliable. The recent criticism of Catlin has not necessarily called into question the accuracy of specific details, but it has called into question the value of his images overall as sources of information about Native Americans. I find that it is precisely in certain details where the value of Catlin's work may lie, because they assist us in reconstructing the material culture of the 1830s Mandan. The objects that the Mandan made and used are historical records of their culture. These artifacts are the documents that most directly provide information about the Mandan (see Glassie 1988). As I continue, I will show how details in Catlin's paintings can help us to identify these Mandan-created documents.

The method I am using (namely, comparing Catlin's images with independent sources for corroboration) is a form of "triangulation"—that is, the determination of one point by establishing its distance from two other points. This is a technique that I know best from another context, the creation of site plans for historic farmsteads, and it is one that is familiar to surveyors and archaeologists. In order to plot one point—for example, the corner of a building in relation to another building—it is necessary to measure its distance from at least two other points; one measurement by itself does not provide enough information. Only by using the two measurements as two sides of a triangle is it possible to determine the location of the third point. Of course, the analogy is not perfect; in this study the subjects are not rigidly fixed points. However, from my experiences with triangulation, the comparison is appropriate. Although the technique promises precision in the two-dimensional planes of trigonometric abstraction, when one translates from the actual measurements taken in the field to the scale drawing on the drafting table, the lines do not always converge. In real-world practice, triangulation is approximate, not exact. In this study Catlin's painting is the first measurement, so to speak, and the evidence juxtaposed for comparison—archaeological information, a painting by another artist, or an artifact—constitutes the second measurement. I am crosschecking multiple lines of evidence with one another in order to see where they concur. In doing this, I do not view any one line of evidence as more reliable or definitive on its own; rather it is the convergence of two or more that increases the significance of each. Finally, agreement of multiple sources does not provide an absolute proof. Instead, the conclusions reached by this method remain relative and contingent.

Analysis of Catlin's Paintings

In *Bird's-eye view of the Mandan village* (fig. 11.1), Catlin displays an abundance of detail for the viewer's consideration. A 1986 archaeological survey of the Fort Clark historic site (fig. 11.2) reveals the town that the Mandan had occupied from about 1822 to 1837. The survey discovered archaeological remains of about sixty-five Mandan earth-covered dwellings, arranged around an open area (i.e., a plaza). (The dwelling in the middle of the plaza was built after the Mandan period of occupation.) There was also evidence of a wooden fence (or palisade) enclosing the twelve-acre site (Wood 1993). All of these elements also appear in Catlin's painting. The work of Swiss artist Karl Bodmer, who visited the Mandan during the winter of 1833–34, provides a number of useful comparisons for Catlin's Mandan scenes (see Hunt and Gallagher 1984). His drawing of the Mandan village (fig. 11.3) likewise shows the dwellings and the plaza, the barrel-like shrine in the center, and a pole wrapped with fur and feathers and topped with a wooden head (representing a sacred figure). Bodmer, however, draws something not in Catlin's depiction—the frames used for drying meat. Perhaps Catlin omitted them for the sake of clarity. He obviously was attempting to pack as much into this image as possible, while at the same time trying to keep it legible. This would also account for Catlin's elevated vantage point in contrast to Bodmer's eye-level view. On the rooftop in the foreground (and in some other locations), Catlin displays a bullboat, consisting of bison hide stretched over a wooden frame. A similar example of a Mandan bullboat occurs in a watercolor study by Bodmer (see Hunt and Gallagher 1984:289, fig. 297). Beyond the wooden fence, in the background, Catlin represents above-ground burial plat-

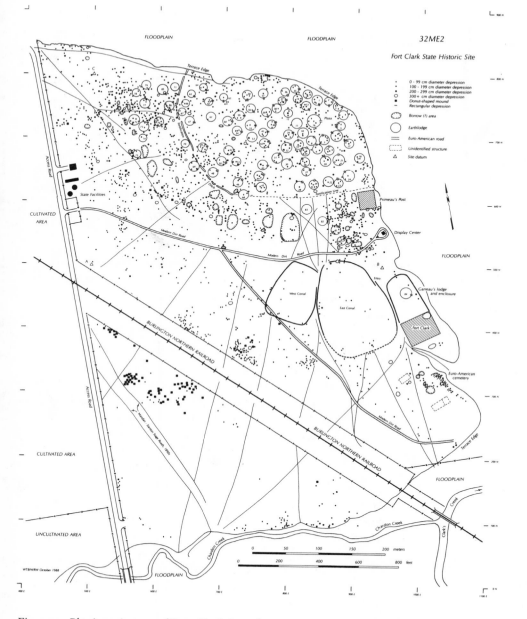

Fig. 11.2. Planimetric map of Fort Clark State historic site, 1986. From W. Raymond Wood, "Integrating Ethnohistory and Archaeology at Fort Clark State Historic Site, North Dakota," *American Antiquity* 58(3) (1993):549. Reproduced by permission of the Society for American Archaeology and the author.

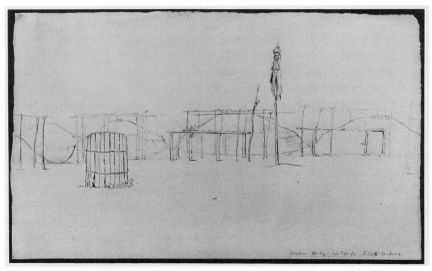

Fig. 11.3. Karl Bodmer, *Mih-Tutta-Hang-Kusch, Mandan Village,* ca. 1833. Ink and pencil on paper, 10¾ × 17″. Joslyn Art Museum, Omaha, Nebraska; gift of the Enron Art Foundation.

forms that are also visible in the background of a watercolor by Bodmer (see Hunt and Gallagher 1984:293, fig. 302).

In contrast to his treatment of artifacts and structural elements, Catlin's portrayal of the inhabitants of the community—in anecdotal vignettes—seems firmly rooted in the Euro-American tradition of scenes of everyday life. This artistic tradition is represented, for example, in the work of John Lewis Krimmel (e.g., *Fourth of July in Center Square, Philadelphia,* ca. 1810; see Craven 1994:157, fig. 11.6) and Francis Guy (e.g., *Winter Scene in Brooklyn,* ca. 1817; see fig. 11.4). In particular, note Catlin's presentation of small groupings of people (and sometimes animals) engaged in ordinary activities—children running on the rooftop (comparable to Krimmel's children playing around the fountain) or various figures engaged in conversation (as present in Guy's painting), and so on. It is no surprise that Catlin would base his composition on earlier models. He learned to paint in an era when art instructors and guidebooks advised artists to learn their craft by studying the successes of previous masters, to make drawings from casts of ancient sculptures, and to copy the works of recognized artists. This practice is also evident in a series of drawings (see Truettner 1979:84, figs. 72–75)—representing the expressions of a smile, sadness, wonder, and anger—that Catlin made based on examples in a book by the 17th-century French artist Charles LeBrun. Similar expressions appear on the faces in Catlin's painting. Clearly, the fact that Catlin was a Euro-American artist determined what he chose to depict and how he represented his Native American subjects. Considering Catlin's reliance on Euro-American traditions of representation, it is unclear what if anything we can learn about the historical Mandan from the activities or expressions of the figures in the composition. Aside from this, however, the details of the painting seem plausible. Catlin has manipulated the arrangement in order to present legibly as many elements as possible, but otherwise he has faithfully described the material culture.

With *Interior of a Mandan lodge* (fig. 11.5), Catlin provided the interior counterpart of his village genre scene.[2] Once again Bodmer created a comparable work, *Interior of a Mandan Earth Lodge* (fig. 11.6). There are differences between the two, but also some significant similarities. First, both show a similar arrangement of posts and beams supporting the roof and a fire pit below the smoke hole in the center of the ceiling. This location for the fire pit was also confirmed by the 1986 archaeological inves-

Fig. 11.4. Francis Guy, *Winter Scene in Brooklyn,* ca. 1817–20. Oil on canvas, 58¾ × 75" (acc. no. 97.13). The Brooklyn Museum, Brooklyn, New York; gift of the Brooklyn Institute of Arts and Sciences.

Fig. 11.5. George Catlin, *Interior of a Mandan lodge*, 1832–33. Oil on canvas, 23¼ × 28" (neg. no. A93867). © The Field Museum, Chicago.

Fig. 11.6. Karl Bodmer, *Interior of a Mandan Earth Lodge*, 1833–34. Watercolor and ink on paper, 11¼ × 16⅞". Joslyn Art Museum, Omaha, Nebraska; gift of the Enron Art Foundation.

Fig. 11.7. Mandan pot, 18th century. Earthenware, 5½ × 5½ ". Logan Museum of Anthropology, Beloit College, Beloit, Wisconsin.

tigations. Wood (1993:550) reported that "depressions in the house center invariably produced burned earth and ash when they were cored with a soil probe, and clearly are central hearths." Second, the two paintings depict similar pottery vessels (to the right in Catlin's interior and near the fire pit in Bodmer's). The general profile of the pottery as represented by the two artists corresponds with a Mandan example from the 18th century in the collection of the Logan Museum of Anthropology in Beloit, Wisconsin (fig. 11.7). Third, both scenes include the storage posts for bison masks and weapons (to the rear in Catlin's work and in the right foreground in Bodmer's). Fourth, the two works show the enclosed beds (along the rear wall in Catlin's and barely visible in the right background in Bodmer's). The interior, therefore, like the exterior, provides apparently reliable renderings of some common elements of 1830s Mandan material culture.

Catlin's portrait of Mahtotohpa, or *Four Bears, second chief, in full dress* (fig. 11.8), contains some of the most significant information for this study. The pose of the figure relates to standard Euro-American portrait

Fig. 11.8. George Catlin, *Four Bears, second chief, in full dress,* 1832. Oil on canvas, 29 × 24". National Museum of American Art, Smithsonian Institution, Washington, D.C.; gift of Mrs. Joseph Harrison, Jr.

styles—for example, Catlin's portrait of *William Clark* (fig. 11.9). Both are full-length views with the figure facing to the viewer's right, each is accompanied by artifacts attesting to his status and achievements, and each stands with his weight shifted slightly to one foot in a *contrapposto* stance common among classical sculptures.[3] In addition, Mahtotohpa, like the statue of Apollo Belvedere (see Janson 1991:195, fig. 222), also stands with his left arm outstretched, holding a weapon, and his right arm down at his side. Even the fringe of Mahtotohpa's left sleeve echoes the sculpture's draped robe. That Catlin's portrait of Mahtotohpa resembles both a revered example of European sculpture and Catlin's painting of a

Fig. 11.9. George Catlin, *William Clark*, 1832. Oil on canvas, 28½ × 23½". National Portrait Gallery, Smithsonian Institution, Washington, D.C.

respected American explorer might suggest how highly Catlin thought of Mahtotohpa or, at least, how he wanted viewers of the image to perceive the chief. Because the pose so thoroughly reflects artistic convention, however, this aspect of the portrait does not necessarily tell us anything about the actual person. Bodmer also did a portrait of the chief (see Hunt and Gallagher 1984:308, fig. 317) entitled *Mató-Tópe* (a German rendering of his name, with the same pronunciation), in which he wears similar clothing. In particular, Mahtotohpa wears a horn bonnet that resembles a Mandan example with ermine tails (dating from the mid-19th century) in the collection of the Denver Art Museum (fig. 11.10). Both paintings also show him dressed in a leather shirt and leggings comparable to a Mandan

Fig. 11.10. Mandan split horn bonnet, ca. 1850s. Skin, horn, ermine, wool; 33 × 10 × 13½". Denver Art Museum, Denver, Colorado; exchange with Peabody Museum, Cambridge, Massachusetts.

outfit (ca. 1880) in the Chandler-Pohrt Collection at the Detroit Institute of Arts (figs. 11.11 and 11.12).[4] The shirt, as Catlin represents it, is red on Mahtotohpa's right side and yellow on his left side. In another portrait by Bodmer (fig. 11.13), the chief's face paint around the eyes, chin, and scalp line are likewise red on his right side and yellow on his left side. Bodmer also collected some watercolor self-portraits executed by Mahtotohpa that are useful in this analysis. In the first, Mahtotohpa represents himself in hand-to-hand combat with a Cheyenne chief (see Hunt and Gallagher 1984:358). Of particular interest to the way that Catlin portrays him is

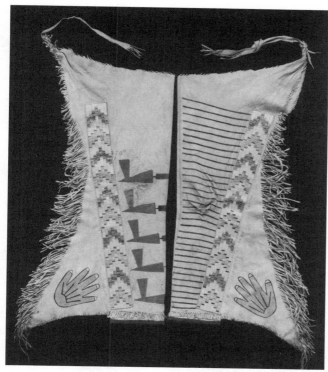

Fig. 11.11. Mandan man's leggings, ca. 1880. Buckskin, porcupine quills, pigment; 32 × 17". Collection of Richard and Marion Pohrt. Photograph © The Detroit Institute of Arts, Detroit, Michigan.

Fig. 11.12. Mandan man's shirt, ca. 1880. Buckskin, wool stroud, porcupine quills, human hair, horsehair, pigment; 42 × 26". Collection of Richard and Marion Pohrt. Photograph © The Detroit Institute of Arts, Detroit, Michigan.

Mahtotohpa's careful delineation of the streamers on the tips of the headdress feathers and on the tails attached to his heels, features that Catlin
also recorded. Catlin thereby captured some of the same elements that the
chief himself considered an important part of his image. Another self-
portrait (fig. 11.14) exhibits the same red and yellow division of the body
mentioned above. By recording such details, Catlin, even if he was not
aware of it, was communicating an evidently important part of the way

Fig. 11.13. Karl Bodmer, *Mató-Tópe, Mandan Chief*, ca. 1833. Watercolor, 13¾ ×
11¼". Joslyn Art Museum, Omaha, Nebraska; gift of the Enron Art Foundation.

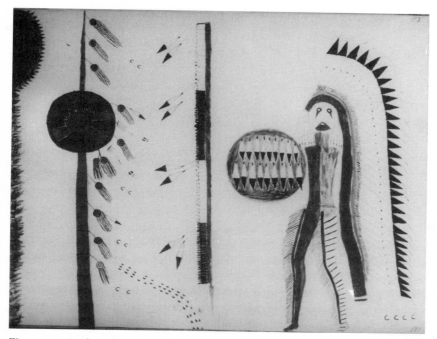

Fig. 11.14. Mahtotohpa, self-portrait, ca. 1834. Watercolor and pencil on paper, 12⅜ × 15⅝". Joslyn Art Museum, Omaha, Nebraska; gift of the Enron Art Foundation.

that Mahtotohpa thought about himself. In details such as these, we begin to get the insider's perspective of Mandan culture—the ways in which the Mandan perceived themselves.

Conclusions

In looking to George Catlin's paintings for information about Native Americans, we must be careful not to underestimate the fundamentally problematic character of this source. Failure to take seriously the Eurocentric biases identified by recent criticism is to err on the side of keeping the soiled bathwater along with the baby. Nevertheless, the three cases I have analyzed here provide some measure of the potential for using Catlin's paintings as historical evidence in spite of their flaws. They illustrate that from Catlin's paintings of the Mandan, when examined in conjunction with other sources, it is possible to learn not only about Catlin and his culture but sometimes also about the historical Mandan. Indeed, these documents can yield information unavailable from other ethnohistorical sources. Catlin's paintings are firmly rooted in Euro-American traditions of portraits and scenes of everyday life and therefore are not necessarily useful sources of information concerning behavior. The works are nevertheless important for their representation of details of Mandan material culture—that is, the Mandan-created documents through which they present their own stories. Through these elements of the paintings, we have the opportunity to learn about more than simply George Catlin's culture. From these details, at their best, we can also learn about the Mandan that Catlin visited in the 1830s.[5]

Notes

1. "Cartoon" comes from an Italian word for paperboard (or a large sheet of paper). Sometimes it refers to a full-size drawing created as a preparatory step, prior to producing a finished work, but that is not necessarily how Catlin was using it.

2. The version of *Interior of a Mandan lodge* illustrated here is probably not Catlin's original painting of the subject (see Truettner 1979:288). I have not yet been able to locate the current owner of the other painting. Instead of a doorway on the right, that painting displays a bullboat leaning against the wall.

3. Art historians often use the Italian term *contrapposto* to refer to a pose that features a weight-bearing leg opposite a non-weight-bearing leg (and sometimes also an arm that carries something opposite one that is free). This compositional strategy was developed by ancient Greek sculptors to provide their figures with a more naturalistic or lifelike appearance.

4. A shirt from the Catlin collection, now at the Smithsonian Institution (Dept. of Anthropology, Cat. No. 386505), is reportedly the one worn by Mahtotohpa in Catlin's portrait of him. Bill Holm (1992), however, provides substantial evidence that this was not Mahtotohpa's shirt and instead was likely produced by Catlin using Native American materials that he collected elsewhere.

5. Concerning the application of these findings to the rest of Catlin's work, each painting or subseries must be evaluated individually. For other analyses (each using a select group of Catlin's work), with varying conclusions, see Krebs (1990), Moss (1999), and Picha (1999).

Acknowledgments

I am grateful to the following people for their willingness to critically engage with this topic and for their timely assistance at various stages of the project: the members of Wayne Craven's fall 1993 seminar, Gabrielle Lanier, Thomas Rocek, W. Raymond Wood, Anna Andrzejewski, Beth

Parker Miller, and the editors of this book. I was able to present this work in Kalamazoo, Michigan, at the 1995 annual meeting of the American Society for Ethnohistory, thanks to travel grants from the American Society for Ethnohistory and from the University of Delaware's Department of Art History.

References Cited

Antliff, Mark, and Patricia Leighten. 1996. Primitive. In *Critical Terms for Art History*, ed. R. S. Nelson and Richard Shiff, 170–84. University of Chicago Press, Chicago.

Bowers, Alfred W. 1950. *Mandan Social and Ceremonial Organization.* University of Chicago Press, Chicago.

Bruner, Edward M. 1961. Mandan. In *Perspectives in American Indian Culture Change*, ed. E. H. Spicer, 187–277. University of Chicago Press, Chicago.

Cash, Joseph H., and Gerald W. Wolff. 1974. *The Three Affiliated Tribes (Mandan, Arikara, and Hidatsa).* Indian Tribal Series, Phoenix.

Catlin, George. 1841. *Letters and Notes on the Manners, Customs, and Conditions of the North American Indians.* 2 vols. George Catlin, London.

Craven, Wayne. 1994. *American Art: History and Culture.* Brown and Benchmark, Madison, Wis.

Dippie, Brian W. 1990. *Catlin and His Contemporaries: The Politics of Patronage.* University of Nebraska Press, Lincoln.

Ewers, John C. 1956. George Catlin, Painter of Indians and the West. In *Annual Report of the Board of Regents of the Smithsonian Institution, 1955*, 483–528. U.S. Government Printing Office, Washington, D.C.

———. [1867] 1967. Introduction: An Appreciation of George Catlin's *O-kee-pa*. In George Catlin, *O-kee-pa: A Religious Ceremony and Other Customs of the Mandans.* Reprint, Yale University Press, New Haven.

Fagan, Brian. 1995. *Ancient North America.* Thames and Hudson, New York.

Glassie, Henry. 1988. Meaningful Things and Appropriate Myths: The Artifact's Place in American Studies. In *Material Life in America, 1600–1860*, ed. R. B. St. George, 62–92. Northeastern University Press, Boston.

Hight, Kathryn S. 1990. Doomed to Perish: George Catlin's Depictions of the Mandan. *Art Journal* 49 (Summer):119–24.

Holm, Bill. 1992. Four Bears' Shirt: Some Problems with the Smithsonian Catlin Collection. In *Artifacts/Artifakes: The Proceedings of the 1984 Plains Indian Seminar*, ed. G. P. Horse Capture and S. G. Tyler, 43–59. Buffalo Bill Historical Center, Cody, Wy.

Hunt, David C., and Marsha V. Gallagher. 1984. *Karl Bodmer's America.* Joslyn Art Museum, Omaha, Neb.

Janson, H. W. 1991. *History of Art.* 4th ed. Revised and expanded by Anthony F. Janson. Harry N. Abrams, New York.

Jennings, Francis. 1993. *The Founders of America*. W. W. Norton, New York.

Krebs, Edgardo Carlos. 1990. George Catlin and South America: A Look at His "Lost" Years and His Paintings of Northeastern Argentina. *American Art Journal* 22(4):4–39.

McCracken, Harold. 1959. *George Catlin and the Old Frontier*. Dial Press, New York.

Metcalf, Fay D. 1992. *Knife River: Early Village Life on the Plains*. Teaching with Historic Places, National Trust for Historic Preservation, Washington, D.C. Reprinted in *Social Education* 56(5) (September):312 ff.

Meyer, Roy W. 1977. *The Village Indians of the Upper Missouri: The Mandans, Hidatsas, and Arikaras*. University of Nebraska Press, Lincoln.

Mitchell, David D. 1853. Letter to Henry R. Schoolcraft, January 28, 1852. In *Information Respecting the History, Condition and Prospects of the Indian Tribes of the United States*, vol. 3, comp. Henry Rowe Schoolcraft, 253–54. Lippincott, Grambo and Co., Philadelphia.

Moss, Madonna L. 1999. George Catlin among the Nayas: Understanding the Practice of Labret Wearing on the Northwest Coast. *Ethnohistory* 46(1):31–65.

Peters, Virginia Bergman. 1995. *Women of the Earth Lodges: Tribal Life on the Plains*. Archon Books, North Haven, Conn.

Picha, Paul R. 1999. George Catlin among the Mandans, 1832: Chronicles in Visual Representation and Written Text. Paper presented at the annual meeting of the American Society for Ethnohistory, Mashantucket, Conn.

Schimmel, Julie. 1991. Inventing "the Indian." In *The West as America*, ed. W. H. Truettner, 149–89. National Museum of American Art, Washington, D.C.

Truettner, William H. 1979. *The Natural Man Observed: A Study of Catlin's Indian Gallery*. Smithsonian Institution, Washington, D.C.

Will, George F., and Herbert J. Spinden. 1906. The Mandans: A Study of Their Culture, Archaeology and Language. *Papers of the Peabody Museum of American Archaeology and Ethnology* 3(4):81–219.

Wood, W. Raymond. 1993. Integrating Ethnohistory and Archaeology at Fort Clark State Historic Site, North Dakota. *American Antiquity* 58(3):544–59.

———. 1995. Personal communication to author, October 11.

Wood, W. Raymond, and Thomas D. Thiessen, eds. 1985. *Early Fur Trade on the Northern Plains: Canadian Traders Among the Mandan and Hidatsa Indians, 1738–1818*. University of Oklahoma Press, Norman.

III

Ritual, Iconography, and Ideology

12

Images of Women in Native American Iconography

Larissa A. Thomas

Iconography is an important source of insight into the roles of women in Native American societies before written documents became available with the arrival of Europeans. During the Mississippian period (ca. A.D. 900–1500), Native Americans in the southeastern United States created many objects displaying images of women. These objects hold great potential to shed light on the lives of Native southeastern women. However, with few exceptions (see C. Brown 1982; Drooker 1994; Koehler 1997; K. Smith 1991), gender has not been a central focus in studies of Mississippian iconography. This chapter presents some preliminary observations on the role and participation of women in Mississippian ritual and cosmology based on their depiction in various forms of iconography.

Human images in archaeological remains provide a unique opportunity to examine how artists in past societies chose to portray people—in mundane activities, as well as in sacred and supernatural contexts. In isolation from other sources of information, however, iconography can be difficult to interpret. Witness the drastically divergent interpretations of so-called Venus figurines of Europe's Upper Paleolithic (e.g., Abramova 1967; Collins and Onians 1978; Conkey 1983; Dobres 1992; Marshack 1991; McDermott 1996). For archaeologists interested in the Native American societies that existed shortly before European contact, a wealth of early historic documents can be used to help interpret iconography from previous periods. European descriptions of indigenous lifeways and beliefs make possible greater specificity in our understanding of the meaning and use of Native iconography.

Using information from the historic period can be problematic, however. Ceremonial life in the Mississippian Southeast was not monolithic, and the meanings of iconography probably differed somewhat from one chiefdom to the next (Brose 1989:31). Therefore, one cannot use ethno-historic information to make highly specific interpretations about archaeological materials. It is more appropriate to focus on general themes. In fact, it has been argued that despite language differences among historic-period southeastern groups, people shared a similar worldview across the Southeast (Hudson 1976:122). A larger problem with ethnohistoric information, however, is that European contact changed the way people in southeastern societies attached meaning to iconography and ritual, and affected the way they understood the relationship between the natural and supernatural world (Brose 1989:31–32). Furthermore, the changing political landscape effected changes in myths and stories, as the need for legitimizing ideologies was transformed (Keyes 1994:113–14). Despite such changes, the entirety of southeastern ritual and belief was not wiped away by the arrival of Europeans. One remarkable example of the persistence of ritual practice is the fact that in the 1990s some Creeks still bury deceased family members under house floors (Moore 1994:136). Because of continuities in tradition, some general themes and meanings can be extracted from the ethnohistoric literature on southeastern ritual and belief. Obviously source criticism must be used to evaluate any ethnohistoric information (Vansina 1989:343–47; Wood 1990). Used critically, ethnohistoric information complements archaeological data and permits richer, more penetrating understandings of the past.

Images of Mississippian women can be found in numerous archaeologically recoverable media including ceramic effigy vessels, carved stone effigies and pipes, embossed copper plates, and in shell art. There is considerable variability in the ways women are represented. The variability in the depictions of women in Mississippian art parallels the variability in social roles occupied by Native southeastern women—both real and mythical. The gender-based division of labor in southeastern societies made women responsible for domestic duties (e.g., Swanton 1946:709–18). However, women were not restricted exclusively to lives as homemakers. The earliest ethnohistoric sources tell us that some women occupied the very highest positions of leadership in southeastern societies (Clayton et al. 1993a:229, 278–81, 290; Clayton et al. 1993b:285–86, 294–95). Some women were shamans and healers (e.g., Swanton 1946:768, 795). We also know that in some circumstances women took part in warfare (Clayton et al. 1993a:294; Clayton et al. 1993b:342–43; Swanton 1946:650). Women's social positions were differentiated by the kin group to which they belonged, their age, their own skills as craftspeople, and possibly other attributes such as beauty or the ability to sing or tell stories. Women also occupied different roles simultaneously and at different times during their lives—daughter, sister, wife, mother, and elder, for example. There were also many different roles for mythical women, from Corn Mother to evil spirits from the nether world (Swanton 1929:9–15, 146–47, 168, 230–40; Witthoft 1949).

Here I offer an initial examination of the ways women were represented in different classes of Mississippian art. My objective is to summarize images of women that appear in artifacts from across the Mississippian Southeast, and then to consider what can be learned from the objects' context of use and the meanings the objects communicated. Mississippian iconography was not disconnected from its social context. It shaped and was shaped by social ideals regarding gender and other social relations. Thus, the way women were represented in iconography is directly connected to the way Mississippian societies viewed gender roles. Viewing female representations from this perspective can help to illuminate the place of women in Mississippian ritual practice and belief.

The Study Sample and Methodology

For this study, I examined published photographs and drawings of seventy-two objects of stone, ceramic, copper, and shell that appear to depict female human figures (table 12.1). The objects include statues or figurines, smoking pipes, effigy bottles, an effigy appendage for a vessel, shell gorgets, shell cups, and copper plates. Figure 12.1 shows the locations of sites from which the artifacts came. These items do not constitute an exhaustive inventory of Mississippian artifacts bearing female representations. The objects were selected for inclusion in the sample as they were encountered in a thorough but unsystematic search undertaken by the author. Any object with a possible female representation created during the Mississippian period, from any site in the Southeast or Midwest, was included. No geographical restrictions were imposed given the relatively small number of available specimens. The resulting sample captures a large range of depictions in various media, including well-known artifacts as well as more obscure pieces. Although the objects considered here do not constitute a random sample, a random sample is not needed to address the questions of this study. To explore what iconography can tell us about women in Mississippian society and ideology, it is most important to examine a broad range of images. This study does not rely on statistical

Table 12.1. Archaeological objects depicting women in the Southeast used in this study

Object	Count
Stone statues/figurines	13
Stone smoking pipes	3
Ceramic effigy bottles	36
Vessel effigy appendage	1
Ceramic figurines	3
Shell gorgets	9
Shell cups	3
Copper plates	4
Total	72

comparisons of the frequency of attributes and artifact types; instead it considers the range of female images created in the Mississippian period and what those images might mean.

The primary criteria by which objects were identified as female were the depiction of breasts and genitals. Additional criteria include kneeling posture, hairstyle, and skirts. Some of the objects identified as possibly female in this study may be considered male by other researchers. Using expansive selection criteria has allowed me to think about Mississippian gender relations in new ways. It is hoped that this endeavor will allow other scholars to examine unstated assumptions, even if the result is to contest the premises and conclusions offered in this paper.

For each artifact in the sample, the following information was recorded:

1. provenience;
2. a detailed description of the figure's appearance, including posture and position of body parts, facial features, hairstyle, clothing, and ornaments;
3. the activity in which the figure is depicted (e.g., kneeling, grinding corn, and so forth);
4. objects or symbols depicted in association with the figure;
5. the medium of the object (e.g., ceramic, engraved shell, and so forth);
6. the type of object (e.g., bottle, figurine, gorget, and so forth); and
7. techniques used to execute the piece.

The study considers objects made of different materials, objects used in different social contexts, objects made by different artisans (men for some

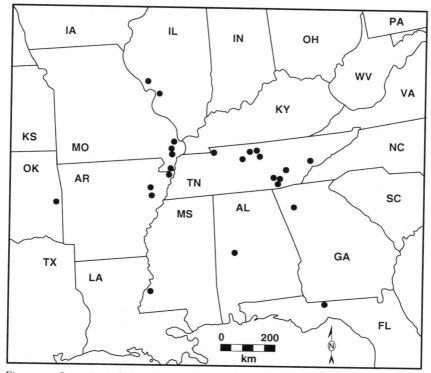

Fig. 12.1. Location of sites that produced objects used in this study. Some sites provided more than one object.

and women for others), objects depicting women in different settings, and objects in which women are depicted in different ways. The diversity among these artifacts defies meaningful and concise summary.

Male Bias in Iconographic Interpretations

The male-dominated tradition of North American archaeology has influenced the tone and content of discourse on female representations in Mississippian iconography. Typically, male bias has been subtle and implicit. As a result, some objects that likely display female figures have been overlooked. A researcher's assumptions can strongly affect how images are interpreted. To illustrate this fact, I discuss two examples from Phillips and Brown's (1978, 1984) volumes on shell engravings from Spiro—not to condemn their exemplary work, which is one of the most thorough treatments of Mississippian iconography ever attempted, but to offer alternate interpretations of these unusual pieces. One example is a shell cup featuring representations of four dead bodies (Phillips and Brown 1978:Plate 21), two of which appear to me as female based on the representation of genitals. In their commentary on these figures, Phillips and Brown state, "A particular anatomical monstrosity, situated in the groin, is worthy of mention only because it is the sole attempt at the depiction of human genitalia in the entire sample. 'Human' is hardly the word, but they are in the right place, insusceptible of any other interpretation" (Phillips and Brown 1978:Plate 21). What is susceptible to other interpretation is whether these genitals are male or female. Although not stated in the text, Brown believes them to be male. I believe they are female. The figures are not realistic in a photographic sense because of the conventions of Mississippian art and the limitations of the medium. This makes them open to differing interpretations. Another example is a gorget from Spiro depicting two symmetrical figures holding a central pole with one hand raised and both mouths open (Phillips and Brown 1984:Plate 135B). Phillips and Brown's caption contains the following description: "Two slightly grotesque individuals with beer bellies and pool-table legs." An alternate interpretation is that the gorget features a naturalistic representation of two pregnant dancers. By changing the sex of the figures, the way we interpret the scene is vastly different. In this paper, I explore the implications of viewing such figures as female in order to assess how our understanding of Mississippian society and ideology is expanded or changed by this new perspective.

For decades archaeologists have uncritically used masculine pronouns for images in Mississippian art that might actually represent women. The best example is a host of figures variously called falcon dancers, falcon impersonators, and falcon warriors that appear on shell cups, shell gorgets, and embossed copper plates. Objects displaying the conventionalized falcon warrior have been associated with high-status burials across the Southeast, and the figures have been assumed to be male. In a little-known, yet groundbreaking article by Catherine Brown (1982), this tacit attribution of male gender came under challenge. Brown made the observation that on copper plates depicting the falcon warrior, some individuals were shown with a breast (fig. 12.2) while others were not. Among the small number of copper plates that she examined, there also were differences in dress elements between those figures with breasts and those without: crescent-shaped necklaces were only shown on the figures without breasts (C. Brown 1982:4). According to Brown, both men and women personified the falcon warrior in Mississippian art.

Fig. 12.2. Copper plate from Etowah in northwestern Georgia. Note the breast shown in profile on the left. (Catalogue no. 91117.) Department of Anthropology, Smithsonian Institution, Washington, D.C.

I have found that Brown's observation also holds for a variety of human forms in shell art. Many of the gorgets and cups that I examined have not been heretofore acknowledged as possible depictions of women. Taking into consideration all of the female representations in Mississippian iconography, including those recognized through Brown's insight, one finds that women are present in all iconographic media, and they are depicted in many different roles. Attributing female gender to the various figures with breasts on copper headdress ornaments, shell gorgets, and shell cups permits a reinterpretation of women in Mississippian ceremonial life and status hierarchies.

Feminist perspectives have played a major role in forcing us to reconsider firmly established notions about gender roles in ancient lifeways. Another major reinterpretation of gender in southeastern archaeology can be found in Watson and Kennedy's (1991) discussion of the development of horticulture in the Eastern Woodlands. They describe how gender bias excluded women from scenarios reconstructing the domestication of starchy and oily seed plants, cucurbits, and the Northern Flint variety of maize. Watson and Kennedy (1991:258–59) cite ethnohistoric documentation regarding women's primary involvement in horticulture and plant collecting in the Eastern Woodlands, as well as cross-cultural data showing that women are usually responsible for plant-food production in small-scale societies. In view of the evidence for women's involvement in horticulture in the Eastern Woodlands, they point out that it is striking that women are absent in explanations for the origins of horticulture, and they attribute this absence to the stereotype of passivity associated with women. They critique Bruce Smith's (1987) explanation of indigenous weedy plant domestication for the way it removes intention and innovation from the scenario such that the plants "virtually domesticate themselves" (Watson and Kennedy 1991:262). They also critique Guy Prentice's (1986a) theory that male shamans were responsible for domesticating gourds on the basis that his scenario removes women "from the one realm traditionally granted them [plant production], as soon as innovation or invention enters the picture" (Watson and Kennedy 1991:264). In addition, they challenge the idea that after maize was introduced to northern latitudes it slowly (independently) adapted to the new day length, temperatures, moisture cycles, growing season, and soil conditions. Instead, they argue that the rapid spread of maize after A.D. 900 suggests that farmers (women) had been actively nurturing the species (Watson and Kennedy 1991:266). Women, they contend, had been working to acclimatize maize to the conditions in the Eastern Woodlands by planting it deeper or shallower, earlier or later, and in hilled or ridged fields, and by crossing varieties to create, enhance, and suppress traits (Watson and Kennedy 1991:266).

As Watson and Kennedy show, gender biases can obscure our understanding of the past. Women have often been viewed as passive recipients of culture, leading to a belief that they could not have been instrumental in the innovation of horticulture. Likewise, some have assumed that women could not have occupied high-status positions (real and mythical) in Mississippian society, such as those represented by the falcon dancer. In either case, a closer reading of the data opens up the possibility that women played more important roles in the past than had been previously acknowledged.

Although women's roles have often been underestimated, women have not been entirely absent from earlier studies of Mississippian iconography. In Thomas Emerson's discussion of Mississippian religious symbolism, he states that although women were often influential in southeastern societies, their social importance was not reflected in iconography (1989:61). Based on Brown's revelation, one is forced to recast Emerson's statement as follows: women were influential in southeastern societies, and their social importance was indeed reflected in diverse media of Mississippian art. The present study takes into account Brown's (1982) revelation and reinterprets a large corpus of iconography on that basis. It focuses specifically on Mississippian women in iconography, rather than on more general topics such as "religion" or "elite ideology." However, this study builds on distinguished research by a number of archaeologists interested in Mississippian iconography (e.g., Emerson 1989, 1997a, 1997b; Knight 1986; Pauketat and Emerson 1991; Prentice 1986b; K. Smith 1991). While this body of work has not focused specifically on women, many insights about Mississippian women emerged from it.

The Southeastern Cosmos

Fundamental to any discussion of iconography is an orientation to the belief system in which it was produced (see also Brotherton, chap. 13). Obviously, we cannot access the Mississippian belief system directly, but must infer aspects of it from ethnohistorical information about southeastern peoples in later times. The best summary of southeastern beliefs can be found in Charles Hudson's (1976) book, *The Southeastern Indians*. Hudson's (1976:122–36) description of the southeastern cosmos is relevant to my interpretations of female iconographic imagery.

Native southeastern peoples viewed the cosmos as divided into three main parts: an Upper World, This World, and an Under World (Hudson 1976:122). They believed that This World was suspended from the vault of the sky that arched above them. Over and beyond the sky vault was the Upper World of harmony, stability, and purity (Hudson 1976:123–25). The Upper World was associated with the ancestors and past time (Dye 1989:322; Hudson 1976:127–28). The Under World existed beneath the earth and the waters and was linked to disorder and change (Hudson 1976:125). The Under World contained monsters and danger, but it was also the source of water, fertility, and the means of coping with evil (Hudson 1976:166). As such, it was associated with the darker side of human relations (Dye 1989:322). The Upper World and the Under World in Cherokee mythology were opposed to each other; the chief beings of each realm—Tlanuwa, a bird of prey from the Upper World, and Uktena, a composite Under World monster—were mortal enemies (Hudson 1976:136). The humans living in This World attempted to strike a balance, often playing one side against the other in this cosmic conflict (Hudson 1976:128, 136). The southeastern conception of the cosmos is reflected in the iconography of the Mississippian period through various media including stone, ceramics, copper, and shell.

Images of Women in Stone

Female representations in stone consist of large statues, figurines, and smoking pipes. All of these objects were likely used in ritual contexts, although the nature of the rituals differed for stone statues as opposed to figurines and pipes. The large stone statues (e.g., Fundaburk and Foreman 1957:Plate 95, Plate 97; Perryman 1966:41; K. Smith 1991:126; Willoughby 1932:14), such as the one shown in figure 12.3, have long been interpreted as ancestor figures used in mortuary ritual, an explanation based upon early ethnohistoric accounts of their presence in temples (Waring 1968). For example, Garcilaso de la Vega, writing about the de Soto expedition, describes the statuary encountered in a southeastern temple:

> Lowering their eyes from the roof, our captains and soldiers saw that along the highest part of the four walls of the temple were two rows, one above the other, of statues of figures of men and women corresponding in size to the ordinary stature of the people of that country. ... On the floor against the walls, on very well-made wooden benches, as was everything in the temple, were the chests that served as sepul-

Fig. 12.3. Female ancestor figure from the Etowah site. Note the kneeling posture, knee-length skirt, and dark paint on the torso and face. Reproduced with the permission of the Parks, Recreation and Historic Sites Division, Georgia Department of Natural Resources.

chers, in which were the bodies of the curacas who had been the lords of that province of Cofachiqui. (Clayton et al. 1993b:301–2)

An extensive description of the temple ensues. Of course, Garcilaso de la Vega (or his informant) exaggerated the size of the figures, and we should not embrace the description of the temple as a photographic image. But it is reasonable to accept that statues representing chiefly ancestors resided in mortuary temples at sites across much of the Southeast.

In Knight's (1986) exposition on Mississippian cult institutions, he identified temple statuary as an exclusive cult institution represented by seated or kneeling human figures in deathlike poses (Knight 1986:679, 681). The figures were used in public ceremonies that acted to validate elite power by invoking connections to real and supernatural forebears (K. Smith 1991:134). Ancestor figures were perhaps produced by and probably controlled by an exclusive temple-based priesthood (Knight 1986: 679). However, men and women from the entire community participated in public ceremonies involving ancestor figures (Swanton 1946:758–59). In addition to their use in periodic, collective ceremonies involving the ancestor figures, these statues were probably used regularly by chiefs, their wives, and perhaps other family members for purposes of private ritual (e.g., Swanton 1946:779).

While most archaeological examples of ancestor figures are made of stone, statues carved from wood also exist and may have been quite common, although they are less likely to have been preserved (Knight 1986: 679). These statues have been found not only at the larger Mississippian mound centers but at smaller towns as well. The unique style and facial features represented in these pieces suggest that they may have been memorial portraits of real individuals (K. Smith 1991:131). Even so, many aspects of the representations are conventional (e.g., Penney 1985:Plate 141; Perryman 1966:41; K. Smith 1991:126). Kevin Smith (1991:128–30) has discussed some of the conventional characteristics associated with male and female figures. For example, seating posture in female figures is almost always kneeling with legs together, feet tucked behind, and hands resting on the thighs (K. Smith 1991:128). The figures are usually wearing a knee-length, wrap-around skirt and no ornamentation except perhaps body painting (fig. 12.3). Sunken eyes and drawn lips on these figures represent death. Other stone figures do not conform to the conventional model and may or may not have been used as ancestor figures (e.g., Funda-burk and Foreman 1957:Plate 95, Plate 97; Willoughby 1932:14).

In many cases, paired male and female figurines have been recovered.

Fig. 12.4. The Birger figurine from the BBB Motor site in the American Bottom, just east of St. Louis. The woman hoes the back of a serpent coiled around her. Reproduced with the permission of the Illinois Transportation Archaeological Research Program, University of Illinois, Champaign-Urbana.

This suggests that female ancestors were just as important as male ancestors in Mississippian cosmology—not surprising given the likelihood of matrilineal descent in the Mississippian Southeast (e.g., Hudson 1976: 185; Swanton 1946:654). The pairing of figures suggests that the union between the male and female ancestor was of primary importance, again not surprising since the sexual union between a man and woman is responsible for creating descendants in a lineage.

Ancestor figures were part of an exclusive cult for the veneration of chiefly ancestors, periodically playing a role in collective ceremonies in which chiefly rule was legitimized. Other stone figurines and pipes depicting women were probably used in more communal ritual contexts. A number of figurines and pipes with shared themes have been recovered from Mississippian sites. The themes and motifs presented on these objects appear to be linked to the mythical corn or earth mother and probably were used in agricultural rites (Emerson 1989, 1997a; Prentice 1986b). The archaeological contexts of the artifacts suggest ritual use. The Birger (fig. 12.4), Keller, Sponemann, Willoughby, and West figurines were recovered from temple contexts at sites in the American Bottom (Emerson 1989:48–50; Emerson and Jackson 1984; Jackson et al. 1992). The Schild effigy pipe and the "Figure at Mortar" have been recovered from mortuary contexts, probably after having been used in some types of ritual settings (Emerson 1989:54, 56).

Unlike the ancestor statues, which portray a stationary figure, these other stone figures are engaged, explicitly or implicitly, in some activity. It has been argued that stationary figures in iconography embody generalized symbols while active figures express action from myths (Strong 1989:222). In the case of the female figures I will discuss here, it appears that they do indeed express the action and themes of a particular religious myth.

The Keller figurine depicts a woman holding a stalk of some kind of plant with a basket before her; she is kneeling on a base that appears to be made of corn (Emerson 1989:52–53). An object portraying similar themes is the "Figure at Mortar" from Spiro (Emerson 1989:54–56). It is an effigy pipe that may have originated as a figurine (Emerson 1989:56). The "Figure at Mortar" shows a woman also kneeling at a metate holding an ear of corn and a grinding stone. The woman has a pack on her back, much like the pack carried by the woman of the Birger figurine. In the Birger figurine, there are gourds growing up the woman's back on vines that originate as the tail of a serpent coiled around the woman (fig. 12.4). The serpent has feline facial features. The woman is hoeing the back of the serpent, as one would hoe a field. A number of motifs present in the Birger figurine are also present in the Schild effigy pipe (Emerson 1989:56–57). The kneeling woman in this object has a hoe hanging over her shoulder. Her right arm ends in a bulbous form that probably represents a gourd. The Schild effigy pipe also has a serpent. However, the serpent in this case is coiled around the base of a pot, positioned behind the female figure. The head of the serpent is large, bulbous, and featureless, as is the woman's face. Three reconstructed figurine fragments from the Sponemann site—the Sponemann, the Willoughby, and the West figurines—also display the same series of motifs (Jackson et al. 1992:Plates 9.3, 9.7, and 9.10). The remaining portion of the Sponemann figurine depicts a woman wearing a turban (or using a tumpline) with her arms outstretched. The palms of her hands are upturned, with a plant growing from each, arching to either side of the figure's head (Emerson 1997a:200). Similarly, there are branching plant vines in the hands of the woman in the Willoughby figurine (Emerson 1997a:203). As with Keller, there is a basket in the lower portion of this figurine (Emerson 1997a:204). The West figurine is reminiscent of the Birger figurine in the prominence of the serpent motif. The woman has a naturalistically rendered rattlesnake coiled around her head, and she has a backpack, several snake heads, and a tail rattle (Emerson 1997a:204). In addition to the three reconstructed figurines, several recognizable figurine fragments also were recovered from the Sponemann site, including pieces of vines, gourds, baskets, and even lashings on a hoe identical to that in the Birger figurine (Emerson 1997a:204).

Emerson (1989:51–52) has argued that the curled lips and bared teeth of the Birger woman symbolize the concept of death and the supernatural realm to which the figure belongs. He bolsters his argument by comparing the Birger figurine to the stone ancestor figures. In each case the woman is kneeling, wearing a skirt that ends just above the knees, and has a face that might be described as a death mask, with drawn lips, bared teeth, and sunken eyes. These female figures have packlike objects strapped to their backs, which may represent cradle boards (K. Smith 1991:130–31) or the "sacred bundles" described in myths about the earth mother, who carries a pack containing ears of corn as her gift to mankind (Prentice 1986b). The packs may have been depicted in an ambiguous manner to evoke both symbolic associations to coalesce ideas about human and agricultural fertility (K. Smith 1991:131). However, unlike ancestor figures, these pipes and figurines represent a specific supernatural context—a mythical storyline expressed in these figurines. Emerson (1989) has linked these female effigies with the Corn Mother myths that were so central to southeastern mythology (Witthoft 1949). There are different versions of the origin of corn myth, but each shares some essential elements. Generally, the corn mother produces corn from her own body in one or another unappetizing way. When people discover how she is creating the food, they are disgusted and will not eat it; so she sacrifices herself in some way and becomes the corn growing in the fields (Swanton 1929:9–15, 168, 230–40). Her mythical self-sacrifice may account for the death imagery most apparent in the Birger figurine and the Schild effigy pipe.

In the figurines and pipes, the corn mother is associated with various Under World motifs and fertility symbolism (Emerson 1989:58–62).

Snakes and feline-headed snakes were Under World creatures associated with water, lightning, and fertility (Emerson 1989:59–61). Moreover, gourds as rattles were seen as symbolically linked to rattlesnakes (Emerson 1989:61). In most of the figurines and pipes, the central agricultural motifs are the hoes and plants, while in the "Figure at Mortar," the agricultural theme is embodied in the harvested corn being ground. These objects celebrate different phases of agricultural production—coaxing cultigens from the earth, and then transforming them from raw produce into edible food.

The Schild effigy pipe and the "Figure at Mortar," as pipes, were used differently from the figurines, since tobacco and perhaps other materials were smoked in them. Pipes and tobacco smoking played a part in both individual and collective rituals in the Southeast (see also Nassaney, chap. 15). Tobacco was used by individuals in certain hunting taboos (e.g., Swanton 1946:382, 766). Shamans used tobacco as an offering to gods, in ceremonies to absolve people of their sins, as a medicine in certain healing practices (e.g., Swanton 1946:382–84, 745, 759, 797), and in conjuring acts (Hudson 1976:353–54). Shamans smoked tobacco as a kind of "spiritual facilitator" in various ceremonies, a use that can be explained in part by the psychological and physiological effects of *Nicotiana rustica* (Hudson 1976:353). Many characteristics of smoke—its whiteness, the fact that it rises, its similar appearance to clouds—suggest that it was symbolically associated with positive social and spiritual values and with the Upper World. The Upper World connotations of tobacco smoke are juxtaposed to the Under World themes presented in the pipes discussed above. Perhaps the pipes were used in rituals meant to mediate supernatural forces from various realms of the cosmos.

Some female effigy pipes did not communicate agricultural themes. For example, a pipe from eastern Tennessee features a woman in an anatomically impossible position, wrapped backwards around the bowl of a pipe (Fundaburk and Foreman 1957:Plate 101). The pipe might simply be a whimsical portrayal without religious significance. The iconographic content of this piece suggests that pipes and tobacco smoking in the Mississippian period may have taken place in both ceremonial and secular contexts (see also Nassaney, chap. 15). Such was the case in the historic period (e.g., Swanton 1946:383–84), but such evidence alone is not persuasive since tobacco use may have been influenced by the manner of European usage. The style of Mississippian pipes ranged from serious and sacred (for example, the "Big Boy" pipe from Spiro; Museum of Fine Arts, Houston 1965:43) to perhaps humorous (for example, a pipe in the form of a human leg and foot from Nashville; Tennessee State Museum 1985:112, 115). The iconographic variability of pipes can be taken as independent evidence of the diverse contexts in which tobacco was smoked in the Mississippian period. The sample of pipes considered in this study encompasses both sacred and profane female images on objects probably used in contexts dominated by men, although tobacco use by women is noted in one historic account (Swanton 1946:384). The presence of female representations on pipes can be read in two ways: either women participated in rituals involving pipes with female representations, or images of women were present on pipes despite the fact that women did not participate in rituals in which those pipes were used. Ethnohistoric sources are not particularly informative on this issue. But even if women did not take part in rituals involving effigy pipes, they were part of the symbolic content of the rituals expressed in the imagery of the pipes.

Images of Women in Ceramics

Female representations in ceramics consist of effigy bottles and figurines. I will discuss effigy bottles and figurines together because they share themes and styles. In most cases, the entire woman is modeled in three dimensions. Usually the woman is kneeling with her hands on her knees; less often she is squatting. Dress and ornamentation on these figures is usually minimal—often restricted to a knee-length skirt and some kind of hairstyle. The figures rarely hold any kind of prop. However, there are exceptions, including women holding or nursing infants (e.g., Chapman 1980:250; Penney 1985:Plate 106), a woman with a child on her back (Evers 1880:Plate 24, fig. 7), and an effigy appendage for a vessel depicting a woman with a child on her back bent over a grindstone (Morse and Morse 1983:276). In many cases, representations are realistic and individualistic enough to suggest that they could be portraits of specific individuals (Hudson 1985:30; K. Smith 1991:131). However, there is reason to believe that such objects were icons for supernatural individuals.

It is possible that effigy bottles and figurines served in household rituals.[1] Like the stone ancestor figures that were used in mortuary contexts as well as in the temples of chiefly families, effigy bottles may have embodied real or mythical individuals in household shrines (perhaps ancestors), which were later buried with individuals. I use the term *household shrine* to mean any context involved in personal ritual—that is, ritual not participated in or supervised at a community level. There is some documentary evidence for household shrines in the early historic period. About the Tunica, La Harpe states that "their household gods are a frog and a figure of a woman which they worship, thinking that they represent the sun" (Margry 1875–86, 6:247, cited in Swanton 1946:780). Various southeastern groups believed that the sun was female (Swanton 1946:767, 781). Household shrines may have featured naturalistic representations of animals or humans—both female and male. Some household shrines may have been devoted to concerns about fertility. Some bottles likely depict pregnant women (e.g., Brain and Phillips 1996:256; Drooker 1992:79; Dye and Wharey 1989:355; Tennessee State Museum 1985:Plate 3). Some bottles, like the one shown in figure 12.5, depict women nursing infants (Chapman 1980:250; Penney 1985:Plate 106). Could these artifacts be evidence of sympathetic magic used by women who wanted extra help conceiving a child?[2] Sympathetic magic in hunting ceremonies and other situations has been described among historic southeastern groups (e.g., Swanton 1946:766). It is possible that sympathetic magic was practiced in more private contexts as well. It is unlikely, however, that early European observers would have been privy to (or even interested in) the private ritual practices of women; thus it is not surprising that no accounts of such practices exist. It is interesting to note that other ceramic artifacts recovered archaeologically have also been interpreted as folk-magic amulets: a series of sherds with sloppily engraved birdman heads unlikely to have been used in formal ritual contexts (Emerson 1989:80–81).

The possibility that Mississippian people used household shrines is supported by an unusual pair of artifacts from Tennessee (Thruston 1897: 110): a ceramic figurine found in a conch-shell case designed specifically to hold it. The front of the shell was removed, as were the interior whorls and column, down to a point where they were ground off to form a pedestal for the figurine. Shell had complex spiritual and ceremonial significance for people in the Southeast (Claassen 1991:294; Thomas 1996:39–40); the figurine must have had some importance if a shell case was fashioned just to house it. The symbolic connotations of shell may have been conferred on or cognitively linked to the figurine in the shell case.

One unusual bottle from southeast Missouri consists of two female figures, or a Janus-like figure with the two halves facing in opposite directions (Evers 1880:Plate 20, fig. 3). Scholars have interpreted the double-headed figures in shell engravings as warriors, drawing on historic-period use of the title "Doublehead" for alert warriors who could seemingly see in two directions at once (Howard 1968:61). Considering the Janus or "Doublehead" image from a broader metaphorical perspective, one might see such figures, including the bottle from Missouri, as representing indi-

Fig. 12.5. Effigy bottle found near Cahokia in the American Bottom depicting a woman nursing an infant. Reproduced with permission of the Saint Louis Science Center, Henry Whelpley Memorial Collection.

viduals with the ability to negotiate more than one realm—This World, the Upper World, and the Under World. Other than the fact that the bottle depicts two women rather than one, the portrayal adheres to the conventions observed in most female effigy bottles.

Like other female effigy bottles, a particular type of bottle referred to in the literature as the hunchback might also have been used in household ritual (fig. 12.6). Hunchback bottles are usually female (e.g., Chapman 1980:201; Dye and Wharey 1989:330–31; Evers 1880:Plate 21, figs. 2 and 3; Fundaburk and Foreman 1957:Plates 119 and 120; J. Jones 1876: 41; O'Brien 1994:235; Tennessee State Museum 1985:32, 125; Thruston 1897:Plate 3), but rare male versions also exist (e.g., Dye and Wharey 1989:330). Representations of the hunchback are conventionalized and have been found over a large area—from the central Mississippi River Valley across Tennessee. The distinguishing feature of these effigies is the depiction of pronounced spinal curvature, often combined with protruding vertebrae. Ancillary characteristics depicted on some of the figures include very slender arms and protruding chest and clavicle bones. Hunchbacks are often shown squatting with their hands on their knees or over their breasts.

Hunchback figures have often been explained as depictions of individuals afflicted with tuberculosis. While individuals with this condition may have inspired these figures, it is likely that the condition was invested with meaning beyond its physical reality. Because the figures' portrayal is so standardized and so common, it seems likely that the hunchback is a mythical character. Mythical characters or actual individuals with this deformity may have been associated with the supernatural realm because of their deviance from "normal" physical appearance. In the many southeastern myths assembled by John Swanton (1929), older women are more likely than young women to be instigators of action rather than victims or props in the story. An advanced degenerative condition, as might be depicted on the hunchback figures, would correlate with age and with the status age was accorded in southeastern societies. Thus, hunchback effigies may embody individuals, real or mythical, who were seen to have great power.

David Dye (1989:322) explains that portrait vessels and hunchbacks are associated with the Upper World and its emphasis on past time, order, harmony, structure, and stability. Some hunchback bottles also feature symbols that Dye associates with This World and the Under World—bilobed arrows, forked eye surrounds, and concentric circles (Dye 1989: 322)—which appear as tattooing on the face and chest (e.g., Dye and

Fig. 12.6. Female "hunchback" effigy bottle found near Nashville, Tennessee. Reproduced with the permission of the Tennessee State Museum, Gates P. Thruston Collection of Vanderbilt University.

Wharey 1989:330–31). The meanings expressed in the hunchback effigies are unclear. However, they constitute another example in which female iconography was central to belief and ritual practice in Mississippian communities.

All available evidence suggests women rather than men made ceramics in the pre-Contact Southeast. Ethnohistoric information from the southeastern United States describes pottery making as women's work (e.g., Swanton 1946:549–55, 710), and the same is true for the Northeast (Allen 1992:140–41; see also Johnson, chap. 4). At least one Mississippian ceramic vessel actually shows a woman engaged in this activity (Holmes 1903:Plate 28). It is also reasonable that women, who did most of the cooking, would make the tools necessary to prepare food. Many human effigy vessels present intimate portraits of motherhood (e.g., Chapman 1980:201; Evers 1880:Plate 24, fig. 7; Morse and Morse 1983:276–77; Penney 1985:Plate 106), a subject probably of more immediate concern to women artists than to men. In artifacts likely created by men, such as engraved shell, men are the predominant subjects of representation. In ceramic art, however, women predominate.

Considering that women potters were creating these objects, it is not surprising that female representations are more numerous in ceramics than in any other media. The women who made ceramic effigy vessels and figurines were consciously creating images imbued with meanings that revolved around gender, ritual, and cosmology. The meaning of these artifacts is partially revealed through the contexts in which the objects are found: household middens, suggesting use in household ritual and daily tasks; and burials, suggesting use in mortuary practices. Although ceramic effigies are often recovered from mortuary contexts, they are not recovered from those of small infants. While infant burials often contain artifacts, human effigies such as figurines were not buried with children until after the age of two, by which time gender identities were usually well established (K. Smith 1991:134). It seems that gender was an important aspect of the effigies, the meaning they conveyed, and the contexts in which they were used.

Images of Women in Copper

Female representations in copper portray the falcon dancer (e.g., Cotter 1952; Hudson 1976:399; B. C. Jones 1982:30–31; Willoughby 1932:36). The four objects included in this study are from Etowah, the Lake Jackson site on the Florida Panhandle, and the Mangum site in southwestern Mississippi. Copper plates featuring women in the falcon dancer role were used as breastplates and parts of headdresses worn by important individuals. At Etowah, for example, Larson (1971:65) recovered headdresses decorated with copper ornaments as well as hawk skins and feathers, and supported by a framework of wooden splints fastened to a leather headband or cap.

With the exception of the Mangum No. 1 plate (Cotter 1952), the female falcon dancers executed in repoussé copper share many motifs: (1) the wings and tail of a bird appear behind the individual; (2) the individual holds a human head in one hand and a weapon in the other; and (3) costume elements consistently include elaborate headdresses with bi-lobed arrows in the back, necklaces with conch-shell pendants, many beaded bands around arms and legs, bellows-shaped aprons and tassels, beak noses, beaded forelocks, and ear ornaments (see fig. 12.2). In the Mangum plate, the figure is framed by the wings and tail of a bird and has similar costume elements, such as a bellows-shaped apron and beaded ornaments. However, the figure differs in that she is facing to her left rather than her right, her headdress appears to include an antler, and rather than a weapon and a human head, the only associated prop is a pole from which two beaded feathers are hanging. The Mangum plate may represent a different character from the others.

The highly conventional and stylized depiction of the falcon impersonator suggests that it represented a mythical character. Unfortunately, an explicit description of the falcon warrior does not exist in historic-period southeastern mythology. However, Charles Hudson (1976:129) has argued that "Tlanuwa," the monstrous bird of prey in Cherokee oral traditions, may be represented as the falcon beings of Southeastern Ceremonial Complex iconography. Moreover, an explicitly female bird man-being is mentioned in Iroquois mythology (Parker 1923:203, 326, cited in Hammell 1983:9). It is possible that southeastern people during the Mississippian period understood the falcon impersonator differently than their descendants in the historic period did. Greg Keyes (1994) tracked changes in an unrelated southeastern myth between the 1670s and 1880s to illustrate how the legitimizing ideologies of Mississippian elites vanished from the story as the sociopolitical context of southeastern peoples changed. During the Mississippian period, the falcon impersonator may have been interpreted to confer legitimacy on elites by identifying the character with some earthly representative, in a way not manifest in historic-period myths.

Notwithstanding the mythical nature of the falcon warrior, it is clear that in some southeastern societies, certain individuals played or lived the role, at least in certain situations. At Etowah, excavations have exposed burials in which the interred wore nearly all of the costume details depicted in iconographic representations of the falcon warrior. These include copper-covered earspools with dangling wooden knobs and pearls; forelock beads of copper-covered wood; shell beads worn around the wrists, upper arms, and ankles, and below the knees; necklaces of large columella beads and pendants; and hair ornaments with copper bi-lobed arrows and parts of birds' wings (Larson 1989:139–40). The fact that a number of falcon warrior representations are female suggests that women may have occasionally occupied the authority roles linked to the mythical figure. Indeed, early Spanish explorers encountered women as chiefs among a number of southeastern groups (C. Brown 1982:7; Clayton et al. 1993a: 229, 278–81, 290; Clayton et al. 1993b:285–86, 294–95; Hudson 1990; Trocolli 1993). Likewise, Mississippian women may have occupied other important roles in society.

It has been argued that the falcon impersonator filled the war-captain role in Mississippian society (J. Brown 1976:126–27). Alternatively, it is possible that individuals of a particular status filled the falcon impersonator role temporarily in ritual contexts, serving as an intermediary between This World and the Upper World. It is also possible that Mississippian elites traced their descent from a mythical falcon being, thus bolstering their claims to authority through divine kinship and ancestral linkage to the Upper World. That falcon beings may have been divine ancestors to Mississippian elites could explain why there are both male and female representations of these characters. Female falcon beings as elite ancestors may have been particularly important in southeastern societies, which were predominantly matrilineal.

Images of Women in Shell

Whereas copper provided the primary medium for the depiction of falcon impersonators, shell provided the medium in which Mississippian artists depicted individuals impersonating the mythical Under World monster that the Cherokee called Uktena. Drawing on ethnographic observations of Yuchi dances in the early 1900s, Hudson (1976:144–45) has argued that certain Mississippian gorgets depict dancers playing the part of Uktena, a monster with attributes of deer, birds, and serpents. The individuals on these gorgets have antlers, wings, and birdlike claws, and wear breechcloths spotted like snake skins, thus displaying the composite fea-

Fig. 12.7. Gorget from the Hixon site in eastern Tennessee depicting paired fighting female Uktena impersonators. Courtesy of the Frank H. McClung Museum, University of Tennessee, Knoxville.

tures of Uktena. Among the objects included in this study are three examples of paired fighting female Uktena impersonators (Brain and Phillips 1996:47, 48; Willoughby 1932:55) (see fig. 12.7). These gorgets are from eastern Tennessee and Etowah. In each, two female figures are locked in combat, each one grasping the other's ear ornament and raising a baton, knife, or club in a menacing fashion. There are also objects depicting single Uktena impersonators (Brain and Phillips 1996:45; Muller 1989: 20; Penney 1985:Plate 134; Willoughby 1932:54). In these objects, the Uktena impersonator typically has a wing and bird tail behind one side and wears an antler headdress, a spotted snakeskin breechcloth, a beak nose, a conch-shell necklace, wrist and leg bands, and ear ornaments. In each hand, the individual holds a composite animal and a knife. David Dye (1989:322) associates anomalous mythical animals, like the ones held by the Uktena impersonators, with the Under World—the realm of the Uktena itself.

The shell gorgets depicting female Uktena impersonators may reflect the participation of Mississippian women in ritual contexts in which individuals—perhaps as shamans—played the role of the Under World monster. Such contexts include fertility rites, rituals devoted to rain, rituals designed to cope with evil, or other possible ceremonies dealing with Under World themes. Since some southeastern women were shamans and healers in the historic period (e.g., Swanton 1946:768, 795), it is not difficult to imagine women filling the same roles in Mississippian societies. As shamans, they may have evoked Uktena's powers, particularly in fertility rites whose efficacy may have been linked to the procreative powers of women.

In addition to Uktena impersonators, another role in which women are depicted on shell artifacts is that of warrior. For example, a cup fragment from Spiro appears to depict a woman engaged in battle (Phillips and Brown 1984:Plate 163). She is holding a large club or spear, and arrows are raining down on her. It appears that she has been wounded by one of the arrows, which is entering her side, possibly shown X-ray fashion in her torso. Another shell-cup fragment from Moundville also may depict a woman warrior (Brain and Phillips 1996:298). In the Myer gorget from the Castalian Springs site northeast of Nashville, Tennessee (pictured in Hudson 1976:89), the sex of the individual is more ambiguous, but this may be another example of a woman in a warrior role. In this example the individual is depicted with an elaborate headdress that includes a bi-lobed arrow. Other costume elements include a bellows-shaped apron, a necklace, wrist and leg bands, ear ornaments, a weeping eye, and a beaded forelock. The individual holds a severed head in one hand and a mace in the other. This gorget may depict a female warrior, although the profile of the figure's breast is less distinct than those depicted in other shell gorgets and in copper plates.

The representation of women as warriors is consistent with information from various ethnohistoric sources. For example, women's participation in warfare is described in the de Soto accounts as women joined men against the Spaniards in the battle at Mauvila (Mobile) (Clayton et al. 1993a:294; Clayton et al. 1993b:342–43). Garcilaso de la Vega provides a characteristically colorful description of women's role in the battle:

[T]he Indians, seeing how many of their men they had killed by fire and the sword and that for lack of fighters their strength was decreasing while that of the Castilians was increasing, summoned the women and ordered them to take up some of the many arms that were lying in the streets and set about taking vengeance for the death of their people; and if they could not avenge them, they could at least see to it that all of them should die before becoming the slaves of the Spaniards.

When they gave this command to the women many of them had already been fighting bravely for some time along with their husbands, but with this new order not one remained who did not go to the battle, taking up arms that they found lying on the ground, of which there was an abundance. Many of the swords, halberds, and lances that the Spaniards had lost came into their hands, and they turned them against their owners, wounding them with their own arms. They also took up bows and arrows and shot them with no less skill and ferocity than their husbands. They stationed themselves in front of the latter to fight, and resolutely exposed themselves to death with much more temerity than the men. They thrust themselves among the enemy's weapons with great fury and recklessness, showing well that the desperation and courage of women in what they have determined to do is greater and more heedless than that of men. (Clayton et al. 1993b:342–43)

Historic documents also indicate that women who displayed extraordinary personal abilities could occupy leadership roles in the context of warfare. For example, in the 17th century among a group in Louisiana, a woman rose to a position as a charismatic leader who commanded many war parties (Swanton 1946:650).

Other forms of violence and aggression outside of the context of warfare were not inimical to feminine identity among southeastern women. For example, in Rodrigo Rangel's account of the de Soto expedition, one can read about a captive woman using force against a Spaniard in self-defense:

[O]ne Indian woman took a *bachiller* [a recipient of an academic degree] named Herrera, who was alone with her and behind his other companions, and she seized him by the genitals and held him very fatigued and submissive, and perhaps if other Christians had not passed and aided him, the Indian woman would have killed him. It was not that he wished to have intercourse with her as a lustful man, but rather that she wished to liberate herself and flee. (Clayton et al. 1993a:266–67)

Of course, Herrera's assailant would have been more qualified to comment on the *bachiller*'s intentions than Rangel. The more important point for my argument, however, is that southeastern women were willing to exercise force and defend themselves when the situation demanded it. Their toughness is reflected in myths that place real and supernatural female characters in many violent roles (e.g., Swanton 1929:88–89, 115, 146–47, 177–78, 217–22). Although participation in warfare and other acts of violence may not have been common among Mississippian women, it may have assumed great significance on certain occasions, worthy of commemoration in folklore and ritual objects.

Mississippian iconography not only shows women actively participating in warfare, it also depicts women among the dead. A shell-cup fragment from Spiro, mentioned above, may depict at least four shriveled, dead bodies, two of which appear to be female (Phillips and Brown 1978: Plate 21). Arrows are shown X-ray fashion in the women's torsos, suggesting that they were either killed in battle or were sacrificial victims. (Because of the fragmentary nature of the cup, the other [male?] individuals' lower torsos are missing, so that it is unclear whether they also had arrows in that location.) It seems more likely that the figures on the cup fragment represent sacrificial victims, because the two female figures have multiple arrows in the same location of their bodies. Also, the fact that all of the individuals are wearing ornaments such as bead necklaces, beaded wrist, arm, and leg bands, and tassels suggests that they may have been killed as part of some ritual event, although it is equally likely that the bodies were dressed for burial after death. If we agree that the cup depicts a mortuary context subsequent to some ritual sacrifice, then it is interesting to note that the female bodies are strewn among what appear to be male bodies. Whatever the event was that preceded the mortuary context shown on the cup, it seems to have been something in which women and men both participated.

Not all representations of ritual in the medium of engraved shell are as macabre as the preceding cup fragment. For example, a gorget from Spiro depicts two identical pregnant women singing and dancing around a central pole (Phillips and Brown 1984:Plate 135B). The concentric arcs behind each figure are similar to motifs on some Ramey Incised ceramics from Cahokia, and they may represent the sky vault or its manifestation as a rainbow (Pauketat and Emerson 1991:928–29). In either case, the symbols have Upper World connotations. The concentric arcs can be seen to mirror or to stand juxtaposed to the rounded bellies of the pregnant women that may have been linked to Under World themes of fertility and water. Such an interpretation is consistent with the oppositional nature of the southeastern cosmos (Hudson 1976:136).

Women in Mississippian Ritual Practice and Belief

For many years Mayan scholars dismissed the idea that the 260-day sacred calendar might have been based on the period of human gestation (Miller 1988:vii). Ethnographic work among the Quiché Maya eventually established compelling support for the idea (Earle and Snow 1985; Furst 1986), thus forcing the acknowledgment of women's central role in the symbolism of Mayan calendrical ritual. Since then, other researchers have explored the importance of women in various forms of Mayan iconography (e.g., Bruhns 1988; Joyce 1996; Roosevelt 1988:9–10; Stone 1988). Reinterpreting women in Mayan material culture has led to new ways of thinking about Mayan society. Iconography from throughout Mesoamerica and South America has attested to the mythological, religious, and social importance of women in various pre-Columbian societies (Miller 1988:vii). The present study's revisionist survey of Mississippian iconography suggests that in Native societies of North America, women also played important, socially recognized roles, just as they did in the southern half of the New World.

This study has shown that women were important in both the symbolism and ritual practice of Mississippian religion and ceremonial life. We find women associated with Under World themes—particularly those related to fertility—in objects such as the Birger figurine and gorgets depicting Uktena impersonators. We also find women associated with the Upper World, as falcon impersonators and ancestor figures, for example. In various objects, we find women mediating between various realms. The iconographic representation of women in these contexts suggests that actual Mississippian women may have occupied prestigious roles in their societies—from chiefly elite to shaman. The context of use for various iconographic objects further suggests that women were ritual practitioners in both public and private contexts—in community-wide ceremonies, in mortuary ritual, as well as in private, household ritual. Even when women were not in paramount ritual and ceremonial roles, the female images on ritual artifacts expressed and reinforced the symbolic importance of women in Mississippian ritual life.

Mississippian iconography bearing images of women was visible in many social contexts. For example, female representations appear on gorgets worn by important individuals. They appear as ceramic vessels, likely used in household ritual as well as in mortuary practice. They appear as pipes and figurines used by ritual specialists. Female representations occur in many different social contexts; they also were associated with many different themes, from warfare to human fertility, and from agricultural fertility to elite power. And although most images of women in Mississippian iconography are in some way connected to ritual practice and belief, the figures occasionally are shown engaged in ordinary activities such as grinding corn, nursing an infant, or dancing at a festival. Just as women in Mississippian iconography were connected to many different social contexts and symbolic themes, they were likewise depicted in many different ways. Their features, costumes, posture, and props vary from one artifact type to the next. The diverse array of images discussed here had varied contexts of use and meaning. Such iconographic heterogeneity and visibility likely paralleled the visibility and participation of actual Mississippian women in diverse ritual contexts.

Women themselves made some of the articles discussed in this study, such as the ceramic vessels and figurines, although men were probably responsible for most stone, copper, and shell objects. Nevertheless, women were important in the meaning and use of these artifacts, not simply as objects but as actors. The fact that women figure prominently in the iconography created by men makes clear the central place of women in Mississippian ritual practice and belief. Whether life imitates art, or art imitates life, women certainly played multiple, diverse, active, and prominent roles in Mississippian communities and cosmology. Iconography is one way we can begin to understand these roles.

The present study did not seek out regional patterns or temporal changes in the ways women are depicted in Mississippian iconography. I anticipate that with developing interest in gender and Mississippian iconography, researchers will begin to explore and interpret geographic and temporal variability (e.g., Drooker 1994). Such studies may help shed light on the impact of changing political conditions on women's roles in those societies. One constraint on research of that nature is, however, the limited number of objects featuring images of women. Another important future direction for research on women in Mississippian iconography is to compare images of women with images of men in the various iconographic media. Such a comparative analysis is certain to elucidate interesting similarities and differences in the representations, and this would help to further delineate Mississippian gender roles and their interrelation.

Material Culture and Ethnohistory

The study of iconography is just one way material culture can yield unique insights into past societies. Archaeologists have long appreciated the potential of material culture to reveal important information about the societies that created it, as various contributions to this volume demonstrate. Likewise, archaeologists have also drawn on historical documents and ethnohistorical sources to help interpret archaeological materials. While ethnohistorians have traditionally focused on the use of documents and the historical method, it is worth considering any available source of information, including material culture, to elucidate the past (Wood 1990:81– 82). Indeed, in some cases archaeology may be the only means to investigate questions of historical and cultural interest (see Mason and Holman, chap. 9). When material remains are associated with documentary evidence, each can provide independent, complementary sources of information about past societies (Spores 1980:579; see also Nassaney and Johnson, Introduction). Archaeologists investigating societies at the dawn of the historic period are becoming increasingly sophisticated in the use of ethnographic and historic information (e.g., Stahl 1993:246–52). Thoughtful syntheses of information from documents and material culture can provide valuable insights into past societies, including the Native American societies spanning the centuries before, during, and after European conquest. Furthermore, ethnohistorians are finding it fruitful to explore the late pre-Contact period as a means of providing context for historical processes unfolding in the decades after contact (e.g., Galloway 1995; Hudson 1997; Hudson and Tesser 1994; Keegan 1992; Milanich 1995). Such interdisciplinary research deepens our understanding of Native American societies.

Notes

1. The notion of household ritual in Mississippian contexts came to me after hearing Robert Preucel's talk on domestic ritual and high ritual among the Hohokam. Preucel discussed how aspiring elites manipulated worldview and ritual practice to enhance their status and authority. His ideas about the intersection of ritual, beliefs, and political dynamics have since been published (Preucel 1996). Drawing inspiration from Preucel, one can make three points about Mississippian household ritual. First, ordinary Mississippian households could be the locus of ritual activity. Second, artifacts and features commonly explained in economic terms might have been used instead in ritual practices. And finally, there was not necessarily a sharp emic distinction between mundane "economic" activi-

ties and domestic ritual; ritual may have been embedded in economic activities and considered necessary to ensure the well-being of the household.

2. *Sympathetic magic* is Frazer's (1955 [1922]) term for magical practices believed to achieve a desired effect when things act on each other at a distance through secret sympathy. The specific form of sympathetic magic relevant to my discussion is *homeopathic* or *imitative* magic, whereby the magician believes he or she can produce a desired effect by imitating it.

References Cited

Abramova, Z. A. 1967. Paleolithic Art in the U.S.S.R. *Arctic Anthropology* 17:1–179.

Allen, Kathleen M. S. 1992. Iroquois Ceramic Production: A Case Study of Household-Level Organization. In *Ceramic Production and Distribution: An Integrated Approach,* ed. G. J. Bey and C. Pool, 133–54. Westview Press, Boulder, Colo.

Brain, Jeffrey P., and Philip Phillips. 1996. *Shell Gorgets: Styles of the Late Prehistoric and Protohistoric Southeast.* Peabody Museum Press, Cambridge, Mass.

Brose, David S. 1989. From the Southeastern Ceremonial Complex to the Southern Cult: "You Can't Tell the Players without a Program." In *The Southeastern Ceremonial Complex: Artifacts and Analysis,* ed. Patricia Galloway, 27–37. University of Nebraska Press, Lincoln.

Brown, Catherine. 1982. On the Gender of the Winged Being on Mississippian Period Copper Plates. *Tennessee Anthropologist* 7(1):1–8.

Brown, James A. 1976. The Southern Cult Reconsidered. *Midcontinental Journal of Archaeology* 1(2):115–35.

Bruhns, Karen O. 1988. Yesterday the Queen Wore . . . : An Analysis of Women and Costume in Public Art of the Late Classic Maya. In *The Role of Gender in Precolumbian Art and Architecture,* ed. V. E. Miller, 105–34. University Press of America, Lanham, Md.

Chapman, Carl H. 1980. *The Archaeology of Missouri II.* University of Missouri Press, Columbia.

Claassen, Cheryl P. 1991. Gender, Shellfishing, and the Shell Mound Archaic. In *Engendering Archaeology: Women and Prehistory,* ed. J. M. Gero and M. W. Conkey, 276–300. Basil Blackwell, Cambridge.

Clayton, L. A., V. J. Knight, and E. C. Moore, eds. 1993a. *The De Soto Chronicles: The Expedition of Hernando de Soto to North America in 1539–1543.* Vol. 1. University of Alabama Press, Tuscaloosa.

———. 1993b. *The De Soto Chronicles: The Expedition of Hernando de Soto to North America in 1539–1543.* Vol. 2. University of Alabama Press, Tuscaloosa.

Collins, Desmond, and John Onians. 1978. The Origins of Art. *Art History* 1:1–25.

Conkey, Margaret W. 1983. On the Origins of Paleolithic Art: A Review and Some

Critical Thoughts. In *The Mousterian Legacy: Human Biocultural Change in the Upper Pleistocene,* ed. Erik Trinkaus, 201–27. British Archaeological Reports, International Series 164. Oxford.

Cotter, J. W. 1952. The Mangum Plate. *American Antiquity* 18(1):65–68.

Dobres, Marcia-Anne. 1992. Re-considering Venus Figurines: A Feminist-Inspired Re-analysis. In *Ancient Images, Ancient Thought: The Archaeology of Ideology,* ed. A. Sean Goldsmith, Sandra Garvie, David Selin, and Jeannette Smith, 245–62. University of Calgary Archaeological Association, Calgary.

Drooker, Penelope Ballard. 1992. *Mississippian Village Textiles at Wickliffe.* University of Alabama Press, Tuscaloosa.

————. 1994. Representations of Gender in Fort Ancient versus Mississippian Culture Areas. Paper presented at the Third Archaeology and Gender Conference: Women in Ancient America. Boone, N.C.

Dye, David H. 1989. Introduction (to Exhibition Catalog). In *The Southeastern Ceremonial Complex: Artifacts and Analysis,* ed. Patricia Galloway, 321–24. University of Nebraska Press, Lincoln.

Dye, David H., and Camille Wharey. 1989. Exhibition Catalog. In *The Southeastern Ceremonial Complex: Artifacts and Analysis,* ed. Patricia Galloway, 325–82. University of Nebraska Press, Lincoln.

Earle, Duncan M., and Dean Snow. 1985. The Origin of the 260-day Calendar: The Gestation Hypothesis Reconsidered in Light of Its Use among the Quiché Maya. In *Fifth Palenque Round Table,* 1983, vol. 7, ed. V. M. Fields, 241–44. The Pre-Columbian Art Research Institute, San Francisco.

Emerson, Thomas E. 1989. Water, Serpents, and the Underworld: An Exploration into Cahokian Symbolism. In *The Southeastern Ceremonial Complex: Artifacts and Analysis,* ed. Patricia Galloway, 45–92. University of Nebraska Press, Lincoln.

————. 1997a. Cahokian Elite Ideology and the Mississippian Cosmos. In *Cahokia: Domination and Ideology in the Mississippian World,* ed. T. R. Pauketat and T. E. Emerson, pp. 190–228. University of Nebraska Press, Lincoln.

————. 1997b. *Cahokia and the Archaeology of Power.* University of Alabama Press, Tuscaloosa.

Emerson, Thomas E., and Douglas K. Jackson. 1984. *The BBB Motor Site (11-Ms-595).* American Bottom Archaeology FAI-270 Site Reports, vol. 6. University of Illinois Press, Urbana.

Evers, Edward. 1880. The Ancient Pottery of Southeastern Missouri. In *Contributions to the Archaeology of Missouri by the Archaeological Section of the St. Louis Academy of Science,* part 1, Pottery, pp. 21–30. George A. Bates, Naturalists' Bureau, Salem, Mass.

Frazer, James G. 1955 [1922]. *The Golden Bough: A Study in Magic and Religion.* 12 vols. 3d ed., rev. and enlarged. Macmillan, London, 1911–15. Abridged ed., 1922; reprinted 1955 by St. Martin's Press, New York.

Fundaburk, Emma Lila, and Mary Douglass Fundaburk Foreman. 1957. *Sun Circles and Human Hands: The Southeastern Indians' Art and Industries.* Emma Lila Fundaburk, Luverne, Ala.

Furst, Peter. 1986. Human Biology and the Origin of the 260-Day Sacred Almanac: The Contribution of Leonard Schultz Jena. In *Symbol and Meaning beyond the Closed Community: Essays in Mesoamerican Ideas,* ed. G. H. Gossen, pp. 69–76. Institute for Mesoamerican Studies, State University of New York at Albany.

Galloway, Patricia. 1995. *Choctaw Genesis: 1500–1700.* University of Nebraska Press, Lincoln.

Hammell, George R. 1983. Trading in Metaphors: Another Perspective on Indian-European Contact in Northeastern North America. In *Proceedings of the 1982 Glass Trade Bead Conference,* ed. Charles F. Hayes III, Nancy Bolger, Karlis Karklins, and Charles F. Wray, 5–28. Research Records No. 16. Research Division, Rochester Museum and Science Center, Rochester, N.Y.

Holmes, William H. 1903. Aboriginal Pottery of the Eastern United States. *Bureau of American Ethnology Report* 20:1–237.

Howard, James H. 1968. *The Southeastern Ceremonial Complex and Its Interpretation.* Memoirs of the Missouri Archaeological Society no. 6, Columbia.

Hudson, Charles. 1976. *The Southeastern Indians.* University of Tennessee Press, Knoxville.

———. 1985. Iconography of the Thruston Collection. In *Art and Artisans of Prehistoric Middle Tennessee,* pp. 19–36. Tennessee State Museum, Nashville.

———. 1990. *The Juan Pardo Expeditions: Exploration of the Carolinas and Tennessee, 1566–1568.* Smithsonian Institution Press, Washington, D.C.

———. 1997. *Knights of Spain, Warriors of the Sun: Hernando de Soto and the South's Ancient Chiefdoms.* University of Georgia Press, Athens.

Hudson, Charles, and Carmen Chaves Tesser, eds. 1994. *The Forgotten Centuries: Indians and Europeans in the American South, 1521–1704.* University of Georgia Press, Athens.

Jackson, Douglas K., Andrew C. Fortier, and Joyce A. Williams. 1992. *The Sponemann Site II (11-Ms-517): The Mississippian and Oneota Occupations.* American Bottom Archaeology, FAI-270 Site Reports, vol. 24. University of Illinois Press, Urbana.

Jones, B. Calvin. 1982. Southern Cult Manifestations at the Lake Jackson Site, Leon County, Florida: Salvage Excavation of Mound 3. *Midcontinental Journal of Archaeology* 7(1):3–44.

Jones, Joseph. 1876. *Explorations of the Aboriginal Remains of Tennessee.* Smithsonian Contributions to Knowledge 259. Smithsonian Institution, Washington, D.C.

Joyce, Rosemary A. 1996. The Construction of Gender in Classic Maya Monuments. In *Gender and Archaeology,* ed. R. P. Wright, pp. 167–95. University of Pennsylvania Press, Philadelphia.

Keegan, William F. 1992. *The People Who Discovered Columbus: The Prehistory of the Bahamas.* University Press of Florida, Gainesville.

Keyes, Greg. 1994. Myth and Social History in the Early Southeast. In *Perspectives on the Southeast: Linguistics, Archaeology, and Ethnohistory,* ed. P. B. Kwachka, 106–15. University of Georgia Press, Athens.

Knight, Vernon J. 1986. The Institutional Organization of Mississippian Religion. *American Antiquity* 51(4):675–87.

Koehler, Lyle. 1997. Earth Mothers, Warriors, Horticulturalists, Artists, and Chiefs: Women among the Mississippian and Mississippian-Oneota Peoples, A.D. 1000 to 1750. In *Women in Prehistory: North America and Mesoamerica,* ed. Cheryl Claassen and Rosemary A. Joyce, 211–26. University of Pennsylvania Press, Philadelphia.

Larson, Lewis H., Jr. 1971. Archaeological Implications of Social Stratification at the Etowah Site, Georgia. In *Approaches to the Social Dimensions of Mortuary Practices,* ed. J. A. Brown. Memoirs of the Society for American Archaeology 25:58–67.

———. 1989. The Etowah Site. In *The Southeastern Ceremonial Complex: Artifacts and Analysis,* ed. Patricia Galloway, 133–41. University of Nebraska Press, Lincoln.

Margry, Pierre. 1875–1886. *Découvertes et établissements des français dans l'ouest et dans le sud de l'Amérique septentrionale (1614–1754)* [Discoveries and establishments of the French in the West and South of North America (1614–1754)]. Mémoires et documents originaux recueillis et pubiés par Pierre Margry, Paris [Original memoirs and documents collected and published by Pierre Margry, Paris].

Marshack, Alexander. 1991. The Female Image: A Time-Factored Symbol: A Study in Style and Aspects of Image Use in the Upper Paleolithic. *Proceedings of the Prehistoric Society* 57:17–31.

McDermott, LeRoy. 1996. Self-Representation in Upper Paleolithic Female Figurines. *Current Anthropology* 37(2):227–75.

Milanich, Jerald T. 1995. *Florida Indians and the Invasion from Europe.* University Press of Florida, Gainesville.

Miller, Virginia E. 1988. The Role of Gender in Precolumbian Art and Architecture: Introduction. In *The Role of Gender in Precolumbian Art and Architecture,* ed. V. E. Miller, vii–xviii. University Press of America, Lanham, Md.

Moore, John H. 1994. Ethnoarchaeology of the Lamar Peoples. In *Perspectives on the Southeast: Linguistics, Archaeology, and Ethnohistory,* ed. P. B. Kwachka, 126–41. University of Georgia Press, Athens.

Morse, Dan F., and Phyllis A. Morse. 1983. *Archaeology of the Central Mississippi Valley.* Academic Press, New York.

Muller, Jon. 1989. The Southern Cult. In *The Southeastern Ceremonial Complex: Artifacts and Analysis,* ed. Patricia Galloway, 11–26. University of Nebraska Press, Lincoln.

Museum of Fine Arts, Houston. 1965. *Spiro and Mississippian Antiquities from the McDannald Collection.* Museum of Fine Arts, Houston, Texas.

O'Brien, Michael J. 1994. *Cat Monsters and Head Pots: The Archaeology of Missouri's Pemiscot Bayou.* University of Missouri Press, Columbia.

Parker, Arthur C. 1923. Seneca Myths and Folk Tales. *Publications of the Buffalo Historical Society* 27.

Pauketat, Timothy R., and Thomas E. Emerson. 1991. The Ideology of Authority and the Power of the Pot. *American Anthropologist* 93(4):919–41.

Penney, David. 1985. Continuities of Imagery and Symbolism in the Art of the Woodlands. In *Ancient Art of the American Woodland Indians,* ed. David S. Brose, James A. Brown, and David Penney, 147–98. Harry N. Abrams, New York.

Perryman, Margaret. 1966. Stone Effigy Figures from Georgia. *Tennessee Archaeologist* 22(1):40–42.

Phillips, Philip, and James A. Brown. 1978. *Pre-Columbian Shell Engravings from the Craig Mound at Spiro, Oklahoma, Part 1.* Peabody Museum Press, Cambridge, Mass.

———. 1984. *Pre-Columbian Shell Engravings from the Craig Mound at Spiro, Oklahoma, Part 2.* Peabody Museum Press, Cambridge, Mass.

Prentice, Guy. 1986a. Origins of Plant Domestication in the Eastern United States: Promoting the Individual in Archaeological Theory. *Southeastern Archaeology* 5:103–19.

———. 1986b. An Analysis of the Symbolism Expressed by the Birger Figurine. *American Antiquity* 51(2):239–66.

Preucel, Robert W. 1996. Cooking Status: Hohokam Ideology, Power, and Social Reproduction. In *Interpreting Southwestern Diversity: Underlying Principles and Overarching Patterns,* ed. P. R. Fish and J. J. Reid, pp. 125–31. Anthropological Research Papers No. 48. Arizona State University, Tempe.

Roosevelt, Anna C. 1988. Interpreting Certain Female Images in Prehistoric Art. In *The Role of Gender in Precolumbian Art and Architecture,* ed. V. E. Miller, 1–34. University Press of America, Lanham, Md.

Smith, Bruce D. 1987. The Independent Domestication of the Indigenous Seed-Bearing Plants in Eastern North America. In *Emergent Horticultural Economies of the Eastern Woodlands,* ed. William Keegan, 3–47. Occasional Paper No. 7. Center for Archaeological Investigations, Southern Illinois University, Carbondale.

Smith, Kevin E. 1991. The Mississippian Figurine Complex and Symbolic Systems of the Southeastern United States. In *The New World Figurine Project,* vol. 1, ed. Terry Stocker, 123–37. Research Press, Provo, Utah.

Spores, Ronald. 1980. New World Ethnohistory and Archaeology, 1970–1980. *Annual Review of Anthropology* 9:575–603.

Stahl, Ann B. 1993. Concepts of Time and Approaches to Analogical Reasoning in Historical Perspective. *American Antiquity* 58(2):235–60.

Stone, Andrea. 1988. Sacrifice and Sexuality: Some Structural Relationships in Classic Maya Art. In *The Role of Gender in Precolumbian Art and Architecture*, ed. V. E. Miller, 75–103. University Press of America, Lanham, Md.

Strong, John A. 1989. The Mississippian Bird-Man Theme in Cross-Cultural Perspective. In *The Southeastern Ceremonial Complex: Artifacts and Analysis*, ed. Patricia Galloway, 211–38. University of Nebraska Press, Lincoln.

Swanton, John. 1929. *Myths and Tales of the Southeastern Indians*. Bureau of American Ethnology Bulletin 88. U.S. Government Printing Office, Washington, D.C.

———. 1946. *The Indians of the Southeastern United States*. Bureau of American Ethnology Bulletin 137. U.S. Government Printing Office, Washington, D.C.

Tennessee State Museum. 1985. *Art and Artisans of Prehistoric Middle Tennessee*. Tennessee State Museum, Nashville.

Thomas, Larissa A. 1996. A Study of Shell Beads and Their Social Context in the Mississippian Period: A Case from the Carolina Piedmont and Mountains. *Southeastern Archaeology* 15(1):29–46.

Thruston, Gates P. 1897. *The Antiquities of Tennessee and Adjacent States and the State of Aboriginal Society in the Scale of Civilization Represented by Them*. Robert Clarke Company, Cincinnati.

Trocolli, Ruth. 1993. Women as Chiefs in the Southeast: A Reexamination of the Data. Paper presented at the 50th annual meeting of the Southeastern Archaeological Conference, Raleigh, N.C.

Vansina, Jan. 1989. Deep-down Time: Political Tradition in Central Africa. *History in Africa* 16:341–62.

Waring, Antonio J. 1968. The Southern Cult and Muskhogean Ceremonial: General Considerations. In *The Waring Papers*, ed. Stephen Williams. Papers of the Peabody Museum of Archaeology and Ethnology 58:30–69. Harvard University, Cambridge, Mass.

Watson, Patty Jo, and Mary C. Kennedy. 1991. The Development of Horticulture in the Eastern Woodlands of North America: Women's Role. In *Engendering Archaeology: Women and Prehistory*, ed. J. M. Gero and M. W. Conkey, 255–75. Basil Blackwell, Oxford.

Willoughby, Charles C. 1932. Notes on the History and Symbolism of the Muskhogeans and the People of Etowah. In *Etowah Papers I: Exploration of the Etowah Site in Georgia*, ed. W. K. Moorehead, 7–67. Yale University Press, New Haven.

Witthoft, John. 1949. *Green Corn Ceremonialism in the Eastern Woodlands*. Occasional Contributions 13. University of Michigan Museum of Anthropology, Ann Arbor.

Wood, W. Raymond. 1990. Ethnohistory and Historical Method. In *Archaeological Method and Theory*, vol. 2, ed. M. B. Schiffer, 81–110. University of Arizona Press, Tuscon.

13

Tlingit Human Masks as Documents of Culture Change and Continuity

Barbara Brotherton

Naturalistic human masks were among the first items to be collected by early non-Native visitors to the Northwest Coast of North America beginning in the late 18th century. The collecting of masks by casual visitors, settlers, dealers, and ethnographers continued throughout the Contact period. Evidently, most of the Northwest Coast Native groups had well-established cultural traditions that fostered the use of carved wooden humanoid face masks and well-established art systems that distinguished tribal styles from one another. The styles of these masks were not static but were undergoing changes as a result of both internal and external factors. Despite the formidable problems posed by the absence of reliable documentation, there have been notable attempts to define Northwest Coast Native art systems and their origins and developments (S. Brown 1987, 1998; Carlson 1983a; Holm 1983; Sawyer 1984; R. Wright 1985). However tentative these efforts may be, they provide a matrix upon which to plot the general directions of conceptual and visual changes both spatially and chronologically. Using material culture of the northernmost Northwest Coast group, the Tlingit of southeast Alaska, this study is another attempt to build on that framework.

After considerable experience examining masks and other pieces in museum collections, it became apparent to me that one could discern characteristics that linked pieces together, that clearly (or sometimes not so clearly) distinguished them from one another, and that indicated the hands of individual artists. As an art historian, my main tactic was to discern these traits through visual acuity and analytic methods. Quantifying my perceptions and making sense of them culturally, however, was stymied by the vagaries of artifact collecting and often by poor documentation. In an effort to understand the factors that may have contributed to aesthetic change, I significantly broadened my approach to include data derived from ethnohistory, archaeology, ethnography, museum collection history, oral history, and the insights of living Native artists.

In this chapter I focus on a well-documented group of 125 Tlingit shamans' masks that were collected *in situ* from remote gravesites by amateur collector and U.S. naval lieutenant George Thornton Emmons. When Emmons collected the masks and other healing paraphernalia in the 1880s and 1890s, he obtained data from Tlingit consultants and kept the lots together rather than sell the artifacts individually, a more common practice at the time. Emmons was knowledgeable about the Tlingit, was driven by a desire to preserve "old time" Tlingit culture, and, as a naval officer, had access to maps and watercraft that allowed him to explore less accessible areas. He also befriended many Tlingit, who evidently helped him secure some of these grave-house items; they also provided him the names of the shamans' spirits represented by the masks, occasionally identified the clan of the shaman-owner, and explained some of the ritual uses of the masks (Emmons n.d.).

Despite the utility of Emmons's documentation, its reliability is somewhat compromised by his Anglo-Christian beliefs, his habit of "filling in" information in the absence of a consultant, and his lack of interest in artistry, style, aesthetics, or individual artists. In this study I draw upon Emmons's published and unpublished notes, supplementing them with other types of data. The goals are to analyze systematically Tlingit art conventions, identify the styles of individual unnamed carvers, propose a chronology of style development, and identify the ways in which the masks can shed light on cultural change and continuity. A rigorous stylistic analysis of material objects, in conjunction with the scrutiny of texts and collection data, can supplement, contradict, and expand on our existing knowledge of these masks. In tandem, texts and objects reveal wide-ranging ideas about Tlingit world view, cosmology, and aesthetics and the natural or imposed changes brought to bear on them. As such, I have come to see the masks as documents of culture change and continuity at a time of intense social upheaval. This sample of masks is particularly important because of the relatively reliable documentation associated with them and because they bridge the pre- and post-Contact eras when cultural changes were especially prevalent.

Tlingit Culture and History

The Tlingit of southeast Alaska occupy a spectacular landscape of islands and inlets punctuated by steep glaciated mountains. The area is rich in forest resources and harvestable plants. Food was collected seasonally, and its abundance allowed for freedom from subsistence activities during the winter months, the time of the major ceremonies. Mainland areas had large salmon runs where weirs and traps were set up, while the smaller islands and streams required villagers to move to summer camps to harvest salmon and other fish as well as intertidal foods like clams, cockles, and seaweed (Langdon 1993). The eggs of ducks, geese, and other birds were taken from cliff nests, while bears, mountain goats, and other land mammals were hunted in some areas. Long-established routes into the interior provided a conduit for the exchange of goods with their Athabascan neighbors.

Great permanent cedar-plank houses, some as large as forty by sixty feet, contained a large central hearth that was the focal point of daily life for the several related families who lived within. Carved house posts with the occupants' "totems" (also called crests) rose majestically at the four corners, proclaiming the greatness of the family's lineage. Other treasured objects (*at.óow* in the Tlingit language) might be visible, especially at potlatch time, such as carved screens, chests, feast dishes, hats, headdresses, staffs and woven robes, tunics and leggings (fig. 13.1). *At.óow* embodies two principal elements of Tlingit culture—ownership and reciprocity. Together these create balance. *At.óow* refers to both tangible (objects) and intangible (songs, names) properties that are owned by a clan and that reflect patterns of social structure.

The 15,000 Tlingit who inhabited many large and small villages at the time of contact (late 18th century) were divided into sixteen tribes, or *kwáan*. From south to north these were the Tongass, Sanya, Stikine, Henya, Klawak, Kuiu, Kake, Sumdum, Taku, Auk, Chilkat-Chilkoot, Hutsnuwu, Sitka, Hoonah, Dry Bay, and Yakutat (de Laguna 1990). Political cohesion was on the village level, but important ties were reckoned according to membership in matrilineal clans that may have spread among many villages. Clans belonged to two moieties or sides, Raven or Wolf (later called Eagle in some areas). As "opposites," clan members had important reciprocal social and ceremonial responsibilities. Marriages took place between Ravens and Wolves, artists provided ceremonial paraphernalia for their opposites, funerary rites were performed for each other, and

Fig. 13.1. John F. Pratt, photographer. Interior of the Klukwan Whale House, 1890s. Negative no. 3073. Special Collections Division, University of Washington Libraries, Seattle.

shamans could only heal those of the opposite side. Chiefs who controlled clan property, like houses, fishing streams, ceremonial paraphernalia, songs, dances, stories, and other tangible and intangible resources, headed clans. Tlingit society was highly stratified, with a small group of nobles, larger groups of commoners, and an enslaved class at the bottom of the hierarchy.

The principal ceremonial institution, the potlatch, was staged by related clan members to care for the dead, honor a deceased person with the raising of a commemorative pole, observe the naming of children, celebrate a marriage, and in order to neutralize shameful situations. It was also the arena for demonstrations staged by the shaman, usually a male, dressed in his special regalia to assure the village of their spirit powers and to display special pieces of *at.óow*. The potlatch, and its attendant arts, served to acknowledge publicly the origins and histories of the high-ranking families, to recount the great deeds of illustrious ancestors, and to emphasize the generosity of the host in feasting and gift giving. Many carved, painted, and woven items were displayed bearing images of the clan crests or of supernatural animals, humans, and other spirit beings who bestowed privileges on long-ago ancestors through supernatural encounters. Art was an important and very visible element of Tlingit life, from the clan-owned monumental totem poles to shamans' masks. Art production was (and still is) clearly pivotal to the aims of potlatch display, yet the role of the artist in traditional Tlingit society is not well understood. Based on this study, I put forward some interpretations regarding this in later sections of the chapter.

Tlingit ideals of good health, well-being, and positive community relations were nurtured by the practice of the shaman (ixt), usually a man, with the gift of healing and prophecy (Dauenhauer and Dauenhauer 1990). Supernatural forces were believed to be involved in many Tlingit life events, and health and disease were seen to be in direct relationship to human-spirit connections. The antisocial use of power by witches was especially feared, and the shaman was called on to combat the effects of bewitchment. Thus, the shamans' specialized powers to call upon helping spirits (yek) were the key to spiritual balance and social goodwill. Through the use of helping spirits, the doctor could restore health and good luck, predict significant events, assure successes in hunting and warfare, and offer solutions to problems outside of human control. Shamans' yek were derived from spirits who inhabited the land, air, and sea, and represented supernatural animals, natural phenomena, and human ghosts (Veniaminov 1984). These spirit allies were acquired on the shaman's first and subsequent visionary quests and were skillfully depicted by artists on all types of curing accessories that made up the shaman's "kit," including masks, headdresses, rattles, charms, wands, and other implements. A shaman's life-long physical, mental, and spiritual discipline allowed the spirits to overtake him during a trance (loss of consciousness) and work through him.

Shamanism was well developed among the Tlingit, and the wearing of masks and use of extensive paraphernalia set the Tlingit shaman apart from other Northwest Coast Native shamans. The Tlingit shaman occupied a position of considerable authority and autonomy. He was, in the sacred realm, what the chief was in the secular sphere, and could himself become a house head (hitsati) or even a chief. The "calling" to become a shaman was usually in accordance with culturally agreed-upon principles of inheritance. That is, one or more deceased shamans would visit a nephew, sometimes at the funerary feast. The novice would undergo a vigil in the woods accompanied by assistants, then return to the community to demonstrate his newly acquired powers. From this time on, the shaman would regularly stage ceremonies to ensure community well-being and display his powers at feasts and potlatches. The masks examined in this study were used in both the semiprivate setting of a healing séance and the public sphere of the potlatch. The shaman's objects enhanced his ritual performances and gave physical form to the unseen forces at his command, thus bringing the audience into the drama. The art forms also served as a conduit to the spirit world and provided a focus for the awesome energy generated through these contacts. The implements of his "kit" were the tools of his trade and underscored the view that healing was a profession (Wardwell 1996). In addition to being spiritually potent, many of the objects are of the highest aesthetic quality; some were certainly made by the best artists available.

Ethnographic sources indicate that masks were perhaps the most important of the shamans' implements (Emmons 1991). Spirit images depicted on the masks called up the power under the doctor's control. The stronger his powers, the more *yek* at his command, and the more masks he displayed. Extreme illness, caused by soul loss or witchcraft, might require the donning of several masks in succession to increase the efficacy of the cure (Jonaitis 1986). Eight or more masks were ideal. Many are not bored through to allow the shaman to see because his "vision" came from an intangible source. The masks and accompanying costume created the outward appearance of a particular spirit as the shaman subsumed his own identity; his songs, language, and movements during trances were likewise those of the spirit (fig. 13.2). Together the ensemble worked to make visible the invisible. Imbued with the presence of powerful spirits, the shamans' items were not touched by the laity, and they were placed in his grave house away from the village upon his death. Thousands of shamans' items were collected in the late 19th century, when they no longer had a place in Tlingit life. They were stolen directly from the graves or purchased from Christianized relatives or from former shamans themselves.

Contact and Its Aftermath

Throughout the 18th century, the Russians (1741), Spanish (1775, 1791), French (1796), English (1793), and Americans (1780s) came into contact with the Tlingit. However, there were no non-Native settlements in Tlingit

Fig. 13.2. Edward DeGroff, photographer. Medicine man, shaman wearing mask, 1889. Negative no. NA 2517. Special Collections Division, University of Washington Libraries, Seattle.

territory until the early 19th century. The establishment of the commercial Russian-American Company and the Russian Orthodox Church near Tlingit villages brought a new language, new religion, and new trade opportunities, as well as new concepts of health and education. Tlingit participation in the Russian fur trade did not compromise local Native autonomy and political independence (Black 1988). Likewise, the Orthodox Church permitted aspects of Native life to exist side-by-side with missionary activities, which did not begin in earnest until the 1840s. Conversion to Christianity was slow (see de Laguna 1990; Kan 1988). Priests complained that even some Christianized Tlingit still retained beliefs in shamanism, and from other sources it is known that some shamans practiced into the 1930s (Dauenhauer and Dauenhauer 1990).

The greatest changes resulted from the establishment of mission churches and non-Native communities coupled with disease epidemics. Widespread deaths during smallpox epidemics challenged beliefs in Native healers. After the epidemics of 1836–39, in which nearly half the populations of some villages died, there was a massive increase in conversions. The bishop of Alaska, Ivan Veniaminov, described how the ineffectiveness of the shamans in preventing deaths and the demonstrated immunity of the Russians and Tlingits who had been vaccinated helped to attract new converts. The severity of the devastation and widespread death was unlike anything the Tlingit had ever seen and undermined beliefs in the power of the shaman. The "spirits" of the Church, perhaps, were seen as more powerful. In efforts to retain their stature, some shamans incorporated symbols of power taken from the Church, like crucifixes and holy water, or adopted "Russian spirits" as helpers (Kan 1991). Father Veniaminov was perceptive in noting that the deaths of the Tlingit elders, those most vulnerable to the disease, were instrumental in establishing a new religious order. Prior to the epidemics, he found the Tlingits reluctant to abandon traditional beliefs. The onset of epidemics coupled with the hope offered by the Christian Church primed the atmosphere for acceptance of ideas about health and healing outside traditional beliefs, even if it did not mean an end to shamanism.

The withdrawal of Russian officials after 1867 left the Russian church without financial support. An increase in new members in the mid-1880s was largely the result of the more tolerant practices of the Russian church over those of the Presbyterians and other Protestant sects that took strong stands against traditional beliefs. Kan (1991) has effectively argued that the Orthodox Church supported "Native progress" but did not insist on the kind of "Americanization" demanded by Protestantism. For this and other reasons, many elders and traditionalists eventually gravitated to the Russian Church. Today, in many parts of the former Russian America, the Orthodox Church is seen as a "Native institution" (Black 1988).

The most far-reaching effects of non-Native contact became apparent after the purchase of Alaska by the United States in 1867, when settlers, entrepreneurs, and missionaries came to establish permanent settlements. New economic enterprises—businesses like fish salting and canning, mining, and logging—were run by Caucasians using Native labor, bringing incentives for wage labor and the consumption of trade goods. Missionaries like Presbyterian minister Sheldon Jackson at Sitka promoted radical lifestyle changes that encouraged a Protestant work ethic and renunciation of Native customs, especially potlatching and shamanism (Wyatt 1984).

Because Alaska had no civil government for some years after the purchase, the region was under the jurisdiction of the U.S. Army and later the Navy. Soldiers were posted at several forts and aboard Navy ships as a kind of transitional peacekeeping force. (Emmons was commissioned to Sitka in 1882 aboard the *Adams*.) The prospectors, adventurers, and entrepreneurs who flooded into Alaska mistreated the Indians and provoked conflicts that the Navy was forced to adjudicate. With the establishment of commercial fishing, canneries, and mines in the period of the 1870s through the 1890s, Natives and Caucasians were forced into greater contact; and by the end of the century, traditional village life had been severely impacted. Subsistence practices gave way to participation in a cash economy, remote villages were abandoned for prosperous towns, and for many the old religious practices were absorbed by Christian beliefs.

From the literature of missionaries, travelers, military officials, and anthropologists from the 1880–1910 period (e.g., Krause 1956; Scidmore 1893; Seton-Karr 1887; J. Wright 1883), it is clear that the war waged against the shamans by missionaries and government officials was relentless but not entirely successful. The military and the government intervened at the behest of missionaries who hoped to dislodge beliefs in shamanism. They attempted to rescue "innocent" witches who had been accused by the shamans and to expel shamans from their communities. Shamans were publicly humiliated by cutting their hair (a source of power); they were exposed as frauds, subjected to cruel treatment, and even imprisoned (Wyatt 1984). But Tlingits continued to patronize them. It is likely that even some Christianized Tlingits retained older beliefs about illness and healing, allowing the old and the new to coexist on some levels. Unfortunately, Native accounts of their feelings about shamanism were not collected at the time of the greatest change, and when anthropologist Frederica de Laguna asked her consultants about shamanism in the late 1940s, many were reluctant, even fearful, to discuss the subject. In their interpretations of times past, some contemporary Tlingit elders did not see traditional shamans' practices as inferior to Christian ideas but rather as having no place in their current lives (Kan 1991).

Collecting Shamanic Art

Shamans' paraphernalia was collected in the 1880s, but of more immediate appeal to collectors and ethnologists were the spectacular carved totem poles, house posts, and screens, as well as the masks, headdresses, clothing, and other esteemed items that were displayed at potlatches (Cole 1985). These were objects that ethnologists most usually identified with traditional Tlingit culture. The most prolific collector of Tlingit material was George Emmons while he was stationed in Sitka in the 1880s. He continued to be a frequent visitor to Alaska long after his retirement in 1899, and was infamous for providing fine collections to many Canadian and American museums. Between 1882 and 1893, Emmons collected about thirty shamans' kits of healing paraphernalia from the relatives of deceased shamans or directly from the shamans' grave houses, and he sold them to museums in their original lots. Emmons's correspondence regarding his collection of the kits is sometimes vague but suggests that he both acquired kits from heirs and helped himself. Some relatives no doubt had become Christianized and shunned such objects or no longer wanted responsibility for the upkeep of the grave house. The kits contained as few as five objects and as many as forty-five, and included masks, headdresses, clothing, charms, rattles, wands, and other implements. The kits are now in the collections of the American Museum of Natural History in New York, the Field Museum of Natural History in Chicago, and the Thomas Burke Memorial Washington State Museum in Seattle. Emmons aided in the collecting of an additional kit in 1886, which is now in the Princeton Art Museum in Princeton, New Jersey. Emmons's friendly relations with the Tlingit gave him an advantage in his collecting pursuits. With the collecting of shamans' pieces he recognized a source of artifacts that was not yet tapped.

The more than 300 masks and other objects from the shamans' kits provide an important and unique sample. Emmons educated himself about Tlingit culture and was careful to document the region of the grave (or place of purchase), the name and clan affiliation of the shaman if known, and the approximate date of each shaman's death. In addition, he queried relatives and other knowledgeable people about the identities of the spirits represented on the objects and recorded other anecdotal data about the shaman or the pieces. Due to his considerable knowledge about shamanism, he recognized the value the objects had as ensembles, and for the most part he sold the kits intact. Thus, the Emmons collections and associated documentation form a substantial foundation for scholarly analysis. However, like other collectors of his time, he was not interested in artistry, style, or individual artists. And although Emmons was sensitive to Native customs by the standards of his day, he engaged in the deplorable activity of grave robbing. His own religious conservatism, and the belief that adherence to the "superstitions" associated with shamanism prevented Tlingit people from prospering, evidently provided justification for him to empty grave houses.

Tlingit Art and Artists: Meaning and Style

One of the most difficult tasks of the researcher is to connect the thin threads provided by archaeological data, through the enormous void of several centuries, to the ethnographic art of the modern era. If art is a means of communication, and style comprises those visible attributes that occur with rigorous unity over time and space, then each art object forms a piece of the puzzle. Careful observation of formal principles in tandem with ethnographic analogy (Carlson 1983a, b) and the effective use of ethnographic data are needed to interpret the symbolic meanings of ancient objects. Each new study is an attempt to push such inquiry further, even if only general directions can be sensed.

Systematic archaeological investigations on the Northwest Coast were limited until the 1960s due to lack of prominent surface evidence, the difficulty of accessing remote locations, and the wet environment. Based on the archaeological results available to him in the early 1980s, Carlson (1983b) offered a chronology of coastal cultural development: the Early Period, spanning the years 12,000–5,500 B.P.; the Middle Period, in the years 5,500–1,500 B.P.; and the Late Period, from 1,500 B.P. to Contact. The late Middle Period is most significant for art production; it is then that recognizable cultural patterns emerge, including craft specialization and the making of wealth- and status-oriented objects. The waterlogged Lachane site (2,500–1,700 B.P.) on the central British Columbia coast produced boxes, bowls, and baskets of perishable materials, some showing surface decoration, attesting to the presence of extensive woodworking and other crafts at this early date (MacDonald 1983). Bone combs, pendants, and clubs from the same period display incised designs applied over the sculptural forms (fig. 13.3). This rudimentary design system is surely the progenitor of the positive–negative-based graphic design associated with historic-era art. This mode of carving shows an artistic impulse to differentiate background, or "negative" areas, from "positive," image-producing forms. Using these artifacts, Steven Brown (1998) has convinc-

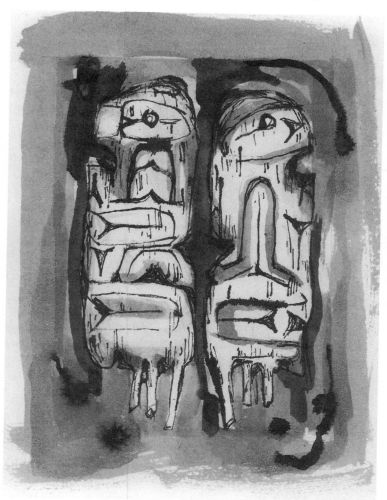

Fig. 13.3. Bone comb (obverse and reverse), ca. A.D. 800. Ink wash and pen drawing by Jill L. Jepsen. Gb To 34-1805. Canadian Museum of Civilization, Hull, Quebec.

ingly sketched out a probable development of the two-dimensional incised-design system from the late Middle Period to its elaborate refinement seen at the time of Contact. Through continual experimentation by artists working throughout the coastal area, several distinctive regional variations emerged, like the "Old Tlingit Style," with its massive surface level elements and small, incised negative elements. This and other styles were not static but continued to evolve after contact toward thinner,

Fig. 13.4. Tlingit chest, early 19th century. American Museum of Natural History E987. Photograph by Barbara Brotherton. Courtesy Department of Library Services, American Museum of Natural History, New York, N.Y.

"positive" form elements (called formlines), the expansion of incised "negative" shapes to facilitate the flow between design areas, and the development of secondary designs (fig. 13.4).

The same impulse, to build and refine simple core elements, is also visible in three-dimensional sculptural forms. Objects found in early sites share stylistic affinities with historic Tlingit art. For example, the bone comb of a wolf in profile depicted in figure 13.5 exhibits simple, compact arrangement in a squat ("hocker") position. There is an economy of carving to show limbs, a prominent ovoid eye, teeth, tongue, and skeletalized ribs. Conventions to indicate specific clan animal totems by emphasizing certain features are important aspects of historic art as well. The rudimentary tools used, such as stone adzes and knives made from animal teeth, account for the paucity of details and shallowness of the relief carving. After contact, when metal became available to fashion better tools, artists responded by carving masks, headdresses, and totem poles with a greater depth and volume, as is seen in mid 19th-century examples. A decidedly anthropomorphic treatment of many animal-crest creatures dating from the historic era is probably linked to mythology in which supernatural animals and humans have shared origins and clan connections and similar social structures. Through public display of art that symbolizes mythic themes, humans acknowledge those connections and boundaries. The shaman moves across such boundaries, however, by assuming the guise of his helping spirits. As Tlingit culture evolved there may have been a need to make distinctions between crest art, which is conventionalized and iconic, and shaman's art, which is naturalistic and narrative.

What do early artifacts tell us about Tlingit shamanism and masking traditions, if anything? By ca. 500 B.C. shared cognitive modes and belief systems were sufficiently developed to be cohesively expressed in images that were physical symbols of clan identity and conduits by which to control spirit forces (MacDonald 1983). Bone pendants, combs, decorated clubs, and slate mirrors found in Prince Rupert Harbour (500 B.C.–A.D. 500) resemble items associated with shamanic ritualism in the historic period. Petroglyphs and pictographs found throughout the Northwest Coast display imagery associated with spirit power, such as humanoid beings with halos, skeletalized anatomies, and what appears to be ceremonial regalia. Two spectacular stone masks, now known to be a pair and clearly made by the same artist (see Duff 1975:188), were found separately in northern British Columbia around 1879 (in Tsimshian territory). The masks were constructed so as to allow the "unsighted" one (without bored eyes) to fit over the "sighted" one (having bored eye holes). Holm (1984) has noted the similarity between the style of the stone masks and early 19th-century Tlingit wood masks, including the rounded facial contours, open eye socket, broad slightly arching brows, thick band-like lips, and carefully delineated ears. It is tempting to speculate that these masks are ancient, that similar masks of wood were being made in this proto-Tlingit style, and for reasons unknown (perhaps this artist was much sought after), the masks ended up outside the Tlingit region.

Unfortunately, archaeology in Alaska has not produced enough specimens to clearly demonstrate regional connections, but it can be surmised that the northern Northwest Coast had regional commonalties. If one could imagine an evolution from the earliest evidence of the art to the sophisticated styles apparent at the time of contact, one might see slow but purposeful changes brought about by cultural and technological developments and by the artists' own innovations (Brown 1998). Some profound alterations did occur as a result of contact, when individual artists were experimenting with new ideas, but these, too, were built up from core

Fig. 13.5. Bone comb, ca. A.D. 800. Ink wash and pen drawing by Jill L. Jepsen. Gb To 36-149. Canadian Museum of Civilization, Hull, Quebec.

attributes that are apparent in the earliest styles. As Northwest Coast peoples continued to define themselves, shared core cognitive and stylistic modes were regionally refined and specified.

What little is known about the role of the artist in Tlingit society comes from the fragmentary archaeological record and sparse ethnographic accounts. As mentioned above, craft specialization evident well before contact suggests that a skilled profession of artists existed and that experimentation with woodworking tool types continued to improve and expand two- and three-dimensional styles. Beaver-tooth and shell knives, as well as stone splitting and planing adzes, were replaced by iron blades as soon as non-Natives provided ready access to these goods through trade and (probably even before contact) via scavenged metal from wrecked ships of Asian origin. Certain regulations were applied to art production: the artistic profession was inherited, art production was gender specified (for example, men were the carvers, women were the weavers), instruction was by an artist of one's own clan, artists made works on commission by their clan "opposites," and they negotiated for remuneration. It is likely that most artists were commissioned to make a variety of objects, and evidently they could achieve reputations outside their own village or tribal group. Continued scholarship will expand our understanding of the artists' role within society as well as identify individual contributions to Tlingit art and style.

A Chronology for Tlingit Art

Based on what information is at hand, is it possible to propose a chronology of Tlingit art using the masks in this study? As Steven Brown (1998) has proposed from his extensive analyses of Northwest Coast styles, the definition of broad temporal categories can serve as an anchor from which to make more exacting temporal attributions. Here I put forward a similar chronology based on analysis of the masks. The three time periods are framed by "benchmark" dates (the end of the maritime fur trade, the transfer of Alaska from Russian to American rule, the last years of potlatching, and so forth). Transitions from one historic (or artistic) era to another are never absolute but are influenced by the complexities of inward and outward growth. A raw chronology cannot assess these complex interfaces, but it can provide a structure from which to gauge stylistic changes.

The Transitional Period (ca. 1750–1820) spans the last years before contact and encompasses the first wave of European presence associated with the maritime fur trade, ending at the shift to land-based trade. If one could paint a broad-brush characterization of this period, traditional means of training artists were adhered to, and the carvers of the naturalistic masks discussed in this chapter were working within well-established aesthetic traditions. Toward the end of this period, art for potlatching and shamanism began a florescence that included more items being produced, the use of trade materials for decorative elements, and style experimentation made possible by the use of metal-bladed tools. One of the most significant features of the period is that Native artists learned that the outsiders were interested in their art.

The Early Historic Period (from about 1820 to the 1860s) is the era of the most accelerated changes to Tlingit folkways. As indicated previously, changes were introduced by Russian and European trading interests, widespread Tlingit participation in a cash economy, the establishment of Orthodox Church missions, and the devastating epidemics that wiped out between 10 and 80 percent of village populations. With the incentive of newfound wealth in cash and trade goods, potlatching was intensified, as was the production of ceremonial items. Artists were called upon to respond, and they did by producing more items, many displaying a greater sculptural boldness and two-dimensional refinement. Ceremonial florescence may have produced a freer arena in which the artist worked, perhaps with challenges to time-honored artistic styles and approaches and a certain premium placed on innovation and uniqueness. Since virtually nothing is known about individual artists of this time, one can only guess that there may have been a greater demand for the "master carvers" and that some artists were building impressive careers. There are indications that some carvers' commissions did not come only from their own village or geographic region. Finally, the seeds of "tourist art" began germinating during this time, and artists responded by incorporating motifs derived from Caucasian culture and by developing new items designed specifically for sale.

The Late Historic Period (from the late 1860s to 1910) witnessed much more intensified Caucasian-Native contact, which ultimately led to radical cultural changes for the Tlingit. The period embraced the end of Russian domination of Alaska, the large-scale establishment of permanent settlements, the rise of Protestant missions, and the establishment of entrepreneurial industries by outsiders. The reservation system was not instituted in Alaska because of the need for a Native labor force to work the canneries, logging camps, and mines. This in turn minimized segregation between the indigenous people and the newcomers (Wyatt 1984). Potlatching, which required days, weeks, or even months of festivities, was at odds with the efforts of the missionaries to convert and educate and with the needs of businessmen to maintain a stable workforce. Although potlatching was never outlawed in the United States, as it was in Canada (1884), it came under severe attack. Some traditional activities—trading, subsistence hunting and fishing, and some types of art production—were absorbed into the new lifestyle, but every effort was made to eradicate those cultural elements most pivotal to the Tlingit belief systems, namely, shamanism and potlatching. Since art production was based on commissions, these must have declined during this time, even though some conspicuous potlatching continued into the early 20th century. I believe that the traditional master-apprentice arrangement must have been severely compromised as well. As epidemic diseases reduced populations, the usual means of transmitting hereditary positions became destabilized, including those of the chief, the artist, and the shaman. Although artists continued to work within existing traditions—perhaps substituting years of instruction with copying objects at hand—it was sometimes without an understanding of design principles and conventions. Exactly when the "breakdown" occurred is difficult to pinpoint. However, mask samples datable to this period indicate that many artists were working under these conditions. Some skilled artists (and we know a few of their names) continued to produce coveted crest regalia as well as shamans' implements alongside their less tutored counterparts. This is evident in pieces commissioned, acquired, and documented by collectors, tourists, and anthropologists.

New choices and challenges for artists appeared with the advent of tourism, which created an additional market for art production. Certainly, the older, more traditionally trained artists participated, but the avenue was open to amateurs as well, in part because of the less discriminating taste of the casual tourist. The steamboats that called at ports in southeast Alaska were met by Natives eager to provide portable, inexpensive curios like miniature totem poles, baskets woven into European forms like teacups and cylindrical bottles, and samples of work in beads, silver, and wood, including masks. Fine-quality carving continued even when the objects were made expressly for foreign consumption because of the personal standards insisted upon by individual artists. For example, Charles Edensaw, a Haida master carver working in the mid-19th century, used the tourist market as an opportunity to recapitulate culturally meaningful images at a time of cultural stress.

More restrictions may have been placed on the reproduction of shamans' paraphernalia for sale than on the reproduction of crest art such as ceremonial masks, pipes, and feast dishes made for sale. Portrait masks of the type used in social ceremonies to honor clan ancestors were made by northern Northwest Coast carvers for the tourist market, but masks derived from shamans' practices were not. Apparently, some artists carved small-scale images meant to depict shamans in trance or death poses, but this practice was limited. Although shamanic iconography appealed to Caucasian collectors, there must have been enough respect for the power and efficacy of this imagery even at this late date to curtail such production.

As we can see, artists negotiated the new terrain of art production in a variety of ways. I see the Late Historic Period as one where clearly drawn aesthetic boundaries were challenged in creative ways, but ultimately in ways that were mediated by outside factors. The new market nurtured new ways of thinking about and practicing art, and these disrupted the relationship between image and meaning, moved away from the direct commission arrangement, and perhaps did not require the same kind of cultural scrutiny and approval. A freer arena in which to create and sell art developed, giving way to an expansion of art types and variations in the adherence to traditional styles and standards of quality.

Research Methods and Sample

Because George Emmons provided important baseline information on the 125 masks he collected (including provenience, dates, function, and identification of subjects and motifs), his notes provide a valuable data set from which to explore previously unexamined questions concerning artists, artistry, style, and stylistic change. To balance the data and minimize the idiosyncrasies that might be present in the collection of a single individual, I also sought out non-kit shamans' masks that had acceptable documentation, bringing the study sample to 150 masks. I constructed a stylistic checklist in order to develop an artistic profile of each mask. The checklist included, for example, the physical attributes of the masks (such as shape, size, sculptural volume), particular treatments of facial features, and the presence of painted or carved details. The overall approach to the rendering of a human or animal visage as naturalistic, semi-naturalistic, or stylized, was also noted. Criteria pertaining to craftsmanship were analyzed, particularly carving quality, degree of finish, and the artist's knowledge of two- and three-dimensional design. Because the identification of individual styles is not a precise science, such a study requires careful examination, recording of data, and extensive post-examination analysis. In every possible case I compared pieces firsthand while conducting research in the museums. Since this was not always possible, I photographed each mask from frontal, profile, and three-quarters views for later comparison with masks not in the same physical location.

After arriving at preliminary groupings, I sought the opinions of several Tlingit carvers, and they provided invaluable information. For instance, when I mentioned how difficult it was to isolate an artist's traits with certainty, they suggested that an artist might slightly deviate from a signature feature in order to satisfy a patron or to indicate an unusual creature, or simply in the spirit of experimentation. I was encouraged to look at the proportional relationships between facial features (e.g., between the orb of the eye and the brow, between the nose and cheek, between the nose and lips, and between the lips and chin), and the relative depth of the carving. One artist who carves masks indicated that these are likely places where the carver expresses an individual aesthetic. In general, the modern carvers were less concerned with aesthetic "quality" and seemed most interested in the visual impact and expressive content of the older pieces and what they might learn from them.

Stylistic analysis of the masks made it clear that the unique handling of elements indicated the hands of particular artists. I then isolated what I believed to be the works of thirteen artists. Five of these carved naturalistic, human-like masks ($n = 33$) and eight carved in a semi-naturalistic to stylized manner ($n = 74$).

Naturalistic Masks in the Sample: An Overview

"Naturalism," a relative term, is best understood by comparison. The two examples in figures 13.6 and 13.7 both use the human countenance as a model for the carved representation. What makes one "naturalistic" and one "stylized" is the degree of adherence to the prototype or model, assuming that the model is the human face. The naturalistic approach attempts to capture an identifiable likeness of a person but allows the artist to add particular nuances for the sake of expressiveness, symbolic meaning, or artistic style. While the stylized work is also shaped by the guiding element of "humanness," the artist has moved further away from the prototype and toward greater generalization. With extremely naturalistic renderings, the identification of individual artists is more difficult than it is for those artists who impart a distinctive stylishness. The type of spirit being depicted would likely affect the artist's approach. This is where reliable documentation is indispensable.

What generalizations can be made from the analysis of the naturalistic masks? First, the key element that distinguishes them is the sensitive, realistic, almost portrait-like approach to the human face. In general, the carving is shallow and spare. Remnants of natural pigments could be seen on some, most usually in the details of brow and inner orb painted in black, and nostrils and lips painted with red, with several exhibiting blue overall surface painting. Some had simple designs or formline designs that represented clan markings painted in black, blue, and red. I determined that five individual artists carved the thirty-three naturalistic masks found in the kits of twelve shamans. All but three of the kits belonged to Yakutat–Dry Bay shamans, accounting for twenty-five of the thirty-three masks. Evidently, some of these artists obtained commissions from outside this region and may have had reputations that crossed tribal boundaries. Emmons (in the 1880s) and de Laguna (in the 1940s) obtained information on some shamans, including Qadjuse from Dry Bay (Xatka?ayi Raven clan), who practiced in the mid-19th century; Setan, from Dry Bay (Lukwax?adi Raven clan), who practiced in the 1860s; and Gutcda, also from Dry Bay (Lukwax?adi Raven clan), who died in the late 1870s or

Fig. 13.6. Carver of the Thin Brows, Tlingit mask of a younger woman. American Museum of Natural History E1629. Photograph by Barbara Brotherton. Courtesy Department of Library Services, American Museum of Natural History, New York, N.Y.

Fig. 13.7. Carver of the Large Eye and Broad Brows, Tlingit mask of a younger woman who lives in the woods. American Museum of Natural History E1601. Photograph by Barbara Brotherton. Courtesy Department of Library Services, American Museum of Natural History, New York, N.Y.

early 1880s. Although I propose that the most naturalistic masks date from the 1750–1820 period, their presence in later 19th-century shamans' kits follows a tradition of passing down important ritual paraphernalia to an heir. Many kits contained masks that varied in date of manufacture; many included both naturalistic and stylized human masks.

I have tentatively named the five naturalistic mask carvers according to their signature characteristics: Carver of the Portrait Faces, Carver of the Crescent Eyes, Carver of the Thin Brows, Carver of the Rimmed Eyelids, and Carver of the Rounded Arched Brows. Hopefully, we will discover their true names one day. Even though the artists likely used bone tools or rudimentary metal blades, the high technical quality and expressive realism of their work indicates that this was an established style that was practiced by highly skilled carvers from Yakutat–Dry Bay area who may have specialized in this type of mask. Similarities in the pieces' formal approaches suggests that the carvers may be linked through training, apprenticeship, collaboration, or geographic location.

Let's turn to the masks and their carvers. The Carver of the Portrait Faces exhibits the greatest degree of naturalism (see fig. 13.8). A strong sense of realism can be seen in the shape and contour of the face, and in the proportions and rendering of features. He shows an effort to depict the varying fleshiness and skeletal structure of cheeks, eyes, and nose. The arching upper edge of the socket clearly suggests bone structure beneath the brow. There is a weightiness about the lid that surrounds an oval eye, expressive of old age or impending death.

The style of the Carver of the Crescent Eyes (fig. 13.9) is closely related to that of Carver of the Portrait Faces, and the two may have worked together in the same village around Dry Bay. Several of his maskettes (small masks) are damaged, but the naturalistic contour of the broad face can be made out. One is struck by the delicate play of convex and concave areas about the eye, while the eye itself is crescent-shaped, simulating the ebbing of life energy at death. The short nose has a rounded tip, and there are ridges on either side of the nose where it merges with fore cheek. This artist preferred a long space between nose and mouth.

Another artist linked in style to Carver of the Portrait Faces is Carver of the Thin Brows (see fig. 13.6). Commonalties can be seen in the overriding naturalism, the simplification of carved and painted forms, and the sensitive articulation of features. Distinctions show up in the brows, which tend to be thin, highly arched on the underside and pointed on top. A thin incised line borders the brows, the eye socket is wide, and the orb is long on the upper side, creating open space between brows and eyes. The distinctive eye is a narrow oval, which is elongated side to side and widely spaced.

The Carver of the Rimmed Eyelids makes use of a square ridge above the center of the upper lip and between the nose, a feature also seen in masks by "Portrait Faces" and "Thin Brows" (fig. 13.10). The brows are rounded, of medium width, and edged by an incised line. The eye is deeply set at the bottom. Heavily rimmed eyelids gave this particular artist his moniker. The planes of the face are angular with a straight-sided head and a squarish jaw, but the chin is rounded. Angularity also defines the lower cheek and mouth area, and the lips are thick.

A fine example by Carver of the Rounded Arched Brows can be seen in

Fig. 13.8. Carver of the Portrait Faces, Tlingit mask of the spirit of a dead man. American Museum of Natural History E414. Photograph by Barbara Brotherton. Courtesy Department of Library Services, American Museum of Natural History, New York, N.Y.

figure 13.11. The overall expression of the forms is round and flowing; the forehead is rounded, the eye is open and unconstricted at the corners, and the brows arch strongly on the under and upper sides. The under brow is an arching ridge that forms a curving arc from the bridge of the nose to the outer eye, where it blends smoothly with the cheek. The face is broad across the cheek plane, and an aquiline nose with down-turned tip complements the fullness of the face. The nostril is not as flaring as others, and the chin comes to a point.

In summary, the high artistic and technical quality of the naturalistic

Fig. 13.9. Carver of the Crescent Eyes, Tlingit maskette of a dying man. American Museum of Natural History E1936. Photograph by Barbara Brotherton. Courtesy Department of Library Services, American Museum of Natural History, New York, N.Y.

masks indicates that this mode of working was strongly established and was practiced by master carvers, many of whom, no doubt, were influenced by one another. Perhaps the masks referred to particular, known individuals. Were some of them actual portraits of deceased matriarchs, esteemed warriors, and powerful shamans who had been visited by the shaman during his vigils and from whom he drew his healing powers? Interestingly, the artists whom I asked about this thought that the expression of "humanity" was more important than an exacting portrait, but that it was possible that some masks were meant to be individual likenesses. It may be that the naturalistic mode, with its emphasis on particulars, was more suited to the shaman's pantheon of spirits, while a more stylized mode made a better fit within a conventionalized iconography of clan totems. Each approach was important to the evolution of Tlingit artistic expression. What seems clear is that the extreme naturalism present in shamans' art gave way to the stylized mode after contact, perhaps influenced by the florescence of crest art. After the mid-19th century, as art systems began to disintegrate, some artists who were less tutored in the techniques and styles of traditional art made less skillful attempts at depicting human spirits.

Fig. 13.10. Carver of the Rimmed Eyelids, Tlingit mask of an older woman. American Museum of Natural History E1626. Photograph by Barbara Brotherton. Courtesy Department of Library Services, American Museum of Natural History, New York, N.Y.

Fig. 13.11. Carver of the Rounded Arched Brows, Tlingit mask of the spirit of a Tlingit. American Museum of Natural History E412. Photograph by Barbara Brotherton. Courtesy Department of Library Services, American Museum of Natural History, New York, N.Y.

Stylized Masks in the Sample: An Overview

Of the eight stylized mask carvers, two were identified as having semi-naturalistic approaches (Carver of the Chilkat Kit and Carver of the Princeton Kit). Six exhibit a decidedly stylized mode in the imaging of human, animal, and spirit figures (Carver of the Auk Kit, Carver of the Cheek Ridge, Carver of the Large Eyes and Broad Brows, Carver of the Yakutat Kit, Carver of the Pinched Eye Corners, Carver of the Burke Kit). The first two mask carvers were skilled artists who, it seems, were pushing the naturalistic style toward a synthesis of exactitude and stylishness, while the other six made use of a generalized and stylized mode, some with greater skill than others. Perhaps this style followed a course whose seeds had been planted in pre-Contact clan-oriented art, and was intensified by responses to external changes. The works of the artists discussed below most certainly contributed to the ascendancy of the stylized mode of representation.

The Carver of the Chilkat Kit utilized a combination of boldly sculptural facial forms with delicate incising and painting on their surfaces (fig. 13.12). The entire surface is painted with well-executed formline designs in black and red as a display of ceremonial facial markings. The eye is particularly distinctive in its broad, open socket with a long space between

Fig. 13.12. Carver of the Chilkat Kit, Tlingit mask of an old woman. American Museum of Natural History 19/851. Photograph by Barbara Brotherton. Courtesy Department of Library Services, American Museum of Natural History, New York, N.Y.

brow and lid. The large eyes have a carved eyelid line and a unique fold above the upper eye. The artist was clearly in command of his craft and able to infuse variation and expressiveness to these spirit faces. Emmons identified these masks as possibly carved by a Tsimshian artist from Port Simpson, British Columbia. One can see some affinities to Tsimshian humanoid masks, such as the contours of the face that give the impression of skin stretched taut over bone structure. However, the delicacy of features, shallow incising of elements, and the overall economical treatment of forms have commonalties with naturalistic Tlingit masks. This unknown carver had ties to pre-Contact traditions but was also developing a more exuberant, plastic approach. I speculate that a plausible time frame for this artist's career was about 1800 to 1820.

To the Carver of the Princeton Kit I have tentatively attributed four masks now in the Princeton Art Museum, as well as four others (fig. 13.13). Emmons aided in the collection of this kit (taking for himself the four masks not in Princeton) when he ferried a group from the *New York Times*–Princeton Expedition to Yakutat in 1886. This group observed a healing séance by a blind shaman and evidently discovered a shaman's grave in a remote area, probably with Emmons's help (Seton-Karr 1887). The masks depict animal and human spirits and are well constructed, proportioned, and executed. The artist displays elongated oval heads, brows that are rather wide and uniform in thickness, and bulging eye forms. Sheet copper of the type exchanged with European visitors, and considered by the Tlingit to be very valuable, was applied to brows, eyelids, and mouths. The masks depicting animal spirits (like the humanoid shark illustrated here) have an uncanny amalgam of human and animal characteristics and display a compelling blend of both naturalism and stylization, leading me to believe that this artist lived much earlier than the 1886 collection date. There is an overall spareness in conception, an elegance in the relationship of parts, and a delicacy of carving that pinpoint this artist's style to the early 19th century, perhaps around 1820.

Carver of the Auk Kit was also, I believe, one of the innovators of the developing Tlingit style that emerged from pre-Contact times and continued to be refined in the years after Contact, perhaps around 1820–30 (fig. 13.14). This carver made eight spectacular masks for an Auk shaman and chief named Kow-ee (who died ca. 1850). I believe he is also the author of a mask and grave guardian figure from a Yakutat grave, both in the American Museum of Natural History. Emmons noted in a letter to the American Museum that these masks were "not like anything he had come across" (American Museum of Natural History 1900–1902). Emmons

Fig. 13.13. Carver of the Princeton Kit, Tlingit mask of the spirit of a shark. The Art Museum, Princeton University, PU3922. Lent by the Department of Geology and Geophysical Sciences, Princeton University, Princeton, N.J.

evidently recognized the fine carving quality, uniqueness of the spirits represented, and cohesiveness of style. They were also ornamented with copper brows, eyes, lips, and nostrils. This carver's rendering of the human face shows certain traits that have come to be associated with 19th century "Tlingit style," and he may even have been one of the artists responsible for the codification of these characteristics. The facial shape is an elongated oval, with eyes that are undercut deeply on the lower edge. There are smooth junctures between the eye, cheek, and mouth areas. A short nose

Fig. 13.14. Carver of the Auk Kit, Tlingit mask of a spirit called "Kan-nah-nah tchitch ge yake." American Museum of Natural History E2683. Photograph by Barbara Brotherton. Courtesy Department of Library Services, American Museum of Natural History, New York, N.Y.

arches abruptly from its indented bridge to meet flaring red nostrils. The nostril and upper lip are separated by a short space, and projecting, rounded lips of uniform width stretch along the sides of the face. The masks of this carver, I believe, represent the ability of the artist to synthesize realism and stylization and to contribute boldly to the more exuberant sculptural style that marked Tlingit cultural florescence in the years after

Contact, when artists had traditional training but were also responding to exciting new changes.

Six masks from the Field Museum and one from the American Museum (fig. 13.15) are attributed to the Carver of the Cheek Ridge. All purportedly are from Dry Bay. A seventh, owned by the Museum of the American Indian, has been identified as Yakutat. The approach of this very effective artist is an amalgam of human realism and bold convention. Some signa-

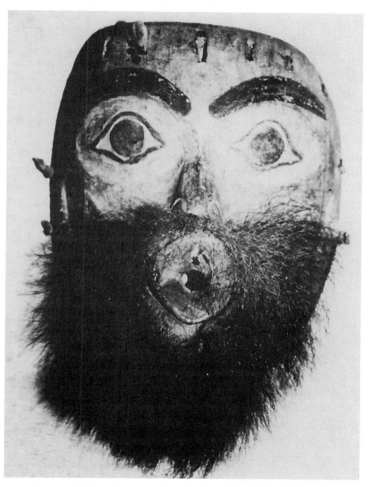

Fig. 13.15. Carver of the Cheek Ridge, Tlingit mask of the spirit of a devilfish. American Museum of Natural History E396. Photograph by Barbara Brotherton. Courtesy Department of Library Services, American Museum of Natural History, New York, N.Y.

ture characteristics of this carver are the broad face, a strongly defined arched brow ridge that connects to a very sculptural nose, rounded orbs that have "cinched in" eyelid corners, smooth cheek and mouth planes, boldly carved and animated mouths, and a squared chin. Surface painting in red and blue is prominent, and in some cases the artist has carved auxiliary creatures on the mask. A generality in the sculpting of the facial characteristics moves his style away from the subtle modeling of the naturalistic carvers. This artist may have produced these masks between 1830 and 1850.

The Carver of the Large Eyes and Broad Brows served at least five different Dry Bay shamans, as evidenced by his masks in the kits belonging to Qadjuse, Setan, and Gutcda, Raven clan shamans who lived between 1830 and 1880 (fig. 13.7). By traditional reckoning, this artist may have belonged to an "opposite" Eagle clan and perhaps worked in the Dry Bay area around the years 1850–70. One characteristic that links the masks is the thick brows that arch considerably on the underside, retaining nearly the same width except for a slight rounded point in the center of the upper contour. The brows terminate in blunt, angular edges near the nose. A delicately incised line borders the brow. Characteristically, the eyes are very large, open, and placed almost directly under the brow. A large, nearly round orb floats in the center and has been drilled through. The lids are rimmed with carved lines and have a loose, unconstricted shape. The rims are painted black, accentuating the prominence of the eye as a distinctive feature of the face. The bridge of the nose is strongly indented and the nose itself carved in a bold, abbreviated way, terminating in flaring nostrils. The mouth, also rudimentary in its treatment, shows carved teeth and a labret (lip plug). Geometric incisions on cheek and forehead areas of the faces of the masks of this artist may indicate clan facial paintings. This artist developed a bold style: he gives us an idea of a woman but not the lifelike presence of one.

The Carver of the Yakutat Kit made eleven masks in a single kit belonging to an unknown Yakutat shaman (fig. 13.16). I think he also carved two other masks not associated with particular kits. I have dated this carver's career to around 1850–70 based on his fully stylized approach, volumetric carving, and elaborate painting (especially the use of white paint). Formline designs indicating facial paintings show a lack of understanding of design principles. Six of the masks are of human beings, two are of *kushtakas* (drowned humans turning into land otters), and the others represent the animal realm (owl, eagle, mosquito, bear). The artist effectively rendered the brows, eyes, nose, and mouth of each different creature to suggest its unique attributes. The faces are broad with little contour, the brows are thick and angular, the eye shape is a rounded triangle with a large circular orb inside, the noses are blocky and carved with an exaggerated nostril, and the open lips show a roughly shaped oval. This artist was cognizant of the art principles but perhaps not sufficiently trained to have developed a command of the techniques of carving and painting. He was talented at boldly visualizing the spirits of what was most certainly a very

Fig. 13.16. Carver of the Yakutat Kit, Tlingit mask of a Tlingit singing. American Museum of Natural History 19/874. Photograph by Barbara Brotherton. Courtesy Department of Library Services, American Museum of Natural History, New York, N.Y.

Fig. 13.17. Carver of the Pinched Eye Corners, Tlingit mask of the spirit of an angry man. American Museum of Natural History E403. Photograph by Barbara Brotherton. Courtesy Department of Library Services, American Museum of Natural History, New York, N.Y.

powerful patron. While artistry and mastery of technique is important to us modern-day observers, it may have been less so to this shaman.

The Carver of the Pinched Eye Corners was also patronized by a number of Dry Bay shamans, perhaps as many as eight (fig. 13.17). This artist shared certain conventions with the Carver of the Burke Kit (not shown here), such as deeply carved eye sockets, a large, flat eye form with eyelids that are pinched at the corners, rather blocky noses and mouths, short chins, and patterns of black lines trailing around the nose, cheek, and mouth. Also, many have open mouths that are carved completely through. Both may have worked within the same time frame as the Carver of the Large Eyes and Broad Brows, 1850–70. Most facial shapes by this artist are rounded ovals with few contours to mark protruding cheeks or tapering chins. The brows are rounded and carved into a ridge that forms the bridge of the nose. Eyes are formed with large, flat orbs that are flatter at the bottom edge; they are placed within an eyelid line that mirrors the rounded upper edge and lower flatter edge of the eye shape. The eyelid corners taper to points well below the center of the eye and are very constricted or pinched. The intense, wide-eyed countenance expresses a kind of spirit presence that would have been desired by the shaman. Like others of their generation, the Carver of the Pinched Eye Corners and the Carver of the Burke Kit may have been largely self-taught and unable to develop a mature style.

Summary and Conclusions

Here I will summarize some of the conclusions reached in this study, in terms of style and stylistic development, artists and art practices, and the impact of contact on Tlingit masks. Already noted is the large gap in available data between the pre- and post-Contact periods. What can be surmised from extant artifacts is that over the span of several centuries, artists working in wood and other materials continued to refine the sculptural and surface elements evident in pre-Contact examples. European and Russian collections from the 18th century indicate that principles of sculpture and surface decoration were codified, and tribal styles are in evidence. A conservative art nurtured by respect for the traditional means of acquiring skills, masks nonetheless bear the distinctive stamps of individual artists. A decidedly naturalistic approach informed the work of the earliest mask carvers in this study; individual artists' preferences were identified through style analysis. Other masks, helmets, and headdresses tentatively dated to the Transitional Period suggest that a more stylized idiom may have been present for crest art, whose purpose was clan identification.

Shamans' spirits, on the other hand, were specific deceased humans, animals, and other beings that visited the shaman during vigils, suggesting that a greater particularity may have been required for the sacred arts. Indeed, some of the shamans' masks appear to be exacting portraits. My examination of 125 masks within their respective kits revealed that some shamans may have sought the services of a small number of trusted artists, usually from their own geographic region. The extreme naturalism of the

Yakutat–Dry Bay shamans' masks may indicate a regional preference that was refined from a general naturalistic tendency. Several of the mask carvers identified in this study may have been part of regional "schools" of artists whose approaches were nurtured, at the least, over several generations via the master-apprentice relationship or through actual collaboration. Initial research and the opinions of contemporary carvers indicate that some carvers, and maybe most, were commissioned to produce both sacred and secular art.

Sometime after 1820 the most naturalistic modes declined. In the ensuing decades there is a perceptible shift toward stylization, more exuberant sculpting, and an elaboration of surface decoration and painting. Easier access to metal tools, greater wealth from participation in trade and a cash economy, and the intensification of the potlatch all served to stimulate the arts. The shaman may have increased the number of implements in his kit, as suggested by Emmons, and adopted new types in response to this florescence. The depiction of human ancestors in mask carvings continues into the Early Historic Period, indicating the persistence of the Tlingit worldview even if the means of expressing it had changed. Thus, a stylized representation of an esteemed ancestor conveyed spirit power, as had the earlier naturalistic masks. This supports the claim that the Tlingit retained significant links to their traditional beliefs during a period of intense social upheaval. Art continued to serve its purpose as a bridge between past and present, between the ancestors and the living. The fact that Setan and other shamans practicing between 1850 and 1880 continued to inherit masks from their shaman predecessors implies that the spirits represented in the masks remained viable even when the practice of shamanism was under severe attack.

By the Late Historic Period, the Tlingit aggressively protected their independence despite widespread population losses, increased non-Native settlements, and government interference in Native lifestyles that eventually undermined Tlingit autonomy. The shaman was especially targeted, and unlike other social practices that were somewhat tolerated by Caucasians, there was no mechanism for the incorporation of shamanism into Europeanized Tlingit culture. Shamans continued to administer to traditional Tlingit, but their practice must have gone underground. While the shamans were alive their healing paraphernalia was, no doubt, kept away from the prying eyes of authorities; upon their deaths, it was secretly buried with them in remote locations. Time-honored methods of assuming the hereditary position of an artist and of acquiring art training were also impacted. The rise of the tourist market meant that avenues were open to amateur artists who might not have knowledge of design principles. Some of the carvers studied here exhibit a less methodical, less well-tutored use of their tools and a lack of understanding about art conventions. This phenomenon appears to increase in the late 19th century. We do not know how these carvers' work was received, but several Tlingit shamans evidently sought after it. Continued research may elicit more substantive data on this subject.

The expertly crafted portrait-like masks of the 1750–1820 period represent the apex of an established naturalistic tradition based on internal aesthetic concerns and time-honored ideas about deceased ancestors. More stylized versions continued into the Contact era, transformed by internal and external changes, but carrying the same significance and efficacy. Despite the impacts of contact, Tlingit shamans' masks track the persistence of religious, historical, and artistic traditions well into the 19th century. The masks are not mute. Rather, they continue to have much to tell us about culture continuity and change.

Acknowledgments

I would like to thank Michael Nassaney and Eric Johnson for their diligent editing of this volume and for their insight that those of us in cognate disciplines do, indeed, have much to say to one another. I continue to enjoy exchanges of ideas with Michael, my colleague at Western Michigan University, whom I look to as a mentor.

I must also thank several individuals who assisted with the acquisition and production of the images that accompany this chapter: Laila Williamson, Paula Willey, and Matthew Pavlick at the American Museum of Natural History; Carla Rickerson and Kris Kinsey at the University of Washington; Nicole Chamberland and Isabelle Poulin at the Canadian Museum of Civilization; and Karen Richter at the Art Museum, Princeton University. Robert Anemone and Antonios Proios made magic happen with computer imaging, and Jill L. Jepsen beautifully illuminated the details of the two bone combs.

This chapter is dedicated to Allen Wardwell (1935–1999), curator, scholar, art lover, and fellow "shamanist." Allen's many published works stand apart because of his gift of seeing the vast as well as the circumscribed. I will always remember that he generously lent me pre-publication notes for his last book, *Tangible Visions,* while I was writing my dissertation on a related topic. Allen's broad range of mind and gentle spirit are greatly missed.

References Cited

American Museum of Natural History. 1900–1902. Accession Folder, Department of Anthropology, New York.

Black, Lydia. 1988. The Story of Russian America. In *Crossroads of Continents: Cultures of Siberia and Alaska*, ed. W. W. Fitzhugh and A. Crowell, 70–82. Smithsonian Institution Press, Washington, D.C.

Brotherton, B. I. 1994. Spirits Like the Sound of the Rattle and Drum: Tlingit Shamans' Kits Collected by George Emmons. Ph.D. diss., University of Washington, Seattle.

Brown, Steven C. 1987. From Taquan to Klukwan: Tracing the Work of an Early Tlingit Master Artist. In *Faces, Voices and Dreams: A Celebration of the Centennial of the Sheldon Jackson Museum,* ed. Peter L. Corey, 156–75. Alaska State Museum and Friends of the Alaska State Museum, Juneau.

———. 1998. *Native Visions: Evolution in Northwest Coast Art from the Eighteenth Century through the Twentieth Century.* Seattle Art Museum and University of Washington Press, Seattle.

Carlson, Roy. 1983a. Change and Continuity in Northwest Coast Art. In *Indian Art Traditions of the Northwest Coast,* ed. Roy Carlson, 199–205. Archaeology Press, Simon Fraser University, Burnaby, B.C.

———. 1983b. Prehistory of the Northwest Coast. In *Indian Art Traditions of the Northwest Coast,* ed. Roy Carlson, 13–32. Archaeology Press, Simon Fraser University, Burnaby, B.C.

Cole, Douglas. 1985. *Captured Heritage: The Scramble for Northwest Coast Artifacts.* University of Washington Press, Seattle.

Dauenhauer, Nora Marks, and Richard Dauenhauer. 1990. *Haa Tuwunaagu Yis, For Healing Our Spirit: Tlingit Oratory.* University of Washington Press, Seattle.

de Laguna, Frederica. 1972. *Under Mount Saint Elias: The History and Culture of the Yakutat Tlingit.* 3 vols. Smithsonian Contributions to Anthropology 7. Smithsonian Institution Press, Washington, D.C.

———. 1990. Tlingit. In *Handbook of North American Indians,* vol. 7, *Northwest Coast,* ed. W. C. Sturtevant, 203–28. Smithsonian Institution Press, Washington, D.C.

Duff, Wilson. 1975. *Images in Stone B.C.: Thirty Centuries of Northwest Coast Indian Sculpture.* Oxford University Press, Toronto.

Emmons, George Thornton. n.d. Catalogue Notes. Department of Anthropology, American Museum of Natural History, New York.

———. 1991. *The Tlingit Indians.* Ed. Frederica de Laguna. University of Washington Press, Seattle.

Holm, Bill. 1981. Will the Real Charles Edensaw Please Stand Up? In *The World Is as Sharp as a Knife: An Anthology in Honour of Wilson Duff,* ed. D. N. Abbott, 175–200. British Columbia Provincial Museum, Victoria, B.C.

————. 1983. Form in Northwest Coast Indian Art. In *Indian Art Traditions of the Northwest Coast,* ed. Roy Carlson, 33–45. Archaeology Press, Simon Fraser University, Burnaby, B.C.

Jonaitis, Aldona. 1986. *Art of the Northern Tlingit.* University of Washington Press, Seattle.

Kan, Sergei. 1988. The Russian Orthodox Church in Alaska. In *Handbook of North American Indians,* vol. 4, *History of Indian-White Relations,* ed. W. C. Sturtevant, 506–21. Smithsonian Institution Press, Washington, D. C.

————. 1991. Shamanism and Christianity: Modern-Day Tlingit Elders Look at the Past. *Ethnohistory* 38:363–89.

King, J.C.H. 1979. *Portrait Masks from the Northwest Coast of America.* British Museum, London.

Krause, Aurel. 1956. *The Tlingit Indians: Results of a Trip to the Northwest Coast of American and the Bering Straits.* Translated by Erna Gunther. University of Washington Press, Seattle.

Langdon, Steve J. 1993. *The Native People of Alaska.* Greatland Graphics, Anchorage.

MacDonald, George. 1983. Prehistoric Art of the Northern Northwest Coast. In *Indian Art Traditions of the Northwest Coast,* ed. Roy Carlson, 99–120. Archaeology Press, Simon Fraser University, Burnaby, B.C.

Olson, Ronald. 1961. Tlingit Shamanism and Sorcery. *Kroeber Anthropological Papers* 25:207–20. University of California, Berkeley.

Sawyer, Alan R. 1984. Toward More Precise Northwest Coast Attributions: Two Substyles of Haisla Masks. In *The Box of Daylight: Northwest Coast Indian Art,* ed. Bill Holm, 143–47. Seattle Art Museum and University of Washington Press, Seattle.

Scidmore, Eliza Ruhamah. 1893. The First District from Prince Frederick Sound to Yakutat Bay. In *Report of Population and Resources of Alaska at the Eleventh Census: 1890,* 42–53. U.S. Bureau of the Census, Washington, D.C.

Seton-Karr, H. W. 1887. *Shores and Alps of Alaska.* Sampson, Low, Marston, Searle, Rivington, London.

Veniaminov, Ivan. 1984. Notes of the Koloshi. In *Notes of the Islands of Unalaska District,* pt. 3, section 2. Translated by Lydia Black and R. H. Goeghegan. University of Alaska, Fairbanks, and Limestone Press, Kingston, Ontario.

Wardwell, Allen. 1996. *Tangible Visions: Northwest Coast Indian Shamanism and Its Arts.* Monacelli Press, New York.

Wright, Julia McNair. 1883. *Among the Alaskans.* Presbyterian Board of Publication, Philadelphia.

Wright, Robin Kathleen. 1985. Nineteenth Century Haida Argillite Pipe Carvers: Stylistic Attributions. Ph.D. diss., University of Washington, Seattle.

Wyatt, Victoria. 1984. *Shapes of Their Thoughts: Reflections of Culture Contact in Northwest Coast Indian Art.* Peabody Museum of Natural History, Yale University, New Haven, Conn.

14

One Island, Two Places

Archaeology, Memory, and Meaning in a Rhode Island Town

Paul A. Robinson

There it was, word for word,
The poem that took the place of a mountain.
Wallace Stevens, "The Poem That Took the Place of a Mountain"

Places, like families, tribes, and states, can have many histories. Some of these are written and memorialized, while others are forgotten, concealed, or simply ignored. Histories of places are shifting stories, negotiated among people with different perspectives on the same geographic area. The poet Wallace Stevens wrote of this fluidity of meaning, how the perspective of the observer or narrator replaces the place itself, or someone else's idea of place, with something else. In this essay I explore the making and remaking of the ideologies and themes that comprise the histories of a small island community in Rhode Island as told and memorialized by two groups of people—the Narragansett Indians and the town's non-Indian residents.

Until recently the two stories existed quietly side by side without much public discussion or debate. Since 1988, however, when Jamestown school officials proposed a school addition in an area adjacent to a recorded ancient Narragansett cemetery, the version of the town's history held by many Jamestown residents has clashed openly and publicly with the Narragansett one. This conflict included debates within each community concerning the interpretation of the past and appropriate behavior in the present. Archaeological materials and the process of doing archaeology itself have figured importantly in this debate, by undermining some as-

pects of the Jamestown version while strengthening parts of the Narragansett one. The case study presented here demonstrates how archaeological findings are actively implicated in ideological production.

The Factual Place

> Go where we will on the surface of things, men have been there before us.
> *Henry David Thoreau, 1849*

The town of Jamestown, Rhode Island, includes all of Conanicut Island (see Nassaney, chap. 15, fig. 15.1). The island is located at the mouth of Narragansett Bay and measures about nine miles long by one and a half miles wide. It is connected to the mainland by two bridges, allowing local residents to travel easily to the mainland and back, while tourists speed quickly across the island to Newport and Cape Cod. Conanicut Island, with a state park at its southern end that provides expansive and spectacular ocean views, is home to several thousand year-round and summer residents, and for generations has attracted people with its scenic beauty and relaxed pace of life.

The island has several documented Native American burial areas, most of them unmarked and poorly delineated. They date from the 17th century and extend back in time over 3,200 years (McBride 1989; Simmons 1970). In addition to the burial areas, over fifty Native American archaeological sites are recorded in the state's archaeological data base, some of which were substantial and regularly used settlements by 3,200 years ago. Collectively, these archaeological sites document a wide range of Native American uses of the island (Leveillee 1997; Morenon 1983).

The name *Conanicut* derives from that of Canonicus, the leading Narragansett sachem at the time of European contact and settlement in the 1620s and 1630s (LaFantasie 1988:75). English settlers obtained grazing rights on the island from Canonicus in 1638 for a small sum of wampum (Bartlett 1865:45–49). Nineteen years later, in 1657, a group of colonists sought clear and absolute title to the land, and in their view obtained it for a quantity of wampum valued at 255 pounds sterling. The deed of conveyance specified that the Narragansett sachems would "remove all the Indian inhabitants, and clear them off from the foresaid Island Quononaqutt" (Jamestown, R.I. *Land Evidence,* 1:12). That some Narragansett stayed, however, is documented in town records from the 18th century (Herndon and Sekatau 1997:439–40; Simmons 1970:39).

The 1657 proprietors divided the land and made plans for a village in the central part of the island, where the main settlement grew through the 18th and into the 20th century. In the center of this village was a large Narragansett Indian burial ground, or perhaps several burial areas, which archaeological studies in 1966 and 1989 showed to be one of the largest recorded Native American cemeteries in New England (McBride 1989; Simmons 1970). Mortuary rituals through the centuries have left evidence of the graves of nearly 300 people. Throughout the years the village has grown within and around this major burial place, periodically disturbing Indian graves. Any construction within the town center risks encountering Narragansett burials, as was the case for school construction in the 1950s and excavations for a municipal water line in 1995.

The Plurality of Place

Our roots belonged here . . . our ancestors were buried here just as deep, if not deeper than the Indians.

Caroline Wright, a prominent Jamestown resident, at dedication ceremonies of Sydney Wright Museum, Jamestown, R.I., 1971 (Wright, 1971)

This island . . . was the place of the summer homes of the Narragansett sachems . . . [when I come here] there is much emotion that is involved . . . sometimes I stop and sometimes I hurry through. When I stop I look for the oldest things that are present— the stones and [some] trees . . . that bore witness to [my ancestors].

Dr. Ella Sekatau, Narragansett Indian tribal ethnohistorian and medicine woman, at the excavation of the Joyner site, Jamestown, R.I., 1991 (Leveillee 1992)

In the more than 360 years since English colonists obtained grazing rights from Canonicus, different traditions or histories have been told and written about the settlement and growth of the town and its original Indian inhabitants. The Jamestown version includes written and oral traditions; the Narragansett is largely oral, although in the last decade official tribal letters, public presentations, and comments at public meetings have provided another glimpse into Indian ideas about the island. Each group has constructed its own ideology to legitimize access to the island and the right to call it "home."

The Jamestown History

The Jamestowners' view, recorded by local historians in the 19th and 20th centuries, memorializes and praises the original Narragansett Indian inhabitants led by Canonicus, but disconnects and discredits most, if not all, Narragansett people who lived in the area after the 1657 purchase. The

Jamestown story is summarized in a "History of Jamestown" written by J. R. Cole and published in Richard Bayles's *History of Newport County* in 1888 (Cole 1888). According to Cole, a local antiquarian who lived in Newport, Rhode Island, Canonicus was a "wise and peaceful ruler" who befriended the colonists by providing refuge from the "oppression of their own countrymen." Moreover, he sought to "advance his people in the arts of civilized life as he saw them in operation among his pale-faced neighbors" (1888:724). Although the Narragansett sachem was not as culturally advanced as the English, he nevertheless possessed a "rudimental education [that] greatly ameliorated [the Indians'] barbarous condition. It is even said that he had conceived some sort of notion of civilization before the coming of the whites, and was actually striving to bring his subjects to a higher plane of life" (Cole 1888:724).

Cole not only ascribed an enlightened wisdom to Canonicus but also gave him the aesthetics of the elite and educated Jamestown establishment. Canonicus, like many of the more affluent residents of the late 19th century, summered on the island. William Trost Richards, a marine artist from Philadelphia, who built an island cottage in 1881, had high praise for the place: "certainly there is no place more lovely than Conanicut in all the world" (quoted in Nebiker 1995:19). Although not quite as cultured as Cole's contemporaries, Canonicus too appreciated the island's beauty: "Even the untutored [Indian] mind seems to have had some sense of appreciation of the beautiful, as evinced by their love of this little gem of the waters" (Cole 1888:724).

In most versions of the Jamestown story, Canonicus (who died on the mainland in 1647) is the last Narragansett Indian on the island. Some authors, however, mention the next generation of Narragansett leaders, but suggest they were less intelligent and more barbarous than Canonicus. Scuttop and Cojonoquant "misunderstood" the original intention of William Coddington and the other colonists who purchased the land in 1638, and demanded a second payment in 1657. This point is particularly important to Jamestowners: the island was not stolen or taken by military conquest, but rather was purchased fairly from the Indians, not just once but twice. Implicit in this story is the position that the second purchase was not legally necessary but was done to clear the air and end the "troubles" with the Indian sachems (Meras 1984:35; State of Rhode Island 1982:131–33; Steinberg and McGuigan 1976:249; Taylor 1925:3).

Following this second "purchase" the Narragansett are, in most published histories, gone from the island, cleanly folded into and made part of the rustic beauty of the place. Soon, all that was left of the Indians were "mute records . . . stone arrow heads and rounded stone weights" (Taylor 1925:3). A passage from an island history written by a resident in 1949 summarized the end. From the highest hill on the island, one can see both Cocumscussoc, the site of Canonicus's main village and Roger Williams's trading post where the first "purchase" was transacted, and Newport, home of William Coddington: "As we gaze on the peaceful scene of beauty before us the dim past seems to come to life and a panorama arises before our mental vision. Across the bay we see the Indian chiefs assemble at Cocumscossoc to negotiate for the sale of the island, and then in Coddington's house in Newport the same assemblage again gathers to sign the deed and the Indians give up possession in their own colorful ceremony . . . to the white man" (Watson 1949:103).

The final part of the Jamestown story is about Narragansett cemeteries and burials. J. R. Cole noted that "here [the Narragansett] had extensive burial grounds [and] oftentimes, by accident or otherwise, skeletons of this early race have been unearthed, but the citizens always respecting their notions of the happy hunting ground beyond, have buried their bones again in a decent manner" (1888:724–25; see also Taylor 1925:2). With the Indians gone—Taylor referred to the "mute records" of ancient Indians found "all over this island"—Jamestowners, according to Cole, assumed the task of caring for the ancient Narragansett graves.

The idea that local residents have cared for Narragansett graves was suggested to me when human remains were found during archaeological investigations for a housing project in December 1994. A long-time island resident suggested that the bones might be a reinterment because "there were many burials in the area and sometimes disturbed burials were reburied nearby." According to this person, Narragansett Indians have taken an interest in the burials only recently. Even William Simmons's well-publicized and reported excavation of Narragansett graves in 1966–67 was publicly ignored by the Narragansett until Simmons himself approached the Tribal Council and arranged reburial of the remains on the island in 1972 (Simmons 1970). It was with this sense of stewardship that Caroline Wright worked for several decades, from 1936 into the 1970s, to protect the major concentration of Narragansett graves on school property while the Indians, according to Wright, were on the mainland, busy with their yearly "summer pow-wow" (Wright 1971:3).

The Narragansett History

While the contemporary Narragansett Indian view shares some elements of the Jamestowners' story, it differs in most respects. Both stories identify the island as a summering place for the Narragansett sachems and identify Canonicus as a wise and able leader. Both stories also agree that the sachems Cojonoquant and Scuttop were less able, a development that the Narragansett version attributes to the corrupting influence of contact with the English.

The Narragansett history is seamless and continuous. It is, for the most part, an oral history composed of living traditions, but it is also contained in letters and expressed at public meetings, primarily by members of the Narragansett Indian Archaeological and Anthropological Committee. Their history tells of a direct and uninterrupted connection between Narragansett people in the 1990s and those who used the island for at least the last three millennia. The sachems, in particular, lived on the island in the summer. During these millennia, the island was also a sacred place used for the burial of Narragansett people. Narragansett oral tradition tells that people who lived on the island were "caretakers" for the sacred areas.

The Narragansett never left the island, the story continues, nor did they forget about the burial areas. After European settlement, tribal people continued to visit the burial grounds regularly, but did so quietly because protests over non-Indian violations were almost always fruitless and sometimes dangerous. Modern Jamestowners and their predecessors are not viewed as benevolent stewards of the land and burial areas but rather as "intruders" who continually and knowingly have disturbed and mistreated Indian burials in a variety of ways.

An Archaeology of Forgetting

> Historians are the professional remembrancers of what their fellow citizens wish to forget.
> *Eric Hobsbawn, 1994*

In her introduction to *The Geography of Identity*, Patricia Yaeger argues that the study of places include an "archaeology of forgetting" (1996:24). After Martin and Mohanty (1986), she suggests that the "comforts" of space invite "political acts of forgetting" that conceal or obscure a clear understanding of the past and the political and social struggles that occurred. Yaeger, a professor of English, is optimistic that a critical historical memory might be awakened by literary texts. She uses a provocative example from Thoreau's *Walden* in which each railroad tie is a "sleeper" whose "dreams have bound America together." Thoreau's sleepers are the "bodies of dead or mangled Irish workers who labored to install the iron path in conditions of incredible suffering and peril. Thoreau describes the forgotten effects of spatial melancholia—the unmourned phantoms that still hover, dreaming and cursing, in geography's thoroughfares" (Yaeger 1996:27).

In Jamestown, historical memory was awakened and the everyday comforts of place were shattered for some residents soon after school officials began planning in 1988 to build an addition to the existing school. In this instance and in the years that followed, archaeological investigation combined with competent and thorough historiography provided a means for bringing to public debate the claims of each side to tell the "whole story" about the island's past.

In 1988 the Town of Jamestown obtained a federal loan to expand and renovate its facilities to accommodate an increasing school population. Some classes were held in hallways, the nurse's office was in a janitor's closet, music was taught in the gymnasium, and band classes were held in a community room, which disturbed nearby classes. In 1966–67 William Simmons had excavated fifty-nine Narragansett burials and cremation pits on school property, only 200 feet west of the existing building (Simmons 1970). The proposed addition was in this area. The town's federal loan triggered a review of the project by the State Historic Preservation Officer (SHPO). The officer determined that the town should conduct an archaeological study to see if the proposed addition would impact any graves or other archaeological resources (Sanderson 1988).

The study, conducted with Narragansett Indian participants, used a combination of shovel tests and machine scraping to survey the area. These investigations located 195 graves on school property (McBride 1989). Survey and testing continued off and on for twenty-one months, and ultimately found a parcel of land in the northwest corner of the school property that contained no burials, where a separate school building was built (McBride 1990). All the burials were preserved in place, although the skeletal remains in one grave were accidentally disturbed during machine testing.

The process of demarcating the area that contained burials involved difficult and lengthy discussions with the Narragansett Indian tribe and the SHPO. It was a process that was unsettling for some town residents. Nearly 200 Narragansett Indian graves were now known to exist in the general area of Simmons's excavations, an area that many people hoped or had "known" was empty of additional graves. When combined with Simmons's work that had recovered cremation burials about 3,200 years old, the new study suggested that school lands had been used sporadically from 3200 B.P. into the 17th century. During the course of the study we also learned that construction of the original school in the 1950s had disturbed Indian burials. With that in mind, one tribal member at a meeting with town officials in September 1989 made the ironic point that the Town Council had purchased the land in 1937 to provide recreation and "to prevent further desecration of the Indian burial ground thereon" (*Newport Daily News,* April 12, 1937, cited in Simmons 1970:8). The townspeople, it seemed, had decided and then neglected to protect the burial place.

Indian burials have been disturbed repeatedly on the island since the earliest European settlement. Newspaper clippings, letters, and notes on file at the Jamestown Historical Society indicate several such occurrences in the Antham Avenue area between 1888 and 1915. According to one local resident, some of the skeletal remains from this area were collected by the Conanicut chapter of the Institution of the Grand Council, Royal Arcanum of Rhode Island, and used in this fraternal organization's secret rituals. Municipal workers laying a new water line, despite a warning from the town historian, disturbed burials along Antham Avenue again in 1995.

Caroline Wright's recollections of the 1936 discovery of burials at the Watson farm, on what would become school property and the site of William Simmons's excavations, provide another perspective on attitudes toward Indian burials. Wright, a Jamestown resident descended from a long line of prominent East Coast families, was instrumental in protecting burials in the school area from continued desecration after they were unearthed. She rescued many of the artifacts from local collectors and antique dealers, sponsored Simmons's excavations in 1966, and established the Sydney Wright Museum to house the collection in 1971. Her address to the Jamestown Historical Society in June 1971 described the "bedlam" that ensued when excavators struck Indian burials:

Now, on a day in October, 1936, some of Jack Smith's men were in there digging, and standing by watching was a fellow named Roy Johnston. . . . he was young then and, as a distributor of the *Providence Journal,* he had learned a lot of odds and ends, as people who have to do with newspapers are apt to do. While he was watching, the men dug against something and, going deeper, found bones . . .

but the general reaction of the diggers was "Oh well, these are just some of Devil Dan's victims." (Now remember, I don't think old Mr. Watson *had* victims, but this was what was quoted to me at the time.) "No," said Johnston, "These bones are flexed. They are Indians," whereupon the men began digging in real earnest with the idea that there was monetary value attached to this find and that instead of water lilies, they could sell Indians to the summer people. (1971:6)

The artifacts and bones were scattered among island residents and museums. Caroline Wright, with the help of friends, tracked down some of the contents from many of the estimated seventeen burials that had been disturbed and kept them together until the museum was established following the Simmons excavations (Simmons 1970:8–9). Taken together, the Antham Avenue incidents and Caroline Wright's account of the Watson farm excavations undermine the Jamestown idea that bones uncovered accidentally are always reburied carefully and respectfully by local residents.

Absent from Wright's recollections was any mention of contemporary Indian people on the island. She did, however, recall a trip to Charlestown, Rhode Island, in the early 1930s to visit the "campgrounds . . . where descendants of the original Indians have their summer pow-wows" (1971:3). Some tribal members say that Narragansett people visited the area regularly, but did not complain about the mistreatment of the Indian burials because of past failures in the Rhode Island courts. In the 1860s the tribe brought a suit against several men who had excavated Native American graves on the mainland. The men were arraigned but never prosecuted (Rubertone 1994:31). It was difficult, some Narragansett say, for a group of people who were discriminated against because of color and economic class to find a sympathetic hearing for any of their grievances. Many, if not most, non-Indians also believed that 19th- and 20th-century Narragansett had lost their Indian identities through marriage with non-Indians and with the sheer passage of time since European contact (Campbell and LaFantasie 1978). Caroline Wright, by noting that descendants of the original Narragansett were still living on the mainland, may have been one significant exception to this prevalent belief. Many tribal members were surprised and gratified, therefore, when William Simmons approached them in 1972 and offered to rebury the skeletal remains of the individuals he had excavated just a few years before.

Political conditions changed soon after that. The Narragansett began working systematically with the state in 1978 on burial discoveries, and on April 11, 1983, they gained federal recognition. In the summer of that year they participated fully in the excavation and study of a Narragansett cemetery and established a tribal committee two years later to work with archaeologists (Nassaney 1989, chap. 15; Robinson 1994; Robinson et al. 1985). Moreover, by 1987 state and federal historic-preservation regulations required Indian participation on public construction projects that had the potential to damage Native American archaeological resources. In 1988, when the Jamestown school committee proposed its project, the Narragansett Indian tribe was eager to get publicly involved in the review of the project. At the time, the tribe was divided, its leadership contested. Both factions, despite the problems they had with each other, participated actively with the town and the state and persuaded town officials to build a new school on a piece of school property that contained no graves (Rowland 1989).

The involvement of late 20th-century Narragansett people with ancient Indian remains was difficult for some Jamestowners to understand. At an afternoon library talk given by the Narragansett ethnohistorian and me in 1993, some in the audience were dismayed that the tribal representative combined modern social and political concerns with ancient traditions. She was not, in the words of one listener, a "real Indian." In this view, real Indians remained tied forever to their mythic, precolonial past, defined on that fall afternoon by a Jamestowner's idea of Narragansett history (see also Carlson, chap. 10).

The new, aggressive approach by the Narragansett toward protecting the burials of their ancestors was also evident at an Antham Avenue reburial ceremony conducted in January 1995 by John Brown, the understudy to the tribe's chief medicine man. Two or perhaps three burials had been disturbed during the installation of a water line, and the state and town had worked with the tribe for three weeks to identify the extent of the disturbance. The Narragansett felt that since burials had been disturbed in this location several times over the years, this most recent instance could have been avoided with careful planning. In fact, the town historian had cautioned town officials that burials were located along the street. Some townspeople, however, were shocked and offended that John Brown was not grateful for their assistance after the disturbance; on the contrary, he had insulted them by calling them "intruders" and by accusing them of "willful desecration." Brown's behavior did not fit with the Jamestown idea of the "real" Indian—symbolized by the peaceful and civilized Canonicus, who had welcomed the original Jamestowners, who in turn had, after all, purchased the land not once but twice from the Indians.

And how are we to understand this original purchase? In the spring of 1638, a group of Rhode Island colonists led by William Coddington and Roger Williams gave the Narragansett sachems forty fathoms of white wampum and a "few gratuities" for Aquidneck Island and for grazing rights on several smaller bay islands, one of which was Conanicut. At this time, the Indians hoped that the English would live according to Narragansett ideas of social etiquette and responsibility. Most of the colonists, however, came to see the land transaction as a simple sale and considered the land to be under colonial control. Twenty years later, a new generation of Narragansett leaders complained that the English had not met their obligations. The sachem Scuttop, grandson of Canonicus, told the English that the Narragansett wanted only what was expected of any people living in Narragansett country. Roger Williams reported the demand in a letter: "That we should furnish them with poison to dispatch Uncas [a rival Mohegan sachem]; that we should send English soldiers against Uncas; that we should send up contributions to their nicommoes [social gatherings]. On these and other such abominable terms they have offered to consent, and that *without any other payment*" (Lafantasie 1988:489; emphasis added).

For the Narragansett the wampum that accompanied the original transaction affirmed their ideas about social obligations and the jurisdictional rights of the sachems. In return for grazing rights, they wanted the English to help them settle their feud with Uncas and they expected the colonists to send gifts to the social gatherings and feasts called *nicommoes*. As Roger Williams observed in his report of Scuttop's remarks, the Narragansett did not want payment for the land; rather they wanted the English to live agreeably with them on Narragansett terms.

The English, however, considered the land sold and would not recognize the essential Narragansett idea. Probably realizing the futility of convincing or compelling the English to act appropriately, the Narragansett in the 1650s demanded and received large sums of wampum for their land. They used the wampum partially in an attempt to create and maintain alliances with Indian communities in the upland sections of Massachusetts and with the Mohawks. And like the English, who had failed to live according to Narragansett values, this time the Narragansett openly ignored the English idea of land sales: they simply accepted the wampum and stayed on the land (Robinson 1990:192–95). That they stayed is amply documented by the many times the Jamestown Town Council dealt with

The preference for pipes of Native manufacture for ritual purposes among Natives has been documented elsewhere on the frontier of eastern North America in the 18th century, suggesting that the pattern was not confined to southeastern New England (see Trubowitz 1992). By maintaining a decided preference for using their own pipes as opposed to those introduced by trade, men may have sought to limit tobacco use to themselves. "The Silver Pipe" may be an expression of expected or idealized behavior that associated male positions of power and authority with stone or otherwise special pipes and their ritual meaning.

Elsewhere I have argued that the content and configuration of the RI 1000 cemetery served to express ideal social relations in aboriginal society (Nassaney 1989:88). In other words, the tribal mortician may have used mortuary space to express traditional social relations that were being threatened by a new social order. Thus, even though women and children may have had access to tobacco and participated in recreational smoking through the use of European clay pipes, all of the pipes recovered from RI 1000 were found associated with men. These included nine pipes of the European variety, a Native-manufactured clay elbow pipe in imitation of a European form, and the soapstone pipe from burial 38. The distribution of pipes in the cemetery suggests that smoking was a male activity and pipes of all varieties were prescribed for male use in the afterlife. Although gender roles may be blurred in everyday life, they are most likely to be thrown into stark relief and portrayed stereotypically in highly ritualized settings, such as those associated with mortuary activities or when large populations aggregate for social displays and group interaction (see, for example, Conkey 1991).

Summary and Conclusions

The presence of a single stone pipe in the RI 1000 cemetery suggests that it was an important and powerful artifact. When it was first discovered in 1983, the pipe caused great excitement among the descendant community, and it triggered a series of ritual acts before the tribe appropriated this ideologically charged object. For unknown reasons, the male interred in burial pit 38 was not buried with "his" pipe at the time of his death. (Incidentally, this male exhibited brown staining on two teeth and teeth notching that is consistent with the habitual smoking of a pipe.) Perhaps his spouse or someone else retained the pipe to benefit from its use after his death, as suggested by the oral account of the Silver Pipe. When the keeper of the pipe decided to return it to its proper owner, he or she may accidentally have dug into burial 18. This burial had occurred significantly earlier, as evidenced by the fact that the head easily became disarticulated by the intrusive disturbance. If the wrong individual were initially disturbed, this would imply that the burials were not marked or that excavation took place when burial locations were difficult to discern, perhaps after dark. The excavator refilled the pit when he or she realized the mistake. Excavations into the second grave (burial 38) to the southwest identified the pipe's rightful owner and the two were reunited.

In an earlier discussion of the tobacco-smoking complex in the Northeast, Turnbaugh (1977:68) doubted whether surviving narratives could illuminate the "extent of ritualism associated with ceremonial pipe smoking." Admittedly, oral accounts cannot always be taken at face value (see, for example, Staeck, chap. 3; Vansina 1985). However, the close correspondence between the "The Silver Pipe" and the archaeological record lends support to the idea that the memorate collected in the late 19th century describes a practice that Native peoples actually engaged in as early as the mid-17th century. Furthermore, the oral account hints at the struggles that existed between men and women in Native society, some of which may have emerged or became exacerbated as a result of transformations in social relationships brought about by changes in access to material goods. Change in gender roles precipitated by new economic avenues for resource acquisition is a well-developed theme in Lauriston Sharp's (1952) now-classic study, "Steel Axes for Stone Age Australians." While the ramifications of tobacco and pipes were perhaps not nearly as profound for Narragansett society as steel axes were among the Yir Yoront of Australia, new trading patterns, partners, and opportunities were nevertheless potentially disruptive to traditional society. The lessons that emerged from conflicts between men and women as social roles and relations became restructured were codified and passed on to subsequent generations through oral traditions.

In her paper "Grave Remembrances," Patricia Rubertone (1994:40) suggested that ritual events such as those described here represent "a ceremony of continuance through which the Narragansett sought to communicate with the ancestors." It seems rather peculiar that no other archaeological evidence for such ceremonies has been recovered from mortuary contexts in southern New England. While early investigators may have neglected to notice or report features such as intrusive pits, work conducted at the West Ferry site by William Simmons (1970) in the late 1960s would have identified grave offerings made after the initial interment. Of course, the West Ferry cemetery was abandoned (ca. A.D. 1640–50) at a time when the English maintained a much more tenuous presence in southeastern New England and their long-term fortunes could not be predicted. As with all cultural practices that were recorded in the turbulent 17th century, we must ask to what extent the postmortem interment of grave goods is an expression of the persistence of ancient beliefs, or whether it may have developed in response to sustained contact with Europeans. Fortunately for investigators of the Contact period, multiple lines of evidence can be brought to bear on questions regarding change and continuity in the sacred and profane worlds of Native North Americans. By integrating these various sources of information, scholars can bring the study of Native American history into clearer focus, as Trigger advocated more than a decade ago.

Acknowledgments

I was fortunate to have the opportunity to participate in the RI 1000 Burial Project, which has inspired my research on the Contact period. Conversations with John Brown and Paul Robinson have influenced my thinking on this site and cultural interactions in innumerable ways. This essay has benefited from critical readings by Eric Johnson, Paul Robinson, William Turnbaugh, and Dena Dincauze. Thanks to Chris Bassett of the Western Michigan University (WMU) Computing Center for assisting me in preparing figure 15.3. The final draft of this chapter was completed while I was on sabbatical leave (1998–99) from my teaching duties at WMU. I dedicate this chapter to my father, Joseph Nassaney, who taught me that material objects are only a means to an end.

References Cited

Asch, David L., and Nancy E. Asch. 1985. Prehistoric Plant Cultivation in West-Central Illinois. In *Prehistoric Food Production in North America,* ed. R. I. Ford, 149–203. Anthropological Papers no. 75. Museum of Anthropology, University of Michigan, Ann Arbor.

Axtell, James. 1981. Last Rights: The Acculturation of Native Funerals in Colonial America. In Axtell, *The European and the Indian,* 110–28. Oxford University Press, Oxford.

Bradford, William, and Edward Winslow. 1841. Bradford and Winslow's Journal. In *Chronicles of the Pilgrim Fathers of the Colony of Plymouth,* ed. Alexander Young, 109–252. Charles C. Little and James Brown, Boston.

Brenner, Elise M. 1988. Sociopolitical Implications of Mortuary Remains in 17th-Century Native Southern New England. In *The Recovery of Meaning,* ed. M. P.

Leone and P. B. Potter, Jr., 147–81. Smithsonian Institution Press, Washington, D.C.

Brown, James A. 1971. The Dimensions of Status in the Burials at Spiro. In *Approaches to the Social Dimensions of Mortuary Practices,* ed. J. A. Brown, 92–112. Memoirs of the Society for American Archaeology no. 25, Washington, D.C.

Butterworth, Hezekiah. 1893. The Silver Pipe. In *Exercises under the Auspices of the Thalia Club, Warren, R.I, 16.* Massasoit Monument Association, Providence, R.I.

Conkey, Margaret W. 1991. Contexts for Action, Contexts for Power: Material Culture and Gender in the Magdalenian. In *Engendering Archaeology: Women and Prehistory,* ed. J. M. Gero and M. W. Conkey, 57–92. Basil Blackwell, Oxford.

Crosby, Constance A. 1988. From Myth to History, or Why King Philip's Ghost Walks Abroad. In *The Recovery of Meaning,* ed. M. P. Leone and P. B. Potter, Jr., 183–209. Smithsonian Institution Press, Washington, D.C.

Garman, James C. 1994. Viewing the Color Line through the Material Culture of Death. *Historical Archaeology* 28(3):74–93.

Hodder, Ian. 1982. The Identification and Interpretation of Ranking in Prehistory: A Contextual Perspective. In *Ranking, Resource, and Exchange: Aspects of the Archaeology of Early European Society,* ed. Colin Renfrew and Stephen J. Shennan, 150–54. Cambridge University Press, Cambridge.

Johnson, Eric S. 1993. "Some by Flatteries and Others by Threatenings": Political Strategies among Native Americans of Seventeenth-Century Southern New England. Ph.D. diss., University of Massachusetts, Amherst.

MacNeish, Richard S. 1952. The Archaeology of the Northeastern United States. In *Archaeology of Eastern United States,* ed. J. B. Griffin, 46–58. University of Chicago Press, Chicago.

McBride, Kevin A. 1989. *Phase I and II Investigations, West Ferry Site, RI 84, Jamestown Elementary School.* Jamestown School Committee, Jamestown, R.I.

———. 1990. *Phase I Archaeological Reconnaissance Survey, Northwestern Section, Jamestown Elementary School.* Jamestown School Committee, Jamestown, R.I.

McGuire, J. D. 1899. Pipes and Smoking Customs of the American Aborigines, Based on Material in the U.S. National Museum. *Annual Report of the United States National Museum, 1896–97,* 351–645. Washington, D.C.

McManamon, Francis P., James W. Bradley, and Ann L. Magennis. 1986. *The Indian Neck Ossuary.* Cultural Resources Management Study no. 17. Division of Cultural Resources, North Atlantic Regional Office, National Park Service, Boston.

Nassaney, Michael S. 1989. An Epistemological Enquiry into Some Archaeological and Historical Interpretations of 17th Century Native American–European

Relations. In *Archaeological Approaches to Cultural Identity,* ed. S. J. Shennan, 76–93. Unwin Hyman, London.

Nassaney, Michael S., Uzi Baram, James C. Garman, and Michael F. Milewski. 1996. Guns and Roses: Ritualism, Time Capsules, and the Massachusetts Agricultural College. *Old-Time New England* 74(262):59–80.

Peebles, Christopher. 1971. Moundville and Surrounding Sites: Some Structural Considerations of Mortuary Practices II. In *Approaches to the Social Dimensions of Mortuary Practices,* ed. J. A. Brown, 68–91. Memoirs of the Society for American Archaeology no. 25, Washington, D.C.

Preucel, Robert W., ed. 1991. *Processual and Postprocessual Archaeologies.* Occasional Paper no. 10. Center for Archaeological Investigations, Southern Illinois University, Carbondale.

Robinson, Paul A. 1990. The Struggle Within: The Indian Debate in Seventeenth-Century Narragansett Country. Ph.D. diss., Binghamton University.

Robinson, Paul A., Marc A. Kelley, and Patricia E. Rubertone. 1985. Preliminary Biocultural Interpretations from a Seventeenth-Century Narragansett Indian Cemetery in Rhode Island. In *Cultures in Contact,* ed. W. W. Fitzhugh, 107–30. Smithsonian Institution Press, Washington, D.C.

Rogers, J. Daniel, and Samuel M. Wilson, eds. 1993. *Ethnohistory and Archaeology: Approaches to Postcontact Change in the Americas.* Plenum Press, New York.

Rubertone, Patricia E. 1994. Grave Remembrances: Enduring Traditions among the Narragansett. *Connecticut History* 35:22–45.

Sainsbury, John A. 1975. Indian Labor in Early Rhode Island. *New England Quarterly* 48:378–93.

Sharp, Lauriston. 1952. Steel Axes for Stone Age Australians. *Human Organization* 11(2):17–22.

Simmons, William S. 1970. *Cautantowwit's House: An Indian Burial Ground on the Island of Conanicut in Narragansett Bay.* Brown University Press, Providence.

———. 1986. *Spirit of the New England Tribes: Indian History and Folklore, 1620–1984.* University Press of New England, Hanover, N.H.

Spinden, Herbert Joseph. 1950. *Tobacco Is American.* New York Public Library, New York.

Thomas, Peter A. 1985. Cultural Change on the Southern New England Frontier, 1630–1665. In *Cultures in Contact,* ed. W. W. Fitzhugh, 131–61. Smithsonian Institution Press, Washington, D.C.

Trigger, Bruce G. 1986. Ethnohistory: The Unfinished Edifice. *Ethnohistory* 33:253–67.

———. 1989. *A History of Archaeological Thought.* Cambridge University Press, Cambridge.

Trubowitz, Neal L. 1992. Thanks, But We Prefer to Smoke Our Own: Pipes in the Great Lakes–Riverine Region during the Eighteenth Century. In *Proceedings of the 1989 Smoking Pipe Conference: Selected Papers,* ed. C. F. Hayes III, 97–111. Research Records no. 22. Rochester Museum and Science Center, Rochester, N.Y.

Tuma, S. John. 1992. Contact Period Mortuary Practices of the Massachusett and Narragansett Speakers. Paper presented at the 32d annual meeting of the Northeastern Anthropological Association, Bridgewater, Mass.

Turnbaugh, William A. 1975. Tobacco, Pipes, Smoking and Rituals among the Indians of the Northeast. *Quarterly Bulletin of the Archaeological Society of Virginia* 30(2):59–71.

———. 1977. Elements of Nativistic Pipe Ceremonialism in the Post-Contact Northeast. *Pennsylvania Archaeologist* 47(4):1–7.

———. 1984. *The Material Culture of RI-1000, A Mid-17th-Century Narragansett Indian Burial Site in North Kingstown, Rhode Island.* Department of Sociology and Anthropology, University of Rhode Island, Kingston, R.I.

———. 1992. Post-Contact Smoking Pipe Development: The Narragansett Example. In *Proceedings of the 1989 Smoking Pipe Conference: Selected Papers,* ed. C. F. Hayes III, 113–24. Research Records no. 22. Rochester Museum and Science Center, Rochester, N.Y.

———. 1993. Assessing the Significance of European Goods in Seventeenth Century Narragansett Society. In *Ethnohistory and Archaeology: Approaches to Postcontact Change in the Americas,* ed. J. D. Rogers and S. M. Wilson, 133–60. Plenum Press, New York.

Vansina, Jan. 1985. *Oral Tradition as History.* University of Wisconsin Press, Madison.

von Gernet, Alexander D. 1988. The Transculturation of the Amerindian Pipe/Tobacco/Smoking Complex and Its Impact on the Intellectual Boundaries between "Savagery" and "Civilization," 1535–1935. Ph.D. diss., McGill University, Montreal.

West, George A. [1934] 1970. *Tobacco, Pipes and Smoking Customs of the American Indians, Part I.* Greenwood Press, Westport, Conn.

Williams, Roger. 1827. A Key into the Language of America. *Collections of the Rhode Island Historical Society* 1, Providence.

Willoughby, Charles C. 1935. *Antiquities of the New England Indians with Notes on the Ancient Cultures of the Adjacent Territory.* Peabody Museum of Archaeology and Ethnology, Harvard University, Cambridge, Mass.

Wilson, Samuel M. 1993. Structure and History: Combining Archaeology and Ethnohistory in the Contact Period Caribbean. In *Ethnohistory and Archaeology: Approaches to Postcontact Change in the Americas,* ed. J. D. Rogers and S. M. Wilson, 19–30. Plenum Press, New York.

Winters, Howard D. 1969. *The Riverton Culture.* Report of Investigations no. 13. Illinois State Museum, Springfield.

Wobst, H. Martin. 1978. The Archaeo-Ethnology of Hunter-Gatherers, or The

Tyranny of the Ethnographic Record in Archaeology. *American Antiquity* 43:303–9.

Wood, William. [1634] 1977. *New England's Prospect*, ed. A. T. Vaughan. University of Massachusetts Press, Amherst.

Yarnell, Richard A. 1964. *Aboriginal Relationships between Culture and Plant Life in the Upper Great Lakes Region.* Anthropological Papers no. 23. Museum of Anthropology, University of Michigan, Ann Arbor.

Selected Bibliography

Andren, Anders. 1998. *Between Artifacts and Texts: Historical Archaeology in Global Perspective*. Plenum Press, New York.

Appadurai, Arjun, ed. 1986. *The Social Life of Things: Commodities in Cultural Perspective*. Cambridge University Press, New York.

Arkush, Brooke S. 1995. *The Archaeology of CA-Mno-2122: A Study of Pre-Contact and Post-Contact Lifeways among the Mono Basin Paiute*. Anthropological Records vol. 31. University of California, Berkeley.

Axtell, James. 1988. *After Columbus: Essays in the Ethnohistory of Colonial North America*. Oxford University Press, New York.

Barth, Fredrik, ed. 1969. *Ethnic Groups and Boundaries*. Little, Brown, Boston.

Beaudry, Mary C., ed. 1988. *Documentary Archaeology in the New World*. Cambridge University Press, Cambridge.

Birmingham, Robert A. 1984. Dogtown: A Historical and Archaeological Study of a Late Historic St. Croix Chippewa Community. *Wisconsin Archaeologist* 65(3):183–300.

Bradley, James W. 1987. *Evolution of the Onondaga Iroquois: Accommodating Change, 1500–1655*. Syracuse University Press, Syracuse, N.Y.

Bragdon, Kathleen J. 1996. *Native People of Southern New England, 1500–1650*. University of Oklahoma Press, Norman.

Brain, Jeffrey P. 1979. *Tunica Treasure*. Papers of the Peabody Museum of Archaeology and Ethnology 71. Harvard University, Cambridge, Mass.

———. 1988. *Tunica Archaeology*. Papers of the Peabody Museum of Archaeology and Ethnology 78. Harvard University, Cambridge, Mass.

Carlson, Roy, ed. 1983. *Indian Art Traditions of the Northwest Coast*. Archaeology Press, Simon Fraser University, Burnaby, B.C.

Ceci, Lynn. 1982. The Value of Wampum among New York Iroquois: A Case Study of Artifact Analysis. *Journal of Anthropological Research* 38:96–107.

Cleland, Charles E. 1971. *The Lasanen Site: An Historic Burial Locality in Mackinac County, Michigan*. Anthropological Series 1, no. 1. The Museum, Michigan State University, East Lansing.

———. 1991. From Ethnohistory to Archaeology: Ottawa and Ojibwa Band Territories of the Northern Great Lakes. In *Text-Aided Archaeology*, ed. Barbara Little, 97–102. Telford Press, Caldwell, N.J.

d'Azevedo, W. L., ed. 1986. *Handbook of North American Indians*, vol. 11, *Great Basin*. Smithsonian Institution Press, Washington, D.C.

Deagan, Kathleen. 1988. Neither History nor Prehistory: The Questions that

Count in Historical Archaeology. *Historical Archaeology* 22(1):7–12.

DeCunzo, LuAnn, and Bernard L. Herman, eds. 1996. *Historical Archaeology and the Study of American Culture.* Henry Francis du Pont Winterthur Museum, Winterthur, Delaware.

Deetz, James F. 1977. Historical Archaeology as the Science of Material Culture. In *Historical Archaeology and the Importance of Material Things,* ed. Leland Ferguson, 9–12. Special Publication 2. Society for Historical Archaeology, Tucson.

Driver, Harold E. 1961. *Indians of North America.* University of Chicago Press, Chicago.

Fagan, Brian. 1995. *Ancient North America.* Thames and Hudson, New York.

Fitzhugh, William, ed. 1985. *Cultures in Contact: The Impact of European Contacts on Native American Cultural Institutions, a.d. 1000–1800.* Smithsonian Institution Press, Washington, D.C.

Fixico, Donald L., ed. 1997. *Rethinking American Indian History.* University of New Mexico Press, Albuquerque.

Galloway, Patricia. 1995. *Choctaw Genesis 1500–1700.* University of Nebraska Press, Lincoln.

Getty, R. M., and K. R. Fladmark, eds. 1973. *Historical Archaeology in Northwestern North America.* Archaeological Association, University of Calgary, Alberta.

Hammell, George R. 1983. Trading in Metaphors: Another Perspective on Indian-European Contact in Northeastern North America. In *Proceedings of the 1982 Glass Trade Bead Conference,* ed. C. F. Hayes III, 5–28. Research Records no. 16. Research Division, Rochester Museum and Science Center, Rochester, N.Y.

Hill, Jonathan D., ed. 1996. *History, Power, and Identity: Ethnogenesis in the Americas, 1492–1992.* University of Iowa Press, Iowa City.

Hoxie, Frederick E., ed. 1996. *Encyclopedia of North American Indians: Native American History, Culture, and Life from Paleo-Indians to the Present.* Houghton Mifflin, Boston.

Hudson, Charles. 1976. *The Southeastern Indians.* University of Tennessee Press, Knoxville.

Hugill, Peter J., and D. Bruce Dickson, eds. 1988. *The Transfer and Transformation of Ideas and Material Culture.* Texas A&M University Press, College Station.

Innis, Harold A. 1930. *The Fur Trade in Canada.* Yale University Press, New Haven.

Jones, Sian. 1997. *The Archaeology of Ethnicity: Constructing Identities Past and Present.* Routledge, London.

Judd, C. M., and A. J. Ray, eds. 1978. *Old Trails and New Directions.* University of Toronto Press, Toronto.

Krech, Shepard, III. 1991. The State of Ethnohistory. *Annual Review of Anthropology* 20:345–75.

Kroeber, Alfred L. 1939. *Cultural and Natural Areas of Native North America.* Publications in Archaeology and Ethnology 38. University of California.

Lightfoot, Kent G. 1995. Culture Contact Studies: Redefining the Relationship between Prehistoric and Historical Archaeology. *American Antiquity* 60:199–217.

Lightfoot, Kent G., Thomas A. Wake, and Ann M. Schiff. 1991. *The Archaeology and Ethnohistory of Fort Ross, California,* vol. 1, *Introduction.* Contributions of the Archaeological Research Facility no. 49. University of California, Berkeley.

Martin, Ann Smart, and J. Ritchie Garrison, eds. 1997. *American Material Culture: The Shape of the Field.* Henry Francis du Pont Winterthur Museum, Winterthur, Delaware.

Mason, Ronald J. 1986. *Rock Island: Historical Indian Archaeology in the Northern Lake Michigan Basin. Midcontinental Journal of Archaeology* Special Paper no. 6. Kent State University Press, Kent, Ohio.

McMullen, Ann, and Russell G. Handsman, eds. 1987. *A Key into the Language of Woodsplint Baskets.* American Indian Archaeological Institute, Washington, Conn.

Milanich, Jerald T. 1995. *Florida Indians and the Invasion from Europe.* University Press of Florida, Gainesville.

Orser, Charles E., Jr. 1996. *A Historical Archaeology of the Modern World.* Plenum Press, New York.

Penney, David W. 1992. *Art of the American Indian Frontier: The Chandler-Pohrt Collection.* Detroit Institute of Arts and the University of Washington Press, Seattle.

Quimby, George I. 1966. *Indian Culture and European Trade Goods: The Archaeology of the Historic Period in the Western Great Lakes Region.* University of Wisconsin Press, Madison.

Quimby, George I., and Alexander Spoehr. 1951. Acculturation and Material Culture. *Fieldiana* 36(6). Chicago Natural History Museum, Chicago.

Robinson, P. A. 1990. The Struggle Within: The Indian Debate in Seventeenth-Century Narragansett Country. Ph.D. diss., State University of New York at Binghamton. University Microfilms, Ann Arbor.

———. 1994. Archaeology, History, and Native Americans: Preserving the Richness of the Past. In *Cultural Resource Management: Archaeological Research, Preservation Planning, and Public Education in the Northeastern United States,* ed. J. E. Kerber, 87–95. Bergin and Garvey, Westport, Conn.

Rogers, J. Daniel. 1990. *Objects of Change: The Archaeology and History of Arikara Contact with Europeans.* Smithsonian Institution Press, Washington, D.C.

Rogers, J. Daniel, and Samuel M. Wilson, eds. 1993. *Ethnohistory and Archaeology: Approaches to Postcontact Change in the Americas.* Plenum Press, New York.

Rubertone, Patricia. 1989. Archaeology, Colonialism, and 17th-Century Native America: Towards an Alternative Interpretation. In *Conflict in the Archaeology of Living Traditions,* ed. Robert Layton, 32–45. Unwin Hyman, London.

———. 1996. Matters of Inclusion: Historical Archaeology and Native Americans. *World Archaeology Bulletin* 7:77–86.

St. George, Robert, ed. 1988. *Material Life in America, 1600–1860.* Northeastern University Press, Boston.

Shennan, Stephen, ed. 1989. *Archaeological Approaches to Cultural Identity.* Unwin Hyman, London.

Spector, Janet, and Elden Johnson, eds. 1985. *Archaeology, Ecology, and Ethnohistory of the Prairie-Forest Border Zone of Minnesota and Manitoba.* J&L Reprints in Anthropology, vol. 31, Lincoln, Nebraska.

Spores, Ronald. 1980. New World Ethnohistory and Archaeology, 1970–1980. *Annual Review of Anthropology* 9:575–603.

Stark, Miriam, ed. 1998. *The Archaeology of Social Boundaries.* Smithsonian Institution Press, Washington, D.C.

Sturtevant, William C., ed. 1988. *Handbook of North American Indians,* vol. 4, *History of Indian-White Relations.* Smithsonian Institution Press, Washington D.C.

———. 1990. *Handbook of North American Indians,* vol. 7, *Northwest Coast.* Smithsonian Institution Press, Washington, D.C.

Swanton, John R. 1946. *Indians of the Southeastern United States.* Bureau of American Ethnology Bulletin 137. Smithsonian Institution Press, Washington, D.C.

Thomas, David Hurst, ed. 1990a. *Columbian Consequences,* vol. 1, *Archaeological and Historical Perspectives on the Spanish Borderlands West.* Smithsonian Institution Press, Washington, D.C.

———. 1990b. *Columbian Consequences,* vol. 2, *Archaeological and Historical Perspectives on the Spanish Borderlands East.* Smithsonian Institution Press, Washington, D.C.

———. 1991. *Columbian Consequences,* vol. 3, *The Spanish Borderlands in Pan-American Perspective.* Smithsonian Institution Press, Washington, D.C.

Trigger, Bruce G. 1985. *Natives and Newcomers: Canada's "Heroic Age" Reconsidered.* McGill-Queens University Press, Montreal.

———. 1986. Ethnohistory: The Unfinished Edifice. *Ethnohistory* 33:253–67.

———, ed. 1978. *Handbook of North American Indians,* vol. 15, *Northeast.* Smithsonian Institution Press, Washington, D.C.

Wedel, Mildred Mott. 1959. Oneota Sites on the Upper Iowa River. *Missouri Archaeologist* 21(204).

Whayne, Jeannie, comp. 1995. *Cultural Encounters in the Early South: Indians and Europeans in Arkansas.* University of Arkansas Press, Fayetteville.

Wobst, H. Martin. 1977. Stylistic Behavior and Information Exchange. In *Papers for the Director: Research Essays in Honor of James B. Griffin,* ed. C. E.

Cleland, 317–42. Anthropology Papers, vol. 61. Museum of Anthropology, University of Michigan, Ann Arbor.

Wood, W. Raymond. 1990. Ethnohistory and Historical Method. In *Archaeological Method and Theory,* vol. 2, ed. M. B. Schiffer, 81–110. University of Arizona Press, Tuscon.

———. 1993. Integrating Ethnohistory and Archaeology at Fort Clark State Historic Site, North Dakota. *American Antiquity* 58(3):544–59.

Contributors

Brooke S. Arkush received his Ph.D. in anthropology from the University of California at Riverside in 1989 and currently is an associate professor of anthropology at Weber State University in Ogden, Utah. Most of his research concerns the Native archaeology and ethnohistory of western North America, especially in regard to communal big-game hunting and Native acculturation in California and the Great Basin.

Barbara Brotherton is an assistant professor of art history at Western Michigan University. She is the author of articles on Tlingit art and culture.

Kathleen H. Cande is a research assistant and senior project archeologist with the Arkansas Archeological Survey. She is a part-time graduate student in the Department of History, University of Arkansas.

Catherine C. Carlson is an associate professor in the Department of Social and Environmental Studies at the University College of the Cariboo, Kamloops, British Columbia, where she teaches archaeology and ethnography.

Charles E. Cleland is distinguished professor of anthropology at Michigan State University. His research interests include the prehistory, historic archaeology, and ethnohistory of the upper Great Lakes region and eastern United States, and he has written widely on these topics, including a recent book, *The Rites of Conquest*, on the Native Americans of the Great Lakes.

Sean B. Dunham is a staff archaeologist and principal investigator at the Commonwealth Cultural Resources Group in Jackson, Michigan, where he specializes in the archaeology of the upper Great Lakes region. His recent publications have appeared in *The Michigan Archaeologist* and in the New Directions in Archaeology series published by Cambridge University Press.

Margaret B. Holman is a research associate at the Michigan State University Museum. She is a specialist in Great Lakes archaeology and has written a number of articles on maple sugaring and its origins.

Eric S. Johnson earned his Ph.D. in anthropology from the University of Massachusetts, Amherst. A specialist in the archaeology and ethnohistory of northeastern North America, he is currently a preservation planner with the Massachusetts Historical Commission.

Alice B. Kehoe retired as professor of anthropology at Marquette University in 1999. Her research interests include the archaeology and ethnology of North American Indians, the history of archaeology, and gender studies in archaeology.

Carol I. Mason earned her graduate degrees from the University of Michigan and is a specialist in Great Lakes archaeology and ethnohistory. She is presently professor emerita at the University of Wisconsin–Fox Valley and adjunct professor of anthropology at Lawrence University.

Mark S. Parker Miller is a doctoral candidate in art history at the University of Delaware. He has concentrated on the study of American and Native American art, architecture, and material culture, and his current research interests concern issues of cultural interaction and exchange.

Michael S. Nassaney received his Ph.D. in anthropology from the University of Massachusetts, Amherst, in 1992; he is currently an associate professor of anthropology at Western Michigan University. His research interests include social archaeology and material analysis in eastern North America. In 1999 he was a research fellow at the John Nicholas Brown Center in Providence, Rhode Island, where he studied 17th-century Native American gender roles in southeastern New England.

Susan M. Neill earned her M.A. in cultural anthropology from the University of Wisconsin–Madison. She received the 1997–98 and 1998–99 Hope B. McCormick Costume Fellowship at the Chicago Historical Society before accepting her current position as the curator of textiles and social history at the Atlanta History Center.

James F. Pendergast is a retired Royal Canadian Artillery officer, Canadian Army Regular, who since 1962 has published extensively in Canada and the United States, making a significant contribution to Iroquoian archaeology, particularly the St. Lawrence Iroquoians. Over the period 1972–78 he was assistant director (Operations), National Museum of Man, National Museums of Canada. In 1976 he was made a doctor of science (Hons. Causa.) by McGill University. In 1991 he received the Crabtree Award from the Society of American Archaeology, and the same year he was made a fellow of the New York State Archaeological Association. In 1994 he received the Emerson Silver Medal from the Ontario Archaeological Society.

Paul A. Robinson is the Principal State Archaeologist at the Rhode Island Historical Preservation and Heritage Commission. He has written many articles on southern New England history and archaeology with an emphasis on the Narragansett Bay basin and Rhode Island.

John P. Staeck is an assistant professor of anthropology at the College of DuPage in Illinois. He holds a B.A. from Beloit College and an M.A. and Ph.D. in anthropology from Rutgers University. His interests include symbolic archaeology, identity marking, and social interaction as seen in the archaeological record.

Larissa A. Thomas is a research archaeologist at TRC Garrow in Atlanta, Georgia. Her research focuses on the Native American archaeology of the southeastern United States.

Index